# The History of Canadian Business 1867-1914

## Volume One

# The History of Canadian Business 1867-1914

## Volume One
## The Banks and Finance Capital

R. T. Naylor
Foreword by Eric Kierans

James Lorimer & Company, Publishers
Toronto 1975

0-88862-092-6 paper
0-88862-094-2 cloth

Cover design: Robert MacDonald
Design: Lynn Campbell

James Lorimer & Company, Publishers
Egerton Ryerson Memorial Building
35 Britain Street
Toronto

Printed and bound in Canada

Published with the assistance of the Social Science Research Council, using funds provided by the Canada Council.

Canadian Shared Cataloguing in Publication Data

Naylor, R. T.
    The history of Canadian business, 1867-1914.

    2 v.

Bibliography:
Contents: v.1. The banks and financial capital. —
v.2. Industrial development.
ISBN 0-88862-094-2 (v.1) ISBN 0-88862-092-6 (v.1) pbk.
ISBN 0-88862-095-0 (v.2) ISBN 0-88862-093-4 (v.2) pbk.

1. Canada - Commerce - History. 2. Canada - Industries
- History. 3. Canada - Economic conditions. I. Title.

HF5349.C2N39 1975  380'.0971
            Vol. 1

69540

# CONTENTS

Acknowledgements  viii

Foreword by Eric Kierans  x

Preface  xvii

List of Abbreviations  xxii

List of Tables  xxiv

**CHAPTER I/Introduction: Canadian Mercantilism, 1867-1914**  2

The Canadian State and the International Economy  2
Economic Development in the "Great Depression"  7
The "Wheat Boom" 10
Notes to Chapter I  18

**CHAPTER II/Revenue, Protection, and the Politics of International Finance**  20

Capital Formation and the State  20
Development of the Canadian Capital Market  22
The Dawn of the Railway Age  23
Financial Forces Behind Confederation  27
Confederation  30
The National Policy Tariff  35
Protection and the Business Community  37
Proponents of the National Policy  40
The Sugar Industry and the West Indies Trade  45
The Textile Industry  46
Protectionist Industries  51
Iron and Steel Policy  52

After the National Policy — Revenue and Protection 55
Conclusions 57
Notes to Chapter II 59

## CHAPTER III/The Evolution of the Chartered Banking System 66

Origins of the Banking System 66
Commercial Operations of the Chartered Banks 69
Finance and Politics 74
Banks and the Commercial Sector 78
Savings Deposit Business 85
Chartered Bank Expansion, Competition, and Mergers 95
The Flow of Funds 99
Banking and Agriculture 104
Banking and Industry 107
Conclusions 110
Notes to Chapter III 111

## CHAPTER IV/Chartered Bank Failures 118

Stability of the Canadian Banking System 118
Bank Failures in the Maritimes 120
Bank Failures in Quebec 126
Bank Failures in Ontario 140
Bank Failures in the West 148
The Record of the Chartered Banks 149
Notes to Chapter IV 150

## CHAPTER V/The Rise and Fall of the Private Banking System 156

Pre-Confederation Patterns 156
Operation of the Private Banks 158
Private Banks in the Maritimes 161
Private Banks in Quebec 165
Private Banks in Ontario 166
Private Banks in the West 174
The Record of the Private Banks 178
Notes to Chapter V 180

## CHAPTER VI/ Financial Institutions and the Accumulation of Capital 186

Financial Intermediaries and the Capital Market 186
Insurance Company Operations 187
The Bond Market 197
The Mortgage Market 199
The Stock Exchanges, the Bucket Shops, and the Money Market 210

Miscellaneous Sources of Funds and the Distribution of Income 219
Notes to Chapter VI 221

## CHAPTER VII/Canada and the International Flow of Finance Capital 228

Patterns of Foreign Portfolio Investment 228
Policy Towards Portfolio Investment 230
The Colonial Stocks Acts 234
Dominion Government Finance 236
Provincial Finance 238
Municipal Finance 243
Public Utilities Investment 246
British Industrial Bond Investments 253
Conclusions 254
Notes to Chapter VII 255

## CHAPTER VIII/High Finance and the Canadian Railways 260

Early Ventures 260
The Pacific Project: I 262
The Saga of Labrador Smith 264
The Pacific Project: II 267
Railway Policy and Politics 279
The New Railways: I 284
The New Railways: II 288
Notes to Chapter VIII 293

# Acknowledgements

The debts to co-operating and encouraging individuals accumulated by the author during the preparation of this book would require yet another volume to acknowledge adequately. Only a few can be mentioned here, and perhaps their contribution to the work is best elucidated by a few remarks on how such a book came to be written.

The credit or the blame, as the case may be, for initiating a process of enquiry that culminated in this book belongs to Abe Rotstein directly and Kari Levitt indirectly. Until the summer of 1970 the author of this book was earnestly wasting his time attempting to extract useful information from a virtually useless subject. This is not to deny that the core material of orthodox economics does have its concrete social application. Clearly it does. For some two hundred years at least, practitioners and perpetrators of the subject have worked diligently to refine a body of precepts and axioms that rivals medieval Catholicism in its scope and ingenuity. Like the medieval theologians they succeeded in producing a set of theorems that does more than just provide all the correct answers — it also provides all the correct questions. For one whose principal interests lie in writing eulogistic rationalizations for the status quo distribution of power and wealth, the body of economic orthodoxy is eminently satisfactory. For someone actually hoping to help shed light on pressing social problems, it is of course less than useless. The author's decision to discard his conventional baggage as completely as possible came as a result of Abe Rotstein's promptings to shift out of the orthodox trap, and as a result of the influence of Kari Levitt's writing on the multinational corporation. From then on it was downhill all the way.

Many other individuals contributed in their own way to the development of the ideas herein expressed. Jack McLeod has been a pillar of support in innumerable ways for as long as I have known him, approximately from the time of the Boer War. R. I. K. Davidson of the University of Toronto Press provided endless encouragement during the gestation period of the book, and indeed the whole concept of turning certain ideas into this book began with him. Mel Watkins pushed me to open up many critical lines of research, and his influence stands out very strongly in the pages that follow. Gary Teeple's importance to this book is also immeasurable, for he, more than anyone else, provided a critical appraisal of many of the key theoretical propositions that underlie the train of thought presented. Cy Gonick played a very major role in rescuing the manuscript from the near oblivion it once reached as a result of a series of mishaps. Professor E. P. Neufeld, though in no way responsible for my handling of the material — he would in all probability take strong exception to both the tone and many of the conclusions of this book — has nonetheless been a profound influence on me over the years as teacher and author and in discussions on the development of the Canadian capital market. Several colleagues at McGill University spent much time in laboriously examining the manuscript for flaws and suggesting improvements, notably, but by no means exclusively, Paul Davenport, Phil Ehrensaft, John Thompson, Eric Kierans, and Tom Velk.

Numerous individuals suggested sources, lent me materials, endured being used for testing concepts in the process of their epigenesis, and corrected misapprehensions. An even longer list of people undertook to type pieces of the manuscript from handwriting that is frankly appalling. Among these Ilana Kohn, Debra Lamoureux, Colleen Pearce, Beverley Horka, Lynn Boyle, and Vivian Goldstein in particular stand out. McGill University supported the typing with a research grant. Several breweries helped keep the author sane during the work — though they were amply reimbursed.

Jim Lorimer and Dave Berry oversaw the process of production. Without their efforts and dedication, and without Jim Lorimer's gratifying opinion that the project was well worth bringing to light, the book would clearly have been impossible.

# Foreword

There is not much difficulty in attempting to understand the structure of the Canadian corporate economy. Each corporation is required to file an annual return with the Minister of National Revenue. These returns are generally prepared by accredited chartered or general accountants and conform to accepted principles of accounting and auditing practice. Thus a mass of unstructured financial information — balance sheets, operating statements, source and application of funds schedules, etc., — is accumulated, standardized and published in a form suitable for tax, financial, and general economic analysis. Given the virtually absolute coverage of the corporate sector, the facts and data needed for a complete picture of the economy are there. We know where we are. The important question of how we got there remains, and this is a task for the economic historian.

This is the way it is. The latest reports by Statistics Canada cover the 1971 operations of 231,536 corporations, divided for analytical purposes into 37 major industry groups.[1] The number is large enough to satisfy any theorist or econometrician, but the significance changes immediately when it is noted that 291 firms (one-eighth of one per cent of the total) controlled 58% of the assets ($159 billion of $275 billion), produced 30% of the goods and services ($48 billion of $162 billion sales), and collected 39% of total profits in the corporate sector ($4.5 billion of $11.6 billion). It is difficult to escape the conclusion that Canada is the example par excellence of corporate concentration and oligopoly dominance of price and output decisions.

This interdependence is clearly evident in the resource sector. There were 3,740 corporations in the mining sector at the end of

1971. Of that number, 34 firms (less than one per cent) controlled 55% of the assets ($9.5 billion of $17.4 billion), sold 61% of Canada's mineral and mining output ($3.8 billion of $6.2 billion), and earned 73% of the profits before income taxes ($693 million of $952 million). More specifically, if the metal mining group is separated from the rest of the resource sector, the 14 largest firms are found to control 73% of the assets, 71% of the sales and received 72% of the profits earned in exploiting Canada's metal mines. This is concentration of economic power with a vengeance.

Nor does Canada's manufacturing sector display the characteristics of a competitive capitalism. In the 21 major industry groups of Canadian secondary industry in 1971, there were 21,998 incorporated firms. Eighty-three of these firms (three-eighths of one per cent) controlled 45.6% of the assets ($22.9 billion of $50.1 billion), 37.5% of the output of goods and services ($22.5 billion of $59.9 billion) and made 43.2% of the profit before income taxes ($1.6 billion of $3.7 billion).

The primary metals industry is one of the 21 major groups within Canada's manufacturing sector. A total of 365 incorporated firms are engaged in the converting and processing of our natural resources. Eight of these firms dominated the group, controlling 81% of total assets ($3.8 billion of $4.7 billion). The same eight firms produced 69% of the output ($2.4 billion of $3.5 billion) and made 80% of the profits before income taxes ($247 million of $309 million). Clearly, these eight firms are not adjusting their price and output policies independently of each other as economic theory would suggest. Again we have the picture of oligopoly capitalism and price leadership.

The facts about the concentration of corporate power in Canada are generally known and understood in the community. Recent spectacular merger moves by Inco, Noranda, Power Corporation, etc., have increased public concern and misgivings about the policies that permit this wave of takeovers. It is only when the political fallout threatens the government's credibility that the Prime Minister announces the creation of a Royal Commission on Corporate Concentration, charged with the task of reporting upon and making recommendations concerning "(a) the nature and role of major concentrations of economic power in Canada; (b) the economic and social implications for the public interest of such concentrations; and (c) whether safeguards exist or may be required to protect the public interest in the presence of such concentrations."[2]

The most glaring deficiency in the terms of reference has been the exclusion of an examination of the federal economic policies which have provided the major impetus to corporate concentration in this country. Perhaps such a reference would not have been acceptable to the chairman of the Royal Commission, for as the single most powerful economic adviser to successive governments since the Second World War he would, in effect, have been asked to judge his own policies, biases, and prejudices. While I would not suggest that Mr. Robert Bryce could not have second thoughts, his commitment to size ("bigger is better") has been too long and too deeply ingrained for him to undergo an intellectual conversion at this time.

Consider again our two volumes of statistics tracing out the shape and structure of the Canadian economy. If economic policy were truly committed to encouraging a competitive environment, one would expect a neutral corporate income tax system or, if not, a system favouring the growth of new, small and medium-sized firms. In fact, the reverse has been true since the corporate income tax became a substantial tool of policy during and after the Second World War. Of all categories in the manufacturing sector, the 83 firms with assets in excess of $100 million paid the lowest effective rate of corporate income tax in 1971, 30.8%. The next lowest rate was paid by firms with assets of more than $25 million but less than $100 million; the effective rate for the 197 firms in this category was 35.6%. The remaining 21,718 firms, i.e. with assets less than $25 million, paid an effective rate of 45.3% on their profits. As far as tax concessions are concerned, "them that has, gets."

Similarly, in the resource sector. The largest 106 firms, with assets over $25 million, provided $68 million for current income taxes in 1971 on profits of $961.8 million for an effective corporate rate of 7.1%. Two hundred firms, with assets between $5 million and $25 million, paid $26.8 million in taxes on profits of $70.1 million in the same year for an effective rate of 38.2%.

The enormous difference in effective rates stems from the nature of tax exemptions and privileges. In all instances, capital cost allowances, depletion, investment credits, exploration and developments, etc., favour the large and profitable firms. This has been the bias in the Canadian tax structure since the Second World War as government policy-makers have equated efficiency with size and discriminated against the employment of labour by favouring capital investment via tax concessions and subsidies.

Similarly, in manufacturing. The 83 largest firms were able to defer the payment of $1.3 billion in taxes out of a total deferral of $1.9 billion for the 21,998 corporations engaged in manufacturing at the end of 1971.

Incredible as it may seem, the pace of concentration did not satisfy the Canadian government. Impressed with the Herman Kahn theme that the multinational corporation would dominate the global economy of the nineteen-eighties, the Honourable E. J. Benson included in his Tax Reform(?) Legislation of 1971 measures that would ensure that the big would get bigger and fewer. Canadian corporations will be allowed a full deduction for interest paid on money borrowed to buy shares in other corporations.[3] In order that there be no misunderstanding about the government's intent, the Minister of Finance went on to explain, "This deduction for interest provides a substantial incentive for Canadian corporations to invest in other corporations and permits them to compete on an even footing with foreign corporations. Assuming a tax rate of 50 per cent, the cost of borrowing money for share purchases will be cut in half."[4]

Observe what is going on here. Clearly the government is addressing the oligopoly firm, i.e. the firm which has sufficient control of its market to ensure, by adjusting price and output, a continuing flow of profits over 10-15-20 years. Borrowing large sums for takeover purposes means annual interest charges for many years. Small firms, medium-sized firms with cyclical profit levels, farmers in the competitive sector need not apply. Nor is the interest-deductible privilege an advantage to firms that do not make profits.

Again we must pay attention to what the government is saying.

The federal government is not telling the large and profitable firms to invest their profits in more productive capacity or even to distribute the profits to shareholders. It is telling Inco, Noranda, Power Corporation, Abitibi, and the rest, to use their existing profits to buy each other out. If they do this, the government will give back the taxes due on profits spent for this purpose, thus financing half the costs of mergers and takeovers. It is quite fascinating to be a member of a cabinet that can put forward this type of tax privilege while affirming stoutly its belief in competition and anti-combines legislation.

Two assertions can be made about Canada's economic structure in the 1970's. In the first place, virtually every sector of the economy is dominated by less than a handful of huge corporations and, secondly, the single most important cause of this concentration of economic power has been and is federal economic policy.

A little reflection, apart from the data and statistics, would suggest that this must be so. The government of Canada has never believed in free trade or in competition. Despite all protestations, politicians want action now, growth in economic activity and employment. An economic structure composed of large numbers of firms busily competing away one another's profits may be advantageous to the consumer but does not throw up the surpluses that can be taxed or reinvested in new capacity and technology. Nature must be made to grow by leaps and bounds, cement and steel, skyscrapers and SSTs. That is the stuff and, to get it, governments go with the few and the large, with concessions and exemptions to force the pace of change.

Governments do not work against — they work with the vested, the established, the giants in place. The two sectors have exactly the same interest, increase the pace of economic activity and the growth of assets. The distribution of that rising product must permit increasing levels of retained earnings and savings out of high incomes to keep the show going. The problems of farmers who might employ an additional hired hand or small business with little surplus to reinvest are of no interest to ministers and their deputies craving policies with high visibility and little else to recommend them.

Politicians and bureaucrats can then point to a rising GNP and corporate chairmen can announce an increase in assets to their shareholders. Only the people are confused as they see little evidence of this increased wealth translated into a better standard of living for them and a more equitable distribution of what the nation does turn out.

With this community of interest between a powerful public sector and a rich and dominating industrial core, it becomes easier to understand the formation of new service corporations such as Reisman and Grandy Ltd. Two of the most powerful bureaucrats, a deputy minister of finance and a deputy minister of industry, trade and commerce laden with honours for their public service and the most generous pension arrangements granted by an unwitting public, take an early retirement, settle in on the tenth floor of the newest Ottawa skyscraper and prepare to guide the oligopolies that can afford them through the labyrinth of the federal bureaucracy and the potential pitfalls of Canada's latest Royal Commission, the inquiry into corporate concentration.

The level of concentration that presently exists in Canada is a direct consequence of government policy. Despite the lip service paid to laissez-faire capitalism, competition and the virtues of individual enterprise and initiative, no Canadian government has ever believed in, to the extent of practising, these principles. They could not afford to wait for the slow procession of natural, diversified and balanced growth. Politicians operate in the short run, and ad hocery is the response of men in a hurry. Re-election makes opportunists of us all.

Professor Naylor shows us how it was in the beginning of our history as a nation. Then, as now, the public and the private sectors were completely intertwined. The political framework was there — a new sovereign nation from sea to sea. It had to be given economic strength and depth, and instantly. Thus, the business of creating this nation fell into the hands of the few — in business. As Professor Naylor describes for us in language that bites, the directions of our growth were imposed upon us by the interests and well-being of particular, mainly commercial, groups. They built themselves into the very structure of the state and the economy could only move forward on their terms. Thus tariffs, capital inflows, subsidies, tax concessions and licences to exploit and export the nation's wealth. Just as the government found that it could achieve its aim of growth by fostering the corporations, so the corporations found in the government the means of ensuring their own development, privileges, and continuing dominance.

This is scholarly work. Professor Naylor does not confine himself to economic activity as such but deals with the institutions of the time, especially that new phenomenon, the corporation, and the inter-relationships of the private and the public sectors. His account of corporate activity, Canadian style, is rich in insights and leads to a deeper understanding of the origin of our most pressing problems, the concentration of economic power and the dominating role of foreign capital.

There is no question that this study reflects the author's personal anxieties about Canada's future. I share many of his misgivings. However, in following out his concerns, I find no evidence that he has allowed his own scale of values to distort or colour unfairly the facts. The scholarship consists in a down-to-earth grasp of what went on in Canadian government-business relations during the critical period 1867-1914. If he calls a spade a spade, then Professor Naylor is recognizing that it is also the business of the historian not only to lay bare the facts but to do so in a manner that communicates the real meaning and import of what did happen.

Eric Kierans
July 27, 1975

# Notes to the Foreword

1. The core publications are Corporation Taxation Statistics (Catalogue 61-208) and Corporation Financial Statistics (Catalogue 61-207), published annually since 1965, Statistics Canada, Business Finance Division. All statistics used in this introduction are based on these reports.

2.  The Royal Commission on Corporate Concentration, Orders-in-Council P.C. 1975-879, April 22 and P.C. 1975-999, May 1, 1975.

3.  Summary of 1971 Tax Reform Legislation, Department of Finance, Business and Property Income, p 49.

4.  *Ibid.*, p. 50.

# Preface

This book has several objectives. It is at once an essay in the
political economy of development, an examination of a colonial
economy in transition with major structural changes in the process of occurring, an enquiry into the causes, distribution, and
effects of foreign investment in such an economy, and a general
commercial, financial, and industrial history — although by no
means completely comprehensive — of Canada from 1867 to
1914, with some considerations of the antecedents and later consequences of development patterns of that period. It is, as well,
intended in some measure as a contribution to the task begun by
Gustavus Myers over half a century ago of examining the factual
as opposed to the fictional foundations of the process of capital
formation in Canada during these years. But above all else, since
history is primarily a way of comprehending the present, the
enquiry is directed towards elucidating the roots of contemporary economic structures.

The most striking characteristic of the contemporary Canadian economy is the enormous volume of American direct
investment in its industrial base, and the facility with which the
country moved from being a satellite of Britain to a similar
status vis à vis the U.S. After World War II the "British connection" was virtually liquidated, and the movement of American
firms into Canada was considerably augmented. In part they
were attracted by the resources boom of the early 1950's, in part
by the growth of the Canadian domestic market. The American
multinationals had begun their global march and Canada was in
the forefront of the new class of "borrowing" country. By 1967,
65% of mining and smelting was foreign-owned, 45% American:
57% of manufacturing was foreign-owned, 45% American; 74%

of petroleum and gas, 60% American. On the other hand, foreign ownership of railways and utilities declined.[1] And the Canadian hold on the financial apparatus saw few challenges.

Aggregate statistics hide a great deal of important differences. Foreign ownership of assets varies considerably between industries. In food and beverages, textiles, and primary iron and steel it has run about 20-30% in the post-war period. In agricultural implements, while foreign ownership has increased considerably over the past two decades foreign control has not, and in terms of ownership its level is still less than the average for manufacturing as a whole. On the other hand, in virtually every other major industrial category the level of foreign control exceeds that of foreign ownership. In chemicals, electrical products, and automobiles, the key modern industries, foreign ownership levels are from 60 to 90%. Similarly high and rising levels exist in mining and smelting, pulp and paper, petroleum and natural gas.

But while in absolute terms the level of foreign, especially American direct investment in Canada has continued to grow, in relative terms Canada since the mid-1950's has received progressively less of the total outflow of American direct investment. In 1955 its share was 60%; in 1967 it was only 13%.[2] European reconstruction and integration made western Europe an attractive field for manufacturing investment.[3] And by 1967 the cumulative return flow of earnings from Canada to the U.S. exceeded the total outflow of direct investment from 1950 to 1967 by over half a billion dollars. At the same time, American branch plants and affiliates relied increasingly on sources of funds within Canada, and less on imports of capital from the United States. In 1965, 71% of their external funds were from American sources, 28% from Canadian; by 1969, 25% were from U.S. sources, 73% from Canadian.[4]

Concomitant with increased foreign ownership has come industrial stagnation. Of fourteen OECD countries between 1964 and 1969, Canada — while boasting by far the highest level of foreign ownership — had an unemployment rate second only to Ireland. In terms of Research and Development expenditure, supposedly the key to capitalist growth, Canada was surpassed in 1967 by all but the four poorest countries of the OECD group; and in three of them, R&D expenditure was growing while in Canada it was not.[5] Its record of patents granted to residents is one of the worst in the world. From 1966 to 1970 about five per cent of total patents granted went to Canadian residents.[6]

"Integration" of the continental capital market went hand-in-hand with industrial domination. Stock markets in Canada remained thin, adversely affecting the liquidity of new issues and hence reinforcing the preference for more stable American securities by big institutional investors. The proliferation of wholly owned subsidiaries especially contracts the supply of industrial equity in Canada, leading to slow growth of the stock exchanges relative to the American ones.[7] At the same time that brokerage costs are much higher in Canada than the U.S., Canadian banks do 50% of the call loan business in New York to sustain Wall Street. Similar problems impede the marketing of new corporate bond issues in Canada.[8]

The response of Canadian governments to the problems inherent in the degree of foreign ownership — especially the employment crisis that has resulted from the overexpansion of resource industries relative to manufacturing, and the drainage of surplus income as service payments for foreign investment instead of its being used to generate new capital formation within Canada — has been surprisingly predictable. Huge and growing tax concessions are heaped on wealthy firms to induce them to expand investment. All manner of cash gifts are offered by all levels of government, often on a competitive basis, to try to tilt the industrial balance in their favour.

Industrial integration with the U.S., reliance on imported technology, the twisting of the capital market on a north-south basis impeding inter-sectoral flows of funds within Canada, and competitive "bonusing" by various levels of government: all these phenomena are rooted deep in the logic of Canadian development strategy. Far from being of post-World-War-II vintage, they derive from the era of the national policy and were cemented in place during the supposed golden age of Canadian growth, the "wheat boom." They are the result not only of the weakness of the Canadian economic structure, but also its strengths, the two being inseparable. The power of commercial and financial capital to exploit the resource base led to weakness in industrial development. This in turn was the result of the "British tradition." Born a colony of the British mercantile system, Canada inherited a class structure and a set of economic institutions appropriate to its colonial status. They also proved remarkably adaptive to the rising American order. It is these roots that this book hopes to illuminate.

The period covered, broadly speaking, is that of the "national policy," the set of national development policies which, while evolving out of past precedents, are assumed to reach their quintessence in the agricultural and industrial development strategies of the Macdonald and Laurier administrations, or more specifically, of the big business interests that controlled those administrations. Countless eulogies have been written about the "national policy." It has been presented by Canada's more sycophantic historians as a triumph of burgeoning nationalism in the face of momentous challenges, when "great men" with bold imaginations perceived the long-term best interests of society as a whole and brought them to fulfilment, just by the remotest coincidence creating a fair array of millionaires in the process. Apart from the occasional rigid party line economist — with the predictable ideological fulminations about mystical misallocations of productive resources supposedly resulting from protection — there is virtual unanimity that the "national policy" era, in its later stage during the opening years of the "wheat boom," represents a golden age of Canadian economic growth and development, and a bold declaration of industrial independence. Under the circumstances, a re-examination of the nature, causes, and consequences of what might be dubbed "Lord Strathcona's Northern Vision" needs no justification.

An effort has been made throughout to analyse the evolution of economic structures and state policies by taking explicit cognizance, wherever possible, of the economic interests that they furthered. Hence the "muck" has certainly not been spared. The level of corruption in the Canadian political process of the period, especially under the auspices of John A. Macdonald, is truly astounding even to the cynic. It remains to be seen in subsequent volumes if this is the case in more recent history.

There is one obvious and enormous omission. No attempt has been made to add to sections on the evolution of the labour market and labour organization — for a number of reasons. Canada has no lack of labour historians at the moment: there seems, however, a shortage of new work on the structure of capital; and to the extent that the two could be divorced, only the second was examined here. Then, too, consideration of space intervened: it is already a very long book. Time was also a factor. This book is intended to contribute to debates currently in process, though it is hoped it will have some long-term worth as well. To add material on labour would have involved several extra years of preparation; for despite the substantial volume of work undertaken on labour, the sum of our knowledge of the evolution of labour markets in the post-Confederation period, as distinct from the structure of labour institutions, seems to be not significantly different from zero. Furthermore, a study of labour markets could adequately be done only in the context of a full-scale industrial history of Canada. While many topics of industrial history are covered in this book, its central orientation remains that of a study of the financing of economic activity and the structure of ownership and control.

# Notes to the Preface

1. Dominion Bureau of Statistics, *Canada's International Investment Position, 1926-1967,* p.151.

2. K. Levitt, *Silent Surrender,* p. 163.

3. R. Mikesell, "Decisive Factors in the Flow of American Direct Investment to Europe," p. 449.

4. Calculated from Department of Trade, Industry and Commerce, *Foreign-Owned Subsidiaries in Canada, 1964-1969.*

5. Canada, Science Council, *Innovation and the Structure of Canadian Industry,* pp. 28, 61-2.

6. *Canada Year Book,* 1970-1, p. 1044.

7. K. Levitt, *Silent Surrender,* p. 140.

8. *The Gray Report,* pp.98, 100-1.

# List of Abbreviations

| | |
|---|---|
| ACBCA | Alberta Commission on Banking and Credit with Respect to Agriculture |
| Brad | Bradstreets' |
| CAR | Canadian Annual Review |
| CBC | Committee on Banking and Credit |
| CE | Canadian Engineer |
| CF | Canadian Finance |
| CFC | Commercial and Financial Chronicle |
| CLR I, II | Cost of Living Report Volume I, Volume II |
| CM | Canadian Manufacturer |
| CMJ | Canadian Municipal Journal |
| CYB | Canada Year Book |
| Ec | The Economist |
| FA | Farmers' Advocate |
| FP | Financial Post |
| GGG | Grain Growers' Guide |
| HCD | House of Commons, Debates |
| IC | Industrial Canada |
| JC | Journal of Commerce |
| LG | Labour Gazette |
| MT | Monetary Times |
| RCFB | Royal Commission on the Farmers' Bank |
| RCLI | Royal Commission on Life Insurance |
| RCRLC | Royal Commission on the Relations of Labour and Capital |
| RCRTC | Royal Commission on Railways and Transportation in Canada |
| RCT | Royal Commission on the Textile Industry |

RCTE            Royal Commission on Technical Education
RCTR           Royal Commission on Trade Relations Between
                     Canada and the West Indies
SACC           Saskatchewan Agricultural Credit Commission
SCC             Select Committee on Combines
SCCD           Select Committee on the Causes of the Depression
SCM (1874)     Select Committee on Manufactures (1874)
SCM (1885)     Select Committee on Manufactures (1885)
SCTA           Select Committee on the Operation of the Tariff
                     on Agricultural Interests
SYB             Statistical Year Book of Canada
TEC             Tariff Enquiry Commission

# List of Tables

| | | |
|---|---|---|
| I | (1) | Dominion Disallowances of Provincial Legislation  I - 6 |
| I | (2) | Unemployment, Migration, and Labour Force Growth  I - 8 |
| I | (3) | Growth of Manufacturing in Central Canada, 1878-1884  I - 9 |
| I | (4) | Wheat Production and Exports, 1891-1913  I - 12 |
| I | (5) | Commodity Exports, 1896-1913  I - 13 |
| I | (6) | Capital Invested in Manufacturing, by Province  I-13 |
| I | (7) | Indices of Growth, 1890-1913  I - 16, 17 |
| II | (1) | Province of Canada Budget, 1858-1863  I - 29 |
| II | (2) | Production and Consumption — Selected Industries, 1870  I - 42 |
| II | (3) | Consolidated Fund Account, 1876-1886  I - 57 |
| III | (1) | Bank Notes in Circulation  I - 73 |
| III | (2) | Commercial Failures, 1872-1879  I - 83 |
| III | (3) | Canadian Business Failures, 1891-1895  I - 85 |
| III | (4) | Failures Due to "Lack of Capital"  I - 85 |
| III | (5) | Chartered Bank Liabilities — Selected Items  I - 87 |
| III | (6) | Relative Shares of Total Intermediary Assets  I - 88 |
| III | (7) | Government Savings Deposits  I - 91 |
| III | (8) | Government Savings Deposits Per Capita, 1895 and 1900  I - 92 |
| III | (9) | Bank Selected Asset Items, Percentage of Total  I - 94 |
| III | (10) | Banks Operating, 1867-1914  I - 96 |
| IV | (1) | Chartered Bank Failures, 1867-1914  I - 121 |
| V | (1) | Private Banks, 1880-1914  I - 162 |

V       (2)     The Fawcett Bank, 1884 I - 171
V       (3)     Private Bank Failures, 1894-1913 I - 179
VI      (1)     Federally Chartered Insurance Companies, 1913 I-187
VI      (2)     Fire Insurance Company Assets, 1900 and 1914 I-192
VI      (3)     Life Company Investments I - 193
VI      (4)     Life Company Asset Items I - 194
VI      (5)     Canadian Bond Issues I - 198
VI      (6)     Mortgage Market Conditions, 1896-1913 I - 209
VI      (7)     Call Money Market Conditions. 1901-1913 I - 217
VI      (8)     Real Income, 1901-1913 I - 220

VII     (1)     New Canadian Public Issues in London, 1896-
                1913 I - 231
VII     (2)     Average Rates of Return on Securities I - 236
VII     (3)     New Public Issues in London by Canadian
                Utilities, 1902-1910 I - 247
VII     (4)     Hydro Power Production, 1900-1914 I - 251
VIII    (1)     Canadian Pacific Railway Finance, 1886 and
                1914 I - 286
VIII    (2)     Canadian Northern Expansion, 1897-1907 I - 292
VIII    (3)     Canadian Northern Bond Guarantees I - 292

IX      (1)     Homestead Entries, 1875-1885 II - 7
IX      (2)     Railway and Hudson's Bay Company Land
                Sales, 1893-1913 II - 11
IX      (3)     Domestic and British Prices of Canadian Flour,
                1913 II - 15
IX      (4)     Freight Rates Per 100 lb., 1901 II - 28

X       (1)     Patents Issued by Country of Residence II - 46
X       (2)     Patents Issued to Canadians, 1868-1885 II - 47
X       (3)     Provincial Distribution of Patents in Canada,
                1874-1885 II - 48

XI      (1)     U.S. Branch Plants, 1870-1887 II - 72
XI      (2)     U.S. Investments in Canada 1910 and 1913 II - 77
XI      (3)     Distribution of U.S. Manufacturing Investments
                in Canada, 1913 II - 77
XI      (4)     The Pulp and Paper Industry II - 81
XI      (5)     Royal Mint Canada Branch Gold Coinage II - 87

XII     (1)     Railway Bonuses, 1859 II - 109
XII     (2)     Iron and Steel Bounties, 1896-1912 II - 113
XII     (3)     Iron and Steel Bounties, 1909-1910 II - 116

XIII    (1)     Sherbrooke Bonuses II - 143

XIV     (1)     Industrial Mergers, 1900-1914 II - 190

XV       (1)     Trade of Canada  II - 208

XVI      (1)     Life Company Foreign Investments,1891-1911 II - 221
XVI      (2)     Bank of Nova Scotia Investments,1906-1910  II - 244
XVI      (3)     Premiums Received by Canadian Fire Insurance
                 Companies Operating Abroad, 1900  II - 245
XVI      (4)     Canadian Railways' U.S. Holdings, 1916  II - 251
XVI      (5)     Canadian Banks in Latin America, 1914  II - 254
XVI      (6)     Life Companies' Policy Business, 1913  II - 256
XVI      (7)     Canadian Life Companies' Non-U.S. Foreign
                 Investments  II - 257

XVIII    (1)     Government Investment in Railways, 1916 II - 287
XVIII    (2)     Ownership of Industrial Securities by Country,
                 1918-1921  II - 293
XVIII    (3)     Distribution of Security Ownership by Type,
                 1921   II - 293
XVIII    (4)     Distribution of Ownership of Industrial Securities
                 by Industry, 1921  II - 295

*We are only Englishmen on the wrong side of the Atlantic.*

Joseph Howe, London, 1862

# CHAPTER I

# Introduction:
# Canadian Mercantilism, 1867-1914

## The Canadian State and the International Economy

The Canadian state was consolidated at a point in history when fundamental transformations in the world economic order were in motion. The first of a series of long waves of economic expansion, which was based on water power and the world hegemony of the British textile industry, had given way by the 1840's to the new age of steam and steel.[1] The steamship, the railway, and shortly thereafter the telegraph revolutionized the structure of the Atlantic economy, and then spread even further afield. The communication and transportation revolution precipitated further transformations. Industrialism ceased to be a British phenomenon, and spread to Europe and North America. Capital markets of an integrated sort assumed national dimensions, and soon began to take on international proportions. The scale of railway enterprise was matched by the growth of national business enterprise and, subsequently, by the rise of centralized mass labour organizations.

British industrial dominance weakened with the growth of rival powers. The new industrial capacity of the U.S. and Western Europe poured forth its products in competition with those of Britain. New agricultural areas were brought within the scope of international commerce by the revolution in transportation. And by 1873 the combination of industrial overexpansion, excess agricultural production, and the commercial integration effected by the new transportation system precipitated a world crisis. Prices fell, and in many countries a defensive protectionism arose. The era of virtual worldwide free-flows of commodities — typical of the period after 1846 during the expansion phase of the age of steam and steel — abruptly ended.[2] In the era that followed, the flow of commodities was eclipsed by the movement of capital and labour abroad — from the industrial centres, especially Britain, to the new marginal areas — and the search for higher rates of return, new raw material resources, and safe markets precipitated a fresh wave of colonial annexations.

While remaining a free-trading country[3] Britain was nonetheless in the forefront of the new imperialism. Nearly five million square miles and some 88 million people were added to an already vast empire between the partial recovery of 1878 and the end of the war for the annexation of the Boer republics.[4] The formerly despised colonies assumed a new importance as markets, as raw material hinterlands, and as outlets for the investment of finance-capital. With the relative diminution of the domestic investment frontier in the face of a highly skewed distribution of income that kept down working-class purchasing power, and with the shrinkage of former foreign markets in the developed world following the advent of new competition, the great accumulations of upper-class savings swelling the vaults of British financial institutions moved abroad on an unprecedented scale. The historical legacy of earlier industrial hegemony—a world monetary dominance and a great merchant shipping capacity— now helped restructure the flow of British economic activity towards its colonies, old and new, formal and informal. Finally, too, the new wave of imperial expansion provided ample recreation grounds for the offspring of Britain's parasitical upper class to pursue their hobbies as military adventurers, colonial administrators, or missionaries. It was in such a world context that Canada's business class came of age.

Canadian capitalism had evolved in the context of the British mercantile system, from the accumulation of capital in the early staple trades of fur, lumber, and grain in Canada proper, timber in New Brunswick, fishing, ship-building, and imperial trade in Nova Scotia. British preferential tariffs and shipping regulations defined the horizons of the colonial capitalist class. During the era of free trade following the dismantling of the colonial system in the 1840's, the traditional growth path of the economy was forcibly changed. With the rise of the new imperialism after the depression of the 1870's, normalcy was restored, and with it a renewed role within the empire.

Two fundamental structural attributes of the Canadian economy in the period from 1867 to 1914 must be made central to analysis. First, it was a colony, politically and economically. In terms of commercial patterns it was a staple-extracting hinterland oriented toward serving metropolitan markets from which, in turn, it received finished goods. In such a structure, any economic advance in the hinterland accrues to the benefit of the metropole and perpetuates the established division of labour, for relative cheapening of the cost of production of staples lowers the cost of production of the finished product in the metropole. Canada's commercial and financial system grew up geared to the international movement of staples, rather than to abetting secondary processing for domestic markets. It was also the recipient of the largest amount of British investment of any country or colony of the period, excluding the U.S.

Canada's social structure, and therefore the proclivities of its entrepreneurial class, reflected and reinforced its innate colonialism. The political and economic elite were men associated with the staple trades, with the international flow of commodities and of the capital that complemented the commodity movements. They were wholesale dealers and bankers in Montreal in particular, and to a lesser extent in Toronto and Halifax.

A second trait of the economy of the period, in part derivative from the first, was that it had only begun to make the difficult transition from a mercantile-agrarian base to an industrial one. Wealth was accumulated in commercial activities and tended to remain locked up in commerce. Funds for industrial capital formation were in short supply. Commercial capital resisted the transformation into industrial capital except under specific conditions in certain industries, in favour of remaining invested in traditional staple-oriented activities.

In 1850, so-called "manufacturing" accounted for about 18% of the total GNP, but of this over 50% consisted of the products of saw mills and grist mills — i.e. primary processing only of the two staples. Moreover, in the remaining manufacturing sector, the factory system proper was virtually absent: production was overwhelmingly undertaken in small shops still organized largely on handicraft lines. By 1870, while the percentage of the GNP accounted for by manufacturing had not changed significantly, the content of the manufacturing sector had. Saw mill and grist mill output was down to about one-third the total. Cotton factories, secondary iron and steel plants, and others were now in evidence. It would be wrong to exaggerate the degree of transition caused by the Civil-War-induced industrial expansion, for the mode of production was still generally very small-scale; nonetheless, the beginnings of a new order of industrialism were certainly present by that date.

The national policy was, on one level, a set of policies designed to facilitate this transition with the use of foreign capital, and often labour as well. It was a colonial equivalent of the type of development policies undertaken in many advanced countries in the seventeenth and eighteenth centuries, subsequently described as "mercantilism."

Mercantilism was a set of policies aiming at internal economic consolidation and/or expansion. It was the economic counterpart of the political process by which states were integrated and strengthened. While there were as many particular variants of mercantilism as there were states engaging in mercantilist policies, the basic common factors were that the policies were undertaken in a pre-industrial context, that production was largely handicraft interlinked with mercantile credit, that entrepreneurial leadership came from a merchant-capitalist class in international trade and finance, and that the dominant economic institution was the mercantile corporation, functioning often as a subordinate arm of government and frequently with a state-sanctioned monopoly. Contrary to the liberal notion of the state as umpire of competition, its active role was to share in directing the development process through regulation of commerce and industry, through public financial assistance to the construction of the commercial infrastructure, and, occasionally, through direct investment in industry. Policies were undertaken to stimulate an inflow or to block an outflow of factors of production, capital, and skilled labour. The world and its resources were regarded as static; hence the only means of increasing the wealth and welfare of the state was to take something away from someone else,[5] for example by shifting the locus of production to the domestic economy from abroad.

Canada's "national policy" fits the description "mercantilism" remarkably well in terms of mercantile domination, pre-industrial context, and policies pursued, but with the critical proviso that the mercantile policies were pursued in a colonial context.

As a white settler state, Canada shared with Australia, New Zealand, South Africa, and the Argentine a privileged position within the Empire, formal and informal, an Empire whose expanse embraced black infants, brown children, adolescent white daughters, and the Great White Mother in one happy, hierarchial family evolved from some bizarre species of political parthenogenesis. But though privileged politically, the essential fact of colonialism remained, and nowhere was it more evident than in the political structures created at the time of Confederation.

The British North America Act was derived from a political theory of branch-plant imperialism: lower levels of government, the colonial legislatures, were formerly weak and dependent on Britain; now they were to be weak and dependent on Ottawa,

which in turn was ultimately answerable to Westminster.[6] The
federation of the colonies was a highly centralized one. In fact,
the degree of independence exercised by the colonial (provincial)
legislatures was reduced by the results of Confederation, which
represented a regression from the degree of autonomy that
Reform administrations had succeeded in achieving. Under the
terms of Confederation, the central government got all important
economic powers — control over currency and banking, commerce, the major tax sources, transportation infrastructure, and
subsequently the lands and resources of the West. The federal
government also assumed all provincial debts.

The centralization of fiscal powers was critical to the nature of
the new federation. All taxation but the politically delicate and
therefore very greatly circumscribed power of direct taxation was
annexed by the federal government, leaving the provinces with
little more than a paltry subsidy of 80c per head plus meagre
royalties from resource exploitation. Strangling the provincial
assemblies' powers over the purse meant that the merchant-capitalist oligarchy who controlled the federal government had no
difficulty raising funds for their development objectives. Liberal
democracy in Canada was thus set back three decades. As an
additional safeguard, the old legislative council, which in the

### TABLE I (1)

#### Dominion Disallowances of Provincial Legislation

| Province | 1867-1896 | 1896-1905 | 1905-1914 |
|---|---|---|---|
| Ontario | 6 | 1 | — |
| Quebec | 4 | 1 | — |
| Nova Scotia | 6 | 0 | — |
| New Brunswick | 1 | 0 | — |
| Manitoba | 26* | 3 | — |
| British Columbia | 20† | 22† | — |
| Prince Edward Island | 2†† | 0 | — |
| Saskatchewan | — | — | 3 |
| Alberta | — | — | 1 |

Source: compiled from Department of Justice, *Memorandum on
Disallowance* pp. 66-75.

\* Includes ten railway charters.

† Includes many efforts to curb import of Chinese labour, to promote local
railways and local development, and efforts to regulate working conditions
in mines.

†† Both attempts to free the Island of absentee proprietors.

colonies had been made elective by Reform administration, was restored to its former grandeur as the federally appointed Senate. And the federal government assumed the imperial government's power of disallowance over colonial (provincial) legislation, a power which it wielded with much more frequency than had the imperium of old.

In terms of policies adopted to promote and foster industrialization, create employment in secondary industry, and expand the economy's factor endowment, Sir John A. Macdonald described the intent of the National Policy tariff as follows:

> We have no manufacturers here. We have no work people; our work-people have gone off to the United States. . . . These Canadian artisans are adding to the strength, to the power of a foreign nation instead of adding to our own. Our work-people in this country on the other hand are suffering from want of employment. If these men cannot find an opportunity in their own country to develop the skill and genius with which God has gifted them, they will go to the country where their abilities can be employed, as they have gone from Canada to the United States. . . .If Canada had a judicious system of taxation they would be toiling and doing well in their own country.[7]

In addition to the tariff, patent laws and direct subsidies were employed to stimulate industrial capital formation, generate the basis of population growth, and attract foreign investment. Even the mercantilist institution of the state-chartered monopoly was added to the slate of mercantilist policies, in the form of the Canadian Pacific Railway. And there was virtually no limit to the supplications of successive governments in their effort to attract British investments into Canada — though the pay-off of all these policies took some time to show itself.

The period from 1867 to 1914 can be logically divided into two phases. The first phase, up to 1896 (properly speaking from 1873 to 1896), was one of secular deflation, the recession phase of the era of steam and steel which has been referred to, rather misleadingly, as the "Great Depression." The second phase, from 1896 to 1914, saw a steady rise in prices as the world economy was transformed by the advent of new industries, based on electricity, chemicals, and the internal combustion engine.

# Economic Development in the "Great Depression"

The notion that the 1873-1896 period was in any way a prolonged depression needs clarification. While the growth of

manufacturing output may have been fairly steady,[8] measured
either by gross value of production or value added in real terms,
a "depression" in the Canadian economy of the period must be
given another interpretation. For the staple-extracting hinterland, "depression" or prosperity hinged essentially on the world
prices of its primary produce and on the rate of population
growth which depended in large measure on those prices. And
growth in manufacturing output certainly does not invalidate the
notion that the period was one of the prolonged recession phase
of the age of steam and steel. Industrial overproduction, leading
to secular price declines and a profit squeeze, manifested itself
throughout the developed world, and showed ample evidence in
Canada as well.

Despite any progress made in manufacturing development,
measured unemployment rates remained high, and these are
chronic underestimates for an essentially farm-based community
whose population had the options of either returning to agriculture or emigrating to the U.S. during bad periods. Furthermore,
the period 1873-1879 was unambiguously one of recession on all
counts — according to contemporary reports, which are a much
more reliable guide than latter-day manipulations of inadequate
statistics. So too were the early 1890's, when even the measured
rate of growth of manufacturing output dipped very low. The
one exceptional period seems to be the boom of 1879-1883 at the
time of the imposition of the National Policy tariff.

**TABLE I (2)**

**Unemployment, Migration and Labour Force Growth**

| Year | Unemployment Rate | Total Net Migration (1000's) | Annual Rate of Growth of Labour Force |
|------|-------------------|------------------------------|----------------------------------------|
| 1870 | 4.03 | (1870-1880) -85 | 2.05 |
| 1880 | 6.02 | (1880-1890) -205 | 1.60 |
| 1890 | 5.02 | (1890-1900) -181 | 1.06 |
| 1900 | 3.99 | (1900-1910)+715 | 4.17 |
| 1910 | 3.00 | | |

Sources: O. J. Firestone, *Development of Canada's Economy*, p.
         229; O. J. Firestone, *Canada's Economic Development*,
         pp. 58, 61.

While the Great Depression lifted temporarily in 1879 until
1883-1884, it is not all clear what role, if any, the National Policy

tariff played in the revival of economic conditions. For the period was one of general world recovery, and the markets for Canadian staples, especially timber, improved. Timber was the leading sector in terms of output and employment among the non-agricultural industries. A little burst of immigration also occurred, but this was associated more with the land rush in Manitoba, and therefore with the state of world agricultural produce markets, than with any increase in employment opportunities in the old provinces. After 1880 came a substantial amount of spending on Canadian Pacific Railway construction, and while the National Policy was instrumental in providing funds, some of the impetus was lost through import leakages, for the CPR syndicate received a blanket tariff exemption on its material requirements.

Still, a substantial growth of manufacturing did occur. While the return to prosperity by itself would have generated a great deal of industrial expansion, and while the data available were deliberately falsified by the Tory government's investigators (by adding to the category of "new factories" factories already in existence but not operating in 1878) in order to inflate the results for public consumption, it is clear that the high tariff did stimulate a fair degree of new manufacturing. In the major cities of Ontario and Quebec capital employed rose 85% between 1878 and 1884, while output expanded 125% in value.

The effects in the Maritimes were much less spectacular, as the Atlantic region underwent a degree of reorientation from its former export basis toward integration with central Canada. The results in the Atlantic provinces did not show the balanced growth that typified central Canadian manufacturing. Growth of sugar refining, cotton, and primary iron and steel for domestic markets was partly offset by a decline not only in shipbuilding and primary timber and other traditional industries associated

**TABLE I (3)**

**Growth of Manufacturing in Central Canada, 1878-1884**

|  | No. of Factories | No. of Hands | Yearly Wages | Gross Value of Product | Capital Invested |
|---|---|---|---|---|---|
| 1878 | 467 | 27,869 | 8,174,900 | 34,131,100 | 26,160,500 |
| same factories, 1884 | 467 | 42,080 | 12,870,900 | 53,554,500 | 36,647,400 |
| new factories, 1884 | 258 | 13,453 | 4,040,900 | 23,712,600 | 11,777,700 |
| increase, 1878-1884 | 258 | 27,664 | 8,736,900 | 43,136,000 | 22,264,600 |

Source: *SCM* (1885), p. 34.

with the British mercantile connection, but also by some losses in a number of consumer goods industries geared to local markets, as a result of central Canadian dumping.

Despite the paeans of joy sung by a Tory Select Committee in 1885 over the multiplicity of alleged benefits of the National Policy tariff, the results in terms of industrial expansion were very short-lived. Late in 1883 or early in 1884, depending upon criteria chosen, the prosperity phase ended. The bottom dropped out of land values in Winnipeg, financial difficulties beset the CPR, and industrial stagnation set in. Ontario, which had seen the greatest expansion, was hit hardest by the results of industrial over-expansion during the boom phase. During 1884, 72 plants shut down completely in 65 urban centres, and total employment fell absolutely by 5,557. Wage levels dropped by 15-20% on average from their 1882 levels. The recession hit all industries, but especially secondary iron and steel, foundries, machine shops, and agricultural implements. In Hamilton, most factories cut back to 75% capacity. Guelph had an unemployment rate of 20%. London, a centre of agricultural implement production, anticipated a winter unemployment rate of 50%.[9] In the Maritimes, the three industries which led the expansion all experienced a drastic recession. Over a million and a quarter dollars were lost in the overextended sugar refineries there; there were big losses in cotton; and the iron and steel industry profits were cut to zero, if not below.[10] In addition there were still the problems already inherent in the stagnation of lumber and shipbuilding to face. Yet the Canadian Manufacturers' Association, with its usual sophistry, claimed that the National Policy was a key factor in mitigating the depression.[11]

Despite such false starts as the 1879-1883 expansion, the period from 1873 to 1896 was one of disappointingly slow growth. Population growth was exceedingly slow, the migration to the United States more than offsetting the inflow of the new immigrants, and hence claiming a large share of the natural increase as well.[12] Sir Richard Cartwright, Liberal finance critic, ventured the opinion that the most prosperous part of the Canadian population was the one-and-one-half million people driven out of the country by the National Policy.[13]

# The "Wheat Boom"

The period from 1896 to 1914 is generally regarded as the golden age of Canadian growth. The year 1896 represented a turning-point in world economic conditions, with prices of agricultural products in particular beginning to turn up. In the U.S., "wheat mining" had led to soil exhaustion, forcing a switch in some areas to the cultivation of corn and coarse cereals at the same time as American and European industrial expansion drew labour off the farm and into factories, raising the demand for food.

In Canada, too, the period around 1896 represented a turning-point. World wheat prices troughed and began to rise, as did wholesale prices in Canada. Exports per capita began to rise even before export prices. Bank note circulation followed prices, domestic and foreign, upwards. Yet homestead entries and population did not begin a marked rise until after 1902, indicating that the phrase "wheat boom" applied to the period hides more than it reveals, in particular a major discontinuity in the pattern of growth of the period. The expansion was led by real exports, but not by wheat. It is absurd to attribute the growth of investment that fed the boom to expectations factors derivative from the change in the trend in world prices;[14] obviously business fixed-capital formation was not undertaken in anticipation of a boom in wheat exports nearly a decade later. Furthermore, in the first phase of the new expansion 1895-1902, and for the only time during the entire period 1867-1914, the Canadian trade balance was in surplus over-all, and net export of capital occurred. After 1902-3, as the West began to fill, the balance of trade went into deficit and a great flood of capital imports followed.

This point is a critical one, for the role of wheat in generating expansion has been badly misinterpreted. In 1891, wheat accounted for 6.3% of total commodity exports: in 1901, six years after the "wheat boom" had begun, wheat accounted for 6.0% of commodity exports. It is true that wheat exports grew absolutely during the early years of expansion, but wheat output grew very little, and in relative terms the upward trend in wheat exports was minor. Wheat production began to accelerate in 1902, and did not reach its "take-off" point until 1906. Exports of wheat and wheat flour did likewise. By 1911, wheat was 21.6% of commodity exports, and by 1913 it reached 30.5%. While prices of wheat showed an upward trend after 1896, it would be ludicrous to impute to that alone any great power to restructure the Canadian economy. Not until 1907 did prices reach the level achieved in 1891. And the over-all rise in prices of wheat over the 1896-1913 period is not out of line with the general index of wholesale domestic prices or the over-all export price index.

In fact, the initial expansion was led not by field crops but by the mineral staples, exports of which rose 500% between 1896 and 1901, while the over-all growth of exports was but 162%.

**TABLE I (4)**

**Wheat Production and Exports, 1891-1913**

| Year | (bushels millions)<br>Wheat Production | Wheat Exports |
|------|------|------|
| 1891 | 42.2 | 3.4 |
| 1896 | 55.7 | 10.8 |
| 1897 | 39.6 | 9.8 |
| 1898 | 54.4 | 24.6 |
| 1899 | 66.5 | 13.9 |
| 1900 | 59.9 | 20.3 |
| 1901 | 55.6 | 14.8 |
| 1902 | 88.3 | 31.0 |
| 1903 | 97.1 | 38.8 |
| 1904 | 81.9 | 23.9 |
| 1905 | 71.8 | 20.6 |
| 1906 | 107.0 | 47.3 |
| 1907 | 135.6 | 46.5 |
| 1908 | 93.1 | 47.6 |
| 1909 | 112.4 | 56.7 |
| 1910 | 166.7 | 67.8 |
| 1911 | 132.1 | 62.4 |
| 1912 | 231.2 | 97.6 |
| 1913 | 224.2 | 115.7 |

Source: M. Urquhart and K. Buckley, *Historical Statistics of Canada,* pp. 364-5.

This expansion was largely at the expense of old staples like fish and forest products, which fell absolutely. A relative decline in the share of animal products was also recorded. And within the minerals sector that led the boom, gold from the Klondike rush dominated. It makes as much sense to call this period the "gold boom" as to give pride of place to wheat.

Later, export patterns shifted again. Agricultural products rose from 13.9% of total exports in 1901 to 42.1% of the total by 1913; animals and their products fell drastically, partly due to the conversion of grazing land into arable; a sharp reduction in the relative importance of minerals occurred; while smaller declines were registered by other categories.

Within the agricultural sphere that rose to new importance, there was a shift in the export patterns, not only towards wheat at the expense of other products, but also to the detriment of exports of wheat flour. In 1901, wheat flour accounted for 36.6%

## TABLE I (5)
### Commodity Exports, 1901-1913

|  | % Total 1896 | % Total 1901 | % Total 1906 | % Total 1910 | % Total 1913 | 1913 as % 1901 |
|---|---|---|---|---|---|---|
| All | 100.0 | 100.0 | 100.0 | 100.0 | 100.0 | 202.2 |
| Minerals | 7.6 | 22.6 | 15.0 | 14.3 | 15.9 | 146.0 |
| Fish | 10.4 | 6.0 | 6.7 | 5.6 | 4.5 | 152.3 |
| Forest | 25.6 | 16.9 | 16.4 | 17.0 | 12.1 | 144.3 |
| Animal | 34.4 | 31.2 | 28.2 | 19.3 | 12.5 | 80.7 |
| Agricultural | 13.3 | 13.9 | 22.9 | 32.3 | 42.1 | 605.2 |
| All primary | 91.3 | 90.6 | 89.6 | 88.8 | 87.8 | 193.1 |
| Manufactures* | 8.7 | 9.4 | 10.6 | 11.2 | 12.3 | 273.1 |

Source: *CYB* (various years); *SYB* (1901), adjusted.

* Includes wood pulp.

by value of total exports of wheat and wheat flour; by 1913 it was down to 18.4%.

The expansion was also accompanied by shifts in the relative economic weight of the various provinces. While Ontario maintained its preponderant position, the provinces to the east declined in relative importance as manufacturing centres, and therefore as producers of goods to meet the demands of the new West. And in the West itself, although the provincial economies were basically oriented to primary products — grains, animal products, minerals, and timber — substantial growth in manu-

## TABLE I (6)
### Capital Invested in Manufacturing, by Province

|  | % of total by Province | | | | |
|---|---|---|---|---|---|
|  | 1870 | 1880 | 1890 | 1900 | 1910 |
| Ontario | 48.9 | 48.7 | 49.8 | 48.1 | 47.6 |
| Quebec | 35.9 | 35.9 | 33.3 | 31.5 | 26.2 |
| New Brunswick | 7.5 | 5.1 | 4.5 | 4.2 | 2.9 |
| Nova Scotia | 7.7 | 6.1 | 5.6 | 7.8 | 6.4 |
| Prince Edward Is. | — | 1.3 | 0.7 | 0.5 | 0.2 |
| West | — | 2.9 | 6.1 | 7.9 | 16.7 |

Source: calculated from *Census of Canada,* Vol. III, 1871, 1881, 1891, 1901, 1911.

facturing capacity occurred as well, helping again to reorient activity away from the eastern provinces.

In surveying the effects of the post-1896 expansion, one elated contemporary commented that "at last Canada's hour had struck,"[15] but it is not at all clear that the tolling was heard in working-class circles. Labour markets began to tighten up after 1900, the unemployment rate dropping while the labour force grew and net migration became positive. But the general level of real wages over the period 1900-1914 fell by 1.9%.[16]

One of the most important prerequisites of industrialization is the existence of an agricultural sector capable of providing both cheap food under conditions of rising productivity and surplus income to the industrial sector.[17] The Canadian economy failed this test abysmally. Food prices in Canada soared during the period when the greatest expansion occurred in its agricultural base, because the new agricultural areas were oriented towards export. Not only wheat, but even stock went to service the food requirements of industrial countries. The cattle ranges provided for the American consumer, rather than helping to stock the mixed farms in Canada.[18]

Moreover, rapid inflation of the cost of distribution of commodities resulted from an overextension of trunk railway lines for long-distance movement of commodities at the expense of local service lines, an excessive number of small traders, and the prevailing patterns of investment. British portfolio investment fed the construction of commercial infrastructure to move commodities internationally. British loans later became available to finance huge industrial mergers which led to oligopoly price increases. And in terms of industrial investment, producers' goods industries expanded quickly while consumers' goods industries lagged. As a result, prices of food, clothing, housing, and lumber for building rose fastest of all in Canada during this period.[19] Food prices in Canada in fact rose much more quickly than those in Britain — which imported a substantial volume of Canadian food production. Even bread prices in Canada exceeded the British price of bread made from Canadian wheat.

In terms of surplus income for industrial capital formation, in fact, the flow of funds ran the other way. Canada's new staple farm sector drained income from industry to be invested in overexpansion of a single cash crop because of the structure of the Canadian capital market, which evolved in such a way as to perpetuate a staple-extracting economy.

The two main structural attributes of the economy, domination by commercial capital and its colonial status as a staple-extracting hinterland, complemented and reinforced each other.

Industrial capital formation was retarded relative to investment in staple development and the creation of the commercial infrastructure necessary to extract and move staples. The character and patterns of transportation infrastructure put in place and the banking and financial intermediary structure bore all the hallmarks of a staple-exporting economy. Overexpansion of trunk lines for the long-distance movement of primary output under federal government direction took precedence over local lines for the development of Canadian market for local industry. Funds flowed freely through the intermediary system into commercial investments, into the development and movement of staples, or into other public utilities and other types of infrastructure, and much less so into industrial capital formation.

The results were evident in the uneven development of various regions. The Maritime provinces attached to Canada at Confederation were drained of surplus income to finance central Canadian development objectives in the West. Savings flowed out of the Maritimes via the intermediary system, and hence away from Maritime industry, to be put to work in building up a dependent single cash-crop frontier in the West. Quebec too lost control of its surplus income during the boom era of the "wheat economy, and with the loss of local savings came the submergence of the Québécois industrial entrepreneur under the wave of anglophone-controlled mergers.

The foundations of the current Canadian economic system can be found in this critical period. The degree of American domination of its industrial base, the primary extractive orientation of its export sector, the relative growth of particular regions, and the socio-economic position of the Québécois are all logical outgrowths of the operation of the "national policy," of the set of policies adopted by central Canadian commercial capitalists to advance their interests within the context of Canada's situation in the British empire.

**Table I (7)**

**Indices of Growth, 1890-1913**

| (1) Year | (1) Domestic Wholesale Prices - Index | (2) Export Prices Index | (3) Value of Exports Per Capita $ | (3) Value of Exports Index | (4) Manitoba No. 1 Northern Wheat Wholesale Price $ | (4) Index | (5) Homestead Entries | (6) Bank Notes Total Index | (7) Per Capita $ | (7) Per Capita Index | (8) British Security Prices Index | (9) Population Index |
|---|---|---|---|---|---|---|---|---|---|---|---|---|
| 1890 | 103.4 | 103.5 | $20.2 | 56.0 | $0.85 | 113.3 | 2,955 | 68.1 | $6.51 | 74.2 | 96.4 | 90.1 |
| 1891 | 104.7 | 104.0 | 20.3 | 56.2 | 0.93 | 124.0 | 3,523 | 69.7 | 6.32 | 72.0 | 95.7 | 91.0 |
| 1892 | 96.5 | 103.0 | 23.3 | 64.5 | 0.80 | 106.6 | 4,840 | 72.5 | 6.98 | 79.6 | 97.8 | 91.9 |
| 1893 | 99.2 | 100.7 | 24.0 | 66.5 | 0.73 | 97.3 | 4,067 | 72.6 | 6.85 | 78.1 | 100.4 | 92.8 |
| 1894 | 92.1 | 101.1 | 23.6 | 65.4 | 0.61 | 81.3 | 3,209 | 66.9 | 6.35 | 72.4 | 102.5 | 93.6 |
| 1895 | 88.3 | 96.5 | 22.6 | 62.6 | 0.72 | 96.0 | 2,394 | 66.1 | 6.10 | 69.5 | 107.3 | 94.6 |
| 1896 | 83.1 | 93.1 | 23.8 | 65.9 | 0.66 | 88.0 | 1,857 | 67.5 | 6.18 | 70.4 | 114.0 | 95.4 |
| 1897 | 85.6 | 90.9 | 26.8 | 74.2 | 0.79 | 105.3 | 2,384 | 73.7 | 6.12 | 69.8 | 111.1 | 96.6 |
| 1898 | 91.1 | 97.0 | 31.6 | 87.5 | 0.93 | 124.0 | 4,848 | 81.3 | 7.29 | 83.1 | 107.7 | 97.6 |
| 1899 | 91.9 | 95.4 | 30.2 | 83.7 | 0.71 | 96.7 | 6,684 | 89.2 | 7.89 | 89.9 | 104.7 | 98.8 |
| 1900 | 100.0 | 100.0 | 36.1 | 100.0 | 0.75 | 100.0 | 7,426 | 100.0 | 8.75 | 100.0 | 100.0 | 100.0 |
| 1901 | 99.8 | 102.5 | 36.4 | 100.8 | 0.75 | 100.0 | 8,167 | 108.6 | 9.36 | 106.7 | 96.6 | 101.5 |

| | | | | | | | | | | | | |
|---|---|---|---|---|---|---|---|---|---|---|---|---|
| 1902 | 101.3 | 104.3 | 38.3 | 106.1 | 0.73 | 97.3 | 14,673 | 118.9 | 10.16 | 115.8 | 97.2 | 103.1 |
| 1903 | 102.6 | 107.6 | 39.8 | 110.2 | 0.79 | 105.3 | 31,303 | 129.3 | 10.61 | 121.0 | 95.0 | 106.6 |
| 1904 | 101.1 | 108.7 | 36.7 | 101.7 | 0.92 | 122.7 | 26,073 | 132.6 | 10.60 | 120.8 | 93.2 | 109.5 |
| 1905 | 106.1 | 105.3 | 33.9 | 93.9 | 0.90 | 120.0 | 30,819 | 137.5 | 10.68 | 121.7 | 93.8 | 112.6 |
| 1906 | 111.8 | 113.4 | 41.6 | 115.2 | 0.76 | 101.3 | 41,869 | 151.9 | 11.44 | 130.4 | 91.7 | 116.0 |
| 1907 | 117.4 | 118.5 | 32.0 | 90.3 | 0.88 | 117.3 | 21,869 | 162.7 | 12.02 | 137.0 | 88.0 | 118.4 |
| 1908 | 116.3 | 124.2 | 43.1 | 119.4 | 1.04 | 138.7 | 30,424 | 153.3 | 11.00 | 125.4 | 90.0 | 122.0 |
| 1909 | 114.9 | 123.5 | 39.1 | 108.3 | 1.04 | 138.7 | 39,081 | 158.8 | 11.04 | 125.9 | 88.6 | 125.8 |
| 1910 | 118.5 | 124.8 | 43.6 | 120.8 | 1.00 | 133.3 | 41,568 | 176.3 | 11.87 | 135.3 | 86.6 | 130.0 |
| 1911 | 121.8 | 123.7 | 41.5 | 115.0 | 0.95 | 128.0 | 44,479 | 193.2 | 12.50 | 142.5 | 85.2 | 134.8 |
| 1912 | 130.9 | 120.7 | 42.2 | 116.9 | 0.97 | 129.3 | 39,151 | 215.0 | 13.41 | 152.9 | 82.9 | 140.3 |
| 1913 | 129.3 | 122.5 | 50.7 | 140.4 | 0.88 | 117.3 | 33,699 | 226.0 | 13.56 | 154.6 | 79.1 | 145.8 |

Sources: (1) K. Taylor and H. Mitchell, *Statistical Contributions to Canadian Economic History*, II, p. 6.
         (2) *Ibid.*, p. 56.
         (3) *Canada Year Book (CYB)*, 1916, p. 255.
         (4) R. H. Coats, *Cost of Living Report (CLR)*, II, pp. 34-5.
         (5) *CYB*, 1926, p. 923.
         (6) *CYB*, 1918, p. 514.
         (7) Calculated from *CYB*, 1918, p. 154; *CLR*, II, p. 946.
         (8) K. C. Smith and G. F. Horne, "An Index Number of Securities 1867-1914."
         (9) *CLR*, II, p. 946.

# Notes to Chapter I

1.  See especially J. Schumpeter, *Business Cycles,* (2 vols.); N. Kondratief, "The Long Waves in Economic Life."
2.  E. Hobsbawm, *Industry and Empire*, pp. 140ff.
3.  A great deal of nonsense has been written about the British "exception" to the general retreat from laissez-faire. In fact the British case is much less exceptional than appears at first glance. British dependence on imported foods, at a time when most European countries and the U.S. chose to protect their farm sectors threatened by falling prices, obviously dictated the preservation of free trade in foodstuffs in an effort to keep down money wages and preserve British industry's competitive position: it was thus indirectly a policy of protection. And free trade in manufactures for Britain meant as well free trade for India whether the Indians liked it or not: it thus served to assure the Indian market would stay open to shore up, as of old, the creaky fortunes of the British textile industry. The iron and steel industry in Britain in fact was protectionist, and the decision to remain "free trade" oriented reflected the superior political power Manchester possessed at the expense of Birmingham.
4.  J. A. Hobson, *Imperialism: A Study,* p. 18.
5.  E. Heckscher, *Mercantilism,* II, p.25.
6.  Cf. D. Creighton, *Dominion of the North,* pp. 306-7.
7.  *HCD,* March 7, 1878, pp. 857-9.
8.  G. Bertram, "Economic Growth in Canadian Industry."
9.  *CM,* Jan. 16, 1885, p. 901.
10. *MT,* May 20, 1887, pp. 1379-80.
11. *CM,* Feb. 20, 1885, p. 988.
12. *HCD,* March 14, 1888, p. 144.
13. *HCD,* March 22, 1892, p. 358.
14. See, for example, J. Stovel, *Canada in the World Economy,* p. 70.
15. O. D. Skelton, "General Economic History," p. 191.
16. H. D. Woods and S. Ostry, *Labour Policy and Labour Economics in Canada,* p. 402.
17. W. W. Rostow, *The Stages of Economic Growth,* pp. 23-4.
18. *CLR,* I, p. 67.
19. *CLR,* II, pp. 20, 377.

*Constitutions, statutes, supreme court and privy council decisions are credit instruments.*

Harold Innis

# CHAPTER II

# Revenue, Protection, and the Politics of International Finance

## Capital Formation and the State

The formation and evolution of the Canadian state structure is fully explicable only when explicit cognizance is taken of the commercial and financial relations of the colony to more advanced economies, notably Britain and the United States. Many of the most critical political decisions taken by the ruling class in the colony were conditioned by the state of Canada's relations with the British capital market. British capital built most of the major works of commercial infrastructure in the provinces; public finance depended upon the pleasure of the imperial government and the London private "merchant" banks; and Canadian development policies and the structure of its capital markets and financial institutions were moulded to ensure the greatest facility of entry of British capital.

The critical, if accidental impetus toward the development of the Canadian state structure in its modern form came from a handful of small businessmen in St. Catharines, Ontario, in the wake of the post-1815 deflation that gripped the province of Upper Canada. This little group of merchants and millers, led by William Hamilton Merritt, conceived of an elaborate irrigation-ditch-cum-canal to maintain the water power for their milling operations. In short order, the project became tied to the grand scheme of the Canadian mercantile class, especially that of Montreal, to complete a system of canals on the St. Lawrence-Great Lakes system in order to draw the American north-west grain trade to Europe down the St. Lawrence via Montreal. The canals were essential to offset the effects of the American Erie

Canal, which threatened to capture the U.S. interior trade for New York and draw it along the Hudson-Mohawk drainage system. This competition of rival drainage systems for the products of the interior, a competition founded in the earlier era of the fur trade, left an indelible mark on Canadian economic structures and the commercial policies of its ruling business class. William´ Hamilton Merritt's scheme for the Welland Canal was initially sold to the government of Upper Canada in 1824 with the assurance that the total cost of the project would not exceed $42,000 and that it would not cost the government a cent! Several million dollars later, in 1840, and with a total public investment of over one million dollars, some major rethinking of the finances of the colony was called for, as bankruptcy appeared imminent.

The Welland Canal episode illustrates many of the critical problems faced by colonial financiers and merchants of the period, and it set a number of important precedents for the future. Its tight interface of government and business was an often-repeated pattern in later years, and led directly to a total compromise of the public finances. The province was bankrupted by the drain on its resources imposed by the canal company. It represented, too, the first *major* instances of several categories of foreign investment in Canada. American direct investment, specifically from one J. B. Yates, an Albany financier heavily involved in early variants of the numbers racket, was essential to its early development. It also prompted the first major influx of foreign portfolio investment into Canadian public securities, the proceeds of which were earmarked for canal finance. Early efforts in 1830 failed to interest the London private banks — the Barings, Glyn, Mills, Rothschilds, or Overend and Co. — in the provincial debt. In 1831 some interim financing was acquired from the Bank of the United States on the collateral of provincial currency debentures, but it was far from satisfactory. Hence in 1835 a major innovation in provincial finance was introduced: the first issue of sterling debentures was undertaken in a deliberate effort to shift the Canadian public debt from the province to England in order to free funds in Canada for other investments. The pattern of financing heavy works of infrastructure abroad by long-term debt, while Canadian capital moved into shorter-term investments, persisted thereafter.

Despite increasing raids on the provincial treasury, the canal swallowed up capital in ever increasing amounts and other expediencies were tried. An effort to float a big loan with some unspecified "European" banking house foundered after William

Lyon Mackenzie, the leader of the Reform party of the province, unveiled a long string of charges of corruption against the company. New York was picked clean. The Assembly of the sister province, Lower Canada, was also under the control of a Reform movement unsympathetic to the machinations of the governing and mercantile cliques of the colonies: it would invest little to begin with, and nothing further as time went by. The private resources of the commercial men of the two colonies were meagre, and were largely refused to the Company. Hence, increasing demands on the state were made until the outbreak of rebellion in 1837 and 1838 caused a complete collapse of provincial credit in Britain.

The canal program and its capital requirements brought the British private bankers, Baring Brothers and Co., to Canada for the first time. And in co-operation with the mercantile elite of the colony a fundamental experiment in public finance was carried out. As it became clear that the government was considering writing off the canal and dumping it on the private shareholders, the private shareholders decided to act first and dump the financial derelict on the government. Nationalization plans followed, to bail out the private investors by exchanging shares for provincial debentures.

But as a prelude to buying out the private investors with more public money, the capital market in Britain had to be made receptive to the now thoroughly suspect Canadian securities. The result was the Act of Union of 1841, whereby the two provinces were united in the expectation that spreading the burden of repayment of the bankrupt upper province's debts over the population of the almost debtless lower province would both reassure existing British debenture holders and widen the revenue base for future issues. In conjunction with an imperial guarantee of the interest of a new issue, the credit of the United Province was established in Britain and the path opened for Canadian finance to cultivate an inflow of British portfolio capital in the future.[1]

# Development of the Canadian Capital Market

The two British private banking houses, the Barings and Glyn, Mills, played a key role in Canada's subsequent financial relations with London. At the time, Canadian banks were geared to the provision of short-term mercantile credit. Hence all British capital destined for Canada for three decades after union came via the Barings and the Glyns, who stood in much the same relationship to the Canadian Finance Ministers as did the Bank of England to the Chancellor of the Exchequer.[2]

The development and regulation of private financial institutions revealed the same type of sensitivity to the state of Canadian credit in the imperial capital market. Banking was regulated first by the Colonial Office and later by the provincial authorities themselves, in such a way as to maintain the confidence of the British investor.[3] The first trust company in Canada, the Trust & Loan Company of Canada, founded by the Kingston mercantile community in 1843, had as a major objective the attraction of British capital. The preamble of its charter noted that:

> Whereas the improvement and advancement of the province are greatly retarded by reason of the deficiency of capital which prevails therein; And whereas the difficulty of ascertaining, with confidence, the money value and legal sufficiency of the security offered by borrowers, has hitherto, to a great extent, precluded capitalists resident in Great Britain from availing themselves of the opportunities constantly offered in Canada for the profitable investment of Capital, And whereas, such difficulties would, to a great extent, be overcome by the establishment of an Incorporated Joint Stock Company . . .[4]

The ability of the company to tap British capital sources was greatly improved after 1850 when Thomas Baring and George Carr Glyn were added to its trustees.

The stock exchanges too were created in part with an eye to promoting the inflow of British capital.[5] Even the introduction of general legislation permitting the principle of limited liability had this objective in mind in 1849.[6] And Francis Hincks, a leading member of the Reform movement, future Prime Minister of the Province of Canada, and future Finance Minister of the Dominion of Canada, even expressed his reluctance to participate in the rebellions of 1837-1838 on the grounds that they were likely to frighten away British investment.[7]

# The Dawn of the Railway Age

Railways became an urgent order of priority in the 1840's with the decline and fall of the old colonial system and its preferential tariff arrangements for Canada, and with the threat that American railroads would turn the commercial balance back in favour of the Hudson-Mohawk system at the expense of the carefully

constructed St. Lawrence commercial empire. It was therefore in
railway finance that the greatest efforts were made to win the
approval of British investors. The Municipal Act of 1848, drafted
by the provincial Inspector-General (Finance Minister) Francis
Hincks, created various municipal units and gave them corporate
power to raise money and construct public works.[8] Following
this, a loan fund which pooled the municipalities' resources was
set up on the premise that the municipalities' combined borrowing powers in London would be greater than the sum of their
individual capacities. And in addition the province itself undertook direct guarantees of the securities of certain favoured
railway companies, notably those on which leading government
members such as Francis Hincks, A. T. Galt, and others served
on the Board of Directors.

Under the auspices of these pieces of legislation, the great
railway projects of the era were built — most prominently the
Grand Trunk. Its contractors were the English firm of Brassey,
Peto, Jackson and Betts, who had built nearly one-third of the
English railways of the period. Thomas Baring and George Carr
Glyn sat on the GTR's London board, virtually the entire Canadian Cabinet on its Canadian board. Though it was initially
planned as a public work, the then Prime Minister of Canada,
Sir Francis Hincks, apparently had a change of heart after being
lavishly "entertained" by Lord Brassey and his colleagues on a
visit to London to raise money for the project.[9] By 1859, Canada
has 2,093 miles of railroad of which 1,112 were the Grand Trunk
lines. The cost to the public, much of it in graft and waste, was
over four million pounds, accounting for nearly half of the total
debt of the province.[10] Operations of the road showed a chronic
and growing deficit.

The construction and financing of the line were appalling
operations even by the standards of the day. The initial distribution of the shares left the two English private bankers together
with the contractors in control of over a third, which was more
than enough to ensure them control of the line. At the time of
the original issue, the stock market (fed by the fancy prospectus
of the line, which featured prominently its tight relations with
the government of the province) was very receptive, but the promoters held back stock to push up the price. Once the stock
bubble burst and the stock fell to a heavy discount, from which it
never recovered, the promoters reneged on their agreement to
take up unsold stock themselves. The province had to fill the gap
in their cash resources by the first of a never-ending series of
special relief measures, some voted in Parliament, some granted
by order-in-council, and some just gratuitously handed out by

particular ministers on their own authority. In addition to sustaining a huge infusion of funds to keep the line afloat, the province in 1858 obligingly reduced its claim to that of second mortgagee. Under the terms of the Relief Act of that year, earnings of the road were to go first to pay the interest on preference bonds, next to other bonds and debentures, next to pay dividends of six per cent on the stock, and only then, after paying dividends, were the funds to be appropriated for paying interest on debts incurred by the province on behalf of the railway. Once this neat arrangement had been made, the next difficulty was to generate some earnings for distribution — no mean problem in light of the constant deficit on operations of the line.

There were essentially two approaches taken to the problem of profits. The first was to scamp on construction as much as possible. Thus, a line which the contractors had decreed would be built on a standard superior to any in North America ran up an astonishing record of steep grades, raising costs of operation by reducing the volume of cargo it could carry, with split and broken rails strewn from one end of the province to the other interpersed with a string of wrecked locomotives and derailed cars. The second approach was that of systematic falsification of the books. Its assets were carefully overstated by adding to them the value of replacement of locomotives smashed, steamships sunk, and all manner of other losses in operation, thus inflating the value of assets by double-counting. Then, to buoy up the profit figures, revenues were inflated by imputing a value to the company's own carriage of its own gravel, coal, and other supplies at the same rate as that charged to the general public. All the while great losses were being incurred by the movement of long-distance international freight at less than cost to build up its position in the American entrepot trade. In addition, there were numerous internal drains on its operating capital through such items as the establishment of a luxury hotel in Sarnia to cater to company high officials. The hotel's expenses were over five times the level of its receipts during the first year of operation; of these expenses some 40% went into alcoholic beverages which were given away virtually free of charge to the officials of the line.

Yet despite incessant financial difficulties, or rather because of them, provincial and municipal aid continued to pour into the company as its Canadian board of directors, who simultaneously controlled the public purse that provided the subsidies, incessantly plundered the line. In turn, the line's financial weakness justified the voting of increasing sums of public money to save it. With each new crisis the managers of the line could plead with the province for the "means . . . to avert a calamity which will affect the interests of the several Shareholders and Bondholders as well as the whole province.""[11]

By 1860 the bona fide English investors reached the limit of their tolerance. A special report unveiled the degree to which the line had been deliberately mismanaged by its Canadian board and illegal and ruinously expensive arrangements with other Canadian companies undertaken. During the year the Canadian directors claimed a profit of $1,472,113, when in fact the line had lost $1,009,491. The reasons for the difficulties were not hard to find. As the auditor euphemistically expressed it, "the present embarrassments of the company have arisen chiefly from its connections with the successive governments of the province, and the necessity thereof of conciliatory political support." [12] One of the examples of "conciliation" of leading politicians cited by the auditors involved a certain Minister of the Crown who went unnamed at the security holders' meeting. Apparently the honourable gentleman was responsible for assuring that a Kingston wharf on which he held a mortgage was purchased by the railway for £15,000 when another route had been offered the company free of charge. In addition, while a member of the provincial Assembly, he had secured the sale of certain public lands near Sarnia to himself at $2 an acre and then sold them to the GTR via their contracting firm on the Toronto-Sarnia branch, the firm of D. L. Macpherson and Casimir Gzowski, at a mere 7,500% markup. John A. Macdonald of course vigorously denied any wrongdoing in both of these jobs.

In 1862 the railroad was completely reorganized, at which time the anxious British bondholders not only tried to secure some voting power but also effected the transfer of its headquarters from Canada to London in an effort to increase their influence.[13] The Canadian government was subjected to insistent claims for new loans. And, obligingly, the provincial Cabinet continued to pour funds into the maw of the railroad which, however, still failed to return dividends to its shareholders.

Yet the reorganization in reality did little to change the power structure of the company. Formerly the company's capital consisted of $13 million in equity and $60 million in debt. The reorganization simply effected a conversion of much of the debt into preference shares such that the company ended up with $40 million in equity and $30 million in debt. The Barings, the Glyns, and the contracting firm remained in control in exchange for a promise to pay off the interest and guaranteed dividends when it became feasible, a promise which they were hard-pressed to fulfil. Nonetheless, the principle of paying dividends on the guaranteed stock no matter what the condition of the line and no matter what political hijinks were required to make the payment feasible became the fundamental law of operation of the line for the next 60 years. The earnings of the line, whether genuine or contrived, whether actual operating profit or derived from capital, were drained out to the last penny to placate the grasping collection of stockholders who controlled the line from London. The railway was left without a reserve fund, with equipment consistently run down to the verge of total collapse; and its involvement with the political structure of Canada became ever deeper.

# Financial Forces Behind Confederation

The railway projects tied the Barings more closely to the Province than they were to any of their other clients, and their power was enormous. In 1851, at the Barings' request, the Province passed an Act stating that the public debt would not be increased without first consulting the Barings and the Glyns. To aid the democratic process, the Barings prevented Canadian securities from being quoted on the official Stock Exchange Lists in London until the Act was passed.[14] Not only did the Glyns and the Barings underwrite, but they advanced large sums to the railroad and the province. By 1860, provincial debts to the Barings alone reached $1,867,650. That year the two banks, obviously beginning to worry, established by legal action their prior claims on the rolling stock of the line.[15]

The Barings and the Glyns were financial agents to the governments of New Brunswick and Nova Scotia as well, though with so much of their resources tied up in Canada they could do relatively little to provide funds for the other provinces. Nonetheless, some debts did exist. In fact, debts to the Barings were about the only thing the British North American colonies had in common before Confederation. A large part of Nova Scotia's debts, too, resulted from the activities of Lord Brassey and his henchmen who, in 1851, had sent out an agent to interfere with a Nova Scotia election ensuring through liberal bribes the defeat of candidates pledged to build Nova Scotian trunk lines as public works.[16] In New Brunswick, too, the English bankers were active in railway and public finance. New Brunswick in 1856 passed the Railway Facility Act, better known as the Lobster Act after the sprawling character of the patronage-dispensing series of feeder lines it spawned by its bonuses of up to $10,000 per mile, partly raised by debenture issues in London through the Barings.[17]

Fiscal policy was inseparable from railway finance. In 1858 and 1859, with the Grand Trunk teetering on the verge of bankruptcy, tariffs were raised. While a great deal of confusion resulted from Finance Minister Sir Alexander Galt's use of the phrase "incidental protection," the objectives of the tariff were in fact clearly revenue-oriented. Galt himself, in his attempt to justify the tariff and to placate the ruffled feelings of British industrialists, stated the revenue objective clearly:

> The fiscal policy of Canada has invariably been governed by considerations of the amount of revenue required. . . . The government have no expectation that the moderate duties imposed by Canada can produce any considerable development of manufacturing industry. . . .[18] I do not believe that the adoption of a protection policy is possible in Canada. . . . It is not proper to create a hot bed to force manufactures.[19]

The purpose of the tariff, he stated baldly, was "to protect those parties in England who have invested in our Railway and Municipal bonds."[20] Some years later, with no British industrialists to placate by conscious deception, Galt tried to clarify even more the revenue objective of the tariff. In 1862 he stated that "the best evidence that could be offered against the charge of protection was that the effect of the tariff had not been to produce manufactures." Imports of many of the "protected" commodities grew very quickly.[21] In 1875 Galt claimed further that "incidental protection" had been a misleading choice of phrase. Rather, the fiscal policy adopted should have been called "modified free trade."[22]

Well might Galt be concerned about the provincial debt, which had risen from $22 million in 1852 to $52 million by 1857, with a total issue of new debentures of $29 million — over half of which was directly due to the Grand Trunk Railway demands. The excessive issue of debentures in part at least was forced upon the province by the failure of the promoters to live up to their agreement and take up unsold stock themselves after their stock-jobbing operations in London collapsed. The result of the provincial issues was to depress the market for provincial bonds. The 1858 Grand Trunk relief bill complicated the situation by demoting the province to the rank of second mortgagee whose claims ranked below those of even the common shareholders. Under the circumstances drastic action was needed.

The results of the tariff were in fact to produce a considerable reduction in the level of the provincial deficits.

**TABLE II (1)**

**Province of Canada budget, 1858-1863**

*(millions of dollars)*

| Year | Revenue | Expenditures | Deficit |
|------|---------|--------------|---------|
| 1858 | $5.3 | $8.6 | $3.3 |
| 1859 | 6.6 | 8.1 | 1.5 |
| 1860 | 7.4 | 9.4 | 1.9 |
| 1861 | 7.5 | 9.5 | 2.0 |
| 1862 | 7.4 | 9.4 | 2.0 |
| 1863 | 8.6 | 9.5 | 0.9 |

Source: Sir Richard Cartwright, *Reminiscences,* p. 12.

Apart from Isaac Buchanan, a Hamilton merchant and railwayman who headed an "Association for the Promotion of Native Manufactures," there was little or no pressure for protection before Confederation, at least in Upper Canada.[23] And Buchanan's "protectionism" which, in a revised fashion, became the model for the National Policy tariff, was of a rather curious genus. Buchanan's policy for "protecting" and building up manufacturing industry in Canada called for free trade in final products with the United States! This policy, bizarre at first glance, contained a profound logic. These fiscal changes would, he felt, ensure an inflow into Canada of British direct investment.

To preserve the Empire, Britain has to yield the selfish principle of centralization which has ruined Ireland and India . . . and cost *us* the old American colonies. *The principle of decentralizing the manufactures of the Empire* is a principle which would secure for the Empire an enormous addition of trade and influence through the instrumentality of some one or other of her dependencies. . . . She could secure free trade for all of her mechanics who chose to go to these favoured localities, with countries that would never agree to free trade direct with England without giving a death blow to their comparatively comfortable population. . . . Why should England be jealous or oppose this? Is not Canada just England in America?[24] [Emphasis added.]

Such a strategy depended upon the willingness of the United States to countenance free trade with Canada, and the existence of freight costs on such a level as to produce sufficient natural protection to make it profitable for British firms to migrate. With

the abrogation by the United States of free trade in natural products in 1866, any hope of extending Reciprocity to include
manufactured goods vanished. After the abrogation, too, Canadian commercial policy changed. Galt, in 1866, budgeted for a
considerable reduction in tariffs to an average *ad valorem* rate of
15%. While this in part was motivated by the need to harmonize
Canadian tariff levels with those of the Maritimes as a prelude to
Confederation, an additional hope was that by reducing production costs in Canada, especially by lowering duties on capital
goods and wage goods, an inflow of foreign industrial investments would be tempted.[25] But none such materialized.

In Lower Canada (Canada East) it was only on the very eve
of Confederation, well after the scheme had been worked out,
that a significant protectionist body arose among the mercantile
and industrial capitalists of Montreal. Late in 1866 there was
formed the Tariff Reform and Industrial Association, called into
existence directly by the reduction in tariffs of the Province of
Canada by Galt as a prelude to federation.[26] An earlier association, formed in 1858, had failed to attract sufficient sympathy to
maintain a continuous existence. And while the new body numbered among its members many leading Tory merchants and
manufacturers — John Redpath, George Drummond, E.K.
Greene, John MacDougall, R. Hersey, A.W. Ogilvie, W.
Clendenning and a fair range of others from hardware, textiles,
footware, and other industries, including too a sizeable number
of Québécois industrialists — nonetheless the Montreal Board of
Trade, where the real political power of the city lay, remained
free-trade-inclined until well after Confederation.

# Confederation

On the eve of Confederation, Canada faced a severe financial
and commercial crisis, which had been temporarily alleviated by
the American Civil War and the resultant expansion of commodity trade, but which now loomed larger than ever before.
The war had initially proved the temporary salvation of the tangled fortunes of the Grand Trunk Railway as the closing of the
Mississippi route diverted American farm produce from the
Midwest states along the St. Lawrence routes. Peace brought the
threat of renewed disaster. The war itself had led to serious dis-
turbance to Canadian securities in London. The market for Canadian debentures tended to be very thin, and it took only a few
panicky sellers, frightened by the possibility of invasion and subsequent repudiation, to throw it into upheaval.[27] By 1864,

Canada, the richest and largest of the British North American colonies, saw its provincial debentures at the bottom of the colonial list in London. In 1866, the failure of Overend, Gurney and Company precipitated a panic in Britain, followed in early 1867 by a collapse of railroad finance there.[28] The Barings and the Glyns were restless because of the amount of interim financing they were required to provide the Province. Further funds for railway projects proved impossible to raise.

Furthermore, soil exhaustion and land monopolization in Ontario led to a great deal of agrarian unrest, which helped to feed the chronic drain of population to the United States. Canada was as much a British immigrant's entrepot as it was a middleman in the flow of grain back to Britain from the agricultural areas of the United States. British capital accompanied immigrants to the U.S. at the same time little would venture into British North America. By 1850, the effects of early alienation of lands into the hands of speculators were felt in earnest, for by that date there was no more Crown land in the united province of Canada suitable for settlement. In 1860 in Upper Canada alone there were at least three-and-one-half million acres of unimproved land held by absentee landlords in other parts of the province. Agitation grew in Canada for the annexation of the territories to the west, held by the Hudson's Bay Company under a charter granted by Charles II. And Confederation tried to reconcile the land hunger of Upper Canadian farmers and immigrants with the capital requirements of the railwaymen by attaching to Canada the territories of the Hudson's Bay Company and the revenues of the Maritime provinces.

For the Clear Grit faction led by George Brown, who had formerly opposed the scheme of Confederation, the change of heart was undoubtedly due in some measure to hopes of using the Maritime provinces as a free trade bloc to assist the agrarian community of Upper Canada in its struggle for lower tariffs. The *Globe* contended that "in the Confederation . . . the free traders of the West in conjunction with those of the Maritime provinces will surely be able to secure a tariff as low as that of Nova Scotia."[29] Even more important was the fact that, for Ontario, Confederation began as an act of separation from Quebec. Confederation freed Ontario of its "French rulers," as the *Globe* was wont to call them. It was not in fact francophone domination per se that the Clear Grits fought, but rather the political intervention of the Church hierarchy, and its alliance with Montreal big business that sent 50 or more *"moutons"* to the Provincial Assembly under George Etienne Cartier's leadership to vote for Grand Trunk Railway jobbery or for tariffs that forced

Upper Canada to buy from Montreal wholesale dealers.[30]

For the Macdonald Upper Canada Tories, Confederation was in part a political expediency. During 1864, the Ministry was under attack for another illegal donation of $100,000 to the Grand Trunk Railway and other facets of its dubious handling of the Provincial finances. Fearful of an election that would be fought on the issue of finance in general and the government's relations with the Grand Trunk in particular, they felt that finding Cabinet seats for three Clear Grits in the grand Confederation Coalition was a welcome way out of the difficulty.[31]

Despite the presence of Ontario agrarian expansionists in the Confederation coalition cabinet, the chief impetus to union was financial. The Bank of Montreal, which had also provided interim finance for the government of Canada, joined the Barings and the Glyns in pushing for federation to defend its advances. The Bank's general manager, E.H. King, sent a letter to the Charlottetown Conference where the terms of federation were worked out, stating that only by the union could the provinces' credit be restored in London.[32] In the Confederation debates of the Province of Canada, A.T. Galt stressed the results that widening the tax base would have on the provinces' power to raise money abroad:

> . . . It must be clear to every member of the House that the credit of each and all of the provinces will be greatly advanced by a union of their resources. A larger fund will be available as security to the public creditors, larger industries will be subjected to the action of the legislature for the maintenance of public credit, and we will see remedied some of the apprehensions which have latterly affected the public credit of this country.[33]

As to the so-called defense argument for Confederation, Galt summed it up neatly:

> . . . the fluctuating quotations of the securities of these provinces in London that apprehension of war with the United States has induced — and which has unfortunately affected the price of Canadian bonds — has not to the same extent affected those of New Brunswick and Nova Scotia . . . and we may therefore hope that the union, while it affords us greater reserves will, at the same time, carry with it a greater sense of security.

The leader of the Reform wing of the Coalition Cabinet, George Brown, expressed a similar sentiment.

> For some time previous to November last our securities had gone very low down on the market . . . Our five per cent

debentures went down in the market as low as 71, but they recovered from 71 to 75, I think, on the day the resolutions for Confederation . . . reached London. . . . The resolutions were published in the London papers [with laudatory editorial comment] . . . and the immediate effect of the scheme upon the public mind was such that our five per cents rose from 75 to 92.[34]

In Nova Scotia much the same opinion was expressed by opponents and proponents alike as to the objective of the scheme. Joseph Howe, the anti-Confederate leader, contended that in Britain pressure for Confederation emanated from a group who

painfully interested in the throes and eccentricities of Canada are too much inclined to favour anything which may be calculated to restore her to financial soundness and give buoyance to stock fearfully depreciated. . . . Despairing of relief from other quarters it is sometimes assumed that if the productive revenues of the Maritime Provinces could be flung into the empty treasury of Canada . . . then prospects of dividends might be improved.[35]

Charles Tupper, the pro-Confederation leader in Nova Scotia, contended in 1865 that "there is nothing . . . that lowers the credit of a country more than the insecurity that attends such isolation as the three provinces exhibit at the present moment."[36] His views were confirmed by practical experience, for when in 1866 he went to England with two million dollars of provincial six per cent bonds to sell to raise funds for the Pictou Railway, Baring and Glyn informed him that the securities would not yield more than 95%. Tupper then told them to withhold them from the market until Confederation was accomplished, and instead to advance him the money at six per cent on the collateral of the bonds. This was done, and after Confederation the bonds sold at 112%.[37] In New Brunswick in 1866 much the same pessimistic forecast as to the ability of the province to market debentures in London in connection with its railroad ambitions was made by the Barings,[38] and the terms of Confederation had the same salutary effect. London was quick to give its assent to the new Dominion. A few months before Confederation, Province of Canada bonds had been virtually unsaleable at any price. An issue placed in London was only partly taken up, and that part only at a heavy discount. Within six months of Confederation, Sir John Rose, the new Finance Minister, placed a loan in London at six per cent which was absorbed without any difficulty. [39]

Opposition to the scheme of federation was rife throughout
the Maritimes, and a variety of techniques had to be devised by
Canadian politicians, the imperial government, and Maritime
railwaymen, merchants, and bankers to engineer unification. In
New Brunswick, the banks in St. John at first opposed the
scheme, fearful as they were of the Bank of Montreal's designs
on the area.[40] But the Fenian raids planned for 1866 had as one
of their primary objectives the robbing of the St. John banks,[41]
and this was undoubtedly a factor affecting their patriotic sentiments. The Intercolonial Railway too was planned to run
through northern New Brunswick to generate patronage and get
the area enthused for the Confederation scheme.[42] In Nova
Scotia, the economy of the province tended to divide into pro-
and anti-Confederate camps on lines that corresponded to the
interior resource industries and the coastal settlements based on
the traditional economy of the sea. The pro-Confederate vote
followed a line along the railway route, including as well the coal
pits of Cape Breton, while the anti-Confederate vote was centred
in the old seafaring centers.[43]

The Prince Edward Island plot is especially revealing. The
island had been given away in a single day in 1767 to a handful
of Board of Trade favourites, and thereafter the problem of
absentee landowners was virtually the sole issue of the Island's
politics. The Imperial Government had disallowed all efforts to
compel the absentees to sell. In 1867 the Island had no debt and
little infrastructure, for its energies were directed towards buying
out the landowners. That year the Imperial Goverment refused
P.E.I. any assistance in floating a loan for railway purposes, and
threatened to erect new barriers to the process of repatriation of
land ownership if the Island did not join the new federation. In
1869 Canada offered to give P.E.I. the $800,000 required to com-
plete purchases of land, for by then the Island had, on its own
volition, bought up some 60%.[44] The Island still held out.

In 1871 new proposals were made for a P.E.I railroad. Some
circles contended that the very act of promoting the railroad was
a pro-Confederate plot, since it was by then quite apparent that
all railroads led to Ottawa no matter in which direction they
pointed. The act passed for its construction provided that the
contractors were to receive in payment provincial six per cent
debentures of a sum not to exceed £5,000 per mile. It neglected,
however, to stipulate how long the railroad was to be, with the
result that its right-of-way "meandered with rare abandon
wherever local influence, low cost of construction, and the probability of a subsidy suggested."[45] Compounding the error, branch
lines were authorized on the same basis in 1872. The contractors

then pledged some $120,000 worth of debentures to the Union Bank of P.E.I. for advances which greatly exceeded the bank's total capital of $97,000. With the crisis of 1873, there was no chance of selling the securities in London.

Yet despite this the Island was flourishing. The crisis did not affect the Island itself until a few years later. Exports were booming, duties were low, the debt of the Island was more than offset by the value of the railroad, and no extra taxes were required to meet the interest payments. However, inability to market the debentures abroad caused the directors of the railroad and the Union Bank, who showed a remarkable similarity to the personnel of the Island's government, some concern about the value of the securities. Under the terms of Confederation, the Dominion would assume all railway debts and those of the province, which had reached $4.1 million in June of 1873.

Just prior to a new vote on Confederation, the Union Bank triggered off a phony financial "crisis," and the bank president appeared at his first and only public meeting to assure voters and depositors of the various banks that only Confederation could save the situation.[46] The will of the people was done, and P.E.I. became a province of Canada. Canada then loaned it $800,000 to finish buying out the absentees at five per cent deductible from the annual subsidy payable to the island out of the heavy tariff charges it was thereafter to endure. The next year, the Dominion Government disallowed the Land Purchase Act, which would have completed the transfer on terms that the proprietors found objectionable, on the grounds that it was "subversive to the rights of property, ruinous to the proprietors, and a dangerous sentiment."[47]

# The National Policy Tariff

Following A.T. Galt's 1866 tariff of fifteen per cent on manufactures with raw materials largely free, there was little change in fiscal legislation until 1879. In 1871, it is true, duties were placed on coal and flour: the first of these was a reward to the Cape Breton coal mine owners led by Charles Tupper for their role in bringing Nova Scotia into Confederation; the second, at least in part, seems to have been designed to placate B.C. farmers who were recalcitrant about Confederation because of the Canadian practice of admitting flour from the U.S. free for the entrepot trade,[48] as well as having a revenue objective. These two duties were removed the next year. Then in 1874 Richard Cartwright's budget included a general *ad valorem* rise of two-and-a-half per cent for revenue purposes. This was followed by a minor upward adjustment, especially in iron and steel rates, in 1874. During all of the period from 1866 to 1879, two themes dominated fiscal debate — revenue and protection. At first the protectionist element remained weak, but by the late 1870's it was a political sentiment of some consequence. Nonetheless even by that late date protection was still an emotion-charged and minority-supported position. The budget debates prompted by the high tariff of 1879 correspondingly show a bewildering array of arguments for and against tariff increases, and a pronounced tendency to subsume the protective facets into a broader set of policy objectives.

It was a time of deep commercial crisis, when business failures reached unprecedented levels, albeit mainly among trades rather than industry.[49] Charges of American dumping were bandied about the Commons and the Senate by the Tories and denied by the Liberals.[50] The debate achieved dizzy heights of sophistry with the contention that protection was evil because it led to a relaxation of morals and

> the people were taught that the Government . . . gave a favoured class the power to plunder the masses by the permission and arrangement of the few. The people would be led to believe that property acquired by that favoured class was got by theft and then, going a step further, they would come to the conclusion that property itself was theft. *Protection naturally led to Communism.*[51]

But through the verbal maze it does become clear that employment was the burning issue of the day. The drain of population to the U.S. continued on an escalating scale, and one of the most politically powerful arguments the protectionist could cite was that protection created employment.[52]

It was more than simply an "infant industry" appeal. The "protective" tariff was to be so constructed as to ensure an inflow of foreign capital and labour. One eminent Tory contended in the Commons that "protection . . . would secure the influx of a large amount of foreign capital for manufacturing purposes that would never reach us as long as our present Free-Trade tariff exists." [53] In the Senate these sentiments were echoed by the Tory whip: "To secure the success of manufactures we must endeavour to encourage the manufacturers and capitalists of Great Britain and the United States to establish workshops in the Dominion."[54] The possibility of tariff increases was noted by American industrialists, who let it be known that if the increase was sufficient, they would make the move.[55]

In terms of the effect on working-class incomes, the argument that price increases would follow a tariff, thus lowering real wages, was repudiated rather bluntly by one Tory M.P. who suggested that one had only to "ask a working man which he prefers, flour at $4.50 and no labour, or flour at $6.00 and plenty of work."[56] Conservative Party organizers managed to create a Working Men's Association of Upper Canada to lobby for tariffs and work for the Tory cause in elections.[57] At the same time, Sir John A. Macdonald campaigned on the grounds that protection would bring 30,000 skilled workers into the country to man the new industrial enterprises.[58]

After the tariffs were up, the contention that they attracted foreign capital was a principal defense. In 1883, steeper schedules were introduced and Sir Charles Tupper claimed that "I can, myself, name one concern which is bringing in a million of British capital to establish an industry as a result of the National Policy."[59] Against such a defense the best criticism the Liberal Party could mount was that foreign investment "will come in anyway for it came into the country before we had the tariff."[60] That year export duties on sawn lumber were called for to force the migration of American mills to Canada.[61] And faced with American implement firms establishing dealerships in the Northwest and underselling Canada's firms,[62] Sir Leonard Tilley's "anti-dumping" proposal took the form of advocating a tariff increase to force the American firms to actually shift their productive apparatus to Canada,[63] to convert the American investment from a simple sales agency to a full-fledged producing branch-plant.

# Protection and the Business Community

The attitude of the business community towards the National Policy was ambivalent, some members being uncompromisingly hostile, some enthusiastic. Most farm opinion, as would be expected, was opposed, but thereafter the stereotypes cease to be applicable, for much of the pressure for protection came not from secondary manufacturing, but from the mercantile community and some major primary producers. This seems a rather surprising development in light of the view that merchants are generally free traders. But in Canada, as in Europe during the mercantile era, tariff policy was designed to a remarkable degree to further the interests of wholesale merchants.

There were essentially two paths, with some minor variants,

that a country could follow on the way to industrialization.[64] Manufacturing industry can grow up "naturally" by a process of capital accumulating in a small-scale unit of production, perhaps even artisanal in character, the profits of which are reinvested in the enterprise to finance its growth from within. A second path implies direct development into large-scale enterprise, often with direct state assistance, and with capital from outside the enterprise, be it commercial capital, state subsidies, or foreign investment, being invested in it to facilitate its expansion. The first path, if successfully followed, leads to the emergence of a flourishing, independent national entrepreneurial class. The second may or may not. The second path may simply reproduce the conservatism of commercial capitalism in a new guise, and lead to the development of an inefficient, non-innovative, and backward industrial structure with a penchant for dependence on foreign technology, foreign capital, and state assistance as its *sine qua non*. In Canada in the early post-Confederation era both paths were available, and both were being utilised. But in the long run only one could dominate the industrialization process. And which one that would be hung in a delicate political balance, as the shifting opinions of Canadian boards of trade demonstrated.

In 1871, a debate on tariffs raged at the meeting of the Dominion Board of Trade. Leading merchants called for protection, while many prominent industrialists were opposed, and demands were heard for repeal of the existing grain and coal duties.[65] The Board passed a resolution in favour of free trade.

In 1876, the Montreal Board of Trade had begun to waver in its commitment to free trade, though it was not yet prepared to abandon it.[66] That same year the Toronto Board of Trade endorsed protection. While the Toronto Board reversed itself in 1877, it changed its mind again in 1878 with a unanimous pro-protection resolution. In this it was joined that year by the Montreal and the Dominion Boards. Yet opinion at the Dominion Board meeting was not unambiguous, for a Reciprocity resolution also passed, and while a sugar protection resolution did succeed, one calling for a coal tariff sponsored by the Cape Breton Board of Trade did not.[67]

After the Conservative victory in 1878, the Ontario Manufacturers' Association (the successor to Isaac Buchanan's group, representing 28 industries) banded together to draft a tariff schedule.[68] Apart from that, there is little evidence of prolonged pressure from secondary industry for protection. Many of the leading industries were quite content with the 17½% rate of the Cartwright tariff and, to many, reform of the patent or copyright laws was more important than tariff increases.

Evidence before select committees of the House of Commons in 1874 and 1876 showed a presumption by many manufacturers in favour of Reciprocity. As far as infant industry pleas were concerned, every witness in 1874 who urged protection was a part of a firm that was already well established and flourishing, and they admitted not only that American dumping was a short-run problem, but also that the "revenue tariff" of 1874 was adequate to ensure their prosperity.[69]

One of the strongest industries of the anti-protectionist group was that of agricultural implements. Located largely in Ontario, it was built up from inside by men who were generally master craftsmen or sons of master craftsmen who had evolved into small scale capitalists. The industry flourished in the prosperous agricultural areas of Ontario: the condition of the industry really depended on the degree of prosperity of the surrounding farmers.[70] Agricultural implement manufacturers asked for no further tariff increases. Their complaint was that the U.S. tariff of 35% blocked them out of the American market.[71] Even in the depths of the depression, with Canadian industry reportedly under fire from American dumping, one firm, Frost and Wood, reported they had driven American competition out of the Maritimes. Every leading firm asked for Reciprocity: commenting on the 17½% tariff rate, the Massey Manufacturing Company declared that "the existing tariff is satisfactory to us, and is sufficient. . . . *Perhaps even a little less would also be.* A still further advance would certainly prove adverse to our interests."

Boots and shoes, a Quebec-based industry, was one of the largest and fastest growing in the Dominion. It had arrived in Montreal in 1828 and for a long time remained English-dominated and largely handicraft in organization. Not until the 1850's did the firm Brown and Child introduce the factory system based on the division of unskilled labour and steam power — innovations fought hard but unsuccessfully by the master shoemen. The industry spread rapidly to other Quebec towns.[72] A number of Québécois trained in New England factories, such as Charles Arpin and Louis Coté, became established in the industry, and led to its eventual domination by Québécois. By 1876 there were fifty firms producing shoes and another hundred doing custom work. Capital invested was four million dollars, and employees numbered 14,000. It was reported content with existing tariff levels and exporting.[73] Its major complaint was that the tariff needed more careful staggering by percentage of domestic value added:

The tariff is wrongly made. The tariff must be made so as to give protection to the labour on the goods made by the factories. . . . In the way it is made here there is just as much duty on the raw material as on goods ready made. There is no protection in the labour, and that is what we complain of . . . . If the raw material were free, 15 per cent would be enough.[74]

One manufacturer stated of Reciprocity with the United States that it "would be very beneficial to the Dominion generally and myself particularly."[75] From 1876 on, the industry continued to grow rapidly, and its capital intensity grew even faster than its output.[76] Yet as late as 1878 it was claimed the industry needed no extra protection.[77]

In secondary iron and steel — foundries, stove works and general hardware — the consensus in 1874 was that the industry could compete in the absence of any tariff changes.[78] It was dominated by small firms just barely evolved out of the handicraft stage. One of the leading entrepreneurs, Edmund Gurney, called for Reciprocity in 1876.[79] In steam engines and machines, again a few firms pleaded difficulty, but others claimed they would benefit from free trade with the U.S. Several firms stressed the need for free raw materials, especially pig and bar iron and coal.[80] Foundry products and engines entered Canada free at that time. Many other instances of firms antagonistic or indifferent to the idea of higher tariffs could be cited — tanneries, lumber mills, salt producers, paper makers, flour millers, oat millers, meat packers, and musical instrument manufacturers.[81]

These results are rather surprising. Even given that some of the firms changed their mind by 1878, not all of them did. And even with those that did, the fact that in 1876, and later, in the trough of a depression, they were advocating Reciprocity or opposing increases in the tariff reveals that the foundations of Canadian industrialism were more secure than the Conservative Party campaign propaganda implied. It also opens up the question of where the pressure for the tariff increases came from, and what its principal objectives were.

# Proponents of the National Policy

To understand the foundations of protectionism in Ontario and the political alliances that resulted, one must consider the effects of the American Civil War on the Province of Canada. For the era of Civil War and Confederation was one of major and rapid change in industrial and agricultural conditions. Unlike the Crimean War period, the U.S. Civil War did not lead to an expansion of demand for Upper Canadian wheat. The rapid growth of the U.S. western farm states filled the American demand for wheat, although Lower Canadian field crops, especially barley and oats, were in strong demand. The tapering off of American demand for Canadian wheat must have helped the rising tide of agrarian discontent in Upper Canada on the eve of Confederation.

Coupled with the demands of the Grand Trunk, which once again tottered on the edge of collapse as a result of the end of the war-inflated carrying trade, the coalition of Canadian agrarian interests with Montreal railway promoters and commercial capitalists and with Nova Scotia railwaymen and coal mine interests carried Confederation[82] — and immediately began to disintegrate. The agrarian radical wing, alienated by land policies in the West, dropped off first. And all semblance of a Liberal-Conservative coalition crashed down in ruin when the 1873 Pacific Scandal broke to lay bare the links of the Macdonald government to railway promotion. The rupture of Toryism in Nova Scotia, between the old economy of the sea and the new economy of coal and railroads, had never fully healed despite a series of major concessions by the early Macdonald government: now it was reopened. In the depths of the Great Depression the Tory party searched desperately for a new coalition of economic interests to repair the damage and return them to power.

An important new force had begun to emerge from the chaos of the American Civil War. Upper Canada, while bypassed as a source of foodstuffs, had its industrial importance enhanced by the destruction of competitive American industry. Even for a few years after the war, the new Canadian manufacturing capacity maintained its position. But by 1873 the combination of the onset of depression, American industrial recovery, the beginnings of a long period of secular deflation reducing costs and therefore prices in the advanced industrial countries, and the condition of the foreign exchanges led to problems for Canadian manufacturing interests.[83]

The Ontario Manufacturers' Association by itself was not sufficient to account for the switch of the Tories to a high tariff policy. Although powerful, this protectionist lobby was certainly not by itself of sufficient political significance to offset the anti-protectionism of the huge farm community and many leading industries. But the fracture in the ranks of Ontario industry, with the smaller but better organized and therefore politically more powerful group pressuring for tariff increases, in conjunction with other economic interest groups, formed an essential element in the new Tory coalition. The other components were provided by the structural changes of the Canadian commercial and financial community forced by the years of depression.

One of the outstanding characteristics of the industries that opposed further protection was the extent to which they had been built up by their owners generally from a handicraft base. Then, too, in virtually every case no outside capital was invested in them. It was quite otherwise with the leading proponents of higher "protection." Apart from the Ontario Manufacturers' Association, five principal business groups pushing for the National Policy merit special consideration: three primary producers — petroleum, coal, and primary iron and steel — and the wholesale merchants involved in the cotton and sugar trades (along with the Dominion's sole sugar refiner). In at least four of the five cases, foreign capital was involved, and in cotton and sugar, and later in primary iron and steel, the tariff was the instrument by which the transition from commercial to industrial capitalism could be made.

The years immediately after Confederation witnessed a great surge in production and investment in the petroleum industry of Southern Ontario. It was, however, a boom-and-burst industry, plagued by problems of over-entry whenever prices climbed (a well cost only $2,400 to sink in 1869), and equally with drastic

**TABLE II (2)**

**Production and Consumption, 1870**

| Industry | %Domestic Production to Consumption | Industry | %Domestic Production to Consumption |
|---|---|---|---|
| agricultural implements | 95 | meat | 88 |
| boots & shoes | 99 | petroleum | 99 |
| breweries | 95 | paper | 82 |
| furniture | 97 | rope and twine | 95 |
| carriages | 99 | saddlery | 95 |
| cheese | 99 | soap and candles | 95 |
| cottons | 24 | stone | 97 |
| distilleries | 97 | sugar | 60 |
| flour and meal | 94 | tanneries | 91 |
| glass | 65 | tobacco | 98 |
| foundry products | 79 | woollens | 85 |
| machines | 93 | | |

Sources: *SCCD*, pp. 268-9; O. J. McDiarmid, *Commercial Policy in the Canadian Economy*, p. 148.

liquidation when the price came tumbling down again. More-over, the very rapidity with which new wells could be dug led to problems of rapid depletion of particular areas.[84]

A long boom began in the industry in August of 1869 with prices rising rapidly.[85] Not until near the end of 1873 did it end, and depression struck the refining centres, Sarnia, London, and Petrolia.[86] By 1876 it was in blossom again and exports were thriving. Then in September of 1878, just in time for the National Policy election, the industry tumbled into one of its intermittent troughs,[87] the price of crude falling to 50¢ a barrel from previous highs of $2.50 before the decline was arrested. By January of 1880, a few months after the National Policy, the price had climbed again to $1.50.[88]

It was one of the few industries in which significant amounts of English capital had been invested. Most of the early ventures had been catastrophic. In 1872, a group of Canadian promoters of the Canada Oil Works Corporation managed to secure a share capital of $1,700,000 and float $800,000 worth of debentures in London. In short order the English price of debentures had fallen from £100 to £54/5, and £25 shares were down to £2/11/6. The promoters, however, walked off with $800,000 profit.[89] It was Canadian financial promoters' first major essay in the art of "water wagon finance." Near the end of 1873, another big Anglo-Canadian venture crashed in a barrage of lawsuits after two years of existence, during which time its promoter, Mayor John Walker of London, had managed to sell one million dollars worth of debentures in England.[90] Walker's promotion methods consisted in giving a group of prominent Englishmen, well spiced with baronets, the money with which to buy directors' qualifying stock in the venture. That is, the directors qualified by the theft of the company's own funds, and this body of hired retainers then gave credence to, and assured the success of, the debenture issue on behalf of "unknown adventurers on the other side of the Atlantic,"[91] as the Lord Justice in London later remarked. The end result of these and other schemes was a large number of English security holders anxious for a return on their investment. A tax on imports of oil to drive up the domestic price was one way of giving it to them.

English capital also figured largely in the Nova Scotia coal industry. The involvement went back to 1825, when George IV made of all the ungranted mines and minerals of the province a birthday present to his brother, the Duke of York. These were later transferred to a firm called the General Mining Association consisting of a handful of court favourites, with the Crown maintaining a right to a share of the profits.[92] Involved with them were a few of the leading Halifax merchants and financiers, including Samuel Cunard, shipping magnate, banker, and Nova Scotia agent of the East India Company.[93] The continued protests of the Nova Scotia legislature led to an agreement in 1857 whereby the existing extensive claims of the Association were secured, and the remaining mineral wealth returned to the province, only to be quickly alienated into the hands of other foreign operations through long-term leases. A number of smaller English companies moved into the province's coal lands, and there was also a substantial American presence in Cape Breton by 1876.[94] Among the indigenous capitalists, Charles Tupper was the leader.

Coal duties were imposed in 1870 and removed in a howl of protest from consumers and industry.[95] But pressure for protection mounted: from 1873 coal output was falling sharply until it reached about 65% of its 1873 level in 1879. A rise in imports of American anthracite occurred,[96] displacing the Nova Scotia bituminous even in the area east of Montreal where it had been competitive. In Ontario before the tariff, no Nova Scotia coal at all was used. Yet during the period from 1876 to 1878 fixed capital invested in the mines had risen 25%.[97] The mine owners banded together to demand a duty of 50 to 75¢ per ton.[98] The Ontario Manufacturers' Association "patriotically" announced it would accept the duty despite the fact it would raise production costs. The Cape Breton Board of Trade urged the duty as a prelude to building a primary iron and steel industry.[99] Tupper in fact made it a campaign promise that heavy industry would migrate to Cape Breton to locate near the coal, rather than having the coal move to the industry.[100] The Nova Scotia industry pressed for duties on anthracite as well as bituminous to ensure this result.[101] Ontario's anthracite came from the U.S. at a pit mouth price of 80¢, while the Nova Scotia bituminous cost as much as $1.50 a ton.[102] Under the National Policy, a specific duty of 50¢ was introduced on both types of coal. The result was a tax on the Ontario producers who continued to import American anthracite, and on the consumers in the area east of Montreal.

Two secondary industries which received a considerable increase in protection were sugar refining and cotton. Yet, of the major industries surveyed in the 1871 census, these two ranked lowest in terms of the percentage of consumption accounted for by domestic production: cottons at 24% and sugar at 60%. While their economic importance would appear to have been marginal, their political importance was not. Furthermore, both illustrate well the role of the tariff in effecting the transition from merchants' capital to industrial.

# The Sugar Industry and the West Indies Trade

At the time of the National Policy there were but two refineries in Canada, a defunct one in Halifax and the Redpath refinery, run by George Drummond, in Montreal. In 1876, Drummond had threatened to close down if protection was not granted. He claimed that the two million dollars of capital collected for the refinery had never been fully employed.[103] In 1878 he threatened that he would close if a duty of one cent per pound was not levied, which would have amounted to a subsidy of nearly one million dollars per year from Canadian consumers.[104] The refinery paid an eight per cent dividend that year, and each year thereafter for a decade.[105] Yet complaints of dumping continued.[106]

Drummond was not the sole investor in the sugar business pressing for protection. A great deal of Nova Scotia commercial capital was tied up in the West Indies trade, of which sugar constituted a major part. By the late 1870's, the West Indies trade in general was in chaos.[107] The sugar trade in particular was disrupted by dumping by the French, German, British, and American refiners. In 1876, failure struck several large houses in Kingston, Jamaica, followed by substantial losses to Halifax firms who extended them credit. Halifax's local sugar refinery was rendered idle by foreign dumping, and Halifax merchants were forced to change their commercial patterns when sugar became an unprofitable trade. Halifax ships lay idle, and exports of fish by the merchants to the West Indies began to move via New York in American steamers.[108] Efforts were made in Ontario and New Brunswick to grow sugar cane in Canada,[109] but that was no solution for the ailing Halifax mercantile community, which suffered continued failures.[110] During the Confederation campaigns, Nova Scotia's traditional seafaring economy had found itself at odds with the coal, steel, and railway interests. But the collapse of the West Indies trade provided the Conservative Party with an opportunity to bring the Halifax mercantile community firmly into the Tory fold.

The National Policy, in addition to the one-cent specific duty demanded by Drummond, included a bonus of 35% *ad valorem* on refined sugar. The sugar duty schedule was carefully staggered by degree of processing. Liberal Party spokesmen promptly declared that the objective of the National Policy was to make Peter Redpath a millionaire.[111] Redpath's refinery was booming within two months of the new tariff.[112] Not surprisingly, five new refineries opened within three years; in Montreal; Walkerville, Ontario; Halifax; Moncton; and Dartmouth.

The Halifax firm was the largest of the newcomers. It was promoted by a group of West Indies merchants led by the Hon. T. E. Kenny and J. F. Stairs. Kenny, a grain exporter and dry goods importer as well as being prominent in the sugar trade, was a leading Nova Scotia Tory, a member of the first Macdonald cabinet, and a founder and director of the Merchants' Bank of Halifax.[113] West Indies merchants were involved in the other new Maritime refineries as well.[114]

So successful was the National Policy that it led to the almost immediate reopening of the West Indies trade. In 1878, Halifax imported some 3,730,000 lbs. of raw sugar,[115] and the trade maintained itself for several years. In one week in May of 1881, 122 of the 205 cars sent from Halifax via the Intercolonial Railway were laden with sugar for Montreal and Moncton. [116]

The sugar refining industry was beset by excess capacity almost from its inception, planned as it was to suit the needs of the Maritime West Indies traders at a time when they were being threatened in their traditional markets. Yet the short-run prospects of high profits behind the tariff were sufficient to induce British capital to join Canadian commercial capital in developing the new industry. The Dartmouth Sugar Refinery had £125,000 of its capital subscribed by British (Liverpool) interests at a time when the Canada Sugar Refinery alone could satisfy half of the existing domestic demand.[117] By the end of 1883, overexpansion of the industry led to collapse.

# The Textile Industry

With the cotton industry, the story was much more complex. Cotton and woollen goods imports into Canada were dominated by a few Montreal wholesale drygoods merchants, notably George Stephen, A. F. Gault, Hugh Allan, and David Morrice, in alliance with British export houses. Canadian textile manufacturers, both the cotton industry and the few large woollen factories, were dependent on these wholesale firms for marketing their products. To understand the relationship between the industry and the Montreal merchants, it is necessary to examine the history of the industry.

The two principal streams of the textile industry in Canada — cottons and woollens—were totally distinct in their origins, structure, and operations until the late nineteenth century; and the confluence of the two in terms of industrial structure and finance elucidates a great deal about the main economic and social forces of the period.

The woollen industry was chiefly handicraft in origin, growing up in the small farm communities in Ontario and Quebec from which it drew its raw material and whose markets it chiefly served. By 1870 Canadian production served 85% of total home demand — the imported component being largely the more luxuriant products geared to wealthier urban middle-class markets.

Factory production of woollen goods in Canada, as opposed to domestic and handicraft systems of production, began in 1837 at Georgetown, Upper Canada. The owner was a rebel during the Mackenzie insurrection and was forced to flee. He sold his mill to a group of former craftsmen from a nearby paper mill. That year, too, another woollen mill began operating in the sawmill and gristmill complex established at Carleton Place by James Rosamond. Some of this mill's employees left a few years later to establish their own mill at Almonte — to which town the parent mill soon migrated. The pattern of employees leaving their firms and establishing their own small-scale manufactories typified much of early Canadian industrialization, and revealed how closely linked it remained to the artisanal mode of production, even towards the mid-nineteenth century. In Ontario it was frequently farmers who became partners in the small-scale factories springing up: their hope was that the factory system would provide for cheaper and more efficient processing of their wool than did the prevailing handicraft system.[118] In Quebec the same pattern seemed to prevail, with the result that the early factories were dominated by Québécois entrepreneurs.

The Civil War marked a watershed point for the industry in many respects. The competition of American products largely ended, and the "cotton famine" of the war impeded the development of rival cotton mills. For some time after the Civil War the growth of the industry continued; for with the abrogation of Reciprocity by the U.S. came a high American tariff on Canadian wool, and therefore a surfeit of cheap raw wool for the Canadian industry. By 1871 there were 271 woollen "mills" in Canada, in which a total of 4,443 people were employed.[119] Many of course were still handicraft shops; but the emergence of large-scale enterprise with outside capital had begun in 1866 when a Sherbrooke businessman named Hugh Paton established a large mill in that town with the financial backing of Montreal magnate George Stephen.[120]

Growth of the industry slowed in the mid-1870's as a recession in the American woollen industry was partially relieved by saturating the Canadian market.[121] A few of the larger English-Canadian-controlled mills in 1874 began calling for some protection on the cheaper lines of production, but on the more expensive items the Canadian industry had, by that date, succeeded in overcoming the resistance of the urban middle-class market to Canadian-made fabrics: hence no protection on those items was required. In 1876 leading mills called not for protection, but for Reciprocity with the U.S.[122] However by that date some major transformations in the industry were evident, as the fate of the larger anglophone-controlled mills became increasingly tied in to that of the developing cotton industry.

The cotton industry's origins were radically different from those of the woollen mills. Dependent as it was on imported raw materials and a more capital-intensive production technique, cotton was on a factory basis from its inception. That beginning came with A. T. Galt's promotion of a mill at Sherbrooke in 1844, a mill which closed a decade later. Two other mills opened and closed before 1860. Then came the Civil War, with two conflicting tendencies. On the one hand, erratic raw material supply would hamper development; on the other, the closing of American mills and the end of their competition opened up a domestic market. During the early 1860's three Ontario mills opened their doors, of which only one survived. In 1861 there came as well a mill in St. John, New Brunswick, the promotion of one William Parks.[123] During the 1870's several new mills were added to the roster, but, as with woollens, the character of the industry was beginning to change.

By the early 1870's the textile industry had become increasingly restless over the control exercised by the Montreal wholesale drygoods merchants over the marketing of textiles in Canada, particularly their preference for imported products.[124] Major textile producers attempted to break the hegemony by establishing commercial travellers of their own and direct links to the retailers.[125] The project was eventually abandoned, partly because the industrialists lacked the financial wherewithal to extend long credit to the retailers, as the wholesale dealers could do. Its failure was also due partly to a process of takeover by the wholesale group, which reduced the manufacturers first to junior partners, then to branch managers, and made production in Quebec and part of Ontario directly tributary to Montreal and the wholesale merchants.

George Stephen led the way into the woollen industry, becoming a partner with Bennett Rosamond of Almonte in 1866 in the Rosamond Woollen Company.[126] Rosamond's interests also included the Almonte Knitting Company, which in 1882 was brought under Montreal control by the establishment of Donald Smith, Stephen's cousin, as president, and other Montreal commercial figures as directors.[127]

Other Montreal mercantile figures followed Stephen's lead in establishing links with the industry. In 1868, Stephen with R. B. Angus and Smith took over the Lomas Woollen Mill and the Quebec Worsted Company.[128] Stephen brought Sir Hugh Allan, Smith, and Rosamond into the Canada Cotton Manufacturing Company at Cornwall in 1872. In 1876 Allan became President of the Cornwall Woollen Manufacturing Co., George Stephen its vice-president, and Donald Smith managing director.[129] In 1874 Victor Hudon, a shipper and drygoods importer, established a mill at Hochelaga which prospered from the beginning, using cheap labour drawn from nearby farms.[130] Even before the National Policy it was paying ten per cent dividends.[131] By 1878 Sir Hugh Allan had become president of Montreal Cotton Company.[132] It was the typical pattern: the presidency of the firm and key directorships would be occupied by a leading Montreal figure with commercial and financial connections, while the industrialist would assume the general manager's or an equivalent post.

The process of domesticating the cotton industry climaxed with the National Policy. The 1878-1880 period was one of chronic stagnation in the English mills that still supplied much of the Canadian wholesalers' needs.[133] The merchants then embarked on a program to bring production under their control. Textile rates rose from 17.5% to 25 and 30%, and as a result the English cotton machinery industry "found it profitable to introduce to Canada capital and machinery for manufacturing purposes."[134] The English textile industry had objected strenuously to the new tariff, and had sent representatives to the Colonial Secretary asking him to interfere with the Canadian tariff, but in vain.[135]

A great boom began in the industry almost immediately[136] fed by a rate of reinvestment of profits estimated to reach as high as 90%,[137] and by imports of English capital, and a series of new ventures was projected. The English cotton machinery manufacturers, faced with recession at home, pushed their wares hard in Canada, using it as a virtual dumping ground for the equipment of the grey goods mills, towards which type of output all the new Canadian factories were therefore geared.[138] The wholesalers thus became promoters of the new enterprises in alliance with English technology and English industrial capital.

Joining Hugh Allan in these new enterprises were all the most prominent of Montreal drygoods wholesale merchants; A. F.

Gault, Jacques Grenier, D. McInnis (whose import house had failed in the commercial instability just prior to the National Policy), S. Ewing, an eminent broker, E. K. Greene, J. R. Thibodeau, Victor Hudon, and the manufacturers' agent, David Morrice. All were involved in a complex of interlocking directorships[139] that often tended to make the mills tributary to Montreal function as an effective unit.

For the first few years after the tariff, dividends were described as "fabulous." In 1880 the Hudon Mill paid a stock bonus of 33⅓%, in 1881 and 1882 it paid 10% on capital again enlarged without subscription, and in 1883 the stock bonus was 100%. Dividends for most firms ran at ten per cent[140] while Coaticook Cotton showed 43½% on its first six months of operation.[141] The flow of capital attracted by such rates of return was enormous. The Kingston Mill was organized in early 1882 and within a few months $197,000 of its $200,000 capital was subscribed. The stock went to a five per cent premium before output began to flow, and applications for $40,000 worth of stock from leading Toronto and Montreal capitalists were refused. The same year, Allan's Montreal Cotton Company announced it could not fill half of the previous year's orders with its existing plant, and increased its capacity with a $350,000 extension and its labour force from 500 to 600.[142] Municipalities tributary to Montreal went on an orgy of competitive "bonusing" — giving gifts of cash, free sites, tax exemptions and many other inducements to attract cotton mills.

In southwestern Ontario and the Maritimes, cotton mills also sprang up. In Brantford, an English firm immigrated and set up shop.[143] In St. Stephen, New Brunswick, the St. Croix Mill was a direct extension of New England mills that had lost business after the tariff went up. Americans controlled a majority of the stock,[144] and supplied most of the circulating capital through bond purchases as well.[145] In Ontario and Quebec, the number of cotton mills rose from four to seventeen between 1878 and 1884, capital invested rose from $1.8 million to $6.8 million, hands employed rose from 1,361 to 4,501.[146] In the Maritimes, the solitary pre-National Policy mill was joined by five others by 1884, including a Halifax mill promoted by Thomas Kenny.[147] The Windsor, N.S., mill had Montreal wholesalers, notably David Morrice, among its leading shareholders, who also undertook to market all its output.[148]

In 1870, Canadian cotton production satisfied about one-quarter of domestic demand; by 1882 it began to exceed the capacities of the domestic market to absorb the output. The Bank of Montreal, which controlled the fate of the mills under the aegis of the Montreal commercial community, began to "advise" restraint in 1882.[149] Organized manufacturers in the Canadian Manufacturers' Association (CMA), another creation of the National Policy, denied the need for restraint, for the cotton orgy represented the fruition of their dreams and aspirations. But within a year even that enthusiastic body began to have its doubts,[150] especially after a crisis late in 1882 led to the predicted collapse of prices.[151] Unsuccessful attempts at cartelization followed in 1883, and the duty was raised to 35% in 1884 to try to restore prices. By the middle of the decade, in spite of China having proved a partial vent for the mill's surplus capacity,[152] the condition of the industry was chronic. The mills, under the prompting of the English machinery firms, had engaged in the production of a few standardized runs rather than diversifying them to meet the various facets of the Canadian demand.[153]

By 1884, the grandiose cotton system was in total disarray following the assignment of David Morrice. The wholesale dealer Morrice had held a virtual monopoly on distribution not only of cotton but of the output of other textile firms from southern Ontario to Yarmouth, Nova Scotia. He was also a leading stockholder in several. The Montreal banks who heavily backed the activities of the Montreal commercial community in their cotton escapade had made large loans to Morrice on the basis simply of consignments from the mills, instead of *bona fide* sales. As long as Morrice got advances from the banks — whose directorates were intimately linked with those of the cotton companies — the accumulation of unsold goods went on. With a collapse of prices and Morrice's assignment, the banks lost $180,000, and 36 mills for whom he acted as agent, another $150,000. Some factories, especially those in the Maritimes, were badly hurt by the failure, and the Park and Sons Mill in Moncton suspended.[154]

Despite the collapse of 1883, the National Policy tariff did succeed in establishing the cotton industry in Canada and furthering the movement of the woollen industry into capitalist forms of organization. Local woollen mills of the handicraft sort, especially in Quebec, underwent secular decline and eventually vanished to all intents and purposes.

# Protectionist Industries

There were a number of other minor pressures for the high tariff policy that are worth noting. In 1871, James Domville, a leading Maritime industrialist, led the free trade forces in the tariff debate in the Dominion Board of Trade meeting, arguing that Maritime industrialists could prosper without any extra tariff.[155] By 1878, as a Tory M.P., he had joined the protectionist camp.[156] Edward Gurney, the founder, who in 1876 argued for Reciprocity, was by 1877 the head of the protectionist Ontario Manufacturers' Association, which in 1879 presented a draft of a new tariff schedule to Sir John A. Macdonald.[157] A few firms had peculiar reasons of their own for preferring a tariff. Some clearly wanted little more than an opportunity to extract more monopoly profit.[158] Canada's two railway rolling stock and locomotive companies on the eve of the National Policy, both controlled by the big railway promoters, joined the scramble for profits and pushed for protection despite the fact that they were fully employed in the late 1870's.[159] The Montreal Rolling Mills — a firm likewise tied into the Montreal railway promotion and commercial capitalist community by virtue of its being controlled by Sir Hugh Allan, Peter Redpath, and George Stephen — protested its need for protection via its directors, who were busy paying themselves dividends of seven per cent in 1878, just when industrial conditions were supposedly blackest.[160]

The salt producers typically favoured Reciprocity, but opted for protection as a second-best solution. As early as 1869, Goderich salt well proprietors were asking for a tariff. During the late 1870's, the industry in general claimed to be in difficulty. In 1878 Americans sent 100,000 bushels to Canada, while Canadian wells sent 800,000 bushels to the U.S. That same year, 2,200,000 bushels of British salt were imported into the Maritimes for use largely in the fisheries, salt which was brought as ballast on ships from Liverpool.[161] At the same time, Ontario salt wells, including at least one British-owned firm, had badly overextended their capacity; for they continued to expand their plant even during the supposedly bad years of 1877 and 1878. The stage was well set for an attempt by the Ontario salt wells to seize the Maritime market, much as Maritime coal mine owners were attempting the same with Ontario's coal market. In the absence of Reciprocity, the salt proprietors demanded $2.00 per ton specific duty,[162] and despite the fact that the result was a heavy tax on the already ailing Maritime fishing industry, this was readily granted.

# Iron and Steel Policy

Perhaps the most important industry of all urging protection, in light of its long-term effects, was the sole major primary iron and steel producer.

The primary iron and steel industry in Canada had a troubled early history. From the start it was completely dependent on foreign capital. In the Maritimes the industry began in 1826 with the Annapolis Iron Mining Co. While the circulating capital of the firm was raised in Nova Scotia, the equity remained in the hands of its American promoters, who alone had the technical knowledge to run the operations — smelting, casting, and manufacturing. In a few years it was abandoned, and thereafter only mining was done in Nova Scotia, with the ore shipped to New England for smelting and re-export back to Nova Scotia. The General Mining Association, too, began and quickly abandoned a Nova Scotia smelter in the 1830's.[163] A blast furnace operated briefly in Woodstock, New Brunswick in 1848.[164] But by 1849 all the pig iron used in Halifax industries was imported.[165] In Ontario, little furnaces began early as 1800 in Leeds and Norfolk counties, but were quickly abandoned. American and British capital was introduced into smelting in the Marmora and Madoc districts in the 1830's, but these led to failure and a reluctance on the part of foreign capital to try again. In Quebec, a couple of little smelters operated sporadically from the French regime on. But the main centre for the industry remained Nova Scotia.

While the Londonderry, Nova Scotia, steel works nominally began in 1840 as the Acadia Mining Co., it was not until 1852 that operations really got underway. From 1853 to 1874, it produced only 20,000 tons of pig. Then in 1873 it was reorganized as the Steel Company of Canada,[166] and greatly expanded after a moderate hike in the iron and steel duties in 1874.[167] This new firm's stockholders were virtually all English, the major exception being George Stephen. Most of the two million dollars capital was subscribed in England.[168] By 1876 new extensions were made, the capacity was up to 700 tons per week, and the plant work force reached five hundred.[169] Efforts were also made, albeit without success, to get English capital into a smelting works near Hull, Quebec, following the duty revision.[170] The Londonderry firm soon announced it had driven British and American products out of Nova Scotia. In June 1878, it announced it was booming;[171] by October it reported itself in "trouble," citing American dumping — a strange charge given that most of the imports of iron into the area were brought cheaply to Canada from Britain as ballast in returning grain ships.[172]

It is difficult to unravel the importance of the National Policy to the industry, or to ascertain the degree to which higher duties were necessary for some other purpose than simply bolstering dividend levels. While the three small forges in Quebec that shared the industry with the Londonderry firm were in difficulty (one of them closed, the others on the verge of bankruptcy), efforts were underway at the same time to promote smelters in Ontario,[173] at least one of which began smelting after the tariff went up.[174] And following the new duty of $2.00 per ton on pig iron, the little Quebec forges all became active again. New works too were undertaken at Hochelega and Drummondville.[175] In Ontario, the duties led to the formation of the Kingston Charcoal and Iron Co., its list of subscribers being headed by Sir Richard Cartwright, the Liberal Party's leading anti-National Policy spokesman.[176] Canadian pig iron began to find its way to the United States.[177] This was followed in 1882 by two joint ventures of American and Canadian capital, the Franco-American Mining and Manufacturing Co., and the New York and Ontario Furnace Co.[178] On balance, the tariff stimulated a boom in the industry for Ontario and Quebec. In Nova Scotia the evidence is more ambivalent. Even before the election, in 1878, the Londonderry works were being enlarged.[179] After the Tory victory but before the new tariff, the expansion continued, at the same time that demands for protection were being made.[180]

Yet despite the increase in iron duties that followed, the firm claimed to still be in "difficulty." At first its troubles were imputed to the coal tariff, which raised costs to the point where shutdown was threatened.[181] Then the lament switched to complaints over freight rate discrimination: the local rate on coal was 65¢ per ton per mile, while the through rate was 20¢.[182] So acute were these problems that profits rose from 17¢ per 100 lb. of pig to 30¢ per 100 lb. between 1879 and 1881.[183] And by 1881, hands employed reached to the 2,000 mark.[184]

Nonetheless, to bail the firm out of its "difficulties" a pig iron subsidy system was introduced on top of the tariff in 1883, and extended in 1887. The firm went into liquidation, in spite of all the lavish assistance, in 1883. Its failure, and the contraction of the industry in central Canada as well, paralleled the drastic liquidations of sugar and cotton of the same year, and to some extent seemed to spring from the same cause — overexpansion under the aegis of the tariff. Then, too, the plant was badly obsolete and so inefficient that when it was offered for sale in 1884 no buyers could be found.[185] Yet in 1881 the Nova Scotia Steel Company at New Glasgow was established with an up-to-date plant and expanded steadily, and in 1880 a Charcoal Iron Works in Upper Woodstock, New Brunswick, also made a successful début.[186] How the newcomers succeeded while the old collapsed is somewhat of a puzzle.

Again, before the 1887 revision, the evidence points to substantial prosperity. In 1886 the Nova Scotia Steel Company announced its intention of doubling its capital.[187] The immediate effect of the 1887 revision, apart from calling into existence in Ontario another American-dominated joint venture to smelt in the Kingston area, [188] was to create a new syndicate (headed by the same George Stephen who had presided over the bankruptcy of the old Steel Company of Canada) to take over the defunct works under the name, the Londonderry Iron Co. Once the reorganization was complete the new syndicate refused to reopen the works unless the 1887 elections returned a Tory majority dedicated to the principle of corporate largesse.[189]

Opinion among users of iron and steel, notably in the secondary iron and steel industry, was far from enthusiastic over the iron and coal duties. The objections flew fast and furious from founders, sewing machine manufacturers, agricultural implement makers, machine and engine works, and even carriage makers.[190] While some secondary iron and steel producers had been protectionist, notably those that had grown out of wholesale hardware merchant firms,[191] as early as 1874 Edward Gurney had expressed their preference by calling for a subsidy program for the primary industry.[192] The 1887 revision called forth protests from secondary producers across Canada. Randolph Hersey, the Montreal nail manufacturer, claimed the new higher duties would force him to close.[193] In 1892, Jonathan Hodgson of Montreal, Canada's only wrought iron tube manufacturer, did fail, ostensibly because of the high duties on his raw material.[194] Not until 1897 was the tariff cut and the subsidy program expanded enough to bring them some relief.

# After The National Policy — Revenue and Protection

Despite the clear "protective" objective of the tariff of 1879, seeking to attract foreign capital into Canadian manufacturing as well as to stimulate domestic industrial capital accumulation, revenue remained an important objective of commercial policy. Revenue actually may have been the single most important goal, for when Leonard Tilley introduced the new duties in Parliament he specified four major objectives. Significantly, the first was the need to raise revenue for the CPR, followed by protection to manufacturers, protection to farmers, and the restoration of the sagging fortunes of the West Indies trade and the China tea trade. He also stated that the use of specific duties in place of many of the old *ad valorem* ones was designed to offset the effects of declining import prices on the revenue of the government.[195] Reciprocity too was an avowed goal, but the idea that the tariff was a bargaining device to retaliate against American tariffs[196] seems to have been propagated to appease Canadian farmers and mollify British industrialists. Sir Francis Hincks wrote to the London *Spectator* in 1879 blaming American reluctance to grant Reciprocity for the tariff increases, and at the same time denouncing British free trade as an underhanded form of protection.[197] The government also contended that expanded demand for food at home would compensate farmers for the adverse movement of manufactured goods prices.[198] But despite such arguments, and the imposition of useless tariffs on grain, farm hostility remained obdurate in Ontario, as the Conservatives' showings at the polls demonstrated.

Revenue was quite another matter, and the sweeping character of the National Policy tariff schedule was prompted as much by revenue as by protective considerations. Shortly after the tariff went up, Senator Campbell, the government leader in the upper chambers, as well as Sir Leonard Tilley in the lower house, emphasized the new revenues expected from the tariff.[199] Sir Charles Tupper contended in 1881 that the only unambiguously protective tariff was the coal duty; all others had a revenue objective as well.[200] Two years later, Tilley contributed the rather tortured argument that protection and revenue would go hand in hand, for as industry grew, income grew, and therefore spending on luxuries subject to customs and excise would increase.[201] Even after the new iron and steel duties in 1887, Tupper claimed that one of their great virtues would be expanded revenue.[202]

In fact the budget, which had shown a chronic deficit from 1876 to 1880, a deficit which had earlier been seized upon by the "protectionists" to reinforce demands for higher tariffs,[203] moved into a substantial surplus in 1881. The funds were put to work in building infrastructure. In 1882 the consolidated fund surplus was $6.3 million; in addition, the land sales and other revenue from the Northwest came to $1.7 million. Of this, $7.4 million was spent on capital account projects, notably the Canadian Pacific Railway. Furthermore, that year some four million dollars in maturing liabilities were redeemed. No new loans were deemed necessary. In fact, together with the proceeds of the government savings bank deposits, the budget surplus was expected to eliminate all need for raising new funds abroad. Tilley claimed that

If we can have a surplus of three or four million a year, and savings deposits of a like sum, we will not from this day to the finishing of the Canadian Pacific Railway require to go to the English market, except to replace those liabilities which matured.[204]

**TABLE II (3)**

**Consolidated Fund Account, 1876-1886**

| Fiscal Year | ($ million) Surplus | Deficit |
|---|---|---|
| 1876 | — | 1.9 |
| 1877 | — | 1.5 |
| 1878 | — | 1.1 |
| 1879 | — | 1.9 |
| 1880 | — | 1.5 |
| 1881 | 4.1 | — |
| 1882 | 6.3 | — |
| 1883 | 7.1 | — |
| 1884 | 0.8 | — |
| 1885 | — | 2.2 |
| 1886 | — | 5.8 |

Source: *Canada Year Book (CYB)*, 1916, p. 537.

For a while the program was a success. The tariff revenue, together with the savings deposits in the government banks, bore out Tilley's claims and seemed sufficient to pay for the major public works. [205] But with the collapse of the brief expansion in 1884 such hopes were dashed as import duty receipts plummeted and the budget went into deficit. Nonetheless the linkages were clear. Revenues from the tariff would accrue to the CPR Syndicate composed of George Stephen, Donald Smith, R. B. Angus, and other members of the Montreal commercial community, whose pressure for the tariff and campaign support were instrumental in producing the National Policy.

# Conclusions

From an early date the process of economic development in Canada displayed a very close interfacing of politics and business, leading to inevitable hopeless compromises of the public finances as the government treasury was plundered with impunity by promoters of various projects. From an early date, too, the Canadian business and political elite displayed a near-paranoid obsession with the attitude of British financiers to their actions. British investment was fundamental to the construction of major works of infrastructure, canals and railways alike, and the full forces of the state were put to work to try to assure a free flow of capital to the colony. Fiscal policy and the financing of infrastructure via public subsidies were inseparable.

In 1841, the Province of Canada was created to abet the process of selling public securities, and subsequent tariff policy aimed to keep the debenture holders reassured. In 1867 precisely the same tactic was tried, with new territory brought within the federal tax collectors' grasp to ensure a steady flow of interest payments to Britain and keep up the quotation of public securities. In 1879, parallelling the fiscal policy of the late 1850's, a high tariff strategy was adopted, a key objective of which was to ensure an inflow of revenue to finance infrastructure and to pay off the public debt.

But over the course of the years that separated the 1858-1859 tariffs and the National Policy tariff, major transformations in the Canadian economic structure had occurred. Industrialization had proceeded along two routes. Small-scale local industries had taken root, especially in Ontario. And especially in Montreal and Halifax key figures of the old economic system, the leading wholesale and import merchants, had begun or were about to begin to move into industrial promotions. It was this group in particular who had the ear of government and it was their policy needs which ultimately were fulfilled. In conjunction with a small but vocal segment of Ontario industry and a group of pressing British investors in certain primary industries, the National Policy tariff was pushed through, setting Canadian industrialization on the path to dependence: dependence on state assistance, on foreign capital, and on foreign technology.

The tariff thus accomplished many things. It protected certain key sectors of the economy and weakened others. It served as the means by which the great commercial capitalists who dominated the new Toryism of the post-Pacific Scandal era could invest in industry. It made Canadian investments profitable for foreign capital, both by bolstering the earning potential of already existing industrial investments, especially British, and by forcing a northward migration of American firms. Moreover, the tariff had an extremely critical, and badly neglected, revenue objective. It was a sweeping tariff that taxed inputs of many industries very steeply as well as taking a heavy toll from the consumer.

The funds were then used to help pay for the enormous requirements of infrastructure necessary to rebuild the commercial empire of the St. Lawrence.

# Notes to Chapter II

1. On the Welland Canal Company, see especially H. G. J. Aitken, *The Welland Company;* see also the exchange of H. C. Pentland, "The Role of Capital in Canadian Economic Development before 1875," H. G. J. Aitken, "A Note on the Capital Resources of Upper Canada," and H. C. Pentland, "Further Observations on Canadian Development." A. T. Galt, "Canada, 1849 to 1859," is useful on canal finance.
2. R. Fulford, *Glyn's,* p. 150.
3. R. M. Breckenridge, "Free Banking in Canada," p. 162.
4. Cited in E. P. Neufeld, *The Financial System of Canada,* p.182.
5. *Monetary Times (MT),* Nov. 18, 1913, p. 742.
6. *The Pilot,* Montreal, June 15, 1850; July 20, 1850.
7. R. S. Longley, *Sir Francis Hincks,* p. 31.
8. S. Leacock, *Baldwin, Lafontaine and Hincks,* pp. 323-4.
9. L. H. Jenks, *The Migration of British Capital to 1875,* p. 200; H. A. Lovett, *Canada and the Grand Trunk,* p. 26.
10. A. T. Galt, "Canada, 1849 to 1859," p. 322.
11. T. E. Blackwell, Managing Director, to the Governor General in Council, August 8, 1860; H. C. Chapman to Hon. Charles Alleyn, August 20, 1860; Canada, Sessional Papers 1861, "Railway Returns, 1861;" T. S. Brown, *The Grand Trunk Railway Company of Canada.*
12. *Globe,* Nov. 29, 1860; Dec. 1, 1860; Dec. 4, 1860; Dec. 28, 1860; Feb. 14, 1861; March 5, 1861.
13. *Ec,* July 13, 1861.
14. R. Fulford, *Glyn's.* p. 153.
15. R. Hidy, *The House of Baring in American Trade and and Finance,* pp.473-4.
16. L. H. Jenks, *The Migration of British Capital to 1875,* p. 200.
17. J. Hannay, *New Brunswick,* II, p. 215.
18. A. T. Galt, "Canada, 1849 to 1859," p. 329.
19. A. T. Galt, "Report to the Duke of Newcastle, October 25, 1859," p. 345.
20. *Ibid,* p. 346.
21. A. T. Galt, "Speech at the Chamber of Commerce, Manchester," September 25, 1862.
22. *MT,* September 17, 1875, p. 322.
23. D. Creighton, *British North America at Confederation,* p. 43.
24. Isaac Buchanan, "Speech at Toronto, 1864," pp. 20-21.
25. O. D. Skelton, *Sir Alexander Tilloch Galt,* p. 134.
26. *Globe,* Oct. 29, 1866; Oct. 30, 1866.
27. *Ec,* Dec. 14, 1861, p. 1374.
28. Viscount Goschen, *Essays,* pp. 60, 65.
29. *Globe,* Oct. 8, 1866.
30. F. Underhill, *In Search of Canadian Liberalism,* p. 44.
31. *Globe,* Oct. 30, 1866.
32. M. Denison, *Canada's First Bank,* I, p. 133.
33. Province of Canada, *Confederation Debates,* February 7, 1865, p. 67.
34. *Ibid,* February 8, 1865, p. 98.

35.  "Confederation Considered in Relation to the Interests of the Empire" in J.
     M. Beck (ed.) *Joseph Howe,* pp. 180-1.
36.  Cited in D. Creighton, *British North America,* p. 48.
37.  E. M. Saunders, *The Life and Letters of the Rt. Hon. Charles Tupper,* p. 118.
38.  New Brunswick, *Journals of the Assembly, 1866,* p. 96.
39.  *Ec,* Feb. 29, 1868, p. 237.
40.  A. Bailey "Opposition to Confederation in New Brunswick."
41.  W. S. MacNutt, *New Brunswick, A History,* p. 440.
42.  *Ec,* Sept. 29, 1900, p. 1366.
43.  D. A. Muise, "Parties and Constituencies: Federal Elections in Nova
     Scotia, 1867-1896," *Canadian Historical Association Historical Papers,* 1971.
44.  P.E.I., *Submission to the Royal Commission on Dominion-Provincial Rela-
     tions, pp. 8.*
45.  Bank of Nova Scotia, *The Bank of Nova Scotia 1832 to 1932,* pp. 63-5.
46.  A Macphail, *History of P.E.I.,* pp. 371-2.
47.  Canada, Department of Justice, *Memorandum on the Dominion Power of
     Disallowance,* p. 15.
48.  British Columbia, Legislative Council, *Confederation Debates,* p. 10.
49.  *Globe,* April 19, 1879.
50.  *HCD,* March 1, 1878, pp. 685-6.
51.  *HCD,* March 8, 1878, p. 921.
52.  *HCD,* March 12, 1879, pp. 1954-5; March 7, 1878, p. 858; Senate, *Debates,*
     May 2, 1879, p. 577.
53.  *HCD,* March 28, 1879, p. 789.
54.  Senate, *Debates,* May 2, 1879, p. 577.
55.  *MT,* March 7, 1879, p. 1113.
56.  *HCD,* March 8, 1878, p. 906.
57.  Senate , *Debates,* May 2, 1879, p. 572.
58.  *Globe,* Sept. 11, 1878.
59.  *HCD,* April 19, 1883, p. 715.
60.  *HCD,* April 3, 1883, p. 390.
61.  *HCD,* March 14, 1883, pp. 209-10, 212.
62.  *HCD,* March 30, 1883, pp. 342-3.
63.  *HCD,* April 19, 1863, p. 714.
64.  See especially Maurice Dobb, *Studies in the Development of Capitalism,* p.
     123; cf. Karl Marx, *Capital,* Vol. III, p. 329.
65.  Dominion Board of Trade, *First Annual Meeting,* 1871, pp. 27-8, 30, 33-34.
66.  Montreal Board of Trade, *Annual Report,* 1876, p. 90.
67.  Dominion Board of Trade, *Eighth Annual Meeting* 1878, pp. 75, 39-40, 80-
     82.
68.  *Globe,* October 24, 1878, *Industrial Canada,* November 1901, p. 82.
69.  Select Committee . . . Manufactures, *(SCM) Report* 1874, p. 3; Select Com-
     mittee . . . Causes of the Depression *(SCCD) Evidence,* 1876, p. 74 *et
     passim.*
70.  The industry was exporting all over the world. Its raw materials, especially
     bar and pig iron, were imported, and duties on bar and pig iron would hurt
     the industry *(SCCD,* 1876, pp. 119, 121-2). In some lines, excess capacity
     existed even before the National Policy, and further tariff increase would
     only have augmented the problem *(MT,* Dec. 13, 1878, p. 744). The only
     important failure in the industry during the depression of the 1870's, L.
     Cosset and Bros. of Guelph, was due to a short-run liquidity squeeze and
     not to American competition *(MT,* Dec. 12, 1879, p. 689).
71.  *SCM* (1874), p. 7.

72. Anonymous, *Canada Under The National Policy,* 1883, p. 123.
73. *SCM* (1874), p. 8.
74. *SCCD* (1876), p. 93.
75. *SCCD* (1876), p. 105.
76. *Journal of Commerce (JC)* April 26, 1878, p. 302.
77. *HCD,* March 8, 1878, p. 882. Yet boots and shoes was the manufacturing industry most plagued by failures, and if "dumping" was the cause of the crisis, it logically stood to gain a great deal from higher nominal tariff rates. Several of the firms recorded more than one failure before the National Policy went up. One of the largest, that of Guillaume Boivin, failed three times in the two years before the new tariff, but Boivin went on record in favour of Reciprocity. And the high rate of failure in the industry continued unabated after the tariffs were up. Its instability was due to the peculiarities of the Canadian credit system rather than an external industrial threat.
78. *SCM* (1874), pp. 11, 17.
79. *SCCD,* p. 178.
80. *SCCD,* pp. 25, 86-87.
81. *SCM,* (1874), pp. 10, 17; *SCCD,* pp. 2-5, 11, 19, 70-77, 158, 186; *MT,* Dec. 8, 1879, p. 642; Jan. 4, 1879, p. 925; April 18, 1879, p. 1296; Sept. 7, 1877, p. 304.
82. See especially D. A. Muise, "Parties and Constituencies."
83. One of the reasons American manufacturers were accused of dumping was that the American greenback remained at a discount in terms of gold for more than a decade as a result of the Civil War finance. Throughout the 1870's the gold premium ran at over fifteen per cent, and hence by itself came close to completely negating the protective incidence of the Canadian duties. On January 1, 1879, convertibility was restored, the U.S. greenback appreciated, and hence U.S. manufacturers lost their considerable advantage in the Canadian market even before the National Policy went up. Given that the National Policy schedule of duties was drawn up before the return of parity, it probably contained some degree of protective overkill based on the supposition of a continued American advantage.
84. *MT,* Sept. 10, 1869, p. 55; Sept. 24, 1869, p. 87; Oct. 1, 1869, p. 104.
85. *MT,* August 27, 1869, p. 24.
86. *MT,* Nov. 21, 1873, pp. 490-1.
87. *MT,* Nov. 17, 1876, p. 563; Sept. 27, 1878, p. 403.
88. *MT,* Jan. 9, 1880, p. 812.
89. *MT,* Aug. 16, 1872, p. 129.
90. *MT,* Dec. 12, 1873, p. 561.
91. *Ec,* June, 12, 1875, p. 698; July 24, 1875, p. 864.
92. D. Campbell, *Nova Scotia,* 1873, pp. 396-8.
93. A. Payne, "Life of Sir Samuel Cunard," p. 79.
94. *SCCD, Evidence,* p. 225.
95. *JC,* May 3, 1879, p. 922.
96. *MT,* January 24, 1879, p. 922.
97. Dominion Board of Trade, *Annual Report,* 1878, pp. 176-7.
98. *HCD,* March 8, 1878, p. 884.
99. Dominion Board of Trade, *Annual Report,* 1878, pp. 169-70, 175.
100. *Globe,* Sept. 11, 1878.
101. *Globe,* July 27, 1878.
102. *HCD,* March 8, 1878, p. 887; *SCCD,* p. 83.
103. Montreal Board of Trade, *Annual Report,* 1876, pp. 39-40.

104.  *HCD*, Feb. 26, 1878, p. 559; March 1, 1878, p. 689.
105.  Select Committee . . . Combines, *(SCC) Evidence*,  1888, pp. 49-52.
106.  *Globe*, June 1, 1878.
107.  W. W. Johnson, *Sketches of the Late Depression*, p. 8.
108.  *MT*, Sept. 8, 1876, p. 272; Oct. 20, 1876, p. 446.
109.  *MT*, Sept. 27, 1878, p. 402; April 18, 1879, p. 1246.
110.  *MT*, Dec. 20, 1878, p. 772.
111.  Senate, *Debates*, May 2, 1879, pp. 563-4, 580.
112.  *MT*, May 30, 1879, p. 1472.
113.  *CAR, Historical Supplement*, 1910, p. 79; *MT*, Oct. 13, 1876, p. 418; May 16, 1879, p. 1414; Oct. 28, 1881, p. 519.
114.  *MT*, January 28, 1898, p. 950. See especially T. W. Acheson, *The Social Origins of Canadian Industrialism*, pp. 73, 78.
115.  *MT*, March 26, 1880, p. 1338.
116.  *MT*, May 20, 1881, p. 1345.
117.  *MT*, Feb. 16, 1883, p. 912.
118.  *CM*, April 28, 1882, p. 159.
119.  *RCT*, p. 42.
120.  *MT*, Sept. 2, 1898, p. 306.
121.  *CFC*, Feb. 27, 1875, pp. 199-200.
122.  *MT*, Dec. 17, 1880, p. 696; *SCM* (1874), p. 9; *SCCD*, pp. 194-5; *Globe*, August 12, 1878.
123.  *RCT*, p. 32.
124.  *SCM (1874), p. 9.*
125.  *CM*, May 15, 1885, p. 1189.
126.  *CM*, June 1, 1888, p. 370.
127.  *MT*, May 26, 1882, p. 1443; *CM*, May 26, 1882, p. 199.
128.  H. Gilbert, *Awakening Continent*, p. 15.
129.  *MT*, Dec. 8, 1876, p. 642.
130.  Royal Commission on the Relations of Labour and Capital  *(RCRLC) Quebec Evidence*, pp. 374-5.
131.  *RCT*, p. 35.
132.  *MT*, October 11, 1878, p. 977.
133.  *Journal of Commerce (JC)*, January 2, 1880, p. 643; *Ec*, February 7, 1880, p. 148.
134.  Anon., *Canada Under the National Policy*,  p. 120.
135.  *JC*, May 2, 1879, pp. 338-9.
136.  *MT*, Oct. 17, 1879, p. 465.
137.  *JC*, August 22, 1879, p. 13.
138.  *MT*, Sept. 14, 1883, p. 292.
139.  *MT*, August 15, 1879, p. 205; Feb. 22, 1878, p. 988; August 8, 1879, p. 751; Feb. 6, 1880, p. 921.
140.  *RCT*, p. 35.
141.  *CM*, August 4, 1882, pp. 410-11.
142.  *CM*, Feb. 27, 1882, p. 57.
143.  *JC*, Jan. 2, 1880, p. 638.
144.  *MT*, Dec. 23, 1881, p. 763.
145.  *JC*, Oct. 26, 1883, p. 306.
146.  Select Committee . . . Manufactures *(SCM), Report,* 1885, p. 32.
147.  *MT*, May 20, 1881, p. 1345; July 15, 1881, p. 64.
148.  *MT*, Sept. 9, 1881, p. 309.
149.  *CM*, June 9, 1882, pp. 209-10.
150.  *CM*, August 24, 1883, p. 605.
151.  *MT*, March 28, 1879, p. 1209.
152.  *RCT*, p. 35.

153. *SCM* (1885), p. 38.
154. *MT,* March 3, 1882, pp. 1076-7; August 4, 1882, p. 120; August 1, 1884, p. 123; August 15, 1884, p. 177; August 22, 1884, p. 233.
155. Dominion Board of Trade, *First Annual Meeting,* 1871, p. 30.
156. *HCD,* March 12, 1878, pp. 1054-5.
157. *MT,* Nov. 2, 1877, p. 529; IC, Nov. 1901, p. 82.
158. Senate, *Debates,* 1879, p. 624.
159. *MT,* Dec. 28, 1877, p. 753; Feb. 22, 1878, p. 988; March 22, 1878, p. 1112; April 22, 1881, p. 1232; August 22, 1884, p. 233.
160. *MT,* Feb. 7, 1879, p. 975.
161. *Globe,* July 26, 1878.
162. Select Committee on the Salt Interest, *Report,* 1876, pp. 1-6.
163. A. Gesner, *The Industrial Resources of Nova Scotia,* pp. 255-8.
164. *MT,* April 30, 1886, p. 1237.
165. A. Gesner, *Industrial Resources,* p. 211.
166. *SCM* (1885), p. 61.
167. *Statutes of Canada,* 1874, 37 Vic., Chap. 6.
168. *Globe,* Sept. 28, 1878; *MT,* April 30, 1878, p. 266.
169. *MT,* Sept. 22, 1876, p. 334.
170. *MT,* Feb. 6, 1874, p. 775.
171. *MT,* June 7, 1878, p. 1424.
172. *Globe,* Oct. 14, 1878.
173. The Snowdon Iron Works were projected in 1878, then leased to a U.S. firm and the ores exported *(MT,* Oct. 4, 1878, p. 434). The entrepreneur responsible for the undertaking denounced the projected National Policy, and announced that if duties were placed on coal he would not be able to proceed with his smelter *(Globe,* April 29, 1878; June 10, 1878). At the same time, early in 1879, a Toronto group of former iron ore exporters secured a charter for a smelter at Port Hope *(MT,* April 11, 1879, p. 1271).
174. *MT,* July 11, 1879, p. 64.
175. *MT,* Dec. 30, 1881, p. 792; August 11, 1882, p. 147.
176. *MT,* April 1, 1881, p. 1149.
177. *MT,* Jan. 16, 1880, p. 832.
178. *CM,* April 28, 1882, p. 145; *MT* April 21, 1832, p. 1289.
179. *MT,* August 16, 1878, p. 207.
180. *MT,* March 21, 1879, p. 1177.
181. *JC,* Oct. 28, 1881, p. 335. *MT,* May 23, 1879, p. 1147.
182. *MT, June 20, 1879, p. 1560.*
183. W. J. Donald, *The Canadian Iron and Steel Industry,* pp. 94-5.
184. *MT,* Dec. 30, 1881, p. 792.
185. *MT,* Dec. 7, 1883; August 15, 1884. p. 203.
186. *MT,* August 20, 1880, p. 204; August 15, 1884, p. 203.
187. *MT,* Oct. 15, 1886, p. 434.
188. *MT,* May 20, 1887, p. 1370; June 3, 1887, p. 1432.
189. *MT,* Feb. 18, 1887, p. 953; May 27, 1887, p. 1402.
190. Senate, *Debates,* 1879, p. 626; *HCD,* April 28, 1882, p. 1223.
191. W. Kilbourn, *The Elements Combined,* pp. 40-1.
192. *SCM* (1874), p. 6.
193. *MT,* May 20, 1887, p. 1373; HCD, 1887, p. 1213.
194. W. J. Donald, *The Canadian Iron and Steel Industry,* p. 99.
195. *HCD* March 14, 1879, pp. 409-413.
196. *HCD,* Feb. 26, 1878, pp. 548-9, *et passim.*
197. *JC,* May 2, 1879, pp. 338-9.
198. Select Committee . . . Operations of the Tariff, on the Agricultural Interests . . . *(SCTA) Report,* 1882, pp. 14-15.

199. Senate, *Debates,* May 2, 1879, p. 460; *MT,* March 21, 1879, p. 1177; *JC,*
     March 28, 1879, p. 176.
200. *JC,* Oct. 28, 1881, p. 334.
201. *HCD,* March 30, 1883, pp. 338-9.
202. *MT,* May 20, 1887, p. 1373.
203. *Ec,* March 4, 1876, p. 278.
204. *HCD,* March 30, 1883, pp. 333-5, 337.
205. *MT,* April 6, 1883, p. 1119.

*Some people say that the Grand Trunk Railway is the Government of Canada. They are mistaken. Mr. Brydges is active, alert, always on the qui vive. But Mr. King carries the purse strings. The Bank of Montreal is imperium in imperio.*

Montreal *Witness,* 1866

# CHAPTER III

# The Evolution of The Chartered Banking System

## Origins of the Banking System

The Canadian banking sytem, like virtually all the country's economic institutions, was a truncated import from a more advanced economy, specifically from England. What is important is not the nationality of the bankers *per se,* (who were largely Scots) nor the legal niceties attached to early charters (which were largely American-derived), but the actual manner of functioning of the banks.[1] And in this respect the Canadian banking system was a colonial variant of London joint stock commercial banking.

The migration of English banking to Canada was not complete. Only part of the system took root in the colony. For purposes of analysis the English banking system can be regarded as comprising four parts. First, the Bank of England, a relic of the era of mercantile monopolies[2] which dealt largely in the public finances. Second, the London-based joint stock commercial banks, which operated a series of branches, and subsequently challenged the Bank of England's issue monopoly. In addition, in London, there existed a group of large private banks, whose origins were in the international movement of commodites, but who increasingly specialized in the marketing of securities, especially international. These were the great merchant banks of the Barings, the Rothchilds, and Glyn, Mills.[3] All of these layers of British banking were essentially financial and commercial in their operations in the strict sense and maintained a fair degree of independence from industrial finance.[4]

However, with the coming of the Industrial Revolution there

arose along with it, and as an integral part of it, a system of country banks. Their existence was brief and chaotic; they failed in great numbers in crises, and they disappeared as quickly as they emerged after the end of the Napoleonic wars. But while they existed they played a critical role in fostering industrial capital formation. They were local, unit banks, that is to say, banks with only one office rather than several branches. And they did a local business in accepting deposits, making loans, and issuing bank notes. Their origins were frequently industrial, being vehicles for a particular industrial entrepreneur to promote his own undertakings.[5] These banks were, then, a crucial source of industrial finance for the economy.[6] Under the social conditions then prevailing, the technology applied to the new industrialism was quite primitive;[7] hence the volume of fixed capital investment required for plant and equipment tended to be low.[8] The fixed capital could be provided from the savings of the men who formed the new entrepreneurial class that led the Industrial Revolution, and by reinvested profits, while working capital for wages and materials would be provided by the country bank. Of course, short-term advances ostensibly for working capital would frequently be renewed more or less automatically, converting them into a long-term investment.

The country banks, and to some extent the American state and local banks, were excellent vehicles for industrialization as long as fixed capital requirements were low. But as the capital intensity of industry grew, nations which lagged behind Britain required different sorts of financial structures to bridge the gap.[9] In some instances the state itself mobilized long-term industrial finance, while in the U.S., Germany, and other countries, the investment bank became a prominent financial instrument. Investment banks on the model of Germany's Dresdner Bank or J. P. Morgan and Co. in the U.S. also involved a close link between industry and finance like the country bank,[10] though of course the scale was vastly different.

The financial structures that evolved in the Province of Canada lacked any tradition of either investment banking or institutions analogous to country banks. As a colony, its banking system evolved in imitation of and through regulation by the metropole. Canada was a staple-extracting hinterland servicing British markets, and its banking system took a form appropriate to facilitating the movement of staples from Canada to external markets rather than promoting secondary processing industries. This evolution was reinforced by the migration of British banking physically to Canada in the form of individual British entrepreneurs who took leading places in Canadian financial

institutions, or in the form of direct investments by British financiers in joint ventures with Canadian commercial capitalists, or
in the form of the operation in Canada of wholly British-owned
imperially chartered banks — the Bank of British North
America and the Bank of British Columbia. In brief, Canadian
banking was a branch plant of English commercial banking,
with the Barings, Glyn, Mills, and to a degree the Bank of Montreal assuming the role of the Bank of England in public finance.
It was the banking model least suited to promoting industrial
development in the colony.

Proposals made just after Confederation for a radical alteration in bank legislation were fought to a standstill.[1] The Minister
of Finance, Sir John Rose (of the Hudson's Bay Company, the
Bank of Montreal, and Morton, Rose and Co.) tried to resusci-
tate the idea of a government note issue or, failing that, a reserve
of government securities to back the chartered bank notes. These
proposals were supported by the Bank of Montreal, which would
control the operation of the scheme, while the other big commercial banks, especially those in Ontario, objected. In Ontario,
bank note issue was highly seasonal; the economy was agricultural, and note issue peaked during crop moving season. During
times of financial stringency the effect of locking up their funds
in government securities would be to put them at the mercy of
Bank of Montreal advances.[12] Not only would the Bank of Montreal then reign supreme, but it might well decide to reign alone,
having already in 1866 managed to destroy Ontario's two largest
banks, the Bank of Upper Canada and the Commercial Bank of
the Midland District by denying them credit.[13]

Essentially what was involved in the debate over note issue
power was a choice between using domestic funds for staple
movements or for the construction of infrastructure, and the
banks preferred to keep up the flow into staples and have the
government rely on imports of portfolio capital from Britain to
build the railroads and canals that were necessary for staple
exports to Britain. This pattern of Canadian capital flowing into
commerce, leading to an over-expansion of staple extraction,
coupled with the necessity of imports of capital from Britain to
build the overextended infrastructure that accompanied that
expansion, was destined to be replicated in one form or another
throughout the period until World War I.

Sir John Rose left the Macdonald cabinet in 1869 to join an
English private banking firm styled Morton, Rose, and Co., a
bank which soon rose to the first rank among the financial over-
seers of the empire. His political demise in Canada marked the
first of a series of abrupt endings to careers of finance ministers

eased, or forced, out of office as a result of the anger of the chartered banks. In the case of Rose it represented a defeat of the
Bank of Montreal by the Ontario banks. Macdonald's willingness to sacrifice a minister so prominent in the Montreal financial elite grew out of his need to maintain a coalition of Ontario-
Quebec and Reform-Conservative interests. Such considerations
also dictated his choice of a new minister on Rose's departure.
His replacement as Minister of Finance was the former leader of
the Upper Canada Reform party, now a de facto Tory, Sir
Francis Hincks, who had recently returned to Canada after a
stint as governor of several Caribbean colonies. The *Monetary
Times,* oracle of the Toronto financial and commercial community, greeted his return as a boon to Ontario, as a "Minister of
Finance whom Mr. King [E. H. King, general manager of the
Bank of Montreal] will be unable to hoodwink or manipu-
late."[14] Alas for Ontario, the old quarrels between the so-called
reformer and the bank were gone. The Bank of Montreal remained government banker. And Sir Richard Cartwright, who
had himself been an aspirant for the position as well as the
president of one of the Ontario banks recently destroyed by the
Bank of Montreal, quit the Tory Party in protest over the
appointment of the notorious Hincks. Hincks, in fact, had to be
given a seat in British Columbia in the subsequent elections, so
hostile was Ontario to him.[15]

# Commercial Operations of the Chartered Banks

The chartered banks of Canada were established with close connections to the commercial community to provide short-term
accommodation for the movement of staple products — furs,
timber, and grain. The Bank of Montreal was established by fur
merchants and dry goods importers; the Bank of New
Brunswick, the Quebec Bank, and the Ottawa Bank by timber
merchants; the Bank of Hamilton by dry goods merchants; the
Bank of Toronto by grain dealers and bill brokers; the Commercial by grain dealers; the Dominion by railwaymen and bill
brokers; the Bank of Nova Scotia by small merchants. They
accepted deposits and issued notes; the note issue function was
always an indispensable and bitterly contested part of their activities. An attempt in the 1840's to introduce a provincial bank to
issue bank notes modelled on British legislation was successfully
defeated, and a later effort to establish a "free banking system"

with a government-bond-backed note issue to help the government raise long-term capital for the construction of railways and canals was a failure.

The notes issued by the early banks were a critically important source of loanable funds. As long as the notes of the bank were accepted in general circulation as money, the bank in effect had managed to borrow from the public at zero interest cost a sum equal to the amount of its notes in circulation. The greater the volume of the bank's notes that could be pushed into circulation, the greater the volume of free money the bank had to lend to customers at interest. Gustavus Myers, observing the American banking scene, made a number of observations which applied equally well to Canada. Of the banks of the period he noted:

> The most innocent of their great privileges was that of playing fast and loose with the money confidently entrusted to their care by a swarm of depositors who either worked for it, or, for the matter of that, often stole it; bankers, like pawnbrokers, ask no questions. The most remarkable of their vested powers was that of manufacturing money. The industrial manufacturer could not make goods unless he had the plant, the raw material, and the labor. But the banker, somewhat like the fabled alchemist, could transmute airy nothing into bank note money, and then, by law, force its acceptance. The lone trader or landlord unsupported by a partnership with law could not fabricate money. But let the trader and land holder band in a company, incorporate, then persuade, wheedle, or bribe a certain entity called a legislature to grant them a certain bit of paper styled a charter and lo! they were instantly transformed into money manufacturers.[16]

Hincks fathered Canada's first Bank Act, which was touted as a "compromise" between the two competing banking factions. Under this Act, the government note issue was restricted to the lowest denominations, while the chartered bank notes remained without a reserve requirement— secured instead by a first lien on the bank's entire assets, including a double liability of stockholders. In every other respect, however, the Act was exactly that drafted by the Bank of Montreal.[17] It put the Maritime banks under federal control and forced them to conform to the Canadian model, and opened up the Martimes to the expansion of the Canadian commercial banks.

The logic of "real bills" concepts of banking became ossified into law. Moulded by the bankers themselves, the legislation governing the actions of the banks conformed to the predeliction of the banks towards very short-term loans.[18] Nor were either their deposits or note issues restricted by the requirement of a mandatory cash reserve, unlike the American system where bank note issues had to be backed dollar for dollar by a reserve of government bonds to defend the value of the notes in case of failure of the bank. Moreover, the Canadian system was supposedly less open to "inflationary" influences than the American.[19] Stripped down to its fundamentals, what this meant was that the centralization of power of the Canadian banking system prevented local and regional interests from using easy credit policies for local development and to fight the vested powers of the main urban centres; that in Canada the money supply in theory adapted passively to the needs of commerce rather than being amenable to manipulation as an instrument of development policy.[20] In fact however the operations of the banks in Canada were considerably less constrained by these precepts than the legislation suggested they should be; and the main result of the so-called passivity of the Canadian credit supply mechanism was to leave the Canadian economy exposed to the vagaries of international commercial fluctuations to a vastly greater degree than in the United States.

While the banks were adamantly opposed to a fixed reserve of cash — gold or Dominion notes — as early as 1888 a Nova Scotia banker proposed that the banks collectively pool a certain percentage of their circulation to insure the public against failure.[21] For despite the notes being a first lien on the entire assets of the bank there were instances when failures of banks led to the loss of most of all of the value of the notes to the holders. The Bank of Montreal continued to press for a fixed reserve ratio, and the efforts of the Conservative Finance Minister, Sir George Foster, to introduce one in 1890 were stopped by the Prime Minister, who was fearful of the ire of the chartered banks on the eve of an election. Foster also sought to make the notes of any bank redeemable at par by any other bank as well as making provision for the redemption of the notes of defunct banks.[22] That was effectively the end of Foster's career as the Minister of Finance. On the return of the Tory Party to power in 1911, Foster, at the request of the chartered banks, was relegated to the Trade and Commerce post, a political scrapheap for those who offended Canada's money magnates.

Instead of Foster's proposed 1890 reforms, the Canadian Bankers' Association was formed and subsequently incorporated with the power to appoint liquidators, to report on the fitness of new applicants for bank charters — an adverse report from them would lead to the refusal of a certificate to operate.[23] The CBA was also empowered to administer a central redemption fund for bank notes. All banks theoretically had to band together to protect each other's note issue, for the notes of a failed bank could be redeemed in the notes of a still solvent bank through the central pool of notes established under the Act. Since the effect of the central fund was to make all notes equally safe in the eyes of the public, the General Manager of the Bank of Montreal, Sir Edward Clouston, promptly denounced it as "communism."[24]

The volume of notes that the banks were permitted to issue was restricted to the amount of their paid-up capital. Hence for a bank to expand its note circulation beyond that point it would have to solicit more shareholdings.[25] That led to one obvious potential problem. More shareholders would mean more possible votes at shareholders' meetings and hence would threaten a reduction in the amount of control exercised by a few top financiers. To resolve that problem, the Bank Act was so written as to give the existing stockholders of a bank the right of first refusal on any new issues of stock; and virtually all new issues before the war were absorbed internally.[26] Furthermore the importance of the capital subscribed by the shareholders diminished as a source of loanable funds as the banks began energetically searching for other sources. The expansion of deposits as a source of funds, while the relative importance of shareholders funds diminished, meant of course ever greater financial power could be wielded with a limited commitment of the shareholders' own funds — the equivalent for the banking system of an industrial company expanding its assets by selling bonds rather than shares. As a result of these forces, it was not until well after the turn-of-the-century boom was underway that the volume of bank notes in circulation began to bump up against the ceiling of the legal limit. And once this happened, instead of a compensating expansion in the banks' capital — which could involve either the possibility of new voting shareholders or a commitment of funds from the existing shareholders — the government was simply induced to lift the ceiling on bank note issues.[27]

After the discomfiture of John Rose and Hincks's "compromise" of 1871, the government's fiscal needs no longer threatened the chartered banks' powers to "manufacture" money. While a small tax had been put on the banks' circulation at the time of Confederation, this remained unchanged. And the banks threatened that if the government ever tried to increase it, they would simply collectively pass on the extra charges to the public in the form of higher interest charges.[28]

Nor did the government note issue provide any real competition for the chartered banks. The government note issue was restricted to a maximum fiduciary (unsecured by gold backing)

## TABLE III (1)

**Bank Notes in Circulation as a Percentage of
Paid-up Bank Capital, 1875-1914**

| October | Notes as % Capital | October | Notes as % Capital |
|---------|--------------------|---------|--------------------|
| 1875 | 39 | 1905 | 92 |
| 1880 | 47 | 1906 | 89 |
| 1885 | 56 | 1907 | 89 |
| 1890 | 61 | 1908 | 87 |
| 1895 | 56 | 1909 | 92 |
| 1900 | 80 | 1910 | 97 |
| 1901 | 85 | 1911 | 99 |
| 1902 | 93 | 1912 | 96 |
| 1903 | 90 | 1913 | 101 |
| 1904 | 91 | 1914 | 92 |

issue of $20 millions in minimum denomination notes. In 1894 an effort was made to raise the government's uncovered issue to $25 million, but the bankers proudly announced they had succeeded in defeating the proposal and had secured agreement from the government to maintain 100% gold reserves for all issues of notes in excess of $20 million. The agreement was obligingly embodied into statute, the chartered banks thus imposing a reserve ratio on the government rather than vice-versa.[29] The struggle to expand the government issue, even though defeated, could not have helped further George Foster's political prospects.

Under the Dominion Notes Act, the federal government was entitled to an issue of low denomination notes of up to $25 million, raised in 1903 to $30 million of which 25% had to be backed by gold or Government of Canada securities, the interest and principal of which were guaranteed by the government of the United Kingdom, and of which the remaining 75% had to be backed by a reserve of Dominion securities. For any issue above $30 million, reserves of 100% in gold had to be held.[30] In effect, gold provided the backing, but the attempt to tie the Dominion reserves to the London capital market is worth noting, especially in light of the fact that the chartered bank voluntary reserves were held in the form of call loans in New York. Canadian monetary conditions were thus linked to financial developments in the two principal metropolitan capital markets. In terms of Dominion note issue, however, despite the fact that the chartered banks active in crop moving were straining the limits of their note issue power from 1908 on, the gold reserve ratio behind all

Dominion notes in circulation rose from 21.8% in 1867 to 80% in 1914.

During the credit squeeze in the 1907-8 crop moving season, the government exceeded the legal limit of its issue, and Liberal Finance Minister W. S. Fielding promised, as a consolation, that thereafter the chartered banks could expand their circulation to 115% of the sum of their capital and reserve funds, the government thus largely abandoning the field to them.[31]

The banks' hostility to government issues went even further. The banks avoided holding Dominion notes even as part of their "voluntary reserve" and would present them for redemption in gold, using the proceeds for investments in New York.[32] And the possibility of the establishment of a Canadian mint, or, more properly, a branch of the Royal Mint in Canada, was vehemently opposed. Sir Edward Clouston of the Bank of Montreal claimed in 1901 that coining of gold would disturb the currency,[33] or, more candidly, compete with the chartered banks' note issue. Sir Edmund Walker of the Bank of Commerce added the argument that since Canada had so many debts to pay to foreign investors, only American and British gold should circulate within Canada.[34] Obligingly, the "Canadian" mint confined itself to bronze and silver until 1912. The struggle to prevent competition in the business of manufacturing money went beyond the struggle over government notes and gold: the fight to prevent express companies from issuing money orders was a long and successful one.[35]

# Finance and Politics

The political power of the larger banks and of the Bankers' Association can hardly be exaggerated. The bank acts were written by the very banks supposedly regulated by them. George Hague, general manager of the Bank of Toronto, provided a candid description of the process of writing the 1871 Bank Act.

> Representatives of the [chartered banks] from all parts of the country . . . sat in conference, day by day discussing the clauses of the proposed act one by one; . . . we sat in one of the committee rooms of the House and discussed the bill with a considerable sense of responsibility, being well aware not only that our conclusions would affect the whole banking interest of the country, but every other interest, commercial, manufacturing, and industrial not to speak of the interest of the government itself.

Were that not sufficient guarantee as to the outcome of the democratic process,

> Many of the directors of the banks and several of their presidents were members of Parliament, some in the Senate, some in the House of Commons. These, of course, sat with us from time to time, so that, though not formally constituted as such, we were really a joint committee of Parliament and banks.[36]

Notable among the "joint committee" members was, of course, Francis Hincks, who doubled as Minister of Finance and as a director and subsequently President of the City Bank. Among them too was the Honourable Louis Davies, Minister of Fisheries and President of the Merchants Bank of P.E.I., an institution which at the time of the 1894 revision of the Bank Act had the Premier of P.E.I. and a provincial cabinet minister also on its board.[37]

The years of George Foster's tenure in the Ministry of Finance saw the consolidation of the banks' collective power, much to his subsequent regret. Nor did the advent of the Liberal Party to power in 1896 alter the influence of the banks in the choice of the Minister. According to the Liberal Party's Ontario bag-man, W. T. R. Preston, the obvious Liberal candidate, Sir Richard Cartwright, had his application for the post rejected by the banking establishment, who sent a delegation to Laurier to threaten to call enough loans to cause a financial crisis if Laurier allowed Cartwright to assume the post.[38] The choice fell on W. S. Fielding, whose credentials for the job were ably summed up in 1911 by the Chairman of the House of Commons Banking and Commerce Committee:

> Sir, businessmen in Canada, even Conservatives, men whose every vote has been cast for the Conservative Party, have hesitated to mark their ballots against this government for the very fear that some man other than the Hon. W. S. Fielding might control the financial affairs of this country. And one of the strongest cards it has been possible to play for the Liberal government in any part of this country is to ask, "If you vote Hon. W. S. Fielding out of office as Finance Minister in Canada, whom do you think you are voting in?"[39]

Relations with Ottawa were formalized in 1894 with the establishment of a permanent Bankers' Association lobby in the capital. Its first representative in the capital was the up-and-coming corporation lawyer Z. A. Lash. His operations bore fruit from the onset, sufficiently so for Sir Edmund Walker, the President of the Executive Council, to be able to report to the Association in 1895 that,

> Some private bills containing clauses objectionable to the

banks were introduced into the Dominion Parliament, and the attention of the proper authorities being called by Mr. Lash to these features they were removed.[40]

The lobby's powers grew steadily, culminating in the incorporation of the Canadian Bankers' Association in 1901 with the astonishing power to pronounce on the fitness of, and, de facto, to block the entry of new banks seeking charters. In the legislative field so successful were its operations that Sir Edmund Walker in 1913 could openly boast that every major change in banking legislation since the first Bank Act had been initiated by the bankers themselves.[41]

Nor were the other legislative bodies left out of their purview. The locations chosen for the annual meetings of the Association were especially suggestive, the usual places being the Parliament Buildings in Toronto and Ottawa, the Legislative Council Chambers of Quebec and Halifax, and of course the Windsor Hotel in Montreal, the standard convention place for price-fixing associations during the late nineteenth century. The lobby operated actively in all the provincial capitals, the report of adverse legislation on the order table being sufficient to bring a high-powered delegation to the provincial capital to fight it.

But of course Ottawa was the most important centre of activity, as it was in Ottawa that the power to legislate on banking and currency matters lay. By 1913 the Ottawa lobby had expanded to five lawyers plus several special parliamentary agents who were put to work during the Bank Act revision hearings, buttonholing M.P.s who looked like they would waver during the Committee debates and gathering up members to join the Committee discussions and vote down unwelcome clauses. When the division bells rang, the bankers' lobby had its own whip on hand to fill the back benches with members who seldom attended sittings. And as a final "check and balance" of the legislative process, the solicitor of the Bankers' Association sat on the Senate floor inside the rail and interrupted and interfered with the discussion at the invitation of the government Senate leader, Alberta's Senator Lougheed. The good relations with·the government shown by the then solicitor of the Canadian Bankers' Association were undoubtedly aided by the fact that his brother sat in the House of Commons as the member for North Oxford.

At that time a few mildly progressive clauses were introduced in the House, clauses calling for a compulsory annual shareholders' audit, the outlawing of bank managers' receipt of gifts of stock from companies they lent funds to, the requirement of sterilization of notes before reissue, and the maintenance of transfer and registry offices in every province where the bank did business. All but the gift clause were struck out by the Senate, the gift clause having an obvious utility in limiting the power of discretion of individual branch managers. The lobby was equally active in committees and in the corridors. In committee, progressive clauses were voted down by members brought in specifically for that purpose.[42] The Minister of the Interior later remarked that it took a great deal of courage to stand up to the lobby. Whoever else had that courage, it is certain he did not; this same minister was later accused of accepting bribes from the Bank of Commerce. Whatever else one may say about the banking cartel's methods, they were certainly thorough.

Power within the banking clique was very unevenly distributed. The extent of the centralization of power, not only vis-à-vis the outside community but also inside the banking group itself, was ably summarized in 1901 by Sir Edmund Walker, the President of the Bank of Commerce. Speaking to the Bankers' Association annual meeting in his capacity as President of its Executive Council, he described the power structure as follows:

> If one visits a meeting of the American Bankers' Association, nothing strikes one so much as the fact that it is practically a great convention; hundreds and sometimes thousands of bankers attend. . . . On the other hand . . . the interest of banking in Canada, of our 36 banks with five or six hundred branches is represented by 40 or 50 men, and practically by the 15 or 16 members of the Executive Council. . . . The consensus of opinion of the bankers of Canada upon any public question can be arrived at without difficulty. We have the great advantage of knowing without coming together, from the fact that we are acquainted with each other, and have often met to discuss subjects, what is the thought upon a public question. For that reason we exercise in this country a force that seems to be out of all proportion to our numbers. The opinion of the banking world of Canada becomes concentrated in the Executive Council, and therefore the consensus is easily arrived at. We cannot judge of the importance of our annual meeting by the number present. *In fact the importance is clearly in inverse ratio to the numbers.*[43] [Emphasis added].

Needless to say, some of the banks failed to show the same degree of enthusiasm as Sir Edmund over the concentration of financial and political power he described. As early as 1899, the Bank of Nova Scotia had withdrawn from the Association[44] as a result of its efforts to enforce the existing spheres of influence agreements and keep the Bank of Nova Scotia out of the western provinces.[45] Although the Nova Scotia was back in the fold by 1902, its relation with the other big banks remained very strained for some time.[46] In 1913, H. C. McLeod, the former General Manager of the Nova Scotia — who had been deposed in 1910 as a prelude to the restoration of peace in the financial heirarchy of Canada — denounced the Association as an instrument in the hands of one man.[47] While he did not specify whom he had in mind, it is certain he was referring to either Sir Edmund Walker of the Commerce or Sir Edward Clouston of the Bank of Montreal. That year, too, the President of La Banque Provinciale described the Association as "a tool in the hands of three or four men who today control the whole of the finance of the country."[48] How they chose to exercise that control had to have an enormous impact on the patterns of economic development of the country.

## Banks and the Commercial Sector

The credit system of Canada was inextricably interrelated with the movement of commodities, both internationally and internally. As early as 1824, William Lyon Mackenzie described the relationship as follows:

> Our foreign commerce, confined and shackled as it is, and has been, is entirely in the hands of the British manufacturers. . . . Our farmers are indebted to our country merchants, our country merchants are deeply bound down in the same manner and by the same cause to the Montreal wholesale dealers. Few of these Montreal commission merchants are men of capital; they are merely the factors or agents of British houses, and thus a chain of debt, dependence, and degradation is begun and kept up, the lines of which are fast bound around the souls and bodies of our yeomanry, and that with few exceptions from the richest to the poorest, while the tether stake is fast in British factories.[49]

As Mackenzie aptly described, during the period of British industrial hegemony in Canada the movement of commodities and the movement of "capital" were inseparable. British firms extended long credits to the Montreal importers who acted as their agents, who, in turn, extended credit to a myriad of country retailers, who, in turn, gave credit to their customers. And the Montreal importers were often the same group who exported staples. The role of the banks was, as George Hague of the Bank of

Toronto described it, "handmaiden and tributary to . . . commerce."[50] They provided short-run accommodation by discounting notes for the wholesale houses or urban retail merchants and facilitated the flow of raw material exports to the U.S. and Britain.[51]

Under this system, imports from Britain exceeded those from the United States by a sizeable margin until 1875. In 1875, the position reversed and the U.S. took the lead, which it never again lost.[52] Such a shift in the Canadian trade pattern presupposed some breaking of the rigid link between commodity and capital flows in the form of long credit. As the Canadian banking system matured, it increasingly assumed the role of financing commodity movements, either alone or in alliance with English commercial banks.[53] Britain became of ever greater importance in providing financial capital rather than mercantile credit.

Internally, the system of "long credits" and the Canadian banking system's obsession with mercantile loans and discounts served to divert capital away from industry into commerce, with the result that between Confederation and World War I Canada had a merchant sector that was clogged with small traders hanging on precariously to the credit extensions of the banks and wholesale houses. In the age before the chain store, the country merchant or small urban merchant fulfilled the function of distributing agent for the wholesale houses. Nominally independent, he was in fact tied by credit lines and contracts to dealing exclusively with one big wholesale firm, and his existence depended on it being too costly or inconvenient for the wholesalers to move directly into distribution through branches in small towns and villages. The wholesale dealers' trade associations regulated prices, and the chief form of non-price competition took the guise of proliferating the number of agents; and among these agents competition involved chiefly credit extensions to the customers. Credit was more common than cash dealings among the retailers in all but the largest urban centres. As late as 1870, cash was seldom seen at all in commodity transactions in Nova Scotia and New Brunswick.[54]

As the Canadian banks moved from loans based on personal notes to those on real bills, their importance as the linch-pin of the system grew. In addition to discounting bills for the wholesale dealers, the accounts of produce dealers and town merchants took on increasing importance over time.[55] The banks were well aware of the consequences of the overextension of mercantile credit — that, in the words of Thomas Fysche of the Merchants'

Bank, it "creates a vast army of impecunious traders who intensely compete until the margin of profit nearly reaches the breaking point." But it was essential that the system be maintained, for without it the banking system would have had no *raison d'être* in the period before the great expansion of 1896: most of its best customers would have vanished.[56]

The "real bills" doctrine, to which the banks ostensibly adhered, supposedly guarded against any imbalance between the volume of credit and the supply of goods. But the reality was more as described by a Montreal financial journal:

> simply degenerating the science and practice of banking into a system of pawnbroking, a system by which any man may import goods on credit, put them in a bonded warehouse, pledge them to a bank for as much as he can raise on them, and cross the border with the proceeds.

There were many cases of borrowing twice or even more on the same goods, and of substituting cheaper or valueless goods for those listed on the receipts.[57] Campaigns launched by the business press to curtail the amount of credit extension fell on deaf ears, for it was an integral part of the competitive system, and however destructive in the aggregate, no single trader or bank could curb the process without losing ground to his competitors.

The problem went back at least to the early post-Confederation period with its enormous overextension of drygoods stores and grocers. In 1869, Chatham, Ontario, Brantford, and St. Catharines each had more stores than Detroit. A little village like Goderich managed to have 37 stores, Woodstock 37, Stratford 21, St. Marys 20.[58] During the depression of the 1870's, great hordes of commercial travellers were sent out by wholesale dealers to force their goods on retailers on generous credit terms, or even to bypass the retailers and "sell" direct to customers.[59]

The chaos was aided and abetted by the state of insolvency legislation, legally a federal responsibility. Before the federal act of 1869[60] which applied only to "traders" and not to incorporated companies, legislation by the various provinces was disparate. New Brunswick had no insolvency legislation at all, and creditors had no recourse except for the long and expensive process of civil suit. The Nova Scotia act was very limited, and passed mainly to ameliorate the extent of imprisonment for debt. The act of Canada on which the federal legislation was based dated only from 1864.[61]

The federal act of 1869 provided that discharge could be obtained after 33⅓% of the claims were settled. While this was subsequently raised to 50% in 1875,[62] the essential problem remained unsolved. By favouring the debtor, the Act tended to expand the vast army of merchants and increase the rate of "failure."[63] If a man could pay nearly the whole of the debt it was better to claim insolvency and settle for fifty per cent, and hence each group of traders who "failed" was succeeded by a new group, often composed of many of the same merchants who had "failed" the last time around. And if a merchant had failed so often that no houses would extend him further credit, it was a relatively easy matter to put his wife in as nominal head of the firm and start the cycle again.[64] Prior to the Act, merchants generally settled for the full 100%. After it, paying the legal minimum or less in cases of difficulty became standard practice. In 1879 one assigned merchant's estate sold for 5½ cents on the dollar; one item nominally worth $108 was auctioned off for 40 cents. A Fredericton debtor in 1876 offered one cent on the dollar, and this was accepted.[65] And legal costs tended to absorb a substantial part of the collectible portion of the estates.[66]

The Boards of Trade, the business press, and especially the banks sought repeal or drastic reform, while the traders pressed for the Act to remain.[67] Given the centralization of financial power in Canada, there was little scope for inflationary credit policies on a provincial and local level, as was typical of American patterns of the period. Hence the struggle of farmers and local merchants against the urban financial oligarchy took, among others, the form of a fight over the terms of insolvency. In 1880, an M.P. called for repeal of the Act on the grounds that "the people of this country are tired of the . . . regime of Official Assignees under which they have suffered for some years past."[68] It is clear that "the people" in his view showed a remarkable similarity to the personnel of the banks and wholesale houses, and little beyond. As for the assignees, business was so good that in Montreal in 1877 they moved to form an organization to regulate their trade.[69] The supply of assignees was fed by the overcrowding of the legal profession due to the structural imbalance of the Canadian educational system.[70] These lawyers, who had to be supported as an additional charge on the cost of distributing commodities, were denounced by one of their victims as typified by

> a miserable creature . . . impressed with the idea that he was born to be a professional man . . . whose best energies were spent in gaining the title which he afterwards degrades, and whose natural abilities, if rightly directed and applied, would have made him a burning and shining light as a feeder of hogs, rather than as a counsellor of men.[71]

Repeal of the law in 1880[72] was followed almost immediately by an escalating campaign for restoration.[73] Among those advocating restoration were British wholesale houses who lost large sums by being unable to claim even the 50% they were entitled to under the old Act.[74] On the other hand, Canadian banks fought hard to prevent any new legislation, for their ability to make claims on the spot permitted them to seize 100% of a failed trader's goods. In 1894 a new insolvency bill was introduced into the House of Commons, the first since the repeal, and the new bill sought to re-establish the 50% rule. It was opposed successfully by the bank cartel and defeated.[75] Not until after the war was a new law enacted.

Several results followed from the vagaries of the credit system during times of financial and commercial crisis. During the 1870's depression, a great wave of failures directly attributable to overextension of the credit system occurred. Farm problems led to a drift to the cities at the same time mercantile houses who had overimported were eager to sponsor large numbers of petty merchants of little capital and less experience to try to get rid of the goods; and the farmers were eager to co-operate. A Select Committee reported that "large numbers of persons have thus been withdrawn from productive industry to the detriment of the public and with no advantage to themselves."[76] The result was cut-throat competition among the many small traders. During the depression, many charges of dumping by American and British firms were heard and the Canadian adverse balance of mercantile debt rose to $75 million with debt charges reaching four million a year. In all probability, however, the problem lay not with the price policies of the exporters but with the credit system, and its effect on landed prices of imports.

Failures escalated until the ratio of liabilities of Canadian failed firms to that of American reached 30% in 1879. But even the advent of depression and failure did not stem the rush. The Montreal Board of Trade reported in 1876 that,

> notwithstanding three years of depression in which failures in Canada have been in greater proportion to the number engaged than in any other country, there is today a greater number of persons engaged in business in proportion to the trade done than in any other country where statistics are available.

If the same rate of failure continued, "in ten years every second businessman in Canada may succumb."[77]

In this commercial chaos, the failures of merchants numbered over three times those of manufacturers — reflecting the huge number of petty traders and their vulnerability to the periodic

## TABLE III (2)

### Commercial Failures, 1872-1879

| Year | Number of Failures | Liabilities | %Canadian/ %U.S. Liabilities |
|------|------|------|------|
| 1872 | n.a. | $ 6,464,525 | n.a. |
| 1873 | 994 | 12,334,192 | 5.4 |
| 1874 | 996 | 7,696,765 | 5.0 |
| 1875 | 1,968 | 28,843,967 | 14.3 |
| 1876 | 1,728 | 25,517,991 | 13.4 |
| 1877 | 1,889 | 25,466,139 | 13.4 |
| 1878 | 1,615 | 23,152,262 | 10.2 |
| 1879 | 2,002 | 39,344,579 | 30.0 |

Sources: Montreal Board of Trade, *Annual Report*, 1876, p. 88; *MT*, Feb. 7, 1879, pp. 978 - 80; Jan. 30, 1880, p. 890; *Brad.*, various issues; *SYB*, various years.

collapse of the credit web:[78] though where manufacturers got involved in overdependence on short-term credit to carry on their line of production, they too could collapse in droves.[79] And to try to salvage their prior investments, the chartered banks fed the maelstrom[80] by reawakening and rebuilding collapsed commercial houses, permitting them to struggle on until yet another failure intervened.[81]

The bizarre operation of the Canadian credit system was not exclusively an urban phenomenon. Not only did farmers overburden themselves with credit based on the pledge of future crops, but often diverted that credit into mortgage lending to other farmers,[82] rather than investing in their own future production. The country merchants, backed by the big urban retail houses, in turn supported by the wholesale firms who relied on Canadian banks and British export houses for credit, extended short-term low-interest credit to the farmers who in turn lent at long term high interest to other farmers on the security of their land. The result, under normal circumstances, would have been to speed up the differentiation of the farmer class into rich rentier "gentleman" farmers and a poorer class of indebted small holders and tenant farmers. But given the regularity of periodic credit collapses, it is more likely that the chain of debt led more to the growth of urban absentee landholders than rural.

Even after the depression, problems remained for farmers because of the lack of ready cash which often forced them to sell their crops well in advance of harvesting. Speculators used to roam the rural areas of Ontario in the lean years of the late 1880's offering to buy grain at some fixed price in the future.

The contract was signed, and by cutting off the top and bottom and having it notarized and enforced by one of the great numbers of lawyers eager for employment, the contract for the speculator to pay the farmer became a promissory note made out to the speculator by the farmer. These notes were then bought by professional dealers who were usually the masterminds of the fraud.[83] The rate of discount would be from 12 to 20%, and proceedings against the farmers who refused to pay up were common. As one witness said of the role of lawyers in the affair with respect to one of his notes, "After it was sold, I thought there might be some trouble about it, seeing that it had got into a lawyer's hands and that they take more out of the farmers than the swindlers do."[84]

Even well after the great depression of the 1870's had passed, the absurdities of the credit system did not abate. It remained clogged with small traders who failed in waves with each successive crisis.[85] By the early 1880's the problem had reached Winnipeg, and with the collapse of the land boom there in 1883 a major wave of failures followed.[86] Nearly all of the chartered banks' customers there, whatever their nominal occupation, were involved in real estate speculation. In one town alone, every single trader failed in the aftermath, and the Merchants' Bank of Canada lost 75% of its discounts there.[87] Yet in 1888 Manitoba and the Northwest reported one trader for every 50 people, while Ontario had but one per 400, and at that was badly overstocked with traders.[88]

Failure waves recurred in 1891 and 1896-7. Between 1891 and 1895 the number of traders rose 6.7% while the number of failures rose 3.8%, making a net increase of 2.9%. In the U.S. in the same period the number of traders rose 3.5%, while failures increased 4.5%, making a net reduction of 1.0%. The crisis of 1907 produced a host of failures in Canada that did not begin to abate until the end of 1909.[89] By January 1908, 1,228 general stores alone had failed in the West due to over-entry and to the credit squeeze applied by the banks and implement dealers after the crisis.[90]

The diversion of resources into short-term credit backed by bank accommodation went hand-in-hand with chronic deprivation of long-term finance to industry. At the same time that the commercial credit system was running amok in Canada, the rate of all business failure due to "lack of capital," including manufacturing failures, ranged between 65 and 75% growing steadily, while during the same period the American rate was less than half of this. The figures given apply to percentage of total numbers, but precisely the same pattern results with percentage of

## TABLE III (3)
### Canadian Failures, 1891-1895

|                      | 1891    | 1892    | 1893    | 1894    | 1895    |
|----------------------|---------|---------|---------|---------|---------|
| Total in business    | 75,589  | 75,860  | 76,856  | 78,783  | 80,666  |
| Total failures       | 1,846   | 1,682   | 1,781   | 1,864   | 1,916   |
| Percentage failures  | 2.44%   | 2.22%   | 2.32%   | 2.37%   | 2.37%   |

Source: *Brad.*, various issues.

total liabilities. The American failure rate due to lack of capital fell over the period, while the Canadian rate rose. Though the Canadian failure rate due to capital "shortage" tended to fall off by 1904-5 when the boom was well underway, it still remained substantially above the American level.

## TABLE III (4)
### Failures Due to "Lack of Capital"

|            | 1890 | 1891 | 1892 | 1893 | 1894 | 1895 |
|------------|------|------|------|------|------|------|
| % Canada   | 55.8 | 66.6 | 65.1 | 69.4 | 68.5 | 71.3 |
| % U.S.     | 37.9 | 39.2 | 32.5 | 33.2 | 34.2 | 33.5 |

|            | 1896 | 1897 | 1898 | 1899 | 1900 | 1901 |
|------------|------|------|------|------|------|------|
| % Canada   | 67.2 | 70.3 | 69.1 | 74.4 | 74.4 | 70.6 |
| % U.S.     | 31.1 | 31.4 | 34.1 | 36.1 | 36.2 | 33.4 |

|            | 1902 | 1903 | 1904 | 1905 | 1906 | 1907 |
|------------|------|------|------|------|------|------|
| % Canada   | 67.0 | 69.6 | 62.2 | 55.2 | 50.6 | 52.5 |
| % U.S.     | 32.8 | 32.5 | 32.2 | 33.4 | 35.9 | 37.1 |

|            | 1908 | 1909 | 1910 | 1911 | 1912 | 1913 |
|------------|------|------|------|------|------|------|
| % Canada   | 43.2 | 42.0 | 46.8 | 49.3 | 50.3 | 41.3 |
| % U.S.     | 34.2 | 34.5 | 33.9 | 31.4 | 29.7 | 29.6 |

Sources: *Brad.*, *CYB*, *SYBC*, various issues.

# Savings Deposit Business

Savings banks in British North America evolved to function as a depository for working-class savings, as a means to "develop thrift among the people."[91] Both private and government savings banks emerged, and for most of their history, until the late

1880's, they were not competitive with the chartered banks, but rather complemented them. The private savings banks often had interlocking directorships with their companion chartered banks and shared their facilities. Thus, the Hamilton and Gore District Savings Bank was linked to the Gore Bank and did its savings business for it. The savings were invested in Ontario bank stocks, in City of Toronto notes and debentures, in mortgages, and other safe securities.[92] Hence, in neither the source of funds (working-class savings deposits rather than merchants' and small business demand deposits and bank notes) nor in the use of funds (stable investments rather than current mercantile loans and discounts) did the two institutions compete. While functionally distinct, their directorship was virtually identical.

Similarly, the Montreal District Savings Bank was founded in 1819 two years after the Bank of Montreal and shared directors and facilities with that institution. In 1856 the savings bank was absorbed by the Bank of Montreal and thereafter it functioned as a separate savings department.[93] Not until 1891, with the growing competition among banks for deposits, was the savings department integrated into the Bank's normal operations.[94]

In Manitoba, on the other hand, there was no private savings bank. However, a federal government savings bank was established in 1879 and it filled the gap, functioning as little more than an arm of the Merchants' Bank of Canada. This chartered bank, as a Tory institution, held all the government accounts in Winnipeg, and supplied the government savings bank with over one million dollars in Merchants' notes a year for circulation.[95]

Precisely when savings deposits became of prime importance to the banks varied from bank to bank. As late as 1889, a Halifax banker attested before a Royal Commission as to the unimportance of general savings deposits in his business:

Q.  Do you receive deposits from the working classes?
A.  No. I don't care to do that sort of business . . . . They put their money in the savings banks where they can secrete it and escape taxation.[96]

For all banks, except for the Bank of Montreal, by 1890 the savings deposit business was the central concern. For the Bank of Montreal the slight lag behind other banks was due to its continued major role in public finance and its still extant dreams of becoming a super-bank on the Bank of England model. Nonetheless in 1891 its savings department was integrated into its general operations.

In 1871, savings deposits and notes were about equal in the banks' liability structure, while demand deposits were by far the most important liability they had. Thereafter savings deposits grew relative to notes, until by 1914 they were six-and-one-half times the level of notes, their greatest acceleration occurring about 1898 to 1900. Savings deposits began to exceed demand deposits in 1883, and the gap grew.

**TABLE III (5)**

**Chartered Bank Liabilities — Selected Items**

|      |         |       | Deposits | |
| ---- | ------- | ----- | -------- | ------- |
|      | *Capital* | *Notes* | *Demand* | *Savings* |
| 1875 | 40.7 | 14.2 | 20.7 | 15.9 |
| 1880 | 33.0 | 15.1 | 23.3 | 20.5 |
| 1885 | 27.0 | 14.3 | 23.0 | 22.0 |
| 1890 | 23.0 | 13.4 | 20.6 | 30.8 |
| 1895 | 19.1 | 10.0 | 20.8 | 36.8 |
| 1900 | 13.6 | 10.3 | 22.2 | 38.2 |
| 1905 | 10.6 | 8.7 | 19.2 | 44.2 |
| 1910 | 8.2 | 7.2 | 23.0 | 44.6 |
| 1913 | 7.5 | 7.1 | 24.7 | 40.7 |

*% total liabilities*

While the precise timing of the shift to savings deposits is difficult to pin down, the forces behind the movement are clear. Beginning with the crash of 1873, over two decades of secular deflation set in on an international scale. As world prices fell, the Canadian price level moved downward with it, a decline uninterruped until 1895-1896. The fall in prices diminished the scope for chartered bank note issues. And as the note issue stagnated the chartered banks lost ground to other financial intermediaries in terms of their over-all importance to the flow of funds in Canada. From 1873 to 1885, the share of chartered banks in the total financial intermediation process in Canada shrank steadily as a result of the decline in their sources of funds engendered by the stagnation of their note issue power. The result was to precipitate a scramble for an alternative source of loanable funds — as well as desperate but generally futile measures to maintain note circulation. And the obvious alternative source of funds was the hitherto badly neglected savings deposit business.

In 1873 when the deflation began, chartered banks dominated the Canadian financial structure to the extent of controlling nearly 72% of total intermediary assets. During the 1870's their share declined precipitously as the note issue fell drastically. There was a brief recovery from 1879 to 1883, but thereafter,

while the note issue did not decline absolutely, it remained virtually stagnant. By 1885, chartered banks controlled only 55% of
total intermediary assets, while government savings banks and
mortgage loan companies who earnestly cultivated the savings
deposit business had grown very markedly.

## TABLE III (6)

### Relative Shares of Total Intermediary Assets

|      | % total assets | | |
|------|----------------------|---------------------------|-----------------------------|
|      | Chartered Banks | Government Savings Banks | Mortgage Loan Companies |
| 1873 | 71.6 | 3.2 | 10.7 |
| 1875 | 69.6 | 2.8 | 13.6 |
| 1880 | 55.4 | 5.4 | 24.6 |
| 1885 | 51.8 | 9.3 | 24.1 |
| 1890 | 49.5 | 7.9 | 24.5 |
| 1895 | 48.0 | 7.6 | 22.3 |
| 1900 | 52.6 | 6.7 | 16.2 |
| 1905 | 57.5 | 5.1 | 12.2 |
| 1910 | 59.6 | 3.2 | 10.9 |
| 1913 | 57.4 | 2.4 | 10.6 |

Source: E. P. Neufeld, *The Financial System of Canada,*
        Statistical Appendix.

By 1885, however, the efforts of the chartered banks to break
into the savings deposit business in a concerted way began to
produce significant results. The new sources of loanable funds
stabilized their position and arrested the decline in their importance. At the same time, the spectacular growth of the government savings banks was reversed. Then after 1895-1896, when
the price level began to trend up again, a rising capacity to issue
notes coupled with their control of the savings deposit business
served as the foundation for renewed chartered bank expansion,
and their domination of the financial structure, while never
attaining the level of the early 1870's, nonetheless grew appreci-
ably.

Savings deposits were clearly the key to the salvation of the
banks during the deflationary years. And the desire to control
the business brought the chartered banks face to face with the
government, and with the need to curtail interest rate competition to prevent costly price wars. Both exigencies dictated the
need for organization, and hence it was directly out of the
struggle for savings deposits that an illegal interest-rate fixing

cartel emerged, which subsequently adopted the name "Canadian Bankers' Association."

Chartered bank collusion on the savings deposit rate was initially conducted on a provincial basis, until the monetary integration of Canada was effected by means of the spread of central Canadian banks east and west, and of Halifax banks to the west. In 1876, Halifax banks cut their deposit rate from five to four per cent,[97] followed some months later by Montreal banks. At the same time, Montreal private bankers and brokers were offering up to seven per cent on savings.[98] But the Montreal private banks catered to the wealthy depositors rather than to working-class savers. While the Merchants' Bank of Canada in 1878 engaged in a campaign to attract depositors, raising its savings rate to five per cent,[99] other banks did not follow suit. In fact, less than a year later the Eastern Townships Bank lowered its savings rate to four per cent.[100] The Merchants' zeal to attract depositors may have been, for peculiar reasons of its own, perhaps not completely unrelated to its speculation in gold in New York,[101] which nearly precipitated its failure.

Further rate reductions in Quebec and the Maritimes initiated by the big banks and followed by the little ones occurred in the late 1870's, [102] until three per cent was the norm by 1880. For the Quebec banks the rate cuts were easier than for those of Ontario, where mortgage loan companies and private banks competed for the savings business with the chartered banks.[103] By 1885, the Merchants' Bank had followed the lead of the other Quebec banks, stabilizing its rate at three per cent.[104] But the banks experienced difficulty in maintaining the rate despite their informal cartel arrangement. By 1890, three-and-one-half per cent was the norm, and some banks continued to break the combine when convenient. When caught secretly offering four per cent, the banks blamed it on the overzealousness of underclerks and local managers.[105]

The formation of a formal bankers' association in 1890 was the signal for energetic moves towards full interest rate normalization. The first objective was a complete agreement on the rate on new deposits only, leaving the banks free to continue to pay the established rate on old deposits. By 1897, the Executive Council reported optimistically on its efforts to establish a uniform rate of three per cent:

> It is to be regretted that your Council cannot yet report a complete agreement in all the provinces to reduce the maximum rate of interest on deposits to three per cent, yet the progress made warrants the belief that the incoming Council will be able to establish a uniform arrangement, and that it

will relate not only to new deposits with which limit the present Council had to content themselves, but to old monies as well.[106]

At the same time efforts were made to stabilize the savings deposit rates offered by the chartered banks, a major attack was mounted on the competition from the government savings banks, commencing in 1885. The rate of interest paid by chartered banks had fallen by one or two percentage points over the previous few years, building society rates were down to four per cent, while the government continued to pay four per cent on its savings deposits, a rate which the banks claimed exceeded the rate at which money could be raised on the open market.[107]

This charge, that the savings rate exceeded the open market borrowing rate together with the claim that it forced up the chartered bank rate and hence increased the economy's credit costs, was used time after time.[108] It was not a particularly sensible argument. The nominal rate of interest on government loans, the rate used for the comparison, was generally much lower than the real rate, since most loans during this period were sold at a substantial discount. And until the mid-1890's the government savings deposits were not comparable to those of the chartered banks either by class of depositor or use of the funds. Since the government savings deposits went into long-term investments, the rate of interest logically should have been higher than that of chartered bank deposits, which were used for commercial loans and discounts. The chartered banks tried to counter this argument by the claim that if they got the extra deposits they would buy more government bonds. In fact, once they got them, their holdings of government securities fell.

Replying to the banks in 1885, the Minister of Finance denied that the rate was excessive, and in fact that year the nominal yield in government bonds was 4.10% on average. By 1885, however, the CPR was largely complete to the Pacific coast, and its raids on the public purse tended to abate. As a result, there was less pressure for the maintenance of government savings banks to help provide funds to give away to railway promoters and their friends. Interest rate reductions in the government bank could be expected to follow, and in 1890 the rate fell to 3.5%. The chartered banks collectively raised their rates to four per cent as the government lowered its rate, with the desired result — a large shift of deposits from the government to the chartered banks. In addition, the policy was initiated of shifting some of the government savings banks into the less convenient post-office banking system.[109]

The banks were still unsatisfied. In 1896, before the Canadian Bankers' Association, Thomas Fysche reiterated the old charge with new numbers: that the government's three-and-one-half per cent rate was pegging the chartered bank rate at too high a level and therefore raising minimum borrowing costs. Only a few sentences before, Fysche had been busily denouncing the long credit system for making credit too cheap in the economy![110] But, undeterred by this patent sophistry, the government obligingly lowered its rate to three per cent.

In 1898, the chartered banks attempted a collective reduction of interest rates to 2.5% on deposits, and tried successfully to induce the government to do the same. The Minister of Finance, W. S. Fielding, attempted to justify the decrease on the grounds that there was no longer a need for special savings outlets for working-class income earners. The opposition protested that the result of a further reduction would be to drive small savers into the hands of "unstable" private banks.[111] Although the rate offered on deposits did not fall further, government savings outlets did undergo a steady decline in importance as the chartered banks launched their assault on the savings deposit business. [112] Government savings deposits were thus lost as a means of financing the construction of infrastructure at precisely the point when new raids on the public purse by railway magnates were in the offing, and as the government's legitimate infra-structural spending responsibilities were on the rise in response to a great influx of immigrants, rapid industrial growth, and the opening of the West.

## TABLE III (7)

### Government Savings Deposits

| | ($ million) | |
|---|---|---|
| Year | Savings Banks | Post Office Banks |
| 1870 | 3.4 | 1.6 |
| 1875 | 7.2 | 3.9 |
| 1880 | 11.1 | 3.9 |
| 1885 | 32.0 | 15.1 |
| 1890 | 19.0 | 22.0 |
| 1895 | 17.6 | 26.8 |
| 1900 | 15.6 | 37.5 |
| 1905 | 16.5 | 45.4 |
| 1910 | 14.6 | 42.8 |
| 1913 | 14.1 | 41.9 |

Sources: *SYB, CYB*, various years.

Although in absolute terms some growth in the total of savings in government banks occurred, it was very small; relative to population the decline in government savings outlets was drastic after 1885. And savings banks proper experienced an absolute decline. It is no accident that the federal government turned increasingly to public issues in London to raise funds at the same time that its access to savings deposits fell off relative to the chartered banks.

The impact of the decline of the availability of government savings facilities was not felt evenly either by geographic area or by class of depositors. Farmers and artisans were by far the leading users of the savings banks,[113] and it was their business that the chartered banks, including those of Halifax, now condescended to tap. The greatest number of savings banks too had been in the Maritimes. In per-capita terms Ontario was the greatest user of the post office savings bank facilities — the system of post office savings banks established in 1867 was not extended to the Maritimes until 1885[114] — but when both of the government institutions are aggregated, the Maritimes show the greatest per-capita usage.

**TABLE III (8)**

**Government Savings Deposits Per Capita**

| Province | 1895 | 1900 |
|----------|-------|-------|
| Ont. | 8.75 | 10.55 |
| Que. | 2.89 | 3.71 |
| N.S. | 18.87 | 17.78 |
| N.B. | 24.09 | 27.35 |
| Man. | 4.70 | 5.41 |
| B.C. | 9.02 | 12.03 |
| P.E.I. | 20.27 | 19.25 |
| Northwest | 0.92 | 1.79 |

Sources: *SYB*, 1895, 1900.

As part of the terms of Confederation, the federal government had assumed control of provincial savings banks. In 1886, of 50 such banks in Canada 45 were in the Maritimes.[115] By 1890, when despite the clear need for such institutions the total had been reduced to 41 in deference to the chartered banks, 37 of these were in the Maritimes. By 1900, 21 of 23 banks were there. The funds taken from the Maritimes were used to further central Canadian development objectives.[116] By 1886, some fifteen million had been taken out of the Maritimes and invested in projects like the Canadian Pacific Railway. Not only were these western and central Canadian commercial projects harmful to the competitive position of Atlantic industry, but the direct effect of the drain seriously damaged the position of the Maritime local chartered banks, which in turn had adverse repercussions on Maritime industrial development. The high rates of interest paid on government savings deposits drained the "lifeblood" of the Maritime banks,[117] rendering them more vulnerable to central commercial bank takeover. And once the central Canadian banks had themselves moved into the area, the government savings banks were phased out. The flow of funds out of the Maritimes was then intermediated by the central Canadian commercial banks.

Yet if the flow of savings deposits out was harmful to Maritime industrial development, it did little or nothing to enhance the industrial prospects of the areas of Canada which received the funds. Canadian banks were well aware of the radical distinction between demand and savings deposits in terms of the balance in their liability structures. Edmund Walker, in 1893, made the distinction clear:

> . . . In Canada, with its banks with forty and fifty branches, we see the deposits of the saving community applied directly to the country's new enterprises in a manner near perfect [sic]. . . . Well managed Canadian banks do not give interest on active current accounts. But all Canadian banks issue interest bearing receipts, and . . . almost all have Savings Departments. These deposits, great and small, are in the nature of investments by the depositors, and are not like the temporary balance of a merchant. They are entitled to interest.[118]

In the United States, savings bank deposits went largely into state, municipal, and carefully selected railroad bonds, into public buildings, and similar investments. In Canada, the government savings bank receipts had done likewise. But the structure changed as the chartered banks displaced the government savings banks. The Canadian banks, while recognizing the nature of the change in their liabilities, in fact channelled the proceeds off into current loans and discounts, exactly as they did with demand deposits.[119] Edmund Walker testified before a Commons committee in 1913 to this effect:

> Q. Does your Savings Bank Department in any way differ essentially from the savings banks as such?
> A. Oh yes, we take the savings money and use it in commercial banking.[120]

There was little movement into long-term assets following the lengthening of the terms of their liabilities. The banks' security

holdings did rise a little, as a percentage of total assets, up to
1900, but thereafter they declined during the great western
expansion—indicating a very substantial shift of bank resources
into moving crops and other staples. Very little long-term
finance to railroads or to governments was made available
through the banks at a time when American banks were holding
about 40% of their assets in the form of long-term bonds of governments and corporations.[121] The twisting of savings deposits
into current discounts aggravated the problem of long-term
finance already implicit in the fact that the note issue had no security backing. When long-term investments did occur, a large
amount went into foreign investments. The problem was especially acute because of the active and aggressive campaign of the
chartered banks for these deposits, which permitted them, with
the federal government's co-operation, to seize the overwhelming
share. By the end of 1905, there were some $620 million in sav-
ings deposits in Canada distributed among the various banks
and loan companies, of which the chartered banks held $512
million.[122]

**TABLE III (9)**

**Chartered Bank Assets — Selected Items**

| | | | | | | | | |
|---|---|---|---|---|---|---|---|---|
| | | | | *% total assets* | | | | |
| | *Securities* | | | | *Loans* | | | |
| | *Municipal* | *Dominion & Provincial* | *Railroad etc.* | *Total* | *Current* | | *Call and Short* | |
| | | | | | *Canada* | *Abroad* | *Canada* | *Abroad* |
| 1873 | — | 0.9 | — | 0.9 | 74.8 | | | |
| 1875 | — | 0.7 | — | 0.7 | 73.3 | | | |
| 1880 | 0.8 | 0.6 | — | 1.4 | 62.6 | | | |
| 1885 | 1.3 | 0.4 | — | 1.7 | 68.9 | | | |
| 1890 | 2.3 | 1.0 | — | 3.3 | 72.3 | | 4.5* | |
| 1895 | 3.0 | 0.8 | 2.9 | 6.7 | 62.9 | | 5.4 | |
| 1900 | 2.3 | 2.3 | 5.1 | 9.7 | 57.1 | 3.7 | 6.7 | 5.5 |
| 1905 | 2.5 | 1.1 | 5.2 | 8.8 | 55.9 | 3.3 | 5.6 | 6.7 |
| 1910 | 1.8 | 0.9 | 4.7 | 7.4 | 53.8 | 3.3 | 5.1 | 9.3 |
| 1913 | 1.5 | 0.7 | 4.3 | 6.5 | 56.9 | 2.9 | 4.6 | 6.5 |

The mortgage loan companies had been subjected to a
squeeze on their savings business parallelling that on the government banks, especially with the business revival of the late
1890's. The bankers had long protested the right of mortgage
loan companies to accept deposits: with the organization of the
Bankers' Association they were finally in a position to do something concrete about it. In 1897, the bankers' Quebec lobby successfully forced the withdrawal of a clause in a provincial mortgage loan company charter that would have permitted it to

receive deposits as a basis for making loans. The same success crowned similar efforts in Ottawa that year directed against a federal loan company charter. The Bankers' Association renewed its call for the blocking of all mortgage loan companies from the deposit business and for forcing them to rely on debenture issues to borrow money. While a blanket prohibition was not achieved, the Bankers' Association continued to register successes in forcing the dropping of savings deposit clauses in new incorporations.[123] The funds thereby diverted from mortgage lending went into orthodox commercial banking at precisely the time when the opening of the West created new demands for mortgage funds. Just as with government finance, the result was an increased reliance on British capital acquired through debenture issues to finance mortgage lending in Canada.

# Chartered Bank Expansion, Competition, and Mergers

There were several ways in which the banking system and its individual components could grow. Each bank could expand its assets and the number of branches. Total assets of the banking system, in fact, grew fifteen-fold over the period 1870 to 1914. But growth was not continuous in relative terms. As a percentage of all financial intermediary assets, the banks' position fell from 1873 for some time, then rose with the recovery and expansion.

Many new charters too were granted, but at the same time mergers and failures took their toll of the existing banks. Prior to 1900 mergers were relatively difficult, but thereafter regulations were relaxed and mergers of institutions that would otherwise have failed became common. The granting of new charters came in waves corresponding to peak periods of railway building. Of the 81 new charters granted from 1867 to 1914, 26 came in the 1871-73 period, 11 in the period 1881-84; and 26 in the 1901-05 period, for a total of 53 in these 11 years. Many of these banks never became operational, and with the mergers and failures, the number of banks operating, while rising by five from 1867 to 1900, fell by fifteen from 1900 to 1914.

Simply examining the number of banks and their branches and mergers does not give a full picture of the amount of bank facilities nor the competitive structure, for it was common for chartered banks in new communities to operate, initially, via a private banker. Moreover, there were some cases of surreptitious control of one chartered bank over another, and of sphere of

**TABLE III (10)**

**Banks Operating, 1867 - 1914**

|           | Failures* | Mergers | New Charters | New Banks Operating | Net Change |
|-----------|-----------|---------|--------------|---------------------|------------|
| 1867-1900 | 20        | 3       | 48           | 28                  | + 5        |
| 1901-1914 | 7         | 19      | 33           | 11                  | -15        |

Source: E. P. Neufeld, *Financial System,* pp. 78-79.

*includes both the Royal Canadian and the City Bank.

influence agreements. But in general, especially after the Canadian Bankers' Association was formalized in 1890, interest rate competition was minimized. Competition thereafter took the wasteful form of proliferation of branches to secure both savings deposits and new clients for loans. It was standard big business behaviour, excess capacity coexisting with a restricted number of units operating behind barriers to the entry of new firms, and refraining from price competition.

This overexpansion of bank capital at the same time it was concentrated in relatively few units in Canada became evident as early as 1876, when the Bank of London and the Bank of North America were both chartered, at the same time as the City and the Royal Canadian merged from weakness and the St. Lawrence reduced its capital.[124] The Bank of North America never got off the ground. By the 1890's, leading bankers like Thomas Fysche and Edmund Walker were calling for a curtailment of the expansion of banks, citing "over-competition,"[125] which was reducing profit margins. It was in expansion of the banks' "plant," not in prices, that competition revealed itself. Price competition would have trimmed costs to a minimum and reduced interest rates to borrowers. Competition by expansion of facilities meant maintaining interest rates and increasing overhead costs. At that time, business was not expanding rapidly enough to accommodate the existing number of banks. Thomas Fysche regarded "competition" as obsolete under the circumstances. He declared:

> It was chiefly necessary in order to make up for the lack of proper organization. When the latter is achieved we may regard the rapid disappearance of competition with comparative equanimity.[126]

But despite the growth of "proper organization" in the form of the Bankers' Association's ability to restrict new entrants or the merger powers after 1900, the diversion of resources into banking did not abate. It simply changed from the creation of new banks to the internal expansion of old.

Some new banks were chartered, but comparatively few. And there were great difficulties in getting them operational. The Monarch Bank, chartered in 1895, tried in vain until 1907 to find enough funds to operate, and then wound up.[127] Even earlier, the Traders Bank had difficulty getting a charter. It was a Toronto-based bank that had to disguise itself as a Bowmanville, Ontario, operation by working through a group in that town who fronted for its promoters, notable among them a notorious broker, H. S. Strathy, who had already been a prime figure in wrecking two earlier banks. The surreptitious approach was rendered necessary by vested banking interests in Toronto who would have opposed and blocked a new Toronto bank.[128] And in 1892 the little Farmers Bank of Rustico, P.E.I., a bank with a perfect record of operation, was denied a charter renewal and forced to wind up.

Prior to the great western expansion, most of the growth of banks was accounted for by those of Ontario and their branches within Ontario. Ontario bank assets doubled between 1881 and 1890.[129] The movement west by central Canadian banks actually occurred in two distinct waves. The first began in 1873, when Sir Hugh Allan's Merchants' Bank of Canada established a branch in Winnipeg in conjunction with his CPR and western ambitions. This was followed by twelve other central Canadian banks and one western one by 1896.[130] By that date, the second movement west was beginning. Banks, like railroads, in the Canadian West moved into areas in advance of the main body of settlement. The little Eastern Townships Bank, which did not establish its first branch outside Sherbrooke until it opened in nearby St. Hyacinthe in 1895, had a branch three years later in Grand Forks, B.C.[131] After 1900 the movement became a flood. Branches and sub-agencies of central and eastern banks west of Ontario grew from 108 in 1900 to 2,962 in 1913.[132] The Eastern Townships alone had 64 branches and 39 subagencies. Virtually all of the expansion was accounted for by a few established banks: the Bank of British North America, the Merchants', the Union of Halifax, the Sterling, and the Standard being the pioneers. The Bank of Commerce and the Montreal were slow in moving west.[133] After the boom ended, overextended facilities had to be cut back, the pioneer banks were weakened, and subsequently they were absorbed by the others who had been more cautious in their expansion.

Individual banks expanded as well, by controlling other banks, by precipitating failure through the withdrawal of support, or by absorption. In the East, the Bank of Montreal attempted to secure control of the Maritime Bank in 1880 by purchasing 1,070 shares and having its agent try to select and appoint an amenable set of officers. The little local bank fought back with a court injunction barring the Bank of Montreal from voting. It claimed that by holding Maritime shares the bank became involved in stock jobbing, and this constituted a breach of trust with the stockholders. It was not a particularly logical argument, and of course the real issue was something else quite distinct. By controlling the choice of directorate, the Montreal and other central Canadian banks could use the local banks as their agents, and the little Maritime banks saw their style of business and their interests as fundamentally opposed to those of the big central commercial banks.[134]

The main wave of central bank expansion into the East came, like the move west, after 1900. But the western expansion was at the expense only of private banks, which were already agents of the central Canadian banks (with the exception of the chartered Northern Bank of Winnipeg, which was taken over by the Crown Bank and moved to Toronto in 1908); the eastern expansion, on the other hand, displaced the existing banks. It was a two-fold process of monetary centralization. At the same time that the central commercial banks were expanding into the Maritimes, the Halifax commercial banks did likewise. Then the Halifax banks, which in their behaviour patterns were not at all typical of the Maritimes, but indistinguishable from the central Canadian ones, shifted their headquarters to Montreal.[135]

The Bank of Nova Scotia absorbed the Union Bank of Prince Edward Island as early as 1882. The Bank of New Brunswick took over the Summerside Bank in 1901. In turn, the Bank of New Brunswick was taken over by the Bank of Nova Scotia in 1913, which had in the meantime shifted its headquarters to Montreal. Through the agency of Max Aitken (Lord Beaverbrook), the Union Bank of Halifax took over the Commercial Bank of Windsor in 1902,[136] and this in turn was absorbed by the Merchants' Bank of Halifax (the Royal Bank) in 1910. The Royal shifted to Montreal, where it established a *modus vivendi* with the Bank of Montreal. The Royal's interests were mainly Maritime and Caribbean, while those of the Montreal were largely central Canadian.[137] During 1911 there were rumours in Montreal of a possible merger between the two under the presidency of Sir Herbert Holt. But while this was never effected, the close relationship persisted.[138]

Before the Royal moved to Montreal, the Montreal had made its own moves into the Maritimes. In 1903 it had acquired the Exchange Bank of Yarmouth, followed by the People's Bank of Halifax in 1905 — a move which netted it 26 branches, 15 in the Maritimes. The People's Bank of New Brunswick was added in 1907. The Bank of Commerce was also active in the Maritimes, taking over the Halifax Banking Company in 1903 and the Merchants' Bank of P.E.I. in 1906. These two central banks, who were most ambitious in the Maritimes, were the two who were initially the slowest to enter the West. But the policy of establishing a prior base in the Maritimes paid handsome dividends once they began their westward march, absorbing the banks that had moved west first.

There were bank expansions via branches in the various centres of central Canada as well, especially rural Ontario. And the central provinces also saw many mergers. But while thirteen mergers occurred involving central Canadian banks and only ten involving Maritime ones, the Maritime ones were much more important in relative terms: together with failures and with the shift of the Royal and the Nova Scotia to Montreal, by 1913 Maritime banking simply ceased to exist.

There were many instances, too, of chartered banks moving into communities after banking space was opened up by the failure of a rival. The Merchants' Bank of Halifax (the Royal) capitalized on the failure of the Bank of Acadia in 1872 and the Bank of Liverpool in 1879. The Bank of Montreal got 26 new branches by taking over the assets of the defunct Ontario Bank in 1906, and moved into St. Hyacinthe and St. Jean after the failure of their local banks in 1908. The Bank of New Brunswick moved into St. Stephen after the local bank failed in 1910. Many mergers in fact represented purchases of banks with losses to the stockholders of the absorbed institution, the alternative to the sale at a bargain rate being outright failure.

The merger movement in banks after 1900 attracted attention and no small amount of consternation from the industrial community who were apprehensive about the reduction in bank competition.[139] The merger movement in banks did not at all correlate with the industrial merger movement in Canada. The two obeyed different rules and were prompted by different circumstances. The bank mergers were the outcome of the forces at work in the "wheat boom" and the interregional flow of funds that resulted from it.

# The Flow of Funds

The power of the big commercial banks was enhanced by their interrelations with other major financial institutions. Unlike the U.S., where the banks tended to be heterogeneous, in Canada there was a great deal of functional specialization among intermediaries who were interlocked via shared directorships. The fiduciary function, for instance, was in Canada performed entirely by trust companies and not at all by banks.[140] However, close relations were established between banks and trust companies, the Bank of Montreal with Royal Trust, the Commerce with National Trust, the Royal with Montreal Trust. Royal Trust, for example was founded in 1892 and of sixteen original directors, nine were members of the Bank of Montreal board; and the firm shared the Bank of Montreal building after 1895.[141] The Montreal Trust was very much a Bank of Montreal creation as well, Donald Smith, E. S. Clouston, and several other eminent Montreal commercial and financial figures being involved in its genesis.[142] National Trust was controlled by George Cox, who in 1892 was president of the Bank of Commerce, and several other directors were shared, including Joseph Flavelle, the president of the trust company. The Eastern Trust Company was established in Halifax in 1893 by T. E. Kenny of the Merchants' Bank of Halifax, T. Fysche of the Nova Scotia and later the Merchants' of Canada, private banker J. C. Mackintosh of Halifax, and J. F. Stairs of the Union Bank of Halifax.[143]

Dominion Trust, established in 1910, functioned for several years in close association with the Bank of Vancouver, so closely in fact that the crash of Dominion Trust in 1914 pulled down the chartered bank with it. The ensuing investigation of the trust company's affairs revealed that its general manager had personally helped himself to $100,000 of the company's cash, that four to five million in trust funds were indiscriminately mixed with the company's own funds and large amounts diverted into investments in highly speculative stocks and bonds in flagrant violation of trust company legislation, and that the company had illegally (under existing legislation) accepted demand deposits against which no cash reserves were held.[144]

All of these trust company promotions around the turn of the century reflected a fundamental new trait of the Canadian socio-economic system, the growth of large and even moderate fortunes held in the form of portfolio investments. A distinct rentier class was taking form from a combination of the hardening of class lines, the inheritance of financial assets, and the development of a Canadian capital market. Until World War I, though, this rentier group's investments, either direct or via the nascent trust companies, tended to concentrate on municipal debentures, real estate, financial institution equity and the like, rather than government bonds.

Nor did the links between various financial institutions stop at banks and trust companies. Sir Herbert Holt's Royal Bank and the Bank of Montreal were complementary institutions, and by the early twentieth century the Bank of Montreal's financial network embraced such firms as Royal Securities and Sun Life Assurance. Sun Life, too, was linked to the Merchants' Bank.[145] The financial empire of Senator George Cox went well beyond the Commerce and the National Trust. Cox was also President of Canada Life Assurance, and founder and almost sole owner of Central Canada Loan and Savings Company, which in turn owned Dominion Securities. He also controlled the Toronto Savings Company, Imperial Life Insurance, and the Provident Investment Company.[146] Cox's intricate system was the most spectacular, but was not unique. And substantial flows of funds occurred between the components of these financial networks, often to evade the legislative restrictions on the activities of one unit in the system.[147] Yet despite the mass of evidence on interchanges of directors, Edmund Walker had the audacity to reply to a question in a Commons committee hearing as follows:

Q.  It is said there is much interlocking of directors.
A.  That is just a phrase gathered from the United States.[148]

The power that such centralized structures gave to a handful of Montreal and Toronto money magnates, and in the early period to a lesser extent to Halifax financiers, was protested by the smaller communities in Ontario, and by the eastern and western provinces. As early as 1883, Manitoba businessmen complained of a financial squeeze imposed upon them at the instigation of central Canadian financial magnates.[149] This agitation contributed a great deal to the creation of the Commercial Bank of Manitoba in 1885 to service the local community. By 1907, agitation was widespread in B.C. for a system of provincial banks. The existing banks were accused of draining surplus funds from the province for the benefit of eastern enterprise while B.C. firms were starved for credit.[150] The Bank of Vancouver was established in 1911 in response to these local needs.

In Alberta, the farmers' organizations long advocated a Provincial Bank of Issue and a system of provincially chartered local unit banks on the American state bank model.[151] In Saskatchewan, a Royal Commission investigating agricultural credit called for increased control of financial institutions within the province and denounced the chartered banks, who conspicuously lacked directors from the western provinces.[152] The little Weyburn Security Bank was held up as a model before the 1913 Committee on Banking.[153] And a western member of the House of Commons that year denounced the Bank Act for facilitating the creation of a "money trust" by encouraging mergers and inhibiting new entrants. What was needed, he claimed, was "more banks, and a scattered management of banks, rather than concentration."[154] These sentiments were repeated by the Grain Growers' Associations.[155]

Even after the Bank of Vancouver was established, it and the Weyburn were the only banking institutions with their head offices in the West, the Northern having moved to Toronto. Even counting the Northern-Crown merger as a western institution, the three at their peak accounted for only one-and-one-half per cent of the total branches , and less than ten per cent of the western branches of Canadian banks.[156]

Small towns in Ontario also opposed the cartelization process. The Western Bank, a small chartered bank, had been headquartered in the town of Oshawa, and the town credited most of its industrial advance to the presence of the bank. The Western was absorbed by the Standard of Toronto, and not only did local control vanish, but all activities towards promoting local industrialization reputedly stopped.[157] The town of Glencoe claimed it had also attempted local industrial developments, but its funds on deposit were siphoned off to Toronto and Montreal where they helped the big established cartels. The local branch managers refused to make advances towards the establishment of a cannery controlled by citizens of the town, and the town eventually had to solicit a branch plant of a Toronto-based canning firm, a client of the same banks that refused to use local deposits for the Glencoe project.[158]

The farm journals, like Peter McArthur's *Farmers' Advocate* which fought for local co-operative banking, were subjected to economic blackmail and censorship by the banks. After McArthur published a series of articles by Alphonse Desjardin on co-operative banking and editorials denouncing the existing banking system, all advertisements, not only of the banks but also of all firms that held accounts with the branches of the banks in his area, were withdrawn. McArthur was told they would stay withdrawn until publication of the articles ceased. Where withdrawing of advertisements did not suffice, loans were called or advances refused to keep the local press in line.[159] In addition, a farm journal called *Canadian Countryman* was established with the funds of Edmund Walker and his associates, and managed by Canadian Northern Railway magnate R. M. Horne Payne, to counteract the criticisms of the banking and commercial elite and the radical policy proposals of the bona fide farm journals.[160]

In the Maritimes, the complaints against the banking system were loudest, and the damage done most in evidence. The example of Massachusetts, whose industrial development had been encouraged by a plethora of savings and hence of cheap money for investment, was before the eyes of the inhabitants of the area. The Maritimes had, on Confederation, been touted as the future cradle of a Canadian industrial revolution. But with the drain of savings deposits from the area, this hope became sheer fantasy. In one town the ratio of deposits to loans by 1913 reached twenty-to-one. Yet Edmund Walker dismissed their complaints as "local grievances against what we regard as the interests of the country as a whole."[161]

The Maritimes was an area of "surplus" savings, deposits exceeding loans, and the great virtue of the branch banking system was supposed to inhere in its ability to transfer funds across the country from surplus to deficit areas.[162] In Halifax, as long as it had been a financial centre, interest rates on borrowings had been as low as in the central metropolitan centres. With the migration of the head offices of banks to Montreal, Halifax interest rates rose to the top of the borrowing range,[163] and the city, too, became a "surplus" area. Elsewhere, P.E.I. experienced difficulty in moving its crops after its last local bank was absorbed. In 1907, for example, the Bank of Commerce effectively blocked the movement of its bumper harvest of corn by refusing to make advances.[164]

The critical instrument for initially effecting the monetary union of the Maritimes and central Canada was the note issue, while deposits followed. As late as 1888, Maritime bank notes were charged a five per cent discount by Toronto banks and merchants while in the Maritimes central Canadian notes passed at discounts of one-quarter to one-half a percentage point.[165] And the Maritime note issue showed a completely different seasonal variation from that of central Canada. Central Canadian banks expanded their circulation to move the crops. Note circulation fell in July and August as they accumulated notes in preparation, and rose from October to December or January, thereafter falling. The Maritime banks' greatest circulation was during the summer months, when industrial activity tended to peak. Once takeover was complete, note issue showed the same seasonal pattern across Canada, even though this pattern was inappropriate to the Maritime economic structure.[166]

The flow of funds was largely from east to west, with the funds undergoing a major transformation between place of origin and place of use. The Maritimes and, to a lesser extent, small towns in Ontario, were the lenders, and the prairie agricultural communities, after the wheat boom was underway, were the chief borrowers. Funds that had previously been used in the Maritimes to sustain the industrial growth that followed the

National Policy tariff were now drained west as short-period accommodation to farmers, or lent to the big milling, shipping, and grain speculating companies. As the West developed agriculturally as a commercial fiefdom of Montreal and Toronto capital, the Maritimes sagged industrially. At the same time, small Ontario towns complained increasingly about the drainage of funds.[167] It was observed in both the Maritimes and small-town Ontario that "men of ability follow capital, able and efficient men who otherwise have remained in the community."[168] The effects of the flow of funds were of course compounded by the growth of banks relative to other intermediaries in this period.

Once out west, the funds returned a rate of interest that exceeded the rate in the metropolitan centres. The excuse was that a branch in the West cost more to run than one in the East[169] — this bald assertion coinciding with eulogies over the virtues of branch banking and its ability to equalize interest rates across the country.[170]

# Banking and Agriculture

The flow of funds from the East to the West bypassed eastern farms — which were generally mixed or dairy farms. Farmers in Ontario and Quebec deposited more than they borrowed, while in the West borrowings considerably exceeded deposits.[171] The percentage of farm loans to farm deposits in Saskatchewan in 1913 was 278%, while the Bank of Commerce reported a loan/deposit ratio for the three prairie provinces of 182%.[172] It was a great change from the 1870's and 1880's when the banks had avoided direct loans to farmers.[173] During the wheat boom, farm loans began to be regarded as the safest and most desirable of all bank business.[174] But this change of attitude reflected the growth of wheat as the leading export staple, replacing timber and other primary products. The banks remained commercial rather than agricultural in their outlook. [175] The western capital market showed a large gap between the long-term mortgage loan and the very short-term advances of the bank.[176] Moreover, such short-term bank advances as were available for agriculture could be easily had only in the staple-producing West. Farmers in Quebec were in dire need of bank accommodation at this time. [177] The lack of funds for central-Canadian mixed farms must have contributed to the stagnation of mixed farming, which drove up Canadian food prices at the same time enormous exports of grains from the West to Europe were occurring.

In the West, the accusations that banks were squeezing the

farmers[178] could not be answered by reference to the volume of bank loans to the West. What had to be examined was the character and distribution of these loans, and the relation of the banks to the wheat economy in general. The banks had extended accommodation to farmers even before the 1913 Bank Act gave legal approval to the all-pervasive practice of loans on security of threshed grain grown on a farm,[179] but they remained much closer to the speculator and the grain-moving interests than to the grain-producing class. This was not a new development. Before Confederation, when the frontier for the wheat staple had been western Ontario, banks refused loans to farmers that would permit them to hold back their crops, but loaned freely to dealers to purchase, and thus forced the farmers to sell almost immediately after harvest at adverse terms of trade.[180] Again, on the prairies, the banks would not loan to farmers to hold grain; notes were made to fall due just before harvest-time, forcing the farmers to sell to the speculators and dealers immediately at the price offered.[181]

The expansion of the banks into the West was rapid after 1900. By the end of 1910, nine leading banks had 653 branches in the East and 622 in the West. The Commerce in particular, after a slow start, made very quick progress and soon challenged the Union Bank for leadership in the West. Bank clearings in Winnipeg rose from $106 million in 1901 to $950 million in 1910.[182] The leading banks' involvement in seasonal crop movements became so heavy that it occasionally stretched their note issue power to the limit even after the authorized increases of 1908. The banks were involved in every stage of the process, financing the purchase of grain by millers or speculators on the security of bills of lading from the railway companies, negotiating "inland drafts" on the export houses and sterling and continental bills of exchange. In cases of non-shipment or delay due to early freeze-ups or due to speculators' holding up grains in expectation of a rise in the Liverpool price, bank funds were locked up for a year.[183] Yet despite their avowed fear of "lock ups," and the obvious risks inherent in financing speculation in primary commodity movements, the banks were eager to drain their eastern customers to service the crop movement. Wheat was almost hard currency in the West, with the result that, according to a Winnipeg financial journal,

> . . . the banks, the elevator companies, the milling concerns, the wholesale and retail merchants, and all the minor elements in the business community [are] particularly united in their determination to use wheat as a medium of exchange and to facilitate [sic] the farmers' interest in that commodity. . . . The whole system of credit in the west, elaborate and

intricate as it is, has been built up from the foundation which recognizes wheat as an equivalent of money.[184]

However enthusiastic the banks and other enterprises may have been about the wheat economy, the position of the farmers was far from enviable. The banks made no loans for farm improvements and stayed out of mortgage lending. Instead they confined themselves to three-month advances on security of chattel mortgages or crops in storage. For other types of finance the farmers faced either a complete void or unsatisfactory *ad hoc* arrangements, for example, with agricultural implements dealers who extended sales credit as part of their system of non-price competition in the West.[185] An effort in 1905 to establish an "Agricultural Bank" in the Northwest met chartered bank resistance and was never established. [186] The Grain Growers Grain Association itself at one point tried without success to obtain a charter for a bank.[187]

The three-month loan system was ideally designed to minimize the convenience of credit, and to maximize the exaction. Farm operations were obviously a twelve-month affair. The three-month loan was generally scheduled to expire at the most difficult season, just before harvesting, when extra security on chattel mortgages could be demanded as a condition of renewal. Renewals were common every three months for up to four years at interest rates as high as 14% compounded every three months, when the legal limit was 7%.[188] Discounting was the normal practice to avoid the usury laws. The bankers would openly and illegally meet annually in Winnipeg to collude on the terms of the discounts. Each branch too, except in the few sizeable communities, tended to have a local monopoly. And bank managers were changed frequently to prevent them from becoming too familiar with their clients and therefore sympathetic to local needs.[189] The practices of arbitrarily seizing deposits for late payment or of illegally deducting expenses for the chattel mortgages out of deposits were widespread.[190] All the banks were involved in these practices, but the Bank of Commerce seemed to win the prize for extortion and usury.

Demands for a switch to mixed farming were frequently voiced.[191] But the prairie area was locked into the staple trap. Funds for the conversion from wheat to mixed farming were not available, for all available finance was poured into moving the crops. Once debt was incurred, the only way to meet the fixed interest charges was to maintain a steady flow of staple output. The deeper the debt of the farm to the external institutions, the greater the flow of staples necessary to discharge the debt; and the greater the quantity of staples moving, the more funds were locked up in the staple trades and the less available to finance diversification of crops in the West, or secondary industry throughout Canada.

# Banking and Industry

The attitude of central Canada's big commercial banks to most industry was one of relative indifference; their adherence to the "real bills doctrine" never wavering. In the 1870's even current loans were more readily available to merchants than the soundest of manufacturers, for it was felt that

> a lock up of capital and growing but unpaid interest ensues, to the disadvantage of other interests, and though secured as well as it can be, makes dividends unsound and depreciates the value of the banks' stock.[192]

The danger from the loan was, in the words of George Hague, that "the funds loaned . . . may be diverted in the direction of fixed property." Hague felt that fixed plant and equipment and "innovation" should be financed from retained earnings and reserves, out of additional equity issued, or from a bond issue. The sole exceptions Hague admitted were flour milling and timber — the great staple industries.[193]

These attitudes persisted, and if anything, hardened. In 1894, Thomas Fysche declared the interests of banks and of growing industry to be fundamentally antithetical. For with the progress of the corporate form and internal financing, industry was outgrowing the need for whatever short-term loans were formerly advanced from the banks to cover goods in movement. Banking in the early 1890's was having increasing difficulty finding the "right kind of borrower," and the more successful firms were, the less their future need for banks, forcing the banks to look all the harder for customers. Fysche declared that, for the banks, he could

> . . . see no permanence in this state of things. Between the diminishing return to capital on the one hand and the increasing difficulty and risk of employing it on the other, we stand a fair chance of being ground between the upper and the nether millstones.

The very success of industry was ensuring that "there will never again be the profit in banking that there has been."[194]

Fysche was speaking at a time of great concern for the banks. Note circulation had been falling since 1891, and continued its decline until 1896. The banks' share of total intermediary assets was falling as well until that date. The alternative to Fysche's gloomy prediction of obsolescence would have been adaptation and movement into the other models of bank behaviour. However, with the great expansion after 1896 the banks were relieved of all responsibility for innovation. The rhetoric of real bills again came to the fore. Bank advances were to be confined to discounting customers' paper representing sale of final goods or secured in raw materials.[195] The manufacturer was expected to "provide his own capital up to the point of acquiring the building and equipment, and a part, at least, of working capital."[196]

As could be expected, the manufacturers did not agree, and complaints of lack of bank accommodation were rife. These were especially pronounced in periods of international crisis when the Canadian banking system's much-vaunted ability to stabilize credit conditions did not seem to impress the manufacturing interests of the country. In fact, the only facet of the bankers' various boasts about their system that seems to have been accurate was the evenness of credit conditions across the country during crisis. Manufacturers and farmers alike in every quarter complained of the scarcity of credit with which to proceed with their production plans.[197] A leading Canadianized American entrepreneur, Francis H. Clergue, castigated the banks for their loan policy:

> The Canadian banks seem to consider those loans to be best which can be made to wheat speculators in Chicago, Minneapolis, or Duluth, or the stock speculators of New York.[198]

Clergue might have added American railroad and industrial bonds to his list, for long-term investments in the U.S. seemed to be exempted from the banks' real bills fanaticism.

There were, of course, noteworthy instances of involvement in industry by the big commerical banks. For example, the first major machinery and engine works in Canada, the Sheldon, Dutcher and Co. Foundry, was destroyed in 1836 when the Bank of Upper Canada foreclosed on a chattel mortgage, broke up the foundry, and disposed of the pieces at a sheriff's sale.[199] It was a disturbing portent.

In the cotton industry there was considerable bank activity, largely because cotton manufacturing was dominated by Montreal wholesalers who were closely allied to Montreal finance in the 1870's. The Exchange and Federal banks both made heavy advances to cotton secured on goods already stockpiled through the Montreal factor David Morrice.[200] The Bank of Nova Scotia did likewise for the St. Croix Mill. But only working capital secured on output was advanced. The St. Croix Mill, for example, had to borrow $300,000 from Rhode Island capitalists to complete its plant.[201]

The Merchants' Bank of Halifax (The Royal) performed an analogous role in the sugar industry — undoubtedly because of its close connection with the Halifax West Indies merchants who pioneered sugar refining in the Maritimes. The Halifax sugar refinery ended up working on bank advances with its stock subscription just sufficient to cover plant and equipment. By 1882, the refinery had run up a debt of $460,000 to the bank, secured on bills of sale for refined sugar and mortgages on the real estate.[202] For the Canada Sugar Refinery, ease of bank accommodation was ensured by the presence first of Peter Redpath, then of George Drummond on the Bank of Montreal directorate.[203]

Similarly, the Montreal Rolling Mills — which had strong links to the Montreal financial community, sharing directors with the Bank of Montreal and the Merchants' Bank[204] — received advances for the purchase of raw materials. The Upper Canada industry, on the other hand, received no bank funds at all and had to grow by reinvested profits and merchants' credit, which gradually took on the character of short-term loans.[205]

The rules were fairly clear. The Montreal commercial community, branching out into cotton manufacturing, sugar refining, iron and steel, and the like, secured bank accommodations through their holding directorships on the banks. This accommodation for the old commercial elite reflected again the bias of the pattern of Canadian industrial development in favour of established wealth and away from the new entrepreneurial class which was promoting industrialization throughout southern Ontario.

In industrial mergers, too, the banks' role was a hesitant one. While the banks, especially the Bank of Montreal, were sometimes involved in interim financing on the security of the underwritings, they seldom bought bonds in the mergers, and did not themselves get active in underwriting.[206] Even the limited role they did play in interim financing was not without criticism, some bankers maintaining that even such a role would lead to lock-ups, and hence a lack of funds when needed for the proper banking business of current loans and discounts.[207] Indirectly, the banks assisted the concentration of industry in some areas by discriminating by size among industrial borrowers. In 1913, small firms paid up to ten per cent for the same accommodation granted large ones for five to six per cent.[208]

In resource industries, similar rules were followed. In mining, the banks would not advance money for development work —

this remained the stockholders' responsibility. After the mine actually began shipping ore to the smelter and getting a return on it, the bank might lend on security of the ore.[209]

These considerations did not apply to the little non-Halifax Maritime banks who were actively involved in promoting industrial capital formation and providing entrepreneurial leadership to the Atlantic provinces. Both private and chartered, the little banks mobilized local savings for local fixed capital formation. But they were gradually squeezed out, or failed, and new entrants blocked by the Canadian Bankers' Association; and the funds which had formerly been used locally for industrial capital formation were shipped via the central Canadian branch banks to the West.

# Conclusions

The Canadian banking system was a truncated import from Britain. Canadian banks were largely the outgrowth of merchants' capital involved in the staple trades of the imperial commercial nexus. It was the economic structure of imperial trade rather than efforts to copy the charters of American banks that determined the role they would play in Canadian development patterns. Their primary function began and remained that of financing commodity movements, and merchants' discounts were long the dominant item on the asset side of their balance sheets.

The sources of funds for the banks' loan and discount activities were several. Despite several concerted efforts by some governments to break into the field, the notes of the chartered banks continued to dominate the circulation of money. Demand deposits were an old and well-established source of funds. However, savings deposits were something different, and not until well towards the end of the nineteenth century did the savings deposit business become an object of primary concern. As secular deflation on a world scale pulled down the Canadian price level with it, bank note circulation tended to fall. And the banks were pushed into the savings deposit business to try to recoup the ground that they were losing. The assault on savings deposits was directed on two fronts. First, interest rate competition had to cease among the banks, the rate-fixing cartel that thus emerged eventually securing official recognition as the Canadian Bankers' Association. Secondly, the main source of potential competition, namely the government savings banks, had to be wiped out. Thus the Canadian government lost both the note issue power for the most part, as well as the great bulk of the savings deposit business, to the chartered banks. These potential sources of long-term finance for government were turned into the foundation for an extension of short-term loans and discounts by the chartered banks. One immediate result was that at the same time Canadian governments were being forced increasingly to turn to London for long-term finance, the chartered banks were diverting capital into a wasteful and chronically unstable system of distribution of commodities that was clogged with petty traders hanging on precariously to economic life by virtue of the system of commercial credit the banks fostered.

With the revival of economic conditions in 1896, the banking system underwent rapid expansion and monopolization. In the East, Maritime banks were destroyed and funds drained out of the area. In the West, branches of the chartered banks covered the prairies and aided and abetted the overexpansion of a single cash crop by their loan policies, based on savings drained from the East. At the same time, the number of chartered banks fell dramatically, while financial control tended more and more to be centred in Montreal and to a lesser extent in Toronto.

# Notes to Chapter III

1. See especially A. Shortt, "The Early History of Canadian Banking."
2. W. Bagehot, *Lombard Street,* p. 90 *et passim.*
3. F. Feis, *Europe, The World's Banker,* p. 8; R. Sayers, *Modern Banking,* p. 51.
4. L. Jenks, *The Migration of British Capital to 1875,* p. 131.
5. L. Pressnell, *Country Banking In the Industrial Revolution,* pp. 14-16.
6. Cf. R. Cameron *et al., Banking and Economic Development,* pp. 7-8.
7. E. Hobsbawm, *Industry and Empire,* p. 60.
8. R. Cameron *et al., Banking in the Early Stages of Industrialization,* p. 52.
9. A. Gershenkron, *Economic Backwardness in Historical Perspective,* p. 353.
10. Cf. J. A. Schumpeter, *Business Cycles,* II, pp. 116-8.
11. See Canada, Committee on Banking and Currency, *First Report 1869.*
12. Hon. D. L. Macpherson, *Letter to the Hon. John Rose,* pp. 7, 14.
13. See A. Shortt, "The Passing of the Upper Canada and Commercial Banks."
14. *MT,* Sept. 24, 1869, p. 85.
15. John A. Macdonald to John Rose, Feb. 23, 1870; Francis Hincks to Macdonald, Sept. 23, 1872, *Macdonald Papers,* Pope edition.
16. G. Myers, *History of the Great American Fortunes,* p. 123.
17. R. M. Breckenridge, *History of Banking in Canada,* p. 95.
18. Senate Select Committee . . . Financial Crisis, *Report* 1867-8, p. 6.
19. B. E. Walker, *History of Banking in Canada,* p. 82.
20. B. E. Walker, "Banking in Canada," p. 17.
21. Royal Commission on the Relations of Labour and Capital *(RCRLC) Nova Scotia Evidence,* p. 221.
22. *MT,* March 21, 1890, p. 1162.
23. B. Beckhart, *The Banking System of Canada* p. 476.

24. M. Denison, *Canada's First Bank*, II, pp. 230, 245.
25. R. M. Breckenridge, *The Canadian Banking System* , p. 279.
26. Canada, "Committee on Banking," 1913, p. 489.
27. All bank data except where otherwise indicated from C. A. Curtis, *Statistical Contributions*.
28. Canada, "Committee on Banking," 1913, pp. 525-7.
29. Canadian Bankers' Association, "Minutes of the Third Annual Meeting," *JCBA*, vol. II, no. 1; *MT*, Oct. 12, 1894, p. 477.
30. *Statutes of Canada* , 3 Ed. VII, Chap. 43, 1903.
31. *MT*, March 21, 1908, p. 159.
32. B. E. Walker to W. Laurier, August 30, 1901 *Walker Papers*.
33. *MT*, Nov. 23, 1901, p. 671.
34. *CBC*, p. 520.
35. Canadian Bankers' Association, "Minutes of the Sixth Annual Meeting," *JCBA*, vol. V, no. 2, p. 171.
36. G. Hague *Banking and Commerce*, p. 365.
37. *MT*, Jan. 26, 1894, p. 930.
38. W. T. R. Preston *My Generation of Politics and Politicians* .
39. *HCD*, Jan., 1911.
40. Canadian Bankers' Association "Third Annual Meeting" p. 13.
41. *CBC*, p. 479.
42. *Farmer's Advocate*, June 12, 1913, p. 1065; *GGG*, June 11, 1913.
43. Canadian Bankers' Association, "Ninth Annual Meeting," *JCBA*, vol. VIII, no. 2, Jan. 1901, p. 102.
44. Bank of Nova Scotia, *History of the Bank of Nova Scotia 1832-1900*, p. 59.
45. Canadian Bankers' Association, "Eighth Annual Meeting," *JCBA,* vol. VII, no. 2; "Seventh Annual Meeting," *JCBA*, vol. VI, no. 2, p. 108.
46. B. E. Walker to D. R. Wilkie, Nov. 24, 1903, *Walker Papers.*
47. *Farmer's Advocate,* April 17, 1913, p. 714.
48. *CBC*, p. 599.
49. *Colonial Advocate*, May 28, 1824.
50. C. Hague, *Banking and Commerce*, p. iii.
51. O. D. Skelton, *Fifty Years of Banking Service*, p. 45.
52. *CYB*, 1915, p. 257.
53. H. Feis, *Europe, The World's Banker*, p. 7.
54. *MT*, Oct. 21, 1870, p. 185.
55. H. M. P. Eckhart, *Manual of Canadian Banking*, p. 48.
56. T. Fysche, "The Growth of Corporations," pp. 201-3.
57. *JC*, Aug. 1, 1879, p. 757.
58. *MT*, April 29, 1869, p. 589.
59. *MT*, March 30, 1877, pp. 1113, 1115; Sept. 27, 1878, p. 407.
60. *Statutes of Canada*, 1869, Chap. 16.
61. Select Committee on Bankruptcy and Insolvency, *Third Report*, 1867-68.
62. *Statutes of Canada*, 1875, Chap. 16.
63. *MT*, April 5, 1878, p. 1165.
64. *MT*, June 11, 1886, p. 1404.
65. *MT*, Oct. 3, 1879, p. 520; Aug. 4, 1876, p. 149.
66. Dominion Board of Trade, *Annual Report*, 1878, p. 194.
67. *HCD*, Feb. 19, 1880, p. 107.
68. *HCD*, Feb. 19, 1880, p. 102.
69. *MT*, June 15, 1877, p. 1443.
70. *CM*, Jan. 19, 1894, pp. 51-3.
71. *MT*, Feb. 6, 1874, pp. 772-3.
72. *Statutes of Canada*, 1880, Chap. 1.

73. *MT*, March 12, 1886, p. 1041; April 2, 1886, p. 1127. See also for example Calgary Board of Trade, *Annual Report*, 1912, p. 26.
74. *MT*, July 8, 1881, p. 36; Aug. 29, 1884, p. 235.
75. Canadian Bankers' Association, "Fourth Annual Meeting," *JCBA*, vol. III, no. 1.
76. *SCCD*, 1876, p. 10.
77. Montreal Board of Trade, *Annual Report*, 1876, p. 89.
78. *SCCD*, 1876, pp. 265-6.
79. *MT*, Sept. 7, 1883, p. 79.
80. W. W. Johnson, *Sketches of the Late Depression*, p. 90.
81. *Ibid.*, p. 9.
82. *MT*, Oct. 8, 1875, p. 407.
83. Select Committee to Consider the Fraudulent Obtaining of Promissory Notes. . . , *Report*, 1888, pp. 19, 27, 39.
84. *Ibid.*, p. 32.
85. *MT*, Nov. 1, 1901, p. 562; Oct. 25, 1901, p. 530; Nov. 15, 1901, p. 625; Feb. 14, 1902, p. 1052.
86. *MT*, Aug. 17, 1883, p. 177; Jan. 26, 1883, p. 820.
87. G. Hague, *Banking and Currency*, p. 383.
88. *MT*, Jan. 20, 1888, p. 906.
89. Failure waves determined from series constructed from data in *Brad.*, *MT*, *SYB*, *CYB*, and *Dun's Review*, various issues.
90. *MT*, Jan. 1908, p. 1228.
91. T. T. Smyth, *The First Hundred Years: History of the Montreal and District Savings Bank*, p. 18.
92. V. Ross, *Bank of Commerce I*, p. 221.
93. M. Denison, *Canada's First Bank*, I, p. 80.
94. *Ibid.*, p. 252.
95. "Memo to the President of the Bank of Commerce from B. E. Walker," May 29, 1879, *Walker Papers*.
96. *RCRLC, Nova Scotia Evidence*, p. 215.
97. *MT*, Nov. 3, 1876, p. 503.
98. *MT*, Sept. 29, 1876, p. 364.
99. *MT*, July 6, 1878, pp. 40-1.
100. *MT*, May 16, 1879, p. 1414.
101. *MT*, July 11, 1878, p. 75.
102. *MT*, Aug. 6, 1880, p. 147; Sept. 10, 1880, p. 298; Sept. 17, 1880, p. 332.
103. *MT*, July 16, 1880, p. 70.
104. *MT*, Oct. 30, 1885, p. 483.
105. *MT*, May 6, 1892, p. 1338; May 27, 1892, p. 1432.
106. Canadian Bankers' Association, "Sixth Annual Meeting," *JCBA*, vol. V, no. 2.
107. *MT*, Dec. 11, 1885, p. 656.
108. *MT*, Feb. 5, 1886, p. 884; Jan. 1, 1886, p. 740; Jan. 30, 1885, p. 857; *JCBA*, vol. IV, no. 1, p. 70.
109. *SYB* 1890, p. 489; *SYB* 1891, p. 414.
110. *MT*, Sept. 11, 1896, p. 366.
111. *HCD* April 18, 1898, p. 3719.; *JCBA*, vol. VI, no. 2. pp. 107-8.
112. *MT*, May 14, 1907, p. 1724.
113. M. Morris, "The Land Mortgage Companies . . .," p. 256.
114. *SYB* 1890, p. 487.
115. *MT*, June 4, 1886, p. 1380.
116. *JC*, Jan. 9, 1880, p. 671.
117. *MT*, June 4, 1886, p. 1380.

118. B. E. Walker, "Banking in Canada," pp. 17, 22.
119. *MT*, Aug. 24, 1906, p. 254.
120. *CBC*, p. 499.
121. H. M. P. Eckhart, *A Rational Banking System*, p. 41.
122. *MT*, Jan. 6, 1906, p. 937.
123. Canadian Bankers' Association, "Sixth Annual Meeting," *JCBA*, vol. IV, no. 1, p. 70; "Ninth Annual Meeting," *JCBA*, vol. VIII, no. 2, p. 107.
124. *MT*, April 21, 1876, p. 1211.
125. B. E. Walker, "A Comparison of Banking Systems," p. 239.
126. T. Fysche, "The Growth of Corporations," p. 202.
127. *MT*, May 16, 1908, p. 1915.
128. *MT*, Dec. 26, 1884, p. 723; Jan. 2, 1885, p. 254, May 22, 1885, p. 1311.
129. *MT*, July 25, 1890.
130. *MT*, May 28, 1897, p. 1569.
131. V. Ross, *Bank of Commerce I*, p. 375.
132. A. B. Jameson, *Chartered Banking In Canada*, pp. 35-6.
133. M. Denison, *Canada's First Bank*, II, p. 271; G. Glazebrook, *Sir Edmund Walker*, p. 28.
134. *MT*, July 23, 1880, p. 99.
135. Information on mergers comes from various sources including Canada, Royal Commision on Banking and Currency, *Report*, 1933; Bank of Nova Scotia, *The Bank of Nova Scotia 1832-1932;* Royal Bank of *Canada, Fiftieth Anniversary of the Royal Bank of Canada;* M. Denison, *Canada's First Bank;* and *MT*, May 29, 1903, p. 1615.
136. A. Wood, *The True History of Lord Beaverbrook*, p. 15.
137. J. I. Cooper, *Montreal, A Brief History*, p. 114; *JC*, Oct. 27, 1899, p. 1903.
138. H. B. Walker to B. E. Walker, Dec. 27, 1911, *Walker Papers*.
139. *IC*, Sept. 1912, pp. 196-7.
140. B. Beckhart, *The Banking System of Canada*, p. 317.
141. M. Denison, *Canada's First Bank*, p. 275.
142. *MT*, Nov. 28, 1890, p. 650; Jan. 30, 1891, p. 928; March 18, 1898, p. 1220.
143. *MT*, April 7, 1893, p. 1188.
144. *MT*, Oct. 16, 1914, p. 10; Nov. 6, 1914, p. 42; Dec. 18, 1914, p. 22.
145. *RCLI, Report*, 1907, p. 20.
146. *RCLI, Report*, 1907, pp. 10-11, 84-85; *CBC*, 1913, p. 560.
147. *RCLI, Report*, 1907, pp. 34, 52-3, 58.
148. *CBC*, 1913, p. 560.
149. *MT*, July 27, 1883, p. 95.
150. *MT*, June 1, 1907, p. 1888.
151. Alberta, Commission on Banking and Credit . . . Agriculture, *Report*, p. 37 (*ACBCA*).
152. Saskatchewan, Agricultural Credit Commission, *Official Synopsis*, pp. 846, 853. (*SACC*).
153. *CBC*, 1913, p. 112.
154. *HCD*, Jan. 21, 1913, pp. 1877-1879.
155. *GGG*, Dec. 14, 1910, pp. 7-10.
156. *CF*, May 3, 1911, p. 371.
157. *CBC*, 1913, p. 113.
158. *CBC*, 1913, pp. 201-2.
159. *CBC*, 1913; p. 211, *FA*, April 17, 1913, p. 714.
160. *GGG*, April 23, 1913; Sept. 10, 1913.
161. *CBC*, 1913, pp. 531-2.
162. B. E. Walker "Banking in Canada," p. 18.
163. *CBC*, 1913, p. 115.
164. *FA*, Feb. 27, 1908, p. 338.

165. *MT*, July 6, 1888, p. 16.
166. Monthly returns giving the circulation of various banks are published in the *Canada Gazette*.
167. *IC*, Aug. 1913, p. 75.
168. *CBC*, 1913, p. 179.
169. *CBC*, 1913, p. 168.
170. H. M. P. Eckhardt, *A Rational Banking System*, p. 115. Eckhart was the Bankers' Association's chief hired eulogist.
171. H. M. P. Eckhardt, *Manual of Canadian Banking*, p. 135; *CBC*, 1913, p. 486.
172. *MT*, Feb. 27, 1914, p. 435.
173. W. T. Easterbrook, *Agricultural Credit in Canada 1867-1917*, p. 35.
174. H. M. P. Eckhardt, *Manual*, pp. 135-6.
175. *SAAC*, p. 831; W. T. Easterbrook, *Farm Credit in Canada*, p. 65.
176. *ACBCA*, p. 44.
177. A. Desjardin, *The Co-operative People's Bank*, p. 7.
178. *MT*, Aug. 31, 1907, pp. 337-8.
179. H. M. P. Eckhardt, "The New Bank Act," p. 301.
180. R. L. Jones, *History of Agriculture in Ontario*, p. 237.
181. *CBC*, p. 371.
182. *CF*, May 3, 1911, p. 371.
183. *MT*, Nov. 16, 1907, p. 798; H. M. P. Eckhardt, *Manual*, p. 138.
184. *CF*, Feb. 1, 1911, p. 97.
185. M. Denison, *Harvest Triumphant*, p. 150.
186. B. E. Walker to W. C. Ward, April 14, 1905, *Walker Papers*.
187. *CBC*, p. 451.
188. *CBC*, p. 142; *ACBCA*, pp. 17-18.
189. *ACBCA* pp. 21, 30.
190. *ACBCA* p. 33.
191. *CF*, Sept. 16, 1911, p. 787.
192. W. W. Johnson; *Sketches of the Late Depression*, p. 82.
193. G. Hague, *Banking and Commerce*, p. 124.
194. T. Fysche, "The Growth of Corporations," pp. 200-1.
195. H. M. P. Eckhardt, *Manual*, p. 135.
196. H. M. P. Eckhardt, "Manufacturers' Use of Bank Funds," pp. 193-4.
197. *LG*, Sept. 1907, p. 283; Oct. 1907, p. 311.
198. F. H. Clergue, "Address . . . Sault Ste Marie," Feb. 19, 1901.
199. K. Lewis, "The Significance of the York Factory," p. 6.
200. *JC*, Oct. 26, 1883, p. 312.
201. *JC*, Oct. 26, 1883, p. 306.
202. *MT*, Feb. 17, 1882, p. 1004.
203. *MT*, March 17, 1882, p. 1138.
204. *MT*, Feb. 7, 1879, p. 975.
205. W. Kilbourn, *The Elements Combined*, pp. 11, 19, 23; *CE*, July 1895, p. 74; March 1900, p. 308.
206. *CBC*, 1913, p. 562.
207. H. M. P. Eckhardt, "Financing the Promotion of a New Industrial Company," p. 75.
208. *CBC*, p. 447.
209. H. M. P. Eckhardt, *Manual*, p. 141.

*They stole themselves rich.*
*Palladium of Labour,* 1883

# CHAPTER IV
# CHARTERED BANK FAILURES

## Stability of the Canadian Banking System

The refusal of the successful chartered banks to undertake a significant role in financing industrial fixed capital formation was justified on the grounds that lock-ups in industry led to failures. But many banks failed that did not become involved in industrial banking. The failure record reflects the pre-war division of the Canadian banking system into two distinct systems. The first embraced the Ontario and Montreal and Halifax banks, whose activities were restricted to orthodox commercial banking. The other included the "French banks," in small centres in Quebec, and the Maritime banks. The banks belonging to the second group had few, if any, branches, were actively involved in promoting local industry, and were dominated by local entrepreneurs. Casualties in the first group resulted from factors inhering in their commercial and financial operations; failures in the second group were due to industrial lock-ups. Only upon failure do these factors come to light, for the true nature of the banks' operations were often disguised by falsified returns. The general manager of the Bank of Nova Scotia, H. C. McLeod, estimated that in January 1905, of 34 banks reporting to the Dominion government, at least nine sent in falsified returns.[1] Then, too, a bank might commit itself to automatic renewal of a short-term accommodation to an industry, and this constituted *de facto* a long-term investment — thus only after failure could an accurate picture of the banks' activities be formed.

Another point that emerges strongly was the chronic instability of the Canadian chartered banking system, a rather startling fact in light of the amount of propaganda about its avowed stability. Of the 72 banks that operated in the period 1867 to 1914, 26 failed, or 36%. Losses to creditors reached $11 million; to shareholders $31 million. Furthermore, these reported losses are from unambiguous failures only, from suspensions followed by permanent closing. They do not include those cases where failure was averted only by selling the bank at a bargain price to some other concern, which was especially common after 1901 when regulations pertaining to mergers were relaxed. If the cases are included in which mergers occurred with losses to the stockholders of the absorbed bank, the total shareholders' losses exceed $40 million and the rate of failure reaches a less-than-modest 50%. At the same time, over the roughly equivalent period from 1863 to 1908, the American banking system, with its reputation for extreme instability, showed a rate of failures of *all* banks of 22½%. If one examines only American national banks, the proper comparison with Canada's federally chartered banks, the rate of failure is five per cent, and the total losses to stockholders about $100 million.[2] In per-capita terms, even taking only the unambiguous failures, Canadian losses to shareholders ran at three-and-one-half times the rate of American. And over the period 1881 to 1908, when Canada's notoriously unstable commercial sector showed a failure rate of 29%, Canada's reputedly stable banks failed at the rate of 41%.[3]

The myth of stability is difficult to account for. While the record after World War I shows only one nominal failure, this is hardly surprising given the small number of banks that survived until the war, and given that it became government policy to encourage mergers of shaky institutions. Before the war, Canadian bankers conducted a campaign of self-edification through the services of hired eulogists in the pages of their *Journal,* which perpetuated the myth of stability as bank after bank came crashing down. It was a clever bit of public relations, for it helped to keep down the pressure for outside inspection. H. C. McLeod, General Manager of the Bank of Nova Scotia, began a campaign for outside inspection around the turn of the century, and he was joined in 1906 by the General Manager of Molson's Bank and in 1912 by the Traders' Bank.[4] In 1909, the stockholders of the Bank of Nova Scotia voted 18,866 shares to 567 in favour of outside inspection, with 445 of the opposing votes being cast on behalf of other banks.[5] In fact, opinion in favour of regulation and inspection ("to prevent so many cashiers skipping to the other side") had been building in some government circles since the late 1880's.[6] But the combined pressure of the other banks and their allies in the financial press[7] prevented any moves in this direction. Sir Edmund Walker of the Bank of Commerce

argued that internal inspection at the will of the stockholders sufficed, a curious argument in light of the fact that the directorate
was assured almost complete autonomy by the close holding of
large amounts of stock in a few hands, and the wide geographic
dispersal of the rest. Thomas Fysche of the Merchants' Bank
added an argument based apparently on Darwin. Failures were
good for the system, he said, and to the extent that outside
inspection prevented failures it was an impediment to efficient
operations:

> Death is as necessary to this world as life, and when efficiency
> has gone out of an institution, in God's name let it die. . . .
> Nature's way of working is to obtain strength and efficiency
> by establishing a struggle for life, and causing the fittest,
> because the strongest, to survive.[8]

While the causes of failure varied from bank to bank — those in
the Maritimes were caused by industrial lock-ups, and those in
Ontario often by stock exchange speculation — they were certainly not as inevitable as Fysche implies. Failures tended to
peak at times of general financial crisis, or just after the worst of
the crisis, as in 1879, in 1887, and in 1908 — indicating the significance of outside forces. The most common explanations for
failures were "fraud" and "mismanagement".[9] While the record
of fraud is appalling, a minimum of 19 of the failures leading to
criminal charges being laid against officers of the banks concerned, fraud *per se* cannot explain failure — only unsuccessful
fraud can, and hence one must look deeper for the cause of the
lack of success. Similarly, "mismanagement" is tautological: all
failures must involve mismanagement, with the benefit of hind-
sight, for a successful mismanagement by definition cannot
occur.

# Bank Failures in the Maritimes

Maritime banks existed in a world apart from their central Canadian counterparts. Both those banks that were absorbed and
those that failed, both private and chartered —all the banks, in
fact, except the big Halifax banks who alone survived — were
actively engaged in promoting local development of industry.
The banks were small, with few, if any, branches, and dominated
by local directors who, as leading entrepreneurs in their respective communities, used the banks' resources for promoting their
own business ventures.

The first to fall was the Commercial Bank of New Brunswick
in 1868, a very small institution with but two branches, at Woodstock and at Miramichi. It had a bad record. In 1865, it came

close to collapsing because of lock-ups and was saved by an English financier who guaranteed £23,000 of its bills. A year later, it had to borrow £7,000 from another institution to tide itself over

**TABLE IV (1)**

**Chartered Bank Failures, 1867-1914**

| Bank | Year | Capital ($) | Losses Share-Holders[1] ($) | Losses Creditors[1] ($) | Criminal Charges[2] |
|------|------|------|------|------|------|
| Commercial of New Brunswick | 1868 | 546,000 | 495,000 | — | |
| Acadia | 1873 | 100,000 | 130,000 | — | |
| Metropolitan | 1876 | 916,180 | 456,180 | — | |
| Mechanics | 1879 | 472,245 | 569,732 | 180,000 | X |
| Stadacona | 1879 | 990,890 | — | — | |
| Consolidated | 1879 | 2,270,081 | 2,002,081 | — | X |
| Liverpool | 1879 | 370,000 | 500,000 | — | |
| Prince Edward Island | 1881 | 210,000 | 310,000 | — | X |
| Exchange | 1883 | 1,000,000 | 1,650,000 | 800,500 | X |
| Maritime | 1887 | 760,900 | 1,082,000 | 974,870 | X |
| London | 1887 | 241,100 | 80,000 | — | X |
| Pictou | 1887 | 250,000 | 163,970 | — | |
| Central | 1887 | 500,000 | 750,000 | 7,100 | X |
| Federal | 1888 | 3,000,000 | 4,469,113 | — | X |
| Commercial of Manitoba | 1893 | 552,650 | 700,000 | — | X |
| du Peuple | 1895 | 1,600,000 | 1,900,000 | 1,718,284 | X |
| Ville Marie | 1899 | 716,920 | 716,920 | — | X |
| Jacques Cartier | 1899 | 2,000,000 | 1,750,000 | 1,341,601 | X |
| Yarmouth | 1905 | 300,000 | 335,000 | — | X |
| Ontario | 1906 | 3,500,000 | 4,191,000 | n.a. | X |
| Sovereign | 1908 | 4,000,000 | 7,600,000 | 3,300,000 | X |
| St. Jean | 1908 | 316,386 | 326,386 | 340,000 | X |
| St. Hyacinthe | 1908 | 331,235 | 334,145 | 400,000 | X |
| St. Stephen's | 1910 | 200,000 | 260,000 | — | X |
| Farmers' | 1910 | 547,579 | 800,000 | 1,400,000 | X |
| Vancouver | 1914 | 445,188 | 600,000 | 300,000 | |
| Total 26 | | | $31,455,397 | $11,362,355 | 19 |

Sources: [1] H. C. McLeod's calculations in B. H. Beckhart, *The Banking System of Canada,* pp. 334-337, with some corrections.
[2] probably an underestimate.

another liquidity crisis. A local businessman obtained such huge loans from the bank's cashier that he began to boast openly that the bank had to stand behind him, for his failure meant that of the bank as well. Due to bad debts, including a $90,000 loss on the one large account, the bank's capital shrank to less than $600,000 from its previous $1,000,000. In November 1868, the cashier, who had been busy endorsing fraudulent sterling bills of exchange, overdrew his account and absconded.[10] The bank suspended, and then was wound up.[11]

The Acadia, founded in 1872, and the Liverpool, founded in 1871, both suspended in 1873 — the Acadia permanently. Both of these banks were promoted by leading Liverpool businessmen drawing on Halifax finance for the express purpose of borrowing from them to sustain their business. Both, too, had American stockholders, the Acadia to the extent of one-eighth its total, the Liverpool one-quarter; and these shares had been "paid" for in promissory notes. The banks, in addition to a connection with a British firm of bad credit, were heavily involved with local lumbermen and shipbuilders, and made a series of advances to them on a system of mutual endorsement. Other bills, drawn on American lumber importing firms and supposed to be covered by lumber shipments, were really met by issuing new bills. Under the guise of short-term accommodation based on commodity movements, the banks were advancing long-term credit, and the funds were used to increase the extent of lumber plant rather than discharging debt or paying for materials, In 1873, the notes of the American firms were protested and the leading Liverpool firm promptly failed, dragging both of the banks down with it.[12]

The Liverpool resumed, then failed again in 1879 in the wake of the great financial crisis of the 1870's. When the accounts were checked, it was discovered that the assets of the bank had been overestimated, and interest accruing but not paid on bad debts had been placed to credit in the profit-and-loss account, with the objective of justifying the continuation of the directors' salaries. The main losses fell on the wealthy Halifax residents who were the leading stockholders. Conditions were regarded as sufficiently adverse that, even with the double liability being enforced, it was not expected to be able to pay all of its debts to the public.[13] But there were difficulties in enforcing the liability. The Bank of Nova Scotia as assignee sued the reluctant shareholders, who defended, unsuccessfully, on the grounds that the Liverpool was never a legal bank. It had failed to meet the requirement that $100,000 of capital had to be paid up before a meeting of provisional directors could be held; nor was the additional $100,000 required within the first year paid.[14]

The crisis of the 1870's had repercussions on Prince Edward Island as well, though it tended to reach there later than the mainland. The Merchants' Bank of P.E.I. got into difficulty in 1879 through the account of one large shipping firm, James Duncan and Co., which failed owing large debts to Sir James Malcolm of Liverpool, England. Other banks on the Island, too, were affected by the failure.[15] The Merchants' suspended, and a call on the stockholders was necessary.[16] As to the principal characters involved, the *Monetary Times* reported that,

> Mr. Duncan has been bailed out of prison, and Sir James Malcolm, an English creditor of the failed firm, left the Island in a tug boat on Wednesday, apparently to avoid complying with a Chancery injunction which required him to hand over certain mortgages which ought to have been the property of the bank.[17]

The entire capital of the bank was locked up for a year in the Duncan account, but the bank did resume.

In 1881, the Bank of P.E.I., the oldest on the Island, collapsed for the last time. (But not the first: in 1858 it had loaned twice its paid-up capital to one shipping firm and was forced to suspend.)[18] In 1881 again over double the capital was locked up in mortgages on ships, land, and factories.[19] The cashier had made large unauthorized advances, of which between $400,000[20] and $665,000[21] were regarded as unrealizable. The final cost to the shareholders was $310,000. The cashier absconded, following a trail already blazed by his counterpart from the Commercial to the United States.

In 1887 came the final collapse of the Maritime Bank, one of the largest in the Atlantic provinces. It was an institution which the *Monetary Times* condemned for its "enterprising style of business,"[22] a very suggestive choice of phrase. In 1880, it had been under the control of James Domville, a leading St. John industrialist, who ran the bank to service his own enterprises. That year, when it closed its doors for the first time, it had a paid-up capital of $680,000. Its assets exceeded its liabilities by $341,000, but of the nominal surplus $291,000 was a loan on the security of a local railway. Its losses in the 1877-8 crisis were $500,000, and a great many lock-ups had resulted.[23] These lock-ups and bad debts all involved firms either owned outright by Domville or associated with his enterprises. Fourteen items for which the nominal value was $490,000 turned out to be immediately worth only $72,000, including: (1) a lien on the entire rolling stock of the Springhill and Parsboro Coal and Railroad Company and bonds of the same; (2) shares and first mortgage bonds of the Cold Brook Rolling Mills; (3) shares of the Maritime Warehousing and Docking Co.; (4) mortgages on the bank's own property; (5) mortgages on a number of other buildings; (6) one-sixth of the shares of the Pictou Iron and Coal Mine.[24] It was a remarkable record for a Canadian bank of the period. The bank had even opened up its own office in London, England. Domville had successfully turned back an attempt by the Bank of Montreal to gain control in a proxy fight[25] despite the fact that a majority of the shares seem to have been held by Ontario and Quebec stockholders.[26]

After the first suspension, the Ontario and Quebec shareholders sold out to Maritime financiers and the bank was reorganized under new management. The shares immediately recovered their value. The St. John's group who took control was headed by Thomas Maclelland, a private banker, under whose auspices the capital was reduced to $400,000, and $75,000 in fresh capital subscribed. In three years most of the old accounts were realized, and a surplus appeared.[27]

Then in 1887 came another suspension following the failure of a large lumber firm, S. Schofield and Co. The bank had locked up a large amount of funds in accounts under the name of several small firms which turned out to be all fronts for the Schofield firm. It had also been involved in "kiting" sterling bills of exchange to maintain itself. A large part of its alleged capital had been paid in by promissory notes, and many of its assets were unrealizable. For example, a "loan" of $100,000 to the Province of New Brunswick turned out to be a debt of $35,000. Two firms drew bills on the bank, the fate of $125,654 of which was unknown at the time of suspension. In all, over $325,000 of its assets were deemed doubtful.[28] The shareholders got into a court fight to avoid paying the double liability, but in the final analysis they lost one million, the creditors an equivalent sum. Regarding the failure, the rector of Trinity Church in St. John advised his congregation, "Lay not up for yourselves treasure upon earth where moths and rust do corrupt, and where thieves break through and steal."[29]

The same year, the little Pictou Bank failed. A series of losses by its main debtors led to lock-ups. The principal account was advances to a tannery which were used to build fixed plant and equipment.[30]

Lock-ups of fixed capital for industrial purposes also brought down the Bank of Yarmouth in 1905. This bank was established in 1865 during a great boom in wooden shipbuilding, of which Yarmouth was one of the world's centres. During the shipbuilding period, the Yarmouth and the other local banks carried the industry on a system of note endorsements.[31] With the decline of wooden ships, the bank moved into other industries, notably W. H. Redding and Son, a large tannery and boot and shoe firm. As with many firms in the Maritimes, the Reddings paid their workers in scrip for merchandise from favoured businesses in the town, the scrip ultimately finding its way to the banks of the city who charged it against the Reddings' accounts. Loyalty to the local banks was strong in the Maritime towns, and when in 1903 the Exchange Bank of Yarmouth was absorbed by the Bank of Montreal, with losses to stockholders, the largest local stockholders refused to accept Bank of Montreal shares, and instead bought those of the Bank of Yarmouth.[32] This was followed by a takeover bid for the Bank of Yarmouth by the Union Bank of Halifax, which ultimately refused to follow through on its offer. The Reddings failed in 1905 and suspension of the Bank of Yarmouth followed shortly. The Reddings owed the bank $490,000[33] while its entire capital was but $300,000. The bank had purchased bills drawn by the Reddings on non-existent parties, had used bank funds for discounting worthless notes of the firm; made large advances on security which the directors knew was valueless, and had permitted the firm large overdrafts.[34] In addition, the directors had illegally purchased and held real estate, and had paid themselves $15,000 in dividends out of capital, when no profits existed, just before failure. The Supreme Court of Nova Scotia found the directors guilty of malfeasance and breach of trust, and ordered them to repay the dividends, and to cover the losses of the Redding account from August 19, 1904, with five per cent interest. The President, a Dominion Senator, was found guilty of falsifying the returns to conceal losses, but given a suspended sentence.[35]

The last of the Maritime banks to pass away, either by insolvency or takeover by a commercial bank, was the St. Stephen Bank in 1910. The bank was closely interlocked with the big industries of the town, and in the words of a financial journal "it may be in the position of forming an excellent illustration of the working of the U.S. banking system in Canada".[36] In addition to its lock-ups with the town's industry, it had purchased bonds in a nearby mine and made advances on a long-term basis to the mine's promoters. Failure followed the collapse of a number of small businesses in the town. Criminal charges were laid but later dropped.[37] It was the end of a distinct form of banking in Canada, the extension into Canada of New-England-style banking based on small-scale operations and interrelations of local finance and industry, and a severe blow to independent industrial development in the Maritimes.

# Bank Failures in Quebec

The crisis of the 1870's took a heavy toll of Quebec's banks. Several banks suspended but recovered, several collapsed completely. The Metropolitan was the first to go under, in 1875. As was the rule with Montreal financial community institutions, industrial lock-ups were not the cause of the problem. The bank had made loans to land speculators and loans on bank stocks and other securities.[38] The leading borrowers from the bank were two of its directors, the Honourable Henry Starnes and Maurice Cuvellier, both of whom had paid for their shares in unsecured promissory notes. Starnes got $113,314 in advances for stock speculations of which $31,984 was lost. Cuvellier got even more and lost $69,286. The bank did not suspend, but simply liquidated with some loss of capital. A suit by shareholders against the directors for malfeasance failed.[39] There is no record of criminal charges, despite the illegality of payment for stock in promissory notes.

The Stadacona Bank too is remarkable for the tranquility with which it expired, in 1876. Its independent existence lasted only two years, and its passing as a result of the failure of some of its debtors in the depression caused no excitement.[40] It appears to have been a voluntary liquidation, and there is no record of shareholder or creditor losses.

It was quite otherwise with the spectacular fall of the Mechanics Bank in 1879. The outgrowth of a private bank, it carried over a large amount of weak paper and poor accounts when it got its charter,[41] and got steadily deeper into a high-risk class of commercial advances. In 1875 it suspended, and reduced its capital by 60%. It was then given a line of credit of $125,000 from Molson's Bank, along with the unprecedented authority to issue preference stock. This exceptional favour may have had a great deal to do with the fact that the bank's president at that time was C. J. Brydges, former General Manager of the Grand Trunk Railway and a future Land Commissioner of the Hudson's Bay Company. This authorized preference issue was for a sum up to $300,000 at eight per cent guaranteed out of earnings for five years, thereafter to be merged with the common stock.[42]

The Mechanics' business was orthodox enough, but its methods of pursuing it were not. In 1877 a stock issue was taken up exclusively by the directors and a few friends, and the bank thereafter engaged in a veritable orgy of branch openings in all manner of Quebec small towns and villages. At one point the president, vice-president, and two directors borrowed two-and-a-half million of the bank's money to bull the stock.[43] It also used some rather curious techniques for expanding its circulation, which by the time of its final suspension was the highest in proportion to capital of any bank in Montreal. It extended very lavish accommodation to customers in exchange for their assistance in promoting its circulation.[44] It maintained agents on steamboats on the St. Lawrence and in hotels in major urban centres, who were paid a premium for getting people to exchange other banks' notes for those of the Mechanics. On suspension its liabilities were $547,000 and its immediately realizable assets $29,638. The directors announced that only 60¢ on the dollar of its other assets would ever be recoverable,[45] an estimate subsequently reduced to 40¢. Charges of malfeasance were made against the directors. The shareholders attempted to dodge the double liability.[46] Over half of them could not meet it, and offered to settle with the creditors for $75,000 or 21% of their liability as their "fair" assessment of the debt.[47] The shareholders were not above a charge of malfeasance themselves, since they had been offered previously $100,000 or 28% for the estate.[48] The ultimate cost to the shareholders was half a million dollars, and 57½% of the value of the notes was lost.

The largest bank to fail during the depression years was the Consolidated Bank of Montreal, and therein lies a tangled tale. The Consolidated was an 1876 merger of two already insolvent banks, the City Bank of Montreal and the Royal Canadian Bank of Toronto, both of whom had devious early histories.

The Royal Canadian began in 1860 in Toronto, a promotion of a group of local merchants. Its bid for a place in the financial sun, as with many Canadian financial institutions of the period, came with the American Civil War and its concomitant opportunities for gold speculation, a business endeavour pursued after the close of the war as well. As with most of the Canadian banks of the time, a very substantial proportion of the loans of the bank took the form of handouts to directors. In the case of the Royal Canadian, the amount of such business seems to have exceeded the norm. And therewith began its downfall.

In 1869 one of its directors, Senator Donald McDonald, applied for a loan that equalled one-tenth of the bank's paid-up capital. McDonald was an inveterate speculator, whose demands in the past had threatened to drive the bank into insolvency. The other directors refused the loan for the good reason that their own accounts were so badly overdrawn that the bank's resources were already severely strained.[49] In the ensuing squabble over the division of the bank's resources between them, McDonald began to write "private and confidential" letters of recrimination to his fellow directors, copies of which, just by the remotest coincidence, happened to fall into the hands of the newspapers. These letters were sent using the free postage facilities available to Canadian parliamentarians for official government business. The equally "private and confidential" replies of the other directors also conveniently found their way to the newspapers.

The depositors of the bank were thus treated to the spectacle of an open scramble for division of the spoils — that is to say, their deposit monies — by the directors to whom such funds had been entrusted. Public distrust mounted. And in June of 1869, following the collapse of a private banking firm, W. R. Brown and Co., to whom both the Royal Canadian and the City Bank had made large advances to further its dealings in New York money markets,[50] the Royal Canadian was forced to suspend. In addition to the systematic drain of the resources by individual directors, it transpired that the bank had been further weakened by large sums being withdrawn to traffic in the bank's own stock to keep up its quotation.

An effort was made to sell the ailing institution to the Dominion Bank, but the directors, anxious to rob the shareholders of the Dominion as well as their own, asked too high a price for the financial derelict.[51] The bank then resumed payments on its own, with a new board — which quickly drove it into insolvency again. Among other operations were a series of loans by the Toronto general manager to a commercial house controlled by a relative. The house failed, paying 15¢ per dollar of liabilities. Nearly a third of the advances, which totalled $160,000, were made on notes without any endorsement.[52] Once the Royal Canadian was merged with the City Bank in a desperate attempt to hide its insolvency, the same officer was left in charge of its Toronto business.

The City Bank, a promotion of the halcyon days of the early 1830's, had a long history of near-collapses. At one point, virtually all of its capital was wiped out. It also had an unenviable record of lawsuits launched by other banks over questionable cheques and bills, and in 1872 one such suit by the Banque Nationale cost the City Bank $100,000 in damages.[53] A year later, however, it struck gold in the person of a new president. Thereafter it began reporting steady and rising profits, the origins of which remained a mystery for several years. In the meantime, the Royal Canadian's bad debts accumulated steadily. In 1876, the two were merged with a combined capital nominally at $3.5 million; in reality this capital was heavily watered and the banks' rest fund already virtually depleted. In 1879 the capital had been reduced to $2.7 million, even that representing a grossly inflated figure.[54]

The merger brought the widespread connections the Royal Canadian had built up among a host of semi-solvent customers together with the large amount of worthless paper that blessed the City's portfolio,[55] and combined them under the presidency of Sir Francis Hincks, whose record for grand larceny was by this point irrefutably established. It was a volatile mixture. As early as 1834, in connection with an audit of the books of the Welland Canal Company, William Lyon Mackenzie had expressed his doubts as to Hincks's ability to resist the lure of quick cash.[56] Later, through an assiduously calculated program of political opportunism, Hincks managed to be carried to the position of Prime Minister of the Province of Canada on the crest of a wave of support from the big business interests, for which interests he had careful regard. Hincks was not only the founder of the corporate welfare state in Canada but one of its early beneficiaries, and his hand was rarely absent from the stock manipulations of the railway companies his government so avidly subsidized. Over the course of four years he enriched himself in a number of operations: by speculating in Crown lands, by the diversion of public funds to improvements on his own property, by a major swindle in City of Toronto debentures in collaboration with the Mayor of the City (the requisite legislation being pushed through the municipal level of government by the Mayor and the provincial level by the esteemed Premier); and especially by the sale of the Charter of the Grand Trunk Railway to an English contracting firm.[57] This last service not only netted Hincks himself a gift of £50,000 in railway stock, but in the process even restored the sagging fortunes of the Governor General, Lord Elgin, who collaborated to push through the required legislation.[58] Elgin's share was reputedly sufficient to pay off some £80,000 in mortgages hanging over his Scottish estates. When Hincks was forced to resign because of revelations of fraud that shocked even Canadian parliamentarians of the period, whose whole *raison d'être* was to maximize their conflicts of interest, his Lordship rewarded his clever first minister by engineering his appointment to the governship of various Caribbean colonies.

Elgin himself went on to bigger and better things, leading the British assault on China during the second and third opium wars, presiding over the systematic looting and burning of the Winter Palace in Peking, and forcing upon the Emperor at gunpoint a Treaty stipulating freedom of commerce in China of both British drug peddlars and British slave traders.[59] Part of Elgin's

Chinese legacy returned to Canada in the form of coolie inden-
tured labour for the coal and gold mines of British Columbia
and for railroad construction, and in the form of looted Chinese
art works for display in Toronto's Royal Ontario Museum.

As to Hincks, he returned to Canada in triumph in 1869 to
assume the Ministry of Finance under Sir John A. Macdonald's
coalition ministry, and his presence so outraged Liberal Ontario
that it effectively destroyed the coalition and helped cost Macdonald his Ontario majority. In his new position, Hincks
fathered Canada's first Bank Act, supervised the selling of the
Maritimes fishing industry to the United States in order to col-
lect cash for distribution to railway magnates,[60] and then put the
cap on his amazing career of fraud and corruption by negotiating the CPR contract with Sir Hugh Allan that led to the
Pacific Scandal. It was his last public act.[61] Back in private business, in addition to his banking activities, Hincks joined the
board of directors who were busy despoiling the Graphics Company and was among those sued for $80,000 each by irate stock-
holders in 1878.[62] With Hincks in the saddle, the fate of the Consolidated Bank was sealed.

Memories, however, were short. When Hincks presented the
1878 annual report, Montreal's *Journal of Commerce* saw it and
the Consolidated as proof of "the extraordinary vitality and
strength which so eminently characterises our Canadian banking
institutions."[63] Hincks's own guarded phrases in the report
pointed to a much less rosy interpretation. And within a few
months the bank was in serious difficulty. Still, the *Monetary
Times* eulogized that:

> The bank has the advantage of being governed by a President
> whose qualifications are never better displayed than in
> making a speech under difficult circumstances.[!] Many a time
> and oft, Francis Hincks has confronted opposing forces in
> Parliament, and he has a perfect mastery of the art of putting
> things in such a light as to disarm suspicion.[64]

All the while Hincks was busy in his old Ottawa haunts trying
desperately to find a formula to salvage his bank. An effort to
write down the capital failed to get through committee as a government measure before Parliament closed. The stumbling block
turned largely on the degree of reduction. The committee members took such a pessimistic view of the affairs of the bank that
they pressed for a 50% reduction, while Hincks argued for 33⅓%.
A compromise of 40% was rushed through Parliament as a private member's bill just before the session closed, with Hincks
personally superintending an operation that involved suspension

of normal House of Commons procedures to deal with his private bill. The bank then resumed the payment of dividends that had been briefly interrupted, and Hincks was duly re-elected to the Presidency.[65]

However, the crisis in the bank's affairs deepened, and it became clear to insiders that the bank continued to operate only by virtue of secret loans from other banks. Early in July, a group of large stockholders led by a stockbroker named E. L. Bond of Messrs. Fenwick and Bond, Montreal, held a meeting to determine policy and to stage a coup d'état.[66] Bond declared that the current management was inept, and as Bond had formerly been the head of the stock brokerage firm of Bond Brothers and Company, which had achieved the distinction of being Montreal's greatest brokerage house failure,[67] his opinion in the matter of managerial incompetence evidently carried considerable weight. News of the proceedings leaked out, and speculators began to "bear" the stock, leading to a depositors' run. Hincks resigned, but the run continued and the bank suspended. The financial chaos that resulted from the failure of an institution of its size set off a panic among depositors that nearly brought down several other banks in its wake.

The revelations that followed led to the *Monetary Times* quickly changing its opinion on the state of the Consolidated's management. "No such exposure of incompetence and misdoing has ever before been made in Canada," it decreed. "Reckless plundering" by "irresponsible schemers and desperate speculators" was its description of the bank's conduct of its business.[68] Others shared the *Monetary Times'* opinion, including a special meeting of lady stockholders who represented the daughters and widows of various leading Montreal tycoons, including one who claimed to be the daughter of an officer who had fought at Waterloo and who thus had a special claim for consideration. Nonetheless the language of the assembled ladies would scarce grace a Victorian drawing room as they denounced "loose and scandalous management" and cited the prior example of a cashier of La Banque Jacques Cartier, who had been sent to prison for conduct similar to that of the officers of the Consolidated. One lady shouted, "For my part I would send the whole lot of them to gaol" and a chorus of voices echoed "and so would I."[69] In the interim, the general manager absconded; the Honourable Alexander Campbell, a director and a Dominion Senator, now assumed the post.

After suspension, the extent of weak accounts carried and illegal transactions effected was revealed. The bank had made loans to a number of mercantile houses which should have been allowed to founder. Some, in fact, wanted to declare insolvency, but were prevented by the Consolidated's former general manager, prior to his sudden departure, who feared that their failure would bring down the bank as well. A full million dollars was locked up in six accounts deemed to be by-and-large lost.[70] The bank had engaged in illegal real estate transactions of which Hincks — along with other directors like Campbell, W. W. Ogilvie, Montreal's leading grain miller, and John Molson, eldest son of the brewing magnate — all denied knowledge.[71] In fact, the spate of denials of knowledge of the bank's operations proceeded to such an extent that it became a mystery as to how the directors could justify their fees. Their protestations of ignorance began to sound somewhat hollow when it was discovered that Hincks no longer held enough shares to legally qualify himself for a director's post, while during the crisis that preceded suspension Campbell had been busily urging other shareholders to hold onto their stock.[72] Suspension caused the value of the stock to plummet, but prior divestiture apparently saved Hincks and other directors of considerable potential involvement in the two million dollars of shareholders' losses that eventually resulted.

Francis Hincks and other directors were brought to trial by the federal government at the instigation of the outraged shareholders. Hincks was charged with fraud under the terms of the very Bank Act he had sired. The falsifications of the bank's returns to the federal government were established in the trial. The bank's returns to the federal government had made no mention of the loans received from other banks. Even the discounted notes used as collateral continued to appear in the asset columns of the Consolidated, and the loans from the other banks were listed as "deposits" up to a total of nearly a million dollars. The Consolidated was thus in the unique position of offering collateral to depositors! A quarter of a million dollars in worthless demand notes were included in the bank's "cash" by the general manager. Over half a million dollars in overdrawn accounts were classified as "notes and bills discounted and current" in the returns to the federal government, while on the bank's own books they were correctly entered as overdrafts. To all of this, Francis Hincks had duly signed his name each month.[73]

The trial attracted a great deal of attention, and the courtroom became a veritable parade ground of Canada's financial and corporate elite. Luther Holton, an old political confrère and fellow speculator in numerous railroad operations including the Grand Trunk job, posted part of Hincks's bail; George Stephen, Montreal wholesale trade magnate, Bank of Montreal president, and railway promoter, posted the rest. Other directors received similar solicitude from Duncan McIntyre, wholesale trader and railway promoter; Honourable J. R. Thibaudeau, railway promoter; Alexander Galt; John Ogilvie of the milling family; and Joseph Hickson of the Grand Trunk Railway. Hincks's defence attorneys were equally illustrious. Jonathan Würtele, who would later rise to the rank of provincial treasurer of Quebec and make his mark in private finance on public time and money, shared the honours with John Abbott, Sir Hugh Allan's bargaining agent in his dealings with Hincks over the Pacific Railway and subsequently Prime Minister of Canada.

As the trial proceeded, the list of eminent personalities lengthened. The then incumbent Dominion Minister of Finance, Leonard Tilley, led the string of notables testifying on Hincks's behalf. R. B. Angus, the general manager of the Bank of Montreal, testified that much of the manipulation that had been applied to the returns of the Consolidated was simply standard banking practice — in light of the fact that, of 26 bank failures between Confederation and the First World War, at least 19 resulted in criminal charges under the Bank Act being laid against directors, Angus may well have been telling the truth. The defence attempted to plead that the 1871 Bank Act applied only to banks listed in a schedule accompanying the Act: since the Consolidated Bank did not appear there, (while its components, the City and the Royal Canadian, did) then the Act did not apply to the Consolidated; and hence Hincks did not violate his own Bank Act by signing the falsified returns![74] It was further contended that Hincks in any event had not been "wilfully" attempting to defraud, and that he had been unaware of the falsifications of his subordinate when he signed. A rather obvious question that arises out of this contention is what, then, was Hincks doing in Ottawa at the end of the spring 1879 session; what was the purpose of the political machinations leading to the passage of his private bill, if he had been so blithely unaware that the condition of the bank did not accord with the sunny picture presented in the returns. It raises the further question of how the bank managed to pay dividends out of its capital without Hincks and the directors being aware of the unprofitable state of its business, given that they authorized the payments and given that the bank's own books reflected its condition more accurately than the falsified government returns. Good questions indeed, it would seem, for Hincks was found guilty of fraud. However, a court of appeals later reversed the verdict on a technicality.

The need for some sort of outside inspection of the operations of the Canadian banking system was revealed dramatically by the Consolidated failure. Yet the bankers and the business press refused to countenance it. The banking system itself was declared sound, and individual moral depravity the cause of disaster, to be checked by criminal proceedings after the damage was done. The *Monetary Times* performed truly dazzling feats of argumentation to prove that the system itself was not to blame. Of the Consolidated failure it noted,

> For the past year the Manager had complained of a peculiar feeling in the right lobe of the brain, and co-incident therewith a numbness or pricking sensation in the left arm, which would point to trouble in the nervous centres sufficient to impair not only his will power but his judgement. . . . There is undoubtedly much in the conduct of the General Manager to suggest the conclusion that his brain was affected: advancing of such sums to such firms was an insane act.[75]

The last of the great English institutions to fail in Quebec was Montreal's Sovereign Bank, which collapsed in 1908 in the wake of the American panic that followed the failure of the Knicker-bocker Trust. Despite the Canadian Bankers' Association's fantasies that the Canadian banks weathered the storm without casualties, the president of the Sovereign imputed the failure directly to the consequences of the panic.[76]

The bank had been founded in 1901 by Sir Herbert Holt, CPR contractor, utility promoter, and head of "the Octopus of Montreal," Montreal Light, Heat and Power Co. Ltd., in collaboration with J. P. Morgan (following the failure of the Morgan empire to secure control of the Royal Bank), and later with the Dresdner Bank, one of the great German industrial banks.[77] It was a unique institution for several reasons. It was the only major case of non-British outside investment in Canadian banking, apart from the very short-lived Banque Internationale, and the little private Weyburn Security Bank. And its Morgan and Dresdner connections went deeper than simply finance, for they imparted to it a capacity for investment banking that made it a phenomenon of Canadian finance. It was the exception that proved the rule with respect to the commercial orthodoxy of central Canadian banking. Instead of simply tiding over established firms temporarily short of cash, as was widely regarded the proper function of Canadian banks, it helped establish and build up new firms.[78] Its vigorous expansion policy — 16 new branches in 1906, 27 in 1907[79] — earned it the enmity and jealousy of the other banks and a condemnation from the *Monetary Times* as a "disturber of the financial peace . . . in this gray world of conservatism."[80]

Holt, himself, got out in 1906 before the crash, and took over the Royal Bank. In June 1906, $700,000 in bad debts were written off. The value of the reserve and securities was reduced by $200,000; $541,000 was set aside for accounts in liquidation, a further $800,000 set aside for unsatisfactory advances whose outcome was at that time unclear. The whole of the rest and one million in capital were wiped out.[81] With the panic and widespread suspension in the U.S., the vulnerable bank went under. In November 1906, one million dollars worth of special deposit receipts matured, of which, under normal circumstances, a large amount would have stayed with the bank. In the exceptional climate, it was all drawn out. In addition, a general drain on deposits occurred and its cash reserves were depleted.[82] Losses concealed by fraudulent returns were revealed at the trial of the directors, as were a great many loan irregularities.[83] It held a full two million dollars in Chicago and Milwaukee Electric Railway bonds, the road itself having gone into receivership and the ultimate value of the bonds being therefore in doubt.[84] The overexpansion of branches was cited by the liquidator as the cause of failure,[85] while the *Journal of the Canadian Bankers' Association* in its usual question-begging style cited "injudicious banking."[86] None of the authorities bothered to mention that since the long-run position of the bank was solid, assistance from the other banks during the crisis would probably have sufficed to rescue it. Their hostility cost the creditors of the failed concern nearly three-and-one-half million dollars. Thirteen chartered banks descended on the wreck and divided up its branches among themselves, though not without a great deal of squabbling over the division of the spoils.[87]

A special class of banks existed in Quebec, known in business circles as "French banks," a term not without ambiguity. On the one hand the phrase was not applied to an institution such as Sir Rodolphe Forget's short-lived Banque Internationale, apparently because Forget was an important established figure in Montreal financial circles and the conception of his bank did no real violence to established precepts of banking. The term seemed to imply small, Québécois-dominated institutions with local roots in small urban centres or Montreal suburbs and few branches. Even here the term is not completely free of problems, for the division was not an absolute. Nonetheless, the "French banks" in general conformed more closely to the Maritime, non-Halifax model of banking than to the orthodox Montreal and Ontario commercial style.

The oldest of these, and the one that had evolved the furthest towards more orthodox commercial banking, was La Banque du Peuple, founded in 1835. It was established as a company *en commandité*, the sole survivor in Canada of this type of bank organization whereby the directors had unlimited liability and the dormant shareholders were only liable to the extent of their equity.[88] It had built up widespread branches throughout Montreal and vicinity. During the depression years it was in trouble, aggravated by the use of its funds by one of its directors, an M.P., for speculating in its own stock as well as a few real estate deals on the side.[89] It collapsed finally in 1895 with the failure of a number of its debtors.

In March 1895, its President, Jacques Grenier, had presented a sunny report to the annual meeting, speaking of expansion and improved profits.[90] By July, the real state of affairs began to come into the open following the resignation of its General Manager and some adverse speculation against the bank's stock by a broker with a personal dislike for Grenier. Minor runs started, and the other banks pledged one million to keep it solvent.[91] The Bank tried to negotiate an agreement with the Bank of Montreal to take over some of its assets,[92] but rumours of the meeting fed the panic. Within a week the million was exhausted and the bank suspended.[93] Lock-ups in real estate were part of the problem.[94] But the main source of difficulty lay in its accumulation of savings deposits on which it paid interest. Not only did this raise its fixed charges, but the deposits were all lent out in the form of time discounts,[95] rather than keeping substantial amounts in call loans and very short-term discounts as other banks of the period did. Moreover, huge sums had been advanced to a few firms — all of its capital was accounted for in three loans, one of which alone absorbed nearly 60%.[96] Efforts to revive it were made, to no avail.[97] Its former general manager, charged with fraud, took off to the United States.

The importance of the bank in sustaining key Quebec industries became evident after its failure, for in the wake of the bank's collapse several prominent firms came tumbling down. The boot and shoe firm of Séguin, Lalime et Cie. of St. Hyacinthe failed almost immediately, the large foundry of William Clendenning and Sons together with its affiliate, Canada Pipe and Foundry, soon afterwards.[98] The big Montreal food processing firm of M. Lefebvre and Co. had an outstanding loan of $400,000, part of which it had diverted to real estate speculation. It carried on for a few months, and then folded up, bringing down a few wholesale grocers with it.[99]

La Banque Ville Marie was founded by Québécois businessmen in 1872 and by 1876 was already in such serious trouble that its capital was cut 50%. It was not an auspicious beginning. Over time the bank was anglicized, and when its final suspension occurred in 1899 its president, general manager, and board of directors were all English-Canadian.[100] Problems had been building for some time. At least since 1892 and possibly well before, the bank had been engaged in illegal transactions in its own stock — *with the full knowledge of the federal government.* [101] These ventures led to a reduction of capital that year, also an illegal act since the government had not authorized it.[102] But again there was no federal intervention. The government even maintained its deposits in the bank against the advice of its own top civil servants.[103]

The collapse was triggered by the theft of $58,000 by a teller, which led to a run and suspension.[104] In the ensuing investigation, it was revealed that the bank's note circulation was well in excess of its legal limit, and the bank's bill case included $300,000 in promissory notes signed by the president, William Weir, on behalf of bankrupt firms.[105] One of its junior officers had used $173,000 of the bank's money in gambling in Montreal "bucket shops."[106] This accountant was charged with theft, but no one from the bank had the courage to appear in court to testify against him. The charge was dropped, but subsequently renewed by the Crown.[107]

The main hardship fell on the depositors in the country branches of the bank, which numbered 14 of the bank's total of 20 branches, who ultimately lost well over a million dollars. Warrants were issued for the arrest of Weir and the other officers and directors, who were charged with theft and making fraudulent returns. Also arrested was a Montreal stockbroker who had arranged most of the bucket shop dealings and had helped the absconding teller skip town. Weir was sentenced to two years by Justice Jonathan Würtele, himself a notorious financial operator in his time. The conviction was appealed.[108] It took several years before Weir could be brought to trial again, the pretext being that "Mr. Weir's mind has given way very much."[109] In the meantime the depositors agitated for government relief, and pressure for outside inspection of banks began to grow. Especially adamant were a group of depositors in Argenteuil who wrote to Prime Minister Laurier that "Liberals of Argenteuil who are also unfortunately depositors of the defunct Ville Marie Bank are finding ourselves in a very embarrassing position as regards the coming elections."[110]

While there is some evidence of industrial activity by the bank, it is marginal. Weir was a promoter of a glove factory; the suspension of the bank brought down a lumber firm directly, and indirectly helped wreck a slipper manufacturer. But its chief activities, and cause of failure, lay in the bucket shop promotions of Montreal brokers such as Wm. Weir and Co.[111]

The Ville Marie troubles led to a run on La Banque Jacques

Cartier, which suspended,[112] resumed, then suspended again. In turn its suspension triggered off runs on La Banque de Hochelega and La Banque Nationale, and brought forth a circular from the Archbishop of Montreal urging the depositors to keep calm.[113] The Jacques Cartier bank had begun operations in 1861 and in 1876 found itself in difficulty. It had made large advances to contractors in connection with Sir Hugh Allan's Northern Colonization Railway, and to a syndicate of land speculators.[114] The stock was reduced by over 50% before resumption. In its difficulties the bank had relied on advances from the other big banks to tide it over. Investigations revealed that its general manager had tried to hide losses and overdue paper by falsifying returns. He had also embezzled funds and used them for stock speculation. The *Monetary Times* referred to the falsified return and the trial as "a rare and strange occurrence,"[115] which in 1876 it may well have been. By the turn of the century, however, it was recurring with tiresome regularity. Prior to suspension, the bank had been the fastest-growing in the Dominion, and some of the momentum was regained — by 1881 its activities included extensive dealings with Cape Breton coal mines[116] — such that when it failed for the last time in 1899 it managed to cost its stockholders $1,750,000.

There was really no good reason for the failure apart from the unstable atmosphere surrounding the "French banks" following Weir and company's depredations. The president of the bank, Alphonse Desjardins, claimed a conspiracy existed to wreck the institution. In any event, it reorganized under the name La Banque Provinciale du Canada, the old stockholders of La Banque Jacques Cartier getting $250,000 of the new bank's equity in return for $500,000 of the old plus the nominal reserve of $300,000. In an effort to put on a stable public front, the new institution established, in addition to its regular board of directors, an advisory board consisting of four provincial cabinet ministers, the chief justice of Quebec, and the Mayor of St. Cunegonde, all Québécois.[117]

One of the most astounding cases in Canadian financial history concerned La Banque de St. Jean. It was largely a family bank founded by one Louis Molleur, who was succeeded at its helm by Hon. Philippe Roy, Speaker of the Quebec legislature. Most of the paid-up capital was controlled by Roy,[118] and the board of directors was completely under his orders. At the time of liquidation it had 900 depositors, whose total credits were $296,000, and notes in circulation came to $216,000. Its total assets were estimated at $301,386, liabilities at $550,000. Once a Quebec government claim of $45,000 and the noteholders were paid off, the depositors might have hoped to get 12 to 15% back. This by itself would have caused considerable hardship. The Roy family owned a waterworks for which the town had offered $200,000, and the depositors tried unsuccessfully to have it sold.[119] In addition, most of the small shareholders could not meet the double liability.[120]

Investigation revealed matters to be much worse than they had seemed initially. Over half a million dollars worth of nominal assets turned out to be valueless. Among them were notes held by the bank from Roy's brother,[121] which, on closer analysis turned out to be Roy's own with his brother's name forged.[122] A total of $650,000 in various forms had been wrongfully included in the bank's assets.[123] All of the deposits had been withdrawn and sunk into firms which Roy either owned or controlled.[124] Creditors' ultimate losses reached $400,000, including all of the deposits.

Roy was arrested, along with the general manager and his assistant. Roy was released on $6,000 bail while the other two, who evidently lacked his political connections, had bail set at $50,000. But a second charge led to their re-arrest, followed by a series of civil suits as well.[125] The antagonism towards Roy in his home community was so intense that at his request the trial was shifted to Montreal.[126] Thereupon it degenerated into a circus. The federal attorney had to have a detective placed with the jury to prevent Roy's allies engaging in bribery and coercion.[127] The trial climaxed with a "suicide" attempt, in which Roy drew his revolver, took careful aim, and shot himself — through the foot. "A most criminal farce," the judge declared.[128]

The defence pleas was astounding. Since the bank had never complied with all the legal requirements for functioning, (and therefore had no legal existence), then Roy could not be guilty of a criminal offence in rendering false returns regarding its operations.[129] The judge apparently did not agree that, since Roy had begun his operation of the bank illegally, illegal functions by an illegal institution did not constitute a breach of the law. Roy was unceremoniously removed from the Speaker's chair in the Quebec Legislature to St. Vincent de Paul Penitentiary, nursing his wounded dignity, not to speak of his foot. But Roy was clearly too important a figure to languish long in prison, and by 1911 he had reappeared as a Senator, as the President of La Caisse Hypothècaire du Canada, and the Canadian Trade Commissioner in Paris.[130]

La Banque de St. Hyacinthe failed in the wake of La Banque de St. Jean.[131] Its president, Senator Georges Dessaulles, was the leading industrialist in his community, and had several major enterprises to his credit. The little bank's demise was due to an excessive lock-up of funds in a local railroad at a time when the small banks were under siege. Prolonged litigation followed the suspension: the stockholders appealed unsuccessfully against the double liability.[132] It was the end of most of the little local Quebec banks that often — though not always — played a significant role in the industrial expansion of their communities. The Bank of Montreal moved into St. Jean and St. Hyacinthe following the failures.

# Bank Failures in Ontario

The Exchange Bank had a short, but colourful career. While its headquarters was in Montreal, and its directors largely from among the wholesale drygoods community there, most of the bank's business and branches were in Ontario. It began in 1872 with one million dollars of capital paid in, and soon ran up a series of weak accounts. In 1878, a drain of reserves began after the defalcation of a cashier and a sharp fall in the value of its holdings of telegraph company stocks forced the passing of the dividend.[133] The Bank of Montreal loaned it $250,000 on the personal guarantee of its directors to try to stop the run, but within a week it suspended[134] in the wake of the Consolidated failure. For a time the directors debated simply letting it fail, but ultimately it was revived.[135] During its three-month suspension it came to light that a lot of illegal stock-speculation with the bank's money had occurred. Its circulation was cut from $488,000 to $148,000, its deposits from $465,000 to $199,500, its liabilities from $1,300,000 to $700,000. The cash reserve was rebuilt, the stock was reduced 50%, and the bank reopened.[136]

In very short order it was in trouble again. But the bank had one asset that did not appear in its books and that it now proceeded to realize. Over half its stockholders were leading Conservative Party members, including one cabinet minister, Senator A. W. Ogilvie. In April 1883, the Tory Finance Minister, George Foster, advanced the bank $200,000 of government money, and in May another $100,000 on the personal guarantee of Senator Ogilvie. The bank was known to be insolvent, but the loans were made in the hope that it would recover and that prominent Conservatives would thus be spared the need to pay up on its double liability.[137] The effect of the advance was to put the depositors at ease, convincing them the bank was sound, with the result that creditor losses reached over $800,000 when the final crash occurred.

One year before the fall, the stock had been selling at 179.

Even six months before, the general manager, Thomas Craig, had managed to sell one unsuspecting investor a block of shares worth $40,000 at 170 each. That the stock prices were so high was due to the fact that Craig had been using the bank's money to manipulate a block of stock amounting to one-quarter of the total. In addition to illegal speculations in the bank's own stock, Craig had helped himself to the bank's funds for his own personal stock speculations, and in 1880 he had managed to build himself a house worth $55,000. The directors never enquired about the source of the funds. In fact, not once in the period of Craig's tenure as general manager was any inspection of the books made. When failure came in 1883, both Craig and $226,000 had disappeared.[138] To add insult to injury, three of the directors, who were legally responsible for the wreck, were appointed liquidators, including one E. K. Greene, formerly of the Royal Canadian and not above suspicion of stock manipulation himself, and the Honourable A. W. Ogilvie as well, who in the final analysis had to be sued by the Laurier government in 1898 for recovery of the federal funds advanced.[139] Court orders were also issued against M. H. Gault, M.P., for $110,000 he had "borrowed" from the bank, of which he was a director.[140] And with the suspension of the Corriveau Silk Manufacturing Co., in which M. H. Gault, Craig, and Ogilvie were stockholders, it was bought at a bargain price from the liquidators by a syndicate headed by A. F. Gault, brother of the director, and resold at a handsome profit almost immediately.[141] As for the depositors' claims, the last of the assets of the bank, nominally worth one million dollars, were sold for $4,700 in 1891. The largest of these was a claim of $259,000 against Craig, which sold for $25.[142]

The career of the Bank of London was even shorter, a scant three years separating creation and destruction in 1887. Its president, one Henry Taylor, involved the bank's assets in the operations of the insolvent Ontario Investment Association, which he controlled. Then, after he had manipulated the reserve figure to try to cover losses on his investments, he attempted to unload the bankrupt institution on the Bank of Toronto. On the eve of the sale he "was to *personally* secure certain final signatures and official deeds in London, but instead of doing so, he personally absconded to an American watering hole." It was an appropriate end to a financial career that began by cheating the Imperial Commissariat.[143] Subsequently Taylor returned to Canada and was arrested. A group of shareholders headed by William Meredith, who had been involved with Taylor in the Ontario Investment Association, successfully opposed the motion to prosecute in the shareholders' meeting. Taylor was charged, but acquitted of all charges of misappropriation and fraud and released.[144]

The Bank of London was not the sole casualty of the 1887-8 crisis in Ontario; two others joined it. The Central Bank was a small institution whose authorized capital was only half a million dollars, but it had big ambitions. It had placed stock in towns outside Toronto where it was headquartered by promising to establish branches if a certain amount were subscribed. It had aggressively expanded its circulation, even paying bribes to agencies to keep its issue out, and it sold deposit certificates at a discount. Moreover, it paid one or two per cent more than the current cartel rate of interest to attract depositors. When it suspended, all seemed well at first. Its accounts appeared to be well secured. Two accounts, the Niagara Central Railway and the Ontario Lumber Company, were too large for the bank's resources, but no losses were expected.[145] Then the truth began to emerge. Loans to directors that could not be realized had been concealed by the manager. One director got $121,000, a broker got $133,000, and a "friend" got $100,000 secured on "diamonds." These three loans absorbed most of the paid-up capital. In addition, the Ontario Lumber Company turned out to be headed by a man who had already bankrupted two similar lumber concerns and was set on maintaining his record. And the circulation, through various devices, had been pushed well above its legal limit. Moreover, the manager had used the bank's funds to buy the bank's own stock in order to keep up the quotation.[146]

This kind of illegal manipulation of bank stock using the institution's own funds, while common in Canadian banks, was especially prevalent in Ontario. The effect of a bank lending on, or buying, its own equity is to pay back the capital, with the bank getting only paper representing it in its place. This increases the burden on the shareholders should the double liability become operative. In the case of the Central Bank, this type of manipulation was complicated by a rash of disclaimers of stock ownership during liquidation to avoid double liability. In addition, the directors had allocated stock to themselves that they did not pay up, and had dropped surplus shares out of the stockbook to cover up overissue.[147]

Three leading bankers, Archibald Campbell, who had been a director of the defunct City and Exchange Banks, William Howland, and George Gooderham, were appointed liquidators, and the comedy increased. Campbell wanted to simply wind up the affair; Howland and Gooderham insisted on an investigation. Campbell was accused of having been involved in the failure. He then ran off to Montreal with a detective on his tail. But in the final analysis, Campbell was exonerated and a certain amount of suspicion fell on Gooderham and Howland instead.[148] Nor was Campbell's quick trip to Montreal unprecedented in the case. The broker who borrowed heavily and who bore the name of E. S. Cox left the city in a hurry "apparently for good"; in fact he soon returned to lead other financial institutions into disaster. The director who had borrowed also skipped town. According to the *Monetary Times,* "the late cashier left Canada Wednesday midnight. The ex-President . . ., who had been at Clifton Springs, New York, for some weeks for his health, has not yet returned."[149]

The last of the Ontario banks to fall in this period was the Federal in 1888. It was also the largest, with a paid-up capital of ostensibly three million dollars. In fact, $500,000 of this capital was never paid in and carried no double liability.[150] In addition, large blocs of stock had reverted to the bank, and a great deal of water existed in the nominal stock, which came closer to two than to three million. A lot of speculation had occurred in the bank's own shares through the Commercial Loan and Stock Company, in which one of the directors held equity. In addition, $100,000 was advanced to Forbes and Lownsborough, private bankers, and Gzowski and Buchan, private bankers and brokers, to deal in the bank's own stock.[151] The brokerage firm of Cox and Worts was also involved, as were several others. These manipulations led to a suspension in 1884, precipitating the failure of one of the several private banks involved. But the chartered bank, then under the leadership of the broker H. S. Strathy, of Strathy and Strathy, resumed only to fail again in 1887 under virtually identical circumstances.[152] All of the directors were aware of the manipulations despite the efforts of some of them, including Edward Gurney, to deny all knowledge.[153] Furthermore, there were large losses in Michigan lumber transactions, lock-ups in real estate in Manitoba, and an overdraft on the Commercial Loan and Stock Company that ran as high as $1,-500,000.[154] These dealings had been hidden by falsifying returns to the federal government, and came to light only after the stock bubble burst again and the bank suspended for good.

One of the principle arguments used to defend the Canadian banking system's pattern of organization against the advocates of small local banks was that small banks were supposed to be more unstable. But while in absolute terms the number of "small" bank failures on any reasonable definition did exceed the number of "large" bank failures, it is clear that it took only a few catastrophes of the order of magnitude of the Sovereign or the Consolidated or the Federal for the argument to lose whatever little truth or relevance it might have had.

The Ontario Bank was another of the large banks which, according to Canadian Bankers' Association propaganda, would not fail — and did just that in 1905. It had been deeply scarred in the depression of the 1870's. In 1875, the head office was moved from Bowmanville to Toronto, ostensibly to ensure proper management, and in 1877 $365,000 was appropriated to bad debts and the dividend reduced to three per cent. In 1881 it was still in trouble. A proposal to reduce the stock by fifty per cent was made by the directors, including Howland and Gzowski, but resisted by the small shareholders. At that time the bank was heavily in debt to the Bank of Montreal, and a large number of its discounts were doubtful. The Ontario's problems were unusual for a big central Canadian bank. Instead of stock speculation or mercantile advances being the cause of difficulty, it had been involved in long-term finance to industry. "Advances made to lumberers and other manufacturers had been used for purposes which required fixed capital, the transfer of circulating to fixed capital necessarily involved a lock-up."[155] These, of course, were a relic of its era as a local Bowmanville bank.

The bank recovered, and proceeded without serious mishap until 1896, when it was forced to write off $310,000 and reduce its capital from $1,500,000 to $1,000,000.[156] A decade later, it collapsed again for the last time, in reality the victim of a revolution in Cuba, for the Royal Bank had been prepared to take over the ailing institution until an insurrection made it fearful of its own assets on the island and reluctant to proceed with any further mergers.[157] But the bid had revealed that the capital of the bank had been wiped out and the collapse served as a loud punctuation mark to H. C. McLeod's campaign for external examination.[158] Only a few days before the failure, H. M. P. Eckhardt, the Canadian Bankers' Association's official eulogist, had an article in the *Bankers' Magazine* entitled "Canadian Banking Practice — the Detection of Fraud," arguing that fraud by a general manager was almost impossible and praising the directors of Canadian banks for the close watch they kept on officers. The general manager of the Ontario, Charles McGill, and the president, G. R. Cockburn, were duly charged with fraud.[159]

Investigation by the liquidators revealed the following instances of "sound banking practice." Under the heading "other securities" appeared $778,000 which simply did not exist. At various times the bank had purchased $220,000 worth of its own shares in the name of "the officers' guarantee fund [sic]" in order to protect prices on the open market. It also had speculative losses of $170,000 in American railway stock. These items and other similar ones summed to $1,653,000, while the bank's paid-up capital was $1,500,000 and its reserve $700,000, leaving only $547,000 to meet any possible losses on $12 million in discounted paper.[160] Further investigations revealed that certain large sums, which appeared on the books as loans to New York brokers, never reached those brokers but were used by McGill and his sons to speculate in stocks in New York — over one million dollars' worth of dealings by McGill with four brokers alone, plus a series of smaller ones.[161] It is noteworthy that the Ontario had, in twenty-five years, learned one lesson. Industrial lock-ups were not the cause of its ultimate demise. The shareholders and depositors who lost their money had the consolation of knowing that they did so according to the best banking principles.

In the aftermath, the Bank of Montreal, guaranteed by the other banks for up to $2,500,000 after the double liability was exhausted, took over the assets of the failed concern. A shareholders' association, formed under the leadership of Sir Casimir Gzowski and other leading Toronto financiers, unsuccessfully fought the Bank of Montreal merger.[162] Cockburn, the president, was actually acquitted of "wilfully" signing the false statements to the federal government.[163] As usual, a junior official became the scapegoat, and McGill got five years.[164]

In 1910 came the collapse of the notorious — even by Canadian standards — Farmers' Bank. The bank was promoted by a Liberal Party organizer and former member of the Ontario legislature, W. Beattie Nesbitt, who was joined by one W. R. Travers as general manager. Travers had formerly been manager of the Merchants' Bank's Berlin branch. When he was shifted to its Hamilton branch, the customers of the Berlin bank gave him $420 in gold as a present.[165] The gold apparently went to his head. The bank had difficulty in selling enough stock to pay the $250,000 deposit necessary to get a certificate to operate from the Ministry of Finance. Travers offered to sell the required stock for a 10% commission. He then lied about the number of shares sold, accepted promissory notes as payment, and on the basis of the notes which he endorsed borrowed $100,000 from the Trustee and Guarantee Company to make up the balance of the mandatory deposit. After he got the $250,000 back from the Treasury Board, he paid off the loan. These sums were all recorded as paid-up capital. Then the fun began. In the words of Sir William Meredith, who headed a Royal Commission of investigation after the debacle,

> the subsequent management of the affairs of the bank was characterized by gross extravagance, recklessness, incompetence, dishonesty and fraud and has resulted in the entire loss of the paid up capital and the whole of the deposits.[166]

Sir William's prior involvement in the Bank of London debacle
undoubtedly made him somewhat of an expert in such matters.
As soon as the bank's certificate was granted, Travers and Nesbitt, joined by a new accomplice, George Wishart, began a series
of mining jobs which encompassed stock speculation in
Wishart's Porcupine mine, another bout of speculations in a
Cochrane mine using a third party as a front, loans secured on
the Helca mine property, and above all, the huge Keeley mine
job into which $1,156,000, twice the paid-up capital of the bank,
was sunk[167] — literally and figuratively. The mine made only one
shipment in its entire life. In addition, Travers forged a minute
from the board of the bank authorizing him to lend to the mine
at his own discretion, and he used $156,000 in bank funds to
make purchases of stock in his own name.[168] He used another
$60,000 to buy himself the Lake Shore Country Club.[169] Money
lost in mines was hidden by revaluing the stock in the bank's
books with assistance from some illegal deals with Continental
Securities Company of Winnipeg.[170]

The beginning of the end came in the sleepy Ontario town of
Lindsay, where a branch of the ill-fated Home Bank opened next
door to the local Farmers' branch. Three of its employees,
including a former general manager of the Farmers', began circulating rumours among local farmers that the Farmers' Bank
was unsound, and that all deposits ought to be transferred to the
Home Bank. The three were charged with conspiracy.[171] Though
actuated by the worst of motives, if they had been successful they
would have managed to save the depositors' money — until the
Home Bank itself failed in 1923.

By the time the conspiracy charges were being heard, the
stock market was no longer enthusiastic about the Farmers'. Travers took $150,000 to Syracuse in the bank's notes, which he lent
to the directorate of the People's Mutual Life Company to purchase shares of the bank's stock at 130 — at a time shares were
being quoted at between 35 and 40 in Toronto and had dropped
as low as eleven.[172] When the collapse came even with the double
liability enforced, a loss of $1,806,437 was expected to result.[173]
The result of the failure was the impoverishment of many depositors.[174] In fact, several branches continued to accept deposits
after the head office was closed.[175] The stock was held in a large
number of small towns and villages in Ontario, and it is doubtful
if many of these stockholders even knew of the existence of the
double liability.[176] It is even more doubtful that small investors
and farmers would have purchased so much of the stock if the
bank had not been given a *de facto* vote of confidence from the
Treasury Board by the granting of the certificate.[177]

How such an institution got a certificate is a good question, and the answer appears to be not completely unrelated to the fact that Travers contributed heavily to a $120,000 testimonial to Finance Minister W. S. Fielding.[178] The Liberal whip had gone with Travers to urge Fielding to grant the certificate, and it proved a successful trip.[179]

The Farmers' failure was the first major test of the central note redemption fund established with such accolades by the chartered banks to "secure" the notes of defunct institutions. For a public uninitiated in the mysteries of banking legislation it was a rude shock to find that in fact the central redemption fund did not defend the value of the notes until every last penny was squeezed out of the failed institution. In the unlikely event that there were then any notes unredeemable from the assets, including all the funds placed in the bank by the depositors, then the other banks would be called upon to pay up through the fund. To make sure that the noteholders did not present their notes and demand restitution from the central fund, the chartered banks cashed $320,000 of Farmers' notes, deposited them with a Toronto trust company drawing six per cent interest, and waited for the liquidator to settle the assets of the bank. Thus the deposits of the failed institution functioned as protection for the redemption fund, rather than the redemption fund protecting the noteholders.

The failure provided useful election material in 1911, and several Tory candidates in rural Ontario promised that the double liability which threatened to ruin many farmers would not be enforced if the Conservative Party won office.[180] This appeal did a great deal to offset the pro-Reciprocity feelings of the farm community. In fact, once in office, the Conservatives did nothing to relieve the distress despite petitions.[181] The shareholders asked the courts for exemption on the grounds that fraud had been used to solicit their subscriptions.[182] The depositors launched a countersuit arguing that any fraud by Travers and company was done as an agent of the shareholders, and they were therefore responsible for the result.[183] The shareholders lost their case and sought an appeal to the Privy Council; the appeal was denied.[184] Warrants were issued for several of the leading participants in the festivities. Travers himself was arrested and charged with theft.[185]

Travers got six years, and Nesbitt had a long holiday in the United States[186] where by now he was sure of the company of many kindred souls.

# Bank Failures in the West

Bank failures in the West were two in number — and both were, in the final analysis, brought on by the eastern banks, who wanted the western interlopers out of the way.

The Commercial Bank of Manitoba was the outgrowth of a private banking firm, McArthur, Boyle and Campbell of Winnipeg, who carried over into the chartered bank all of the business and accounts of the private venture in 1885.[187] A great deal of the stock had been sold in England at a substantial premium.[188] It was an aggressive bank which by the time of its failure in 1893 had nine branches and a paid-up capital of $552,650 in theory, while its reserves of specie and Dominion notes were never more than nine per cent of its circulation at a time when other banks in Canada claimed to be holding 50 to 60%. On suspension, its immediately available cash was only 15% of circulation and deposits.[189] And while the other banks had a paid-up capital of 83% authorized on average, and nearly 100% of that subscribed, the Commercial had only 37% subscribed and 28% "paid-up", much of it purchased with promissory notes.

It was very much a one-man operation. McArthur, its president, had formerly been manager of the Merchants' Bank Winnipeg branch in addition to his private banking experience. All of its business, like that of the private bank, was local, and much of it the older banks refused to undertake. Large accounts for local improvements led to lock-ups and losses, and redemption problems began to occur. It became increasingly dependent upon the Merchants' for advances, and when further advances were refused, suspension followed.[190] At the time of suspension, both McArthur and the general manager were heavy personal debtors to the bank.[191] When wound up, its overdue debts were found to be $415,285 and its bad debts $330,750, out of current loans and discounts of $1,146,383.[192] Ultimately the stockholders lost $300,-000.

The only other western chartered effort (except the Crown Bank, which was absorbed by a Toronto bank) to get off the ground was the Bank of Vancouver, born in 1910, buried in 1914. The fledgling institution got heavily into making loans to local enterprise; while these appeared on the books as short-term loans, they became in fact long-term investments. Of total assets of $2,753,714 in November 1913 before the trouble came out in the open, only $106,068 appeared as railway and other bonds and stocks, while current loans and discounts were $1,704,673.[193] But when it was finally liquidated a full $941,000 of the "current" loans were written off.[194] Troubles began early in 1914, and the large banks refused to grant any assistance to tide it over,[195] and an effort to sell the ailing institution to the Royal did not succeed. The situation was especially delicate at that time because the Province of British Columbia was about to float a loan in London and the failure of a bank would be "certain to reflect upon the credit of the province."[196] In March 1914, the bank's capital was reduced by 50%. In December, rumours began to circulate that it was insolvent, and the scandal-wracked failure of Dominion Trust led to a financial stringency that made it impossible for the bank to realize quickly in some of its outstanding loans. The other chartered banks still refused to help, and a run commenced, leading to suspension.[197]

# The Record of the Chartered Banks

The record of stability of the Canadian banking system is alarming, and the myth of stability sheer propaganda. Nor by any piece of statistical subterfuge, apart from a simple head count, can it be claimed that the small banks had a worse record than the large. The cause of the problem did not lie in individual moral depravity. There was certainly no lack of that, but the banking system itself provided fertile ground in which the swindles could be perpetrated. The problem was the structure of the banking system. Overcentralization of control permitted a few men at the head office to wreck the bank. Every one of the failures occurred because of decisions taken at the head office. This renders ludicrous the frequent assertion in Canadian banking circles that the centralized branch system was better insofar as it prevented the local banking facilities from coming under the influence of local businessmen. The inference that local control would generate instability hardly follows from Canada's appalling record of banks plundered into insolvency by their own directors at the head office. There was no system of outside inspection to check them. Competitive note issue, lacking the restraint of any reserve requirement, along with the logic of non-price competition via that note issue and by a proliferation of branches, lent a deep structural instability to the entire system.

Lock-ups in industry were not the cause of failure in most cases. The bulk of the banks that collapsed overextended themselves in mercantile loans and discounts and manipulations with their call loans, and hence conformed to the principles of the banking school on which the Canadian system was predicated. Apart from the Sovereign — the exception that proves the rule because of its Dresdner and Morgan connections — and the frightening example of the Farmers' Bank, none of the central Canadian or Halifax commercial banks transgressed the precepts of orthodoxy in terms of type of business. (Methods were something else again.) But with the "French banks" in small Quebec centres and the little non-Halifax Maritime banks and those in the West, it was a different story. They were local banks, and closely connected with local industrial capital formation. When they failed, due to lock-ups, they left in their wake a real contribution to their localities' industrial growth. When the commercial banks failed, they left nothing but criminal charges behind them.

There can be no doubt that the comparative ease with which the Maritimers began making the transition from commercialism to industrial capitalism was due in no small measure to the entrepreneurial character of its local banking system. On the other hand, the central Canadian commercial banks served only to perpetuate a staple-extracting commercial economy. When the Maritime banking structure disappeared — by takeovers by central or Halifax commercial banks or by failure, together with the tight control exercised by the central Canadian bankers through the federal government to block the creation of new local banks of issue and deposit — its demise showed a remarkable synchronization with the end of economic and social advance in the area. Maritime underdevelopment and the loss of its financial independence went hand-in-hand.

# Notes to Chapter IV

1.   *CBC*, 1913, p. 264.
2.   Data based on H. C. McLeod, "The Need for Outside Inspection"; *Globe*, Nov. 22, 1906; and B. Beckhart, *The Banking System of Canada*, pp. 334-7.
3.   *CBC*, 1913, p. 352.
4.   *MT*, Dec. 15, 1906, p. 871; *CBC*, 1913, p. 507.
5.   Bank of Nova Scotia, *Annual Report*, 1909, p. 20.
6.   *RCRLC, Nova Scotia Evidence*, p. 220.
7.   See for example *MT*, Dec. 15, 1906, pp. 871-2.
8.   *Montreal Witness*, Dec. 1, 1906; quoted in Bank of Nova Scotia, *Annual Report*, 1907, p. 30.
9.   See for example, H. M. P. Eckhardt, "Causes of Bank Failure" and "A Study of Bank Failures."
10.  *MT*, Dec. 31, 1868, pp. 310, 314.
11.  *MT*, Jan. 14, 1869, p. 342; May 20, 1869, p. 630.
12.  *MT*, July 16, 1873, p. 915; Breckenridge, *Canadian Banking System*, p. 439.
13.  *MT*, Dec. 26, 1879, p. 751.
14.  *MT*, May 20, 1881, p. 1354.
15.  Bank of Nova Scotia, *The Bank of Nova Scotia, 1832-1932, p. 66.*
16.  *MT*, Oct. 18, 1878, p. 504.
17.  *MT*, Oct. 1⅃, 1878, p. 474.

18.   *MT,* Dec. 2, 1881, p. 668.
19.   V. Ross, *Bank of Commerce I,* p. 135.
20.   *Bank of Nova Scotia,* p. 66.
21.   *MT,* Dec. 2, 1881, p. 668.
22.   *MT,* March 18, 1887, p. 1094.
23.   *MT,* Oct. 8, 1880, pp. 418-9.
24.   *MT,* Oct. 15, 1880, p. 444.
25.   *MT,* July 23, 1880, p. 99.
26.   *MT,* Dec. 16, 1881, p. 731.
27.   *MT,* March 11, 1887, p. 1063.
28.   *MT,* April 29, 1887, p. 284.
29.   *MT,* May 6, 1887, p. 1309.
30.   *MT,* Aug. 6, 1886, p. 155.
31.   *CBC,* 1913, p. 324.
32.   *Yarmouth Telegraph,* April 7, 1905; Dept. of Finance, *Yarmouth Bank Liquidation File.*
33.   *MT,* March 10, 1905, p. 1205.
34.   *MT,* April 11, 1908, p. 1708.
35.   *Yarmouth Liquidation File; MT,* Feb. 1907, p. 1223, says that the president was acquitted. This appears to be an error.
36.   *JC,* March 11, 1910, p. 334.
37.   "Report of the Liquidators to the Secretary, Canadian Bankers' Association," March 17, 1910, *St. Stephen's Bank Liquidation File.*
38.   W. W. Johnson, *Sketches of the Late Depression,* p. 79.
39.   *MT,* April 19, 1878, p. 1236.
40.   *MT,* July 16, 1880, p. 70; JC, Aug. 8, 1879, p. 787.
41.   W. W. Johnson, *Sketches of the Late Depression,* p. 78.
42.   *JC,* May 30, 1879, p. 438.
43.   *MT,* July 25, 1884, p. 96.
44.   *JC,* Jan. 20, 1879, p. 544
45.   *MT,* Sept. 19, 1879, p. 355.
46.   *MT,* Nov. 21, 1879, p. 611.
47.   *MT,* Jan. 23, 1880, p. 861.
48.   *MT,* Jan. 30, 1880, p. 893.
49.   *MT,* May 6, 1869, p. 601; June 10, 1869, p. 681; July 18, 1869, pp. 742-3.
50.   *MT,* May 27, 1869, p. 648.
51.   *MT,* June 24, 1869, p. 711; Dec. 24, 1869, p. 294.
52.   J. F. Norris (ed.), *The Consolidated Bank of Canada: A Compilation,* p. 15.
53.   *MT,* June 28, 1872, p. 1029; Nov. 8, 1872, p. 372; J. F. Norris, *Consolidated,* p. 5.
54.   *MT,* June 5, 1874, p. 1255; June 19, 1874, p. 1316; June 11, 1875, p. 1399; June 18, 1875, p. 1427; May 12, 1876, p. 1285.
55.   W. W. Johnson, *Sketches of the Late Depression,* p. 78.
56.   S. Thompson, *Reminiscences of A Canadian Pioneer,* p. 290; R. S. Longley, *Sir Francis Hincks,* p. 23.
57.   Province of Canada, Legislative Council, *Sessional Papers,* vol. XIII, 1854-5, Appendix 2, gives the report of the Select Committee and the evidence in the charges against Hincks. Gustavus Myers, *History of Canadian Wealth,* and R. S. Longley, *Sir Francis Hincks* contain fairly thorough discussions.
58.   Province of Canada, *Confederation Debates,* March 7, 1865, p. 741.
59.   W. Holt, *The Opium Wars* (New York, 1964) contains an account of Elgin's activities in China.
60.   R. S. Longley, *Hincks,* pp. 394ff.
61.   F. Hincks to John A. Macdonald, Feb. 10, 1873, *Macdonald Papers.*

62.  *MT,* July 26, 1879, p. 119.
63.  *JC,* June 7, 1878, p. 487.
64.  *MT,* June 13, 1879, p. 1534.
65.  J. F. Norris, *Consolidated,* pp. 8, 15.
66.  J. F. Norris, *Consolidated,* pp. 15 *et passim.*
67.  *MT,* Dec. 1, 1876, p. 613; Aug. 23, 1878, p. 241.
68.  *MT,* Sept. 26, 1879, pp. 384-5.
69.  J. F. Norris, *Consolidated,* pp. 18ff.
70.  *JC,* Aug. 8, 1879, p. 785; *MT,* Aug. 15, 1879, p. 207.
71.  *JC,* Sept. 1879, p. 177; *MT,* Oct. 24, 1879, p. 495; June 14, 1879, p. 1463.
72.  J. F. Norris, *Consolidated,* p. 27 *et passim.*
73.  J. F. Norris, *Consolidated,* pp. 78, 92 *et passim.*
74.  J. F. Norris, *Consolidated, passim,* gives a detailed account from trial transcripts and judgements.
75.  *MT,* Aug. 15, 1879, p. 207.
76.  *JC,* March 20, 1908, p. 552.
77.  *MT,* May 13, 1911, p. 1918; JC, Jan. 31, 1908, p. 223; Dec. 19, 1902, p. 793.
78.  *JC,* Jan. 24, 1908, p. 163.
79.  *MT,* Jan. 25, 1908, p. 1214.
80.  *MT,* Jan. 25, 1908, p. 1209.
81.  *MT,* June 15, 1907, p. 1977.
82.  *MT,* March 21, 1908, p. 1588.
83.  *MT,* Feb. 13, 1910, p. 1430.
84.  *JC,* Jan. 31, 1908, p. 203.
85.  *CBC,* p. 215.
86.  H. M. P. Eckhardt, "Causes of Bank Failures," p. 49.
87.  B. E. Walker to G. L. Pease, 24 Jan. 1908, *Walker Papers; JC,* Jan. 24, 1908, p. 166.
88.  *MT,* July 12, 1895, p. 48.
89.  *MT,* Dec. 13, 1878, p. 744.
90.  *MT,* March 8, 1895, p. 1165.
91.  *MT,* July 12, 1895, p. 48.
92.  *JC,* July 19, 1895, p. 113.
93.  *MT,* July 19, 1895, p. 78.
94.  *MT,* Oct. 11, 1895, p. 468.
95.  *JC,* July 12, 1895, p. 67.
96.  *JC,* July 19, 1895, p. 114.
97.  *JC,* Oct. 25, 1895, p. 873; *MT,* Dec. 7, 1895, p. 813.
98.  *MT,* Oct. 11, 1895, p. 463; Nov. 1, 1895, p. 558.
99.  *MT,* March 20, 1896, p. 1202.
100. *JC,* July 28, 1899, p. 197.
101. J. M. Courtney, Deputy Minister of Finance, to R. Sedgwick, Deputy Minister of Justice, March 3, 1892, Department of Finance, *Banque Ville Marie Liquidation File.*
102. J. M. Courtney to W. Weir, president of La Banque Ville Marie, July 29, 1892.
103. R. Sedgwick to J. M. Courtney, Sept. 19, 1892.
104. *JC,* July 28, 1899, p. 197.
105. *JC,* Sept. 22, 1899, p. 731.
106. Memo re Bank Ville Marie prosecutions, Jan. 24, 1910, *Liquidation File.*
107. *MT,* Aug. 4, 1899, p. 139; Jan. 12, 1900, p. 912.
108. *MT,* Dec. 8, 1899, p. 743; Jan. 5, 1900, p. 874.
109. M. Hutchins to E. L. Newcombe, May 23, 1901.
110. Liberals of Argenteuil to Sir Wilfred Laurier, Oct. 30, 1900.
111. *MT,* Aug. 5, 1898, p. 171; March 25, 1900, p. 1543; Nov. 9, 1900, p. 588.

112.  *JC,* Aug. 4, 1899, pp. 259-260.
113.  *MT,* Aug. 4, 1899, p. 145.
114.  W. W. Johnson, *Sketches of the Late Depression,* p. 79.
115.  *MT,* Nov. 3, 1876, p. 504; June 8, 1897, p. 1412.
116.  *MT,* July 22, 1881, p. 94; Aug. 19, 1881, p. 206.
117.  *MT,* April 6, 1910, p. 1311; July 20, 1900, p. 83.
118.  *MT,* May 2, 1908, p. 1836.
119.  *MT,* May 30, 1908, pp. 2001, 2007.
120.  *MT,* July 18, 1908, p. 214.
121.  *MT,* May 29, 1909, p. 2120.
122.  *MT,* July 4, 1908, p. 13.
123.  *MT,* May 15, 1909, p. 2051.
124.  F. W. Hibbard to Deputy Minister of Justice, Nov. 3, 1908; *St. Jean Bank Liquidation File.*
125.  *MT,* June 20, 1908, pp. 2115, 2124.
126.  F. W. Hibbard to Deputy Minister of Justice, Nov. 27, 1908.
127.  F. W. Hibbard to Deputy Minister of Justice, May 18, 1909.
128.  *MT,* May 29, 1909, p. 2120.
129.  *MT,* May 15, 1909, p. 2051.
130.  F. W. Field, *Capital Investments in Canada,* p. 45.
131.  *JC,* June 26, 1908, p. 1175.
132.  See Report of the Registrar, Exchequer Court of Canada, vol. 12, no. 1, 1909; *Bank of St. Hyacinthe, Liquidation File.*
133.  *MT,* Aug. 8, 1878, p. 182.
134.  *JC,* July 18, 1879, p. 682.
135.  *MT,* Aug. 8, 1879, p. 182.
136.  *MT,* Nov. 7, 1879, p. 555.
137.  *HCD,* Feb. 7, 1884, pp. 155-6; March 5, 1885, p. 373ff.
138.  *MT,* Dec. 7, 1883, p. 629.
139.  *Exchange Bank Liquidation File;* Supreme Court of Canada, 1898, "The Queen . . . A. G. Canada versus Hon. A. W. Ogilvie."
140.  *MT,* Feb. 4, 1887, p. 892.
141.  *MT,* Dec. 10, 1886, p. 659; Dec. 31, 1886, p. 752.
142.  *MT,* Nov. 20, 1891, p. 602.
143.  *MT,* Aug. 26, 1887, p. 265.
144.  *MT,* Sept 30, 1887, p. 425; Dec. 2, 1887, p. 704; June 1, 1888, p. 1408; Aug. 24, 1888, p. 204.
145.  *MT,* Nov. 18, 1887, p. 640.
146.  *MT,* Dec. 16, 1887, p. 756.
147.  *MT,* June 29, 1888, pp. 1606-7.
148.  *MT,* Feb. 17, 1888, p. 1030.
149.  *MT,* Jan. 27, 1888, p. 937.
150.  *MT,* Aug. 11, 1893, p. 164.
151.  *MT,* June 7, 1889, pp. 1416-7.
152.  *MT,* July 4, 1884, p. 14; July 11, 1884, p. 36; Aug. 8, 1884, p. 152.
153.  *MT,* June 21, 1889, p. 1480.
154.  *MT,* Nov. 21, 1884, pp. 571-2.
155.  *MT,* Dec. 2, 1881, p. 665.
156.  *MT,* April 17, 1896, p. 1334.
157.  *MT,* Oct. 20, 1906, pp. 565-6.
158.  *MT,* Oct. 20, 1906, p. 567.
159.  *MT,* Oct. 20, 1906, pp.565.
160.  *MT,* Oct. 20, 1906, p. 604.
161.  *MT,* Jan. 5, 1907, p. 993; *Globe,* Jan. 1, 1907; Jan. 3, 1907.
162.  *MT,* Nov. 24, 1906, p. 742.

163. *MT,* Feb. 9, 1907, p. 1223.
164. *MT,* March 30, 1907, p. 1524.
165. *MT,* March 2, 1900, p. 1143.
166. Royal Commission . . . The Farmers' Bank of Canada *(RCFBC) Report* 1913, p.7.
167. *MT,* Dec. 14, 1910, p. 2615; Jan. 14, 1911, p. 210.
168. *RCFBC,* p. 7.
169. "Memo in the Matter of the Farmers' Bank," May 3, 1914, *Farmers' Bank Liquidation File.*
170. "Report of G. T. Clarkson, Liquidator and Curator of the Farmers' Bank," pp. 13-20, *Walker Papers.*
171. *MT,* Dec. 14, 1910, p. 2614.
172. *MT,* Dec. 7, 1910, p. 2524.
173. *RCFBC,* p. 5.
174. *Globe,* Jan. 14, 1911.
175. *CBC,* 1913, p. 620.
176. *MT,* Dec. 14, 1910, p. 2615.
177. *Canadian Annual Review, (CAR)* 1911, p. 315.
178. *CAR,* 1911, p. 272.
179. *CAR,* 1911, p. 313.
180. *MT,* Oct. 7, 1911, p. 1520.
181. See for example, "The Farmers' Bank of Canada: Subscribers' and Depositors' Brief," *Liquidation File.*
182. *MT,* Nov. 4, 1911, p. 1934.
183. *MT,* Nov. 11, 1911, p. 2037.
184. *MT,* Nov. 25, 1911, p. 2234.
185. *Globe,* Jan. 1, 1911; Jan. 17, Jan. 18, 1911.
186. *MT,* Jan. 21, 1911, p. 315.
187. *JC,* July 21, 1893, p. 120.
188. *MT,* July 27, 1888, p. 92.
189. *JC,* July 7, 1893, pp. 21-2.
190. *MT,* July 7, 1893, p. 12.
191. *JC,* Sept. 1, 1893, pp. 408-9.
192. *MT,* Aug. 25, 1893, p. 229.
193. "General Statement, Bank of Vancouver, Nov. 29, 1913," *Bank of Vancouver Liquidation File.*
194. E. Buchan Liquidator, to H. T. Ross, Assistant Deputy Minister of Finance, May 13, 1916.
195. General manager, Bank of Vancouver, to T. C. Boville, Deputy Minister of Finance, Feb. 11, 1914; *MT,* Jan. 16, 1914, p. 178.
196. President of the Canadian Bankers' Association to Deputy Minister of Finance, Feb. 14, 1914.
197. *MT,* Dec. 18, 1914, p. 18.

*There is hardly a little town in western Ontario which has not in the last few years been the victim of these so-called private banking enterprises; and many people who have been attracted to them by the higher rates of interest they have been offered have been losers to a very considerable degree. In the city of Toronto, I know of two cases, which are well authenticated of men having actually suicided because of losses they have suffered in these concerns.*

W. H. Bennett
House of Commons, 1898

# CHAPTER V
# The Rise and Fall of the Private Banking System

## Pre-Confederation Patterns

Of the four component parts of the English banking system, the London commercial banks and, to a limited extent, the Bank of England, had their counterparts in Canada; the private "merchant banks" like the Barings or Glyn, Mills did not. An institution that was, on the surface, analogous to the country bank seems to have flourished in Canada—the private bank. But on a deeper view, there were fundamental weaknesses in Canadian private banking compared to the English country bank.

Canadian private banks in general failed to exercise the independent industrial functions of an English country bank, largely because of the tight control over the Canadian financial apparatus held by the chartered banks. Under the law, the private banks were not even permitted to use the term "bank" after 1890. The main impediment was, however, in the note issue power. Unlike English country banks, Canadian private banks, except between 1850 and 1855, could not issue notes. Before 1837 they were stopped by the Colonial Office. In 1837 the Province of Upper Canada banned private note issue, a ban extended to the lower province under the Act of Union, and to each new province entering Confederation after 1871.[1] The lack of issue power was the single most important factor tying the Canadian private banks into the existing chartered bank structure and preventing them from becoming either full-fledged independent industrial or competitive commercial banks.

The exceptional period in the province of Canada came with the passage of the Free Banking Act by the Reform Party administration in 1850. Chartered banks in the province were all subordinate directly or indirectly to big produce dealers and financiers in the major commercial centres—and were largely Tory institutions. The Free Banking Act was copied directly from that of New York, which had emerged from the Bank of the United States struggles,[2] and the experiment was designed to foster competition on both economic and political levels. It drew fire from the Lords of the Treasury, but after the 1846 repeal of the Corn Laws and the granting of fiscal freedom and responsible government it was impossible for the British government to directly force the Canadian financial system back into line. Nor was it necessary to do so, for the Canadian financiers could be depended upon, in the final analysis, to remake themselves in the desired image.

Under the terms of the Free Banking Act, individuals in partnerships or joint stock companies could issue notes. Only unit banking was permitted. The minimum capital was set at £25,000. And as security for note redemption, provincial securities of not less than £25,000 (currency) par value were to be deposited with the Provincial Receiver General. Few banks were ever established under the Act, and of them the three survivors after its expiry, Molson's, Zimmerman's and the Bank of the Niagara District, were all chartered in 1855. Zimmerman's failed in 1857; the Niagara District was absorbed by another bank in 1875; only Molson's had a long independent existence. The results were disappointing to the architects of the policy. But the principal reason for its abandonment turned out to be surprisingly predictable — the free bank experiment scared off British capital. As Sir Francis Hincks, then Prime Minister, explained in the legislature,

> . . . no English capitalist was disposed to furnish money to Canada through the agency of private banks. But English capitalists would recognize the large chartered banks, because these banks had been known for many years as a safe means of investing capital. Capitalists had confidence in them, but they would not have confidence in private banks established under a new banking system.[3]

The need to attract foreign investment thus dictated a return to strict financial orthodoxy.

With Confederation, all chartered bank experiments ceased and the federal government replaced the Colonial Office as the regulator of colonial (provincial) banks. The subsequent bank acts were, to all intents and purposes, written by the very chartered banks who were supposed to be regulated by them. And one of the major objectives of financial legislation was to curb

the activities of the myriad private banking operations that intermittently sprang up across Canada.

# Operation of the Private Banks

The private banks exercised a variety of functions. A very few
did begin to behave like industrial banks, promoting industrial
capital formation in their respective localities. A few evolved into
chartered banks. But the overwhelming majority were simply
appendages of the orthodox commercial banking system. They
performed specialized brokerage and financial functions in the
major urban centres, or they acted as agents of the commercial
banks in small centres. In geographic terms, the private banks
that performed industrial functions were most prominent in the
Maritimes, apart from Halifax where their operations were
orthodox. There were also cases in small towns in Quebec and
Ontario. In Montreal, in most of Ontario, and in the prairies, the
private banks operated in strictly commercial and financial
modes. This geographic division of function corresponded
exactly to that of the chartered banks. Maritime banks, private
or chartered, and Quebec banks in small centres acted on principles diametrically opposed to those of the central Canadian and
Halifax commercial banks.

All of the private banks did a loan and deposit business, their
loans coming out of their own capital as well as deposits, and
from a line of credit most of them maintained with one or more
chartered banks. It was through the credit line that power was
exercised, and the private banks, denied the authority for independent bank note issue, functioned as circulating agents for the
notes of the particular bank with which they dealt. The chartered
bank thus extended a loan to the private bank; the private bank
would make loans to its customers out of its local deposits or out
of the funds loaned to it by the chartered bank; the borrowers
from the private bank would then give the private bank promissory notes and other paper as collateral, which paper the private
bank would deposit with the chartered bank as collateral for the
credit line. The claims of the chartered bank on the private were
preferred claims on its assets, and in effect, the depositors in the
private bank functioned as security for the chartered bank
advances. On the other hand, depositors in the private bank had
no security.[4]

The use of a private bank as an agent of the chartered was an
important feature of the Canadian banking system before the

great waves of chartered bank expansion occurred. It permitted the chartered bank to control the banking business in a small community without assuming the risks and without the expenses of maintaining a branch. Virtually all the prairie and rural Ontario private banks were set up in towns that initially were too small to support a chartered bank. The overhead costs of private banking tended to be lower than those of the chartered banks,[5] partly because private banks were often a part-time occupation of merchants. The private banks' profit rates were typically higher than a chartered bank's—on a much smaller volume of business. They had to be higher, for the private banks paid more for deposits, generally two per cent more than the prevailing cartel rate, and in the 1890's they paid six per cent minimum for advances from the chartered banks. At the same time, their business tended to be riskier.

Profits thus went to the chartered banks indirectly through the agency of the private bank, which functioned as a financial analogue of a licensed venture in industry. The proliferation of private banks, especially in Ontario in the 1880's, was due directly to the chartered banks' encouraging their growth, much as the wholesale dealers' patterns of competition at that time produced armies of commercial travellers and petty retailers. It was the note circulation function that was paramount. As prices fell secularly over the period 1873-1896, the chartered banks were forced into all manner of expediencies to try to keep their notes in circulation. Price deflation meant a diminution in the requirements for a circulating medium, and the response was for the chartered banks, on a competitive basis, to promote the growth of circulation agencies in the form of private banks, since the costs of banking in the smaller communities were too high to justify a branch. The typical small community could only support one small bank; then as business built up, or even in anticipation of expansion, the chartered banks moved in directly, displacing the private bank and taking over its business. The change in the relations of private and chartered banking reflected the shift in the chartered banks' liability structure towards the savings deposit business. The private banks, formerly complementary in the note issue business, became competitors for the community's savings. The result was a campaign of financial annihilation. Small banks were bought up, or destroyed by calling in their credit lines. While the private banks had operated in small urban or rural areas as agents of the chartered, it had meant a net inflow of funds into the locality. The chartered bank credit line and/or notes sent for circulation were a supplement to the local savings mobilized for local investment by the private banker. But once the savings deposits became the prime object of the chartered banks' attention, rather than their note issue, the flow ran in reverse. The chartered banks moved into the localities and drained savings out, especially from rural Ontario as the Canadian agricultural frontier shifted from Ontario to the West.

The little private banks for a while bulked large over-all in the Canadian banking structure. In 1881, when chartered bank branches totalled about 320, there were 174 private banks. In 1890, the chartered banks' branches had risen to 426 while the private banks had grown to only 179. The distribution had begun to change. Maritime private banks were declining and western growing. Private banks peaked about 1895, then began to decline absolutely as well as relatively as the chartered banks begun their rapid western expansion. In Ontario after 1895, when rising prices brought a revival of the note issue business of the chartered banks, the private banks declined rapidly in numbers. The savings business now justified the establishment of a branch, and the note issue power no longer needed the aid of the local private banks to maintain the circulation. The decline of private banking in the prairies came a little later as the prairie communities grew sufficiently to support chartered bank branches. By 1910, the private banks numbered only 97 while chartered banks branches totalled 2,363. Many of the rural Ontario and western private banks had branches as well. In the larger centres in the East, branch operation was absent: in these areas, the private banks functioned more as specialized financial institutions—as brokerage firms for example—rather than as commercial banks in the proper sense of the term.

The rise and fall of private banking reflected the needs of the chartered banking system, and the chartered banks' legislative power. The 1880 revision of the Bank Act began to limit the activities of the private banks, for under the legislation of that period they were required to state clearly on their advertising that they were not incorporated. Some private banks even began to desist from using the term "bank" after that revision,[7] though in fact there was as yet no legal requirement for them to do so. But the rule that their banks be clearly designated as unincorporated was enforced. In 1887, two private banks in Lachute were prosecuted for violating the Bank Act on these grounds.[8]

The next Bank Act revision did abolish the use of the word "bank" altogether.[9] By then the chartered banks were better prepared to undertake more of their business directly. By the early 1890's, the savings deposit business became the central concern of the chartered banks, and the private banks were competitors in the field — the more so since the hundreds of little banks could not be disciplined into establishing savings deposit rates in conformity with those set by the chartered banking cartel. The future of private banking appeared on the agenda for discussion at the second annual meeting of the Canadian Bankers' Association in 1893.[10] And by the time of the sixth annual meeting, the chartered banks were boasting of the efficacy of their spy network, which reported private banks to the Ministry of Finance for prosecution if they carried the word "bank" even on their letterhead.[11]

The heady expansionary years, especially after 1900, ushered in the major and final squeeze on the little bankers. As the chartered banks expanded into small urban centres or rural communities, the private banks were either absorbed directly, failed, or forced increasingly to undertake only the high-risk type of banking — which itself carried a greater chance of failure.[12] Then, too, the relative depopulation of rural Ontario during the rise of the wheat staple in the West reduced the field of operations of the private bankers, who were often very closely attuned to the needs and prosperity of the Ontario farm communities.[13]

To guard their position, the private bankers attempted to organize. Following the all-too-well-known example of their chartered brethren, the Canadian Private Bankers' Association was formed in 1902. Delegates met at Toronto and elected a slate of officers: a president, Thomas H. Cook of Sarnia and a series of provincial vice-presidents. The vice-presidents included several of the best known private bankers in Canada: J. Alloway of Winnipeg, J. C. McIntosh of Halifax, D. H. McDonald of Qu'Appelle.[14] But the difficulties of co-ordinating the hundreds of banks scattered across the country, frequently in the most out-of-the-way areas, were apparently insuperable, for the organization did not appear to get beyond the stage of its preliminary organization. Private banking died quickly. By 1914 only some 60 were left, and these included many of the abundant supply of stockbrokers in the major urban centres who did a client's deposit business on the side.

# Private Banks in the Maritimes

The decline of Maritime private banks is especially noteworthy, for those that survived were all Halifax or St. John banks and performed this type of brokerage function, while those that vanished were industrial banks, a pattern precisely the same as the fate of the chartered Maritime banks.

Maritime private bankers, like their chartered counterparts,

**TABLE V (1)**

**Private Banks, 1880-1914**

|                  | 1880* | 1881* | 1885 | 1890 | 1895 |
|------------------|-------|-------|------|------|------|
| Ontario          | 84    | 143   | 136  | 133  | 151  |
| Quebec           | 10    | 13    | 11   | 12   | 14   |
| Manitoba         | —     | 5     | 15   | 16   | 23   |
| Saskatchewan     | —     | —     | —    | 8    | 5    |
| Alberta          | —     | —     | —    |      |      |
| British Columbia | 1     | 1     | 1    | 3    | 3    |
| Nova Scotia      | 4     | 4     | 3    | 3    | 3    |
| New Brunswick    | 7     | 8     | 3    | 4    | 3    |
| Total            | 106   | 174   | 169  | 179  | 202  |

|                  | 1900 | 1905 | 1910 | 1914 |
|------------------|------|------|------|------|
| Ontario          | 146  | 77   | 51   | 31   |
| Quebec           | 12   | 15   | 13   | 4    |
| Manitoba         | 22   | 20   | 14   | 7    |
| Saskatchewan     | 14   | 17   | 15   | 12   |
| Alberta          |      | 1    | 1    | 2    |
| British Columbia | 2    | 1    | —    | —    |
| Nova Scotia      | 2    | 2    | 1    | 1    |
| New Brunswick    | 3    | 3    | 2    | 4    |
| Total            | 201  | 136  | 97   | 61   |

Source: Dun, Wiman and Co., *Mercantile Agency, Reference Book, Dominion of Canada,* quarterly.

*The growth from 1880 to 1881 is probably due simply to reclassification.

were active providers of "entrepreneurial" ability and capital for long-term investments. In Moncton, for example, the early 1880's saw a boom led by investments in a sugar refinery, cotton mills, gas, iron, and various textiles industries. It was financed chiefly by local capital raised in large measure through the efforts of the Moncton private banks, notably Josiah Wood, a shipper and private banker.[15] Wood's father had been involved in the traditional Moncton industry, shipbuilding. Wood was typical of these new Maritime entrepreneurs in that he put the funds accumulated in the old commercial pursuits to work in the new industries. Wood himself sat on the board of the Moncton Sugar Refinery, and invested in foundries and an enamel works. He was also a promoter of Eastern Trust, and acted as an agent of the Halifax Banking Company as well as operating the private bank.[16]

In Yarmouth a similar role was played by the Hon. L. Baker, again a shipper and private banker, who led the local community of shippers and West Indies merchants into a series of industrial ventures such as textiles, a steamship company, and even a hotel.[17] Baker later became president of the Bank of Yarmouth, into which he merged his private banking business. It is certainly true that traditional economic pursuits such as wooden ship-building were in decline in this period, and Yarmouth was a centre that would be hit especially hard by the loss of the industry. As one indicator, six local marine insurance firms failed in Yarmouth from 1881 to 1886, leaving a Boston firm in complete control of the remaining business.[18] But Maritime capitalists were vigorously making the transaction to a new industrial economy, unlike their central Canadian counterparts, and in this the work of the local banks was indispensable. Of this trend, Yarmouth and Moncton are both excellent examples. The explanation for Maritime decline clearly must be sought elsewhere than in "Acts of God" like the vagaries of world demand for wooden ships.

There were many examples of this kind of industrial private banking in the Atlantic provinces. In St. John, a private bank was instrumental in promoting a tobacco company in 1892.[19] In the same city, Thomas Maclellan merged his private banking business with the Maritime Bank, with its long record of industrial promotions, and as a result the private bank failed in the wake of the collapse of the chartered bank.[20] In Bridgewater, Nova Scotia, a local private banker collaborated with a Boston financier and local mining men to promote a local mining company in 1897.[21]

In the old commercial centre of Halifax, the private banks performed orthodox commercial and financial functions. One of the oldest private banks, and indeed one of the oldest banks of any kind in Canada, was the Halifax Banking Company, established in 1825 and not chartered until 1872. Its founder was Enos Collins, a pre-Revolutionary New England loyalist who earned his fortune in piracy. When he got too old to fight, he set up a business equipping and financing other privateers.[22] Like most of the Halifax mercantile community, his prosperity depended on a continued state of armed hostility. Peace brought depression, and in times of peace the cream of Halifax's commercial community would gather in a coffee house and denounce the government, calling for "loud war by land and sea."[23] In 1814 alone, Collins had a stake in no less than 18 captured prizes. His warehouse was soon full of goods garnered indifferently from piracy or the West Indies trade. The lack of banking facilities in Halifax at the time was of considerable inconvenience to the privateering community, who would wend their way to the private money

changers to exchange the broad assessment of coinage in which
they were rewarded for their economic service. Collins was
prominent among these money changers. His fortune, acquired
in such pursuits, was in quieter times turned to a private lending
business to merchants out of which, in conjunction with leading
merchants like Samuel Cunard, the founder of the Atlantic
steamship line, he evolved the bank.

Other Halifax private banks, active in the 1870's and later,
showed similar business preferences, restricting their activity to
orthodox exchange and financial functions. One of these, Almon
and Mackintosh, failed in 1878 under rather unusual circumstances. While funds had been locked up in real estate and in
shipping, it was not clear whose funds they were. In 1873, when
the firm commenced, they claimed a paid-up capital of $200,000
from Almon's father's bequest. In reality, they had only $30,000,
the rest being lost in speculation. However the losses were kept a
secret, and the public image remained one of solid business
foundation. The myth seemed to have attracted a great deal of
business and several small firms tottered and fell after Almon
and Mackintosh suspended.[24] Out of its ruins grew J. C. MacIn-
tosh and Co., a large investment and brokerage firm, which
spread successfully across the Maritimes and by 1911 had a
branch in Montreal and a seat on the Montreal Stock Exchange.
Its head office remained in Halifax, making it something of an
exception to the prevailing trend towards monetary centralization. It was, however, a perfect case of the Halifax private
banking norm.[25]

Normal in every way was another Halifax bank, James S.
Macdonald and Co., which was brought down in 1882 as a result
of its speculations in ranch lands during the Northwest land
boom. Its account at the Merchants' Bank of Halifax was badly
overdrawn, and the cashier of the private bank vanished, leaving
behind $10,700 in shortages.[26] Equally representative of the
financial and commercial orthodoxy of Halifax private banks
was Huse and Lowell, whose claim to fame — and fortune —
grew out of Greenback speculation during the American Civil
War.[27]

There were exceptions of course. The Halifax firm of Far-
quhar and Forest, bankers and brokers, while mainly involved in
urban real estate speculation, also tied up their funds in a tannery which helped precipitate their failure in 1895.[28] But, in general, the distinction between the Halifax private banks engaged
in currency speculation, real estate deals, commerce, or the
export of funds to other parts of Canada on the one hand, and
the Yarmouth, Moncton, St. John, and other industrial banks on
the other, is very pronounced.

# Private Banks in Quebec

Quebec's pattern of private banking was somewhat unusual. On the one hand, chartered banks were widely distrusted in the rural and small town areas as instruments of anglophone domination and as a means by which the savings of the poor were put at the disposal of the enterprises of the rich — the Montreal commercial community. Moreover, as a result of the high degree of development of Montreal financial institutions, there was less need for private banks performing specialized financial functions in that city. Montreal certainly had an abundance of brokers, but they were relatively less involved in private banking than their Toronto and Halifax counterparts.[29] The great bulk of Quebec private banks were in the small towns.

But the private bank never assumed the importance that these factors would suggest possible in Quebec. Most of them were anglophone, and the obvious alternative, the government savings banks, while suitable outlets for working-class savings, failed to provide either agricultural credit or local control. Hence a unique form of institution — La Caisse Populaire — evolved. The idea of the Caisse Populaire was actualized by Alphonse Desjardins, a leading Liberal and former president of La Banque Jacques Cartier. Desjardins evolved the notion of a co-operative savings bank from European precedents but adapted it to the peculiar socio-economic problems he saw in the Quebec of his day. Reflecting his distaste for the money-lords of the Canadian banking system whom he blamed for wrecking La Banque Jacques Cartier, the Caisse Populaire was premised strictly on local control by its depositors. It was designed, too, to fight against the drain of funds out of farm and small urban communities in Quebec to the major uban centres. All the local workers' and farmers' savings were to be used locally for a number of purposes, above all for farm credit and the general class of small borrower. Desjardins was a populist and a nationalist, and he saw in the notion of a co-operatively and locally controlled savings bank at once an instrument for the economic resurgence of French Canada and a means of offsetting the stifling paternalism of a powerful state structure in the hands of railway promoters and financial manipulators. It would also free the "little man" from the usurious grasp and shameful financial exploitation exercised by the banks over workers in the urban centres.[30] Speculation was explicitly prohibited. The charter of the first Caisse Populaire, that established at Lévis in 1900, had a clause that stipulated, "La Société s'interdit formellement et jamais toute spéculation de bourse ou opération aléatoire quelconque."[31] The movement spread quickly, and by 1914 there were 122 such co-operative banks in Quebec, nineteen in Ontario, and the beginning of a substantial spill-over into the Québécois-populated areas of New England.[32]

In industrial banking a few cases could be mentioned, of which Charles Arpin, the boot and shoe magnate, is outstanding. His St. Jean private bank formed the base not only of the large-scale boot and shoe factory which actively exported to other provinces, but helped support his involvement in numerous other enterprises—a mortgage loan company, grain dealing, railway promotion, an enamel ware factory, and a major navigation company. A similar instance was that of Andrew Somerville, the country registrar in Huntingdon, Quebec, who used his private bank to promote a series of manufactures, in addition to establishing a private trust company business.[33] The collapse of a local organ factory which was put into assignment on the demand of the Eastern Townships' Bank led to Somerville's bank's failure. And this quickly precipitated the collapse of the largest foundry and agricultural implements manufacturing firm in the area.[34]

Various other types of private banks existed in Quebec—some largely in mortgage lending,[35] some in brokerage,[36] others the outgrowth of different types of mercantile activity.[37] However, they were few over-all, and the importance to the evolution of the Quebec economy was marginal.[38] Nonetheless in Quebec, albeit on a very limited scale, the Maritime pattern seems to come out—some instances of industrial banking in small centres, while in the larger centres the private banks performed more orthodox financial and commercial functions.

## Private Banks in Ontario

Several types of private banks existed in Ontario, performing several different functions: some complementary to, some competitive with, and some completely independent of the chartered banks.

One type was the specialist financial broker in large urban centres. Edmund Walker, for example, entered the Canadian financial scene with his uncle's private banking firm and bureau de change. He made his name and greatly improved his uncle's financial position on the day the Bank of Upper Canada failed by speculating in its notes.[39] In 1867, he joined a Hamilton private bank dealing in foreign exchange, bank notes, specie, U.S. government securities, "and all kinds of incurrent money"[40] activities which, with the possible exception of foreign exchange dealings, were non-competitive with the commercial banks. In 1868, Walker joined the Hamilton branch of the Bank of Commerce.

Other notables in Canadian finance started similarly in Ontario private banks and from there launched careers in chartered banks. Henry Taylor, the Bank of London's president, bought his discharge from the British Army in 1863 and went into private banking, from that base becoming involved in a series of financial operations, especially banking, mortgage loan companies, and insurance. [41] Gabriel T. Somers, private banker at Beeton and Cookstown, sold his bank to the Traders Bank, of which he became a director. He also became president of the Ontario Securities Corporation and a promoter of Continental Life Assurance,[42] and in those capacities rose to become a kingpin in the Toronto Liberal Party establishment.

The relationship between chartered and private banks sometimes ran in reverse, especially, though not always, in the wake of chartered bank failures. The former local managers of the Central, Federal, Consolidated, and other banks established their own private banks after the failures, for example, in Norwood, Lucknow, Dresden, and Seaforth.[43] A former manager of the Bank of Commerce established a private bank at Niagara-on-the-Lake, while that at Teeswater was the creation of a former Trader's Bank branch manager.[44]

The function of banker and broker were often inextricably interlocked. The brokerage firm, Gzowski and Buchan, also did a banking business. Among their principal activities was the fraudulent manipulation of Federal Bank stock in collaboration with William Mara and Co., Cox and Worts, and Forbes and Lownsborough, the last of which, as both brokerage firm and private banker, failed as a result of the Federal crash in 1884.

The Federal case was not the only Ontario example of the close link between private bank cum broker and chartered bank. When Brown's Bank (W. R. Brown and Co.) failed in Toronto in 1869, the Royal Canadian Bank and the City Bank were its largest creditors, and the only creditors in fact to come out of the wreck unscathed. Brown's Bank had a tangled history. In 1864, a publishing firm's owner gave the City Bank a $50,000 guarantee of Brown's indebtedness. He then sold out his holdings in the publishing firm, transferred all of his fixed property to his wife, and joined Brown's firm. It was announced that up to $20,000 of new capital had thereby been brought into the bank; in fact, nothing was. But the already insolvent bank's reputation for stability was enhanced, and more deposits were attracted. Funds were then poured into gold speculations in New York on which heavy losses were incurred, followed by losses on American railroad stocks. Apart from the two banks, whose claims were preferred, the estate yielded about five cents on the dollar to the unfortunate creditors and depositors.[45]

Brown's Bank was of course a phenomenon of a major urban centre. It was also a bank of considerable size involved in a fair range of commercial banking pursuits. As the chartered banks grew and increasingly dominated business in the urban centres, and subsequently of course the rural ones as well, the private banks' range of activities became more limited. An example of the shift of activities among the urban private banks is the case of Hamilton's Stinson's Bank, established in 1847 and operating for a long time with a credit line from the Merchants' Bank of Canada.[46] It shifted its activities increasingly into American real estate and out of Hamilton commercial banking. When its owner assigned in 1900, he had over $800,000 in debts. Hamilton deposit money had been poured into Illinois real estate. His holdings of fourteen quarter-sections in the city of Superior alone were valued at six million dollars, but his claim was endangered by the U.S. government's contention that he had used fraud in obtaining the pre-emption rights. While Stinson won the litigation, the Canadian depositors lost their money, and made vain efforts to have him extradited back to Canada to face charges.[47]

The great majority of Ontario's private banks operated in small towns and villages in agricultural areas and performed an essential role in servicing Ontario agriculture, by the provision of deposit facilities for farmers, by making mortgage loans and long-term advances, and by promoting agricultural implement and other farm-oriented industries. Apart from the deposit function, the chartered banks did not undertake these operations once the private banks had been eliminated, and the deposit business the chartered banks took over often meant a drain of funds from the community to the major urban centres or to the prairies.

Some of the private banks became a bit over-eager to perform full banking functions, including the forbidden note issue. A private bank in Bothwell, established by two American farmers with a credit line from the Federal Bank, ran short of funds in 1885 and began counterfeiting. The owners then absconded back to their Dakota farm in a fashion strikingly similar to that pioneered by a good many chartered bank directors of the period. The Federal Bank's account was secured of course, and the burden of the failure fell on the depositors.[48]

The origins of the private banks in the small centres were diverse. As noted, they included several cases of former local managers of chartered bank branches establishing private banks. But much more common were private banks growing out of strictly local business concerns, especially various forms of mercantile activity. Drygoods merchants in several cases established banking firms, as did lumber dealers.[49] Insurance agents sometimes operated the local bank, as did those in Barrie and Tiverton who closed up and absconded in 1883 and 1897 respectively.[50] A number of doctors, lawyers, magistrates, and even postmasters had banking operations.[51] But general stores were among the most common origins of the private banks in Ontario.[52] There were many reasons for this development. The chartered banks' longstanding indifference to farmers' and artisans' savings deposits created a void into which the merchant-banker could logically fit. Moreover, a farmer depositing with a local merchant with whom he had longstanding trade during seasons or times when he had surplus cash, for example, just after marketing the harvest, would be a logical corollary of the merchant providing him with a credit line during times of shortage.[53]

The links between private banking and farm or farm-related economic activities were numerous, and often very close. In some cases the relationship to the farmers did not go beyond the bank backing flour and feed stores.[54] Sometimes it was a grain dealer himself who ran the bank.[55] But frequently the links went much deeper, for instance in the case of private banks deeply involved in mortgage lending and in the promotion and support of food processing, agricultural implement manufacture, and other types of small, local, farm-oriented industries. The Glencoe Agricultural Manufacturing Co. had two private bankers on its board of directors in 1882.[56] In 1883, a private banker joined the directorate of the North American Agricultural Implement and General Manufacturing Co., a large merger of London area firms.[57] From its inception in 1879, the Agricultural Implement Manufacturers' Association of Ontario had J. A. Mahon, a London private banker, on its executive committee.[58] The Mahon Banking Co. collapsed with the end of the Winnipeg land boom, into which it had poured a large part of its assets following the refusal of the Bank of Montreal to extend its credit line. Depositors lost $40,000, and many local firms who had been carried by the big bank were badly squeezed. The failure revealed a large overdraught by the cashier plus some bogus cheques, the funds being used for speculating on his own account.[59]

There were many other cases of private bankers in the implement industry. The Chatham postmaster, Samuel Barfoot of Barfoot's Bank, was also a director of the Chatham (Ontario) Manufacturing Co., which made wagons. W. W. Farran, of the
banking firm Farran and Tisdale, was a partner in Farran, Macpherson and Hovey, the oldest thresher manufacturers in
Canada.[61] And the failure of the bankers South and Co. at Pekin
in 1906 was due to its advances to a local wagon works and
plough shop.

The bankers also made a contribution in other facets of farm-
based business. Some were involved with cattle raising or
dealing.[63] One firm of private bankers promoted a grain and
milling business at Burlington.[64] The Brantford Packing Co.,
established to process both meats and vegetables in 1899, was the
creation of a local farmer along with Lloyd Harris, the implement magnate, who collaborated in the private bank Harris,
Cook and Co.[65]

Several private banks failed because they had overextended
credit to farmers in their area. This problem became especially
acute in 1895, when poor crops and low prices led to the inability
of the private banks to realize on the farmers' notes. Donald
Fraser, a longstanding private banker in Kingston and a former
local manager of the Merchants' Bank, was one of the casualties.
As usual, the chartered bank credit line was secured by customers' paper and other assets, while the deposits were unsecured and left to bear the brunt of failure.[66]

Samuel Barfoot quickly followed the Fraser failure for the
same cause. Barfoot had offered a savings rate higher than the
cartel rate and attracted a lot of deposits away from the chartered banks: this was undoubtedly a factor in their refusal to
extend him further aid. Of his assets, over half were locked up in
real estate mortgages. Of his deposit liabilities, nearly $100,000
were in savings deposits while only $25,000 were in current
account. Barfoot's Bank was sound; the only reason for failure
was the hostility of the chartered banks. The depositors were
completely paid off with three per cent interest.[67]

In real estate speculation and mortgage lending, the record of
the private banks was considerably less praiseworthy. Mortgage
lending to farmers did bring down some banks.[68] But the banks
also had a penchant for urban real estate speculation,[69] and
above all for the lands of the Northwest Territories where speculation during the Winnipeg land boom left an enormous trail of
broken banks, including an insurance broker in Lindsay and a
firm of Ingersoll lawyers.[70] Not only land, but timber and railways in the area drew the bank's attention and precipitated collapse. One Bowmanville banker locked up all his deposits in a

Manitoba railway scheme, went to England to get backing for it, and on being unsuccessful, cabled his associates that the visit had failed. Rumours then flew around Bowmanville that the bank had failed, a depositors' run started, and the bank suspended.[71] But of all the banks to fail in the wake of the Northwest land rush, the Fawcett system was the most spectacular.

No better summary of the essential attributes of Ontario private banking can perhaps be found than an examination of the operation and collapse of the Fawcett empire. W. F. Fawcett's private banking system was the largest in Canadian history. It involved both direct branches and a complex of interlocking partnerships spread throughout southwestern Ontario.[72] When failure hit Fawcett in London in 1884, a total of ten private banks suspended with him with aggregate liabilities that were estimated to run close to a million dollars.[73]

Direct branches under Fawcett's control existed, apart from the London headquarters, at Watford, Arkona, and Alvinston. In addition, with one Charles Livingston, who had joined the Watford branch in 1876, there evolved a partnership, Fawcett, Livingston and Co., with branches at Dresden, Thomasville, and Wardsville. The former manager of Fawcett's Arkona branch opened a bank in New Hamburg with Fawcett as a sleeping partner in 1880. In 1881 a Strathroy group joined Fawcett to establish the Oxford Banking Company at Woodstock. Fawcett was also a partner in W. O. Smith's Bank at Thornbury, in the Mitchell Banking Co., the Dresden Banking Co., and the Millbrook Banking Co. On top of this, Fawcett was a director of the Bank of London, of another chartered bank project which never got off the ground, the London Trust and Stock Co., and the North West Railway.[74]

**TABLE V (2)**

**The Fawcett Bank, 1884**

| Liabilities | | Assets | |
|---|---|---|---|
| deposits | $196,280 | bills receivable & mortgages | $ 37,002 |
| other | 20,000 | current account due | 3,725 |
| | | real estate — Watford | 20,000 |
| Total | $216,280 | real estate — Northwest | 20,000 |
| | | office furniture, etc. | 3,500 |
| | | timber limits — Northwest | 200,000 |
| | | cash on hand | 3,000 |
| | | Total | $287,227 |

When suspension came late in 1884, Fawcett blamed a depression in the cattle trade, claiming that many dealers to whom he had made advances were unable to realize at cost covering prices. He also claimed the first failure of the Federal Bank had cost him a lot. It was not a very credible explanation, especially once the assignees began to examine the books of the banking system. For the five branches directly controlled by Fawcett, nearly 80% of the assets were represented by timber limits or land in the Northwest, the real value of which was very uncertain in the wake of the collapse of the land boom.[75] On his more legitimate business over a decade or more before failure, Fawcett had lost $145,297.

The remaining banks in the empire, for the most part, registered failure shortly after Fawcett himself—W. O. Smith and Charles Livingston almost immediately.[76] Another independent banker at Watford faced a depositors' run after the Fawcett debacle and wound up without losses, while Fawcett's brother, who had a large sash and door factory and was dependent on the bank's advances, also failed.[77] Livingston retired to the post of editing a newspaper in Honolulu[78] while some of the branches of the Fawcett system passed into other hands. The Wardsville branch fell into the hands of two brothers who used all its funds for bucket shop speculations, and then absconded in 1887.[79] The Watford branch, where the expansion of the empire began with Livingston's arrival in 1876, passed to a new private banking firm, who sold out to the Merchants' Bank in 1899.[80]

On balance, the private banks of Ontario clearly played a central role in the agricultural prosperity of the province in the late nineteenth century when Ontario was still the Canadian agricultural frontier. There were always a few cases where the farm communities undoubtedly rued the presence of the banks. To take but one case, the Guelph Banking Company offered six per cent interest on savings deposits, attracted farmers' deposits from a large area, and put the proceeds to work in bucket shops under the auspices of E. S. Cox. When the bank failed, Cox could add the first private bank to his already impressive total of destroyed chartered ones.[81] But the general record of their operations is very favourable.

In addition to agriculture-based activities, which absorbed the great bulk of their assets, certain private banks contributed substantially to the establishment of small-scale local industries in some of the smaller centres. The bank of C. W. Anderson, reputedly Canada's most complete private banking operation,[82] in Oakville and Palmerston, was a case in point. Among other factors precipitating his demise was the bank's involvement of its funds in the local electric light system, a creamery, a mill, and a hay dealing business as well as real estate speculation. The Bank of Hamilton, which extended the credit line, seized everything: the creditors and depositors received nothing.[83] Similarly in 1883 the New Hamburg bank, Denison and Crease, was forced to fail by the chartered bank which held the private bank's paper, and it pulled two woollen factories down with it, in addition to a battery of local traders.[84] Waterford's local private bank, L. Becker and Co., locked up its capital in a local electrical company, the promoter of which was a partner in the bank. The electrical company failed shortly after the bank suspended in 1894.[85]

A complex of private banks in the Formosa-Mildmay area promoted a number of local industries. When Formosa's largest bank, F. X. Messner and Co., failed, it precipitated a run on several of the area's other private banks. Messner was a merchant and a brewer as well as a banker and the chief magistrate of Formosa. He paid six per cent on savings deposits at a time when the chartered banks paid but three, and collected most of the local savings.[86]

Following his failure the Mildmay bank, Carrick Financial Co., went into liquidation when a writ was issued against it by its parent, the Bank of Commerce. Its balance sheet looked very orthodox on the surface. Its liabilities were about $39,000 in deposits and $25,000 in a Bank of Commerce credit line. Its assets were $57,500 in bills, $3,360 in mortgages, and $3,500 in overdue debts. The real meaning of the bills became clear only after the bank failed. One partner had carried on a mill on the side, another a foundry: both firms depended on the bank and both closed upon its failure. The Carrick failure managed to bring down a Walkerton hotel as well.[87] Most of the assets went to the preferred claims of the chartered banks or to legal costs and commissions; the depositors and other unsecured creditors got only 28 per cent of their claims.[88]

One other outstanding case of industrial promotion by Ontario private bankers is worth mentioning, namely that of the Rathbun Company of Deseronto, founded by an American émigré, E. W. Rathbun, who pioneered a long list of industrial innovations in Canada. He was the first to install a roller flour mill, and one of the first to manufacture pre-fabricated housing, wood alcohol, and cement.[89] By as early as 1882, the firm of Rathbun and Son employed 900 men and had achieved a very powerful place in the Ontario lumber business through a series of major railway contracts. The company soon expanded and diversified into everything from shipping, wood products, freight cars, cement, shingles, building supplies, and even matches in competition with the Ottawa Valley lumber baron E. B. Eddy. Electric tramway promotions, flour milling, and finally primary iron and steel attracted the resources of the Rathbuns, who were among the very few examples of local businessmen becoming major tycoons on a national scale in Canada in competition with the established commercial and financial giants of the big cities.[90]

# Private Banks in the West

Private banking in Manitoba was pioneered by W. Alloway and H. Champion, two former militiamen with the Wolsely expedition sent out in 1871 to suppress the Métis unrest. Beginning in freight and moving into real estate loans, they became heavily involved in dealing in Métis land scrip.[91] The Métis land scrip system was an open invitation to fraud,[92] and the ultimate benefit accrued to a handful of land speculators and Hudson's Bay Company officials, who bought it on terms that made the Manhattan Island purchase look like a monument of philanthropy, and sold it to incoming settlers during the western boom. Alloway and Champion did not deal directly in land, but only in scrip, later moving into tax certificates and foreign exchange dealings for immigrants. They also pioneered the small loan business in Winnipeg at a time when the chartered banks were not interested in it.

The Winnipeg land boom ushered in a real growth of private bankers in the province. Even Alloway and Champion do not seem to have regarded banking as serious business until after the boom was underway. In 1881, immigration into Canada was 47,-991; in 1882 it was 112,458; in 1882 alone 70,500 people migrated to the Northwest, generating a real estate boom. One bank estimated that over eight million dollars moved to Winnipeg that year for investment in land.[93] Among the investors were several private banks who failed as a result of their speculation. In addition to the Macdonald Company of Halifax, there was a great wave of Ontario failures as a result of northwest land dealings. And the speculative mania claimed its share of Manitoba banks as well. One Winnipeg private bank with a branch at Portage la Prairie got into trouble over its real estate deals and assigned in 1883 on demand of several chartered banks.[94] Private banks were reported as nonexistent in the West in 1880; by 1883 there were 21 operating, falling to 15 in the liquidation that followed the boom. Even after the boom, land speculation figured as a cause of Manitoba bank failures.[95]

One of the earliest Manitoba private banks, after Alloway and Champion, was that established by Duncan MacArthur, who later promoted the chartered Commercial Bank of Manitoba.

The private bank, MacArthur, Boyle and Campbell, had a rapid growth, for its promoters were well connected with eastern Canadian and British capital. W. Lewis Boyle, for example, acted in 1886 as the collection agent for English debenture holders when certain Manitoba towns were in default on their interest.⁹⁶ But it was MacArthur who was the key factor in the partnership. MacArthur commenced his banking career as the Winnipeg manager of the Merchants' Bank of Canada, which continued to back his private bank and even stood behind the promotion of the Commercial Bank of Manitoba in 1886. So close were the relations of MacArthur to the Allans of Montreal who controlled the Merchants' Bank that in 1885 a member of the Allan family, a cousin of Sir Hugh's, joined MacArthur's private bank as a partner: it thereupon became MacArthur, Boyle and Allan until 1887 when the Allans broke off relations and established a new Winnipeg brokerage firm, Allan, Brydges and Co., in partnership with C. J. Brydges, one-time general manager of the Grand Trunk Railway.⁹⁷ The rupture between the former partners probably resulted from MacArthur's involvement in Manitoba efforts to break the CPR monopoly by establishing competing lines to American roads and via them to the Grand Trunk.⁹⁸

In any event, it is clear that MacArthur's local sympathies grew over time. He was a prominent figure in numerous operations in Winnipeg, taking the lead in mustering local capital for express and telegraph companies, mines (in conjunction with American investors), and local manufacturing. As well, his private bank was strong enough in 1886 to act as the underwriter for the bonds of the Saskatchewan and Western Railway. ⁹⁹ That year the private bank evolved into the Commercial Bank of Manitoba. After the failure of the chartered bank in 1893, MacArthur returned to private banking, in which he was still active as late as 1914. So too, following Ontario precedents, did at least one of his branch managers.¹⁰⁰

Other Manitoba private banks followed the MacArthur pattern of representing an alliance of a Manitoba entrepreneur (usually an Ontario émigré) with the facilities and connections of a central Canadian private banking and/or brokerage firm. Osler and Hammond of Toronto extended into Winnipeg in 1884 with a local partner to form Osler, Hammond and Nanton, a firm still active in 1914 in private banking and brokerage. Montreal banker and broker R. S. Ewing did likewise in 1900 with Simpson, Mitchell and Ewing, a firm which extended into a number of financial operations, trust, loan as well as general brokerage.¹⁰¹

Private banking did not reach Saskatchewan and Alberta until after 1885, and its growth was never as strong as in Manitoba. For in Manitoba banks were established and got on a sound footing well in advance of the main rush of settlement, while in the other two provinces the beginning of the great expansion in 1896 led to such a rapid inflow of chartered banks that there was little space or time for the evolution of a system of private banks. In 1890 the entire Northwest had only four chartered bank branches. By 1914 Saskatchewan alone had 280.

Some of the private banks in the Northwest evolved a branch system, and they tended to spread through the same sort of web of partnerships that characterized Ontario developments. For example, one of the earliest, Lafferty and Smith at Calgary, split up in 1889.[102] In its place came two firms. F.G. Smith, at Calgary, T.N. Christie at Moosomin, and H. Lejeune at Regina formed a new bank, Lejeune, Smith and Co., with branches in all three towns. The other new firm, Lafferty and Moore, established itself in Calgary, Regina, Edmonton, Lethbridge and Moosomin.[103] Several other branches were opened, including one at Vancouver. These branches of both firms were often organized as partnerships between the main firm and a local businessman. The Lejeune, Smith and Co. Regina branch was organized as a partnership between Lejeune and Christie, of the main firm, and a Regina businessman. Their Calgary branch was a partnership of Christie and a merchant of that town.[104]

Prairie private banking bore a striking similarity to that in Ontario. The origins of most of the banks seem to have been mercantile, and very often they were the creation of Ontario émigrés who formed the core of the entrepreneurial class in the Northwest. As in Ontario, a few got into mortgages; some had very close financial connections abroad, permitting them to transact international business in bank drafts; others specialised in emigrants' remittances and the like.[105] The system of branch banking also resembled Ontario's, with the branch network peaking around 1900, a little later than that in Ontario. Thereafter, the chartered bank expansion tended to nibble away at them, branch by branch. While takeovers occurred from an early date — the Merchants' Bank branch at Brandon (1883) was the result of the takeover of a branch of a Manitoba private bank, and the Union Bank's agent displaced Lafferty and Moore in Moosomin in 1890[106] — it was in the later period that the great rush of takeovers occurred.[107]

After MacArthur's bank, a second western private bank that eventually evolved into a chartered bank was the Weyburn Security Bank, founded in 1902 by six Americans who had purchased a large block of Saskatchewan land and begun to do a lumbering business. The bank evolved out of the lumbering enterprise, which was inconvenienced by the lack of banking facilities.[108] It established its first branch in Weyburn, later taking over the facilities and part of the name of the Weyburn Security Company. The bank's business was mainly farmers' loans, on which it charged from eight to ten per cent at a time when the legal maximum was six: however, that still made its loan rate a lot less usurious than that of the chartered bank branches of the period. It grew quickly, and by 1913 it had ten branches. The bank was a boon to local businessmen, who asserted that during the crisis of 1907 the little bank had done more to keep them afloat with its accommodation than had all the four chartered banks with whom it co-existed in Weyburn, including the Commerce and the Montreal.[109]

Gold brought banks into British Columbia in the wake of the rush of prospectors. The first of these was Macdonald's Bank,[110] established in 1859 as a private bank of deposit — and issue, for before Confederation with Canada there was no colonial office prohibition on private note issue in B.C. Several other private bankers followed Macdonald, including two agencies of Wells, Fargo that evolved into independent banks.[111] All of these institutions were essentially extensions of San Francisco gold merchants. In addition, Lafferty and Moore established a branch in Vancouver which lasted only about a year. And the American brokerage firm of John Burke of Tacoma established a branch, J. M. Burke and Co., in Vancouver in addition to its branches throughout Washington and Idaho. The B.C. branch failed in 1893.[112]

Chartered banks began operating in B.C. from an early date. The first were the Imperial Banks, the Bank of British North America, and the Bank of British Columbia. The Bank of British Columbia was chartered in 1858, with a set of directors headed by Eden Colvile of the Hudson's Bay Company, and several directors of other big colonial banks.[113] The Hudson's Bay Company was deeply involved in transportation and commodity trade during the gold rush, and this bank was a logical extension. The colonists themselves tried to float the Colonial Bank of British Columbia but without success. The imperial bank began operating shortly after Macdonald's Bank, and was joined in 1862 by the Bank of British North America. For a while Macdonald had been prosperous, his activities mainly revolved about moving gold to San Francisco, the sale of bills of exchange, and making advances on gold dust. But the new banks pushed him hard. He failed in 1864 and absconded to the U.S. with his creditors in hot pursuit.

After the Macdonald failure the field was left to the two Imperial banks and Garesche, Green and Co., a private bank that evolved out of the Wells, Fargo agencies. Then in 1885 Lord Strathcona drove the last nail in the coffin of the prospects of B.C. private banking, for with the completion of the CPR the eastern chartered banks, led by Strathcona's Bank of Montreal, poured into B.C.

In 1892, Mrs. T.T. Green, widow of the late A.A. Green, partner in the private banking firm, bought out the Garesche estate and became sole owner of the bank, later admitting F.H. Warlock as a partner.[114] The new firm, Green, Warlock and Co. continued to function as the Wells, Fargo agent and conduct a private banking business without issue power for a year. Then in 1893 an American panic led to a drain of gold from New York to London. So tied into the vagaries of world bullion movement was the B.C. private bank that it faced a run, suspended, and failed. Its total liabilities were over $500,000, of which about 70 per cent were deposits.[115]

Settlement of the estate dragged on for years. The chief beneficiaries of the failure, apart from the chartered banks, appear to have been the trustees. These ran up handsome salaries, while after six years the depositors had still not been fully compensated and the owners had not received anything. The trustees were asked to quit, but announced they were "not disposed to do so."[116]

A few minor private banks carried on in B.C. after the Green, Warlock failure, but not on the same magnitude. It was the end of an era in the province's financial history. The last of B.C.'s little private banks passed away in 1907.

# The Record of the Private Banks

The private banks performed a number of functions in the Canadian capital market, generally as an arm of the commercial banking system. They provided commercial bank facilities in small centres which could not support a full-fledged chartered bank branch, but they did not offset the gap left by the chartered banks' aversion to financing industrial capital formation. Only in the Maritimes did private banks perform an important industrial entrepreneurial role in any numbers, and in this respect they parallelled the Maritime chartered banks' behaviour. Only in the Maritimes, and in a very scattered few instances in Ontario and Quebec, did the private banks seem to approximate the English

country bank in their activities. And even then they were constrained by their lack of issue power, which doomed all private
banks to functioning, in part at least, as circulation agents of the
chartered banks who extended them a credit line. In Ontario, the
banks were often very close to the farm community, fulfilling
many banking functions and promoting agribusiness in ways
that the chartered banks who displaced them did not. On the
prairies, with a couple of very notable exceptions, they appear to
have behaved largely as appendages of eastern chartered banks.
In B.C., like the chartered banks, they were involved predomi-
nantly with gold and other kindred financial operations. It can
certainly be claimed that the private banks displayed a greater
innovative and entrepreneurial capacity than the chartered
banks, but their over-all contribution to industrial growth was
badly hampered by the degree of domination the established
banks could exercise.

The private banks were criticized for their instability. In 1898
W. H. Bennett denounced them in the House of Commons as
weak institutions that led to great losses by their unfortunate
depositors.[117] In fact, the charge makes little sense. There were
two great waves of private bank failures. In 1883 and 1884, with
a spillover into 1885, large numbers of failures occurred, the
result of the bursting of the National Policy boom and the collapse of land values in Manitoba. Again, the period 1893 to 1899
brought a second wave of failures whose reasons were more
complex: several B.C. failures depended on conditions in the
gold market; in Ontario the state of grain prices or certain small,
local industries were the major factors. In many cases, too, failures were precipitated by chartered banks who wanted the little
banks out of the way.

**TABLE V (3)**

**Private Bank Failures, 1894-1913**

| Year | Number | Year | Number | Year | Number |
|------|--------|------|--------|------|--------|
| 1894 | 6 | 1901 | 1 | 1908 | 0 |
| 1895 | 6 | 1902 | 6 | 1909 | 0 |
| 1896 | 3 | 1903 | 6 | 1910 | 0 |
| 1897 | 5 | 1904 | 2 | 1911 | 1 |
| 1898 | 5 | 1905 | 4 | 1912 | 0 |
| 1899 | 2 | 1906 | 0 | 1913 | 0 |
| 1900 | 6 | 1907 | 0 | total | 53 |

Source: Calculated from data in *Dun's Review*, 1895-1914.

Even taking the failure data at face-value, the failure rate does
not seem very high. According to privately published figures of

Dun, Wiman — which may not be entirely reliable, but in the absence of federal insolvency legislation were the best collected — in 1895, six failed out of a total of 202; in 1900, six of 199; in 1905, four of 135. Over the period 1894 to 1913, 53 failed. Yet several hundred were likely to have been operating during that period, many wound up without losses, and many were taken over by chartered banks.

The failure data of course includes the many brokers who did a banking business on the side, and who were tightly interlinked with chartered banks. When chartered banks failed, private banks in the major cities would thus fail automatically, and this biases the comparative failure records against the private and in favour of the chartered banks. And the fact that private bank failure was frequently at the whim of the chartered bank also stacks the cards against them. Even ignoring all these factors, and taking as the total of private banks operating the 1895 total of 202 — a procedure which again overstates the instability of the private banks since with sales and voluntary liquidations there were many more than 202 operating over the 1894-1913 period — the private bank failure rate is about 20 per cent. It is thus better than the chartered bank record, even with all the biases. The propaganda about the instability of small, local banks, which was so much a part of the program of self-edification launched by the big chartered banks of the period, fails on these grounds too.

# Notes to Chapter V

1.     E. P. Neufeld, *The Financial System of Canada,* p. 165; *MT,* July 31, 1891, p. 135.
2.     B. Hammond, *Banks and Politics in America,* pp. 572-3.
3.     Cited in R. M. Breckenridge, "Free Banking in Canada."
4.     *MT,* Jan. 29, 1886, p. 859.
5.     *MT,* March 9, 1883, pp. 1003-4.
6.     M. Morris, "The Land Mortgage Companies . . .," p. 264.
7.     *MT,* Oct. 12, 1883, p. 406.
8.     *MT,* Aug. 19, 1887, p. 235.
9.     *MT,* July 31, 1891, p. 130.
10.    *MT,* May 26, 1893, p. 1404.
11.    Canadian Bankers' Association, "Sixth Annual Meeting, Minutes," *JCBA,* vol. V, no. 2.
12.    *Farming World,* Aug. 15, 1905, p. 607; *MT,* March 13, 1903, p. 204.
13.    *CBC,* 1913, p. 182.
14.    *MT,* Aug. 4, 1902, p. 1298; *JC,* April 14, 1902, p. 1711.
15.    T. W. Acheson, *The Social Origins of Canadian Industrialism,* p. 68. This is an excellent examination of some of the forces making for the transformation in the Maritime economy.

16. G. B. D. Roberts and A. L. Tunnell (eds.), *Standard Dictionary of Canadian Biography*, vol. I, p. 552; *MT*, Sept. 11, 1885, p. 288.

17. H. J. Morgan (ed.), *Canadian Men and Women of the Time*, p. 44.

18. S. A. Saunders, *Economic History of the Maritime Provinces*, p. 18.

19. *MT*, May 6, 1892, p. 1332.

20. *MT*, Jan. 11, 1884, p. 1332.

21. *MT*, Jan. 29, 1897, p. 1000.

22. V. Ross, *Bank of Commerce*, I, p. 26.

23. V. Ross, *Bank of Commerce*, I, p. 57.

24. *MT*, March 29, 1878, p. 1149.

25. A. G. Brown and P. H. Morres, *Twentieth Century Impressions of Canada*, pp. 447, 850.

26. *MT*, Aug. 4, 1882, p. 120; Nov. 17, 1882, p. 540; Nov. 24, 1882, p. 568.

27. *MT*, Sept. 7, 1888, p. 262.

28. *MT*, Nov. 29, 1895, p. 685.

29. There were of course private banks operating in Montreal. These tended to display a certain specialization of function to justify their existence, in contrast to the general banking business typical elsewhere. For example, the Chinese importing firm Sue Shang and Co., which acted as the CPR's agents in numerous facets of its Chinese trade connections, did a private banking business specializing in Asian remittances through a series of connections with Chinese banks and foreign banks in China.

30. See Claude Ryan, "Alphonse Desjardins: une Méthode et une Pensèe Très Actuelle," *Le Devoir*, 13 Mars, 1975 which describes the intellectual origins of the movement. See Desjardins' own account in *The Cooperative Peoples' Bank*.

31. Quebec *Sessional Papers*, 1901, vol. III, no. 49.

32. Canada, *Cost of Living Report*, vol. I, p. 835.

33. Anonymous, *Canada Under the National Policy*, p. 125.

34. *MT*, Jan. 26, 1894, p. 923; Feb. 2, 1894, p. 952.

35. For example, the case of R. G. Meckle, one of the Lachute private banks prosecuted in 1887 for not specifying his bank was unincorporated; he failed in 1893 with virtually all his assets in mortgages or land purchases. See *MT*, March 3, 1893, p. 1034; March 17, 1893, p. 1046.

36. For instance, William Weir, of La Banque Ville Marie notoriety, whose private bank and brokerage house collapsed with the chartered bank. *MT*, June 29, 1900, p. 1210.

37. See for example *MT*, March 11, 1898, p. 1187 for an example of a Quebec City coal dealer who got into banking on the side. When he failed in 1898 he brought down a local tobacconist with him.

38. There were a few scattered instances of private banks on the model of the rest of Canada in Quebec. For example, an instance of private investment banking is provided by the early operations of Donald A. Smith (Lord Strathcona), who began as a Hudson's Bay Company chief factor in Labrador. The wintering partners and other officials who received their share of the profits or their salaries while in the posts had little opportunity to spend them. Hence some 85% of the funds found their way into the hands of the Hudson's Bay Company's official banker for safekeeping. But Strathcona, from an early point in his career, began to act as a private banker in competition with the Company. He paid the officers three per cent interest, invested the proceeds in Bank of Montreal shares, and soon became one of the largest shareholders in the bank. However this example is illustrative only of itself — there was no pattern of similar behaviour elsewhere in Quebec or Labrador. (B. Willson, *The Life of Lord Strathcona*

*and Mount Royal,* pp. 145-6; E. E. Rich, *The Hudson's Bay Company,* vol.
II, p. 819.)

39. G. T. Glazebrook, *Sir Edmund Walker, p. 10.*
40. "Misc. Banking Memoranda," *Walker Papers.*
41. *MT,* Aug. 3, 1883, p. 120; May 5, 1893, p. 1313.
42. *RCLI, Evidence,* pp. 1364, 1401-22; *MT,* April 28, 1899, p. 1412.
43. *MT,* Dec. 7, 1888; Nov. 9, 1888, p. 524; June 14, 1895, p. 1604; Aug. 17, 1883, p. 177.
44. *MT,* April 18, 1890, p. 1286; July 13, 1900, p. 38.
45. *MT,* Feb. 25, 1869, p. 442; March 11, 1869, pp. 473-5; April 29, 1869.
46. *MT,* Nov. 3, 1876, p. 499.
47. *MT,* Feb. 9, 1900, p. 1038; Feb. 25, 1900, p. 1106; March 16, 1900, p. 1209; May 11, 1900, p. 1478; June 15, 1900, p. 1636.
48. *MT,* Oct. 2, 1885, p. 372.
49. *MT,* Jan. 22, 1892, p. 864; April 1, 1892, p. 1184.
50. *MT,* March 16, 1883, p. 1028; March 5, 1897, p. 1178.
51. *MT,* June 17, 1892, p. 1516; April 20, 1883, p. 1172.
52. *MT,* Dec. 1, 1876, p. 616; March 9, 1894, p. 1118; March 20, 1896, p. 1202.
53. *MT,* Nov. 8, 1889, p. 552.
54. *MT,* June 22, 1883, p. 1499.
55. For example, in the town of Belmont in 1891 the banker and grain dealer, who had paid a savings rate well in excess of the cartel rate, absconded leaving large losses. Gabriel Somers' bank, too, grew out of his grain-dealing business. See *MT,* July 24, 1891, p. 99; July 31, 1891, p. 128.
56. *MT,* Sept. 1, 1882.
57. *MT,* Aug. 10, 1883, p. 149.
58. *MT,* Nov. 7, 1879, p. 549.
59. V. Cronyn to B. E. Walker, Feb. 26, 1883; R. W. Smylie to B. E. Walker, Feb. 26, 1883; *Walker Papers; MT,* Feb. 23, 1883, p. 936.
60. *MT,* Feb. 14, 1890, p. 999.
61. *Globe,* Nov. 24, 1890.
62. *Globe,* April 3, 1906.
63. *MT,* Oct. 28, 1892; Feb. 24, 1893, p. 1003.
64. *MT,* April 7, 1899, p. 1313.
65. L. Harris to B. E. Walker, Nov. 20, 1902 *Walker Papers; MT,* Aug. 4, 1899, p. 135.
66. *MT,* Oct. 4, 1895, p. 429.
67. *MT,* Oct. 18, 1895, p. 501; Oct. 25, 1895, p. 526; Dec. 4, 1896, p. 741.
68. *MT,* Sept. 1899; July 31, 1885, p. 120.
69. *MT,* May 27, 1898, p. 1542; June 3, 1898, p. 1525; June 17, 1898, p. 1642. It was Toronto land investments for example that absorbed half of the deposits of a Bracebridge banker in 1898 and precipitated his failure when the market collapsed.
70. *MT,* Nov. 16, 1883; p. 540; July 3, 1885, p. 9.
71. *MT,* Dec. 21, 1883, p. 681.
72. The pattern of interlocking partnerships was common throughout Ontario, and was reproduced subsequently in the prairies. It probably facilitated the intercommunal transfer of funds, and certainly facilitated the process of growth, both by bringing in new capital to the bank with the partnership and by bringing in local expertise. Another prominent example, illustrating even greater flexibility than the Fawcett system, was the multiplicity of bank firms in which Loftus Cuddy of Amherstburg was involved. In 1878, a branch of the Johnston Banking Co. of Strathroy was established in Amherstburg in partnership with Cuddy, and which he took over completely in 1883. Cuddy's bank then established a Bothwell branch, which

was closed during the bad years of the mid-1880's. In 1891, Cuddy moved to Cleveland in conjunction with his extensive coal investments there, and was succeeded in Amherstburg by Messrs. Fall Bros. In 1893 Cuddy returned to Canada, and the Amherstburg Bank, then the sole bank in the town, was reorganized as a partnership, Cuddy-Falls Co. See *MT,* May 11, 1883, p. 1255; June 4, 1886, p. 1376; Dec. 18, 1891, p. 719; *MT,* Dec. 17, 1893, p. 970.

73.   *MT,* Sept. 26, 1884, p. 344.
74.   *MT,* Aug. 25, 1876, p. 211; Aug. 27, 1880, p. 232; Feb. 4, 1881, p. 892.
75.   *MT,* Nov. 28, 1884, p. 614.
76.   *MT,* Oct. 17, 1884, p. 429; Nov. 14, 1884, p. 546; Jan. 2, 1885, p. 746.
77.   *MT,* Oct. 17, 1884, p. 429.
78.   *MT,* Aug. 21, 1885, p. 203.
79.   *MT,* July 8, 1887, p. 38.
80.   *MT,* Dec. 8, 1899, p. 735.
81.   *MT,* Feb. 3, 1888.
82.   *MT,* Dec. 19, 1890, p. 740.
83.   *MT,* Jan. 9, 1903, p. 919; March 6, 1903, p. 1199.
84.   *MT,* Oct. 12, 1883, p. 400; Oct. 17, 1883, p. 428; Nov. 2, 1883, p. 484.
85.   *MT,* April 3, 1894, p. 1278; April 20, 1894, p. 1316; Aug. 3, 1894, p. 137.
86.   *MT,* Jan. 1, 1897, p. 874.
87.   *MT,* Jan. 29, 1897, p. 915; Feb. 19, 1897, p. 1107; Feb. 26, 1897, p. 1141.
88.   *MT,* Jan. 28, 1898, p. 980; July 14, 1899, p. 49.
89.   *MT,* Nov. 27, 1903, p. 678.
90.   *MT,* Dec. 22, 1882, p. 680; Dec. 29, 1882, p. 708; Dec. 30, 1887, p. 803; March 20, 1896, p. 1199; Aug. 9, 1895, p. 762; Dec. 3, 1897, p. 752; *CE,* Nov. 1894, p. 248. In addition to the long string of activities already mentioned, the Rathbun's collaborated with another rather powerful Kingston private bank, Folger Bros. and Co., to run the North American Telegraph Co. from 1880 to 1899, when they sold the telegraph to an American syndicate. The Folger Bros. had quite a long record of promotions itself, albeit more in utilities, transportation, and mining than in industry. In addition to the telegraph, the Folger firm ran a line of St. Lawrence steamers, and in 1887 along with Toronto brokers and New York capital it promoted an iron mining operation which was slated to eventually begin smelting. The Folgers were also tied up with George Stephen in the construction of the Pembina branch of the St. Paul, Minneapolis and Manitoba Railway. On the Folgers see *MT,* July 28, 1899, p. 103; July 23, 1897, p. 100; May 20, 1887, p. 1370; Oct. 4, 1887, p. 484.
91.   P. Lowe, "All Western Dollars," p. 17.
92.   See for example D. Creighton, *John A. Macdonald,* II, p. 387; G. F. G. Stanley, *The Birth of Western Canada,* 2nd ed., Chap. XII.
93.   Anonymous, *Canada Under the National Policy,* p. 25.
94.   *MT,* Oct. 27, 1882, p. 452; Nov. 9, 1883, p. 512.
95.   *MT,* Jan. 7, 1898, p. 883.
96.   *MT,* Dec. 24, 1886, p. 725.
97.   *MT,* Sept. 18, 1885, p. 316; Nov. 4, 1887, p. 574.
98.   N. Gilbert, *Awakening Continent,* p. 210.
99.   *MT,* May 23, 1884, p. 1309; Nov. 6, 1885, p. 510; Aug. 28, 1885, p. 232; June 2, 1886, p. 6; Oct. 29, 1886, p. 491.
100.  *MT,* Aug. 24, 1894, p. 233; March 1, 1895, p. 1124.
101.  A. G. Brown and P. H. Morres, *Twentieth Century Impressions of Canada,* pp. 605, 610, 613.
102.  *MT,* March 8, 1889, p. 1032.
103.  *MT,* May 7, 1889, p. 1322.

104. *MT,* Sept 28, 1894, p. 408; June 12, 1895, p. 40.
105. See for example *MT,* June 24, 1892, p. 1549; *CBC* 1913, p. 395. D. H. McDonald and Co. of Qu'Appelle grew out of an old lumber dealing firm that evolved a private banking business on the side and in which McDonald had been a partner. This bank was one of the few to become active in the Northwest mortgage market. Another of Qu'Appelle's private banks, that of S. H. Carswell, grew out of a merchants' business, outbid the chartered banks for deposits, and was able to sell drafts on any place in Canada, the United States, or Britain. See R. C. McIvor, *Canadian Monetary, Banking, and Financial Development*, pp. 47-9, 90, 99.
106. *MT,* May 4, 1883, p. 1228; Dec. 19, 1890, p. 740.
107. One of the largest of the Northwest banks, Cowdry's, opened a new branch as late as 1899 in Pincher Creek. Only three years later, Edmund Walker paid a visit to the West to secure two of the Cowdry branches for the Bank of Commerce. See *MT,* Nov. 17, 1899, p. 640; B. E. Walker to J. H. Plummer, Sept. 15, 1902, *Walker Papers.*
108. *MT,* Oct. 22, 1910, p. 1721; Dec. 24, 1910, p. 2619.
109. *CBC* 1913, pp. 424-6, 112.
110. R. L. Reid, "The First Bank in Western Canada," p. 294.
111. E. O. S. Sholefield, *British Columbia,* I, p. 641.
112. *MT,* July 14, 1893, p. 38.
113. A. Baster, *The Imperial Banks,* p. 142.
114. *MT,* Feb. 5, 1892, p. 928.
115. *MT,* April 6, 1894, p. 1254; March 9, 1894, p. 1118.
116. *MT,* July 26, 1901, p. 101; Aug. 9, 1901, p. 172; Aug. 23, 1901, p. 233.
117. *HCD,* April 19, 1898, p. 3720.

*In every stock jobbing swindle everyone knows that sometime or other the crash must come, but everyone hopes that it may fall on the head of his neighbour, after he himself has caught the shower of gold and placed it in safety. Après moi le déluge! is the watchword of every capitalist and of every capitalist nation.*

Karl Marx, 1867

# CHAPTER VI
# Financial Institutions and the Accumulation Of Capital

## Financial Intermediaries and the Capital Market

The post-Confederation period witnessed the financial integration of Canada. Though the banks played the dominant role in the evolution of the capital market and the creation of a national pattern of flow of funds, other institutions grew up to take on specific roles. Still others declined over the same period, as their roles were displaced by the growth, monopolization, and diversification of other financial institutions. The period from 1873 to 1896 saw the decline in relative importance of the chartered banks and the expansion of private banks and mortgage loan companies. From 1896 to 1914, the relative rates of growth were reversed, chartered banks growing, mortgage companies declining, and private banks approaching extinction. Over the entire period, other types of financial institutions grew steadily, especially insurance companies, the organized stock exchanges, and the fledgling trust companies.

Given the specialization of the banks in commercial loans and discounts, and given their continued domination of the financial structure, it is important to ascertain if the other institutions plugged the holes left behind by the banks. The main financial requirements of the period, apart from commercial loans and discounts, were for mortgage money, long-term debt capital for business and government, and equity financing for industry. Yet despite the growth of financial institutions — which in theory should have been equipped to service these needs, in part at least — the bulk of the new financing went into mortgages, and the supply of loanable funds for long-term debt or equity in Canada remained chronically underdeveloped.

# Insurance Company Operations

### Accident and Fire

While Canadian companies dominated life insurance, there were significant numbers of foreign companies active in it and other fields. British firms were especially strong in fire insurance, a field which attracted American firms, too, in increasing numbers after 1900.

**TABLE VI (1)**

**Federally Chartered Insurance Companies, 1913**

|  | Canadian | U.S. | British | Other | Total |
|---|---|---|---|---|---|
| Fire | 29 | 29 | 24 | 2 | 84 |
| Life | 27 | 10 | 7 | 1 | 45 |
| Other | 26 | 29 | 13 |  | 68 |

Source: *CYB*, 1914, pp. 598-600.

Accident insurance, and to a lesser degree fire insurance companies, are supposedly institutions that do not make a lot of open market investments. The usual rationale is that they are subject to sudden and, compared to life insurance companies, relatively unpredictable demands to pay up on policies, and therefore have to keep a large amount of their assets in ready cash or quickly liquifiable forms.[1] Such is the stereotype — the Canadian reality was a little different.

The origins of accident insurance companies in Canada did not lie in the inspiration of some mythical entrepreneur, altruistically assessing a public need. Rather, the accident insurance companies emerged from the efforts of large employers of labour — notably in the transportation sector, where the emergence of a large-scale labour force came first in Canada — to escape their liability under common law for accidents injuring or killing their workmen. Such a development also permitted the employing company itself to maintain control of the policy funds and put them to work in its own interests rather than placing them at the disposal of an independent institution for open market investments.

The Allan steamship line, for example, wholly owned the Citizens' Insurance Company, and all of the employees of

Allan's transportation empire were docked one per cent of their wages for mandatory coverage. The resulting policy was more expensive than the private ones, the coverage was only operational during the working day, and no document to establish the claim legally was ever issued. In the case of the Grand Trunk Provident Society, the company exacted a disclaimer from its employees, freeing the company from all liability for damages due to death or injury. While the company never contributed anything to the fund, the directors of the Grand Trunk had absolute control over the use of the money. In effect, the employees paid to absolve the company from liability. This plan was held up by the Ontario government as a model on which other accident plans should be based.[2]

The origins of fire insurance companies in Canada were very different from those of the accident companies. In the 1830's the first fire insurance company in the Province of Canada was organized by Francis Hincks in conjunction with the Boults of Liverpool, pioneers in British fire insurance and relatives of Hincks. Like banks, then, fire insurance in Canada was a British transplant. In the decades that followed this beginning, actual organized fire insurance companies operating in Canada were relatively rare: typically the chartered banks, acting as agents and salesmen for British companies, were the source of policies—to the extent business bothered to take them out. By the 1870's, however, a fair array of domestic and foreign-owned fire insurance companies were active in Canada.

Canada was notorious for its huge conflagrations which wiped out large industrial areas and with them, in theory, threatened to destroy fire insurance profits as well.[3] Partly the fires were due to the all-pervasive use of wood as a cheap building material; partly the fires were due to flimsy construction of factories and mills, in turn caused to some extent by the exactions of the fire insurance companies who used the resulting fires to justify huge rate increases.

Fire insurance was a very profitable business in Canada, despite the companies' protestations. From 1867 to 1913, only once, after the great fires of 1877, did the annual losses paid exceed the premiums received. And the premium receipts were rarely less than 30% more than losses; frequently they were double or even more than double the level of loss disbursements.[4]

British companies dominated the business in Canada, though their relative share of premiums declined from 64% in 1869 to 52% in 1912. While in 1869 Canadian-owned companies did 28% of the premium business and American only about eight per cent, by 1912 the Canadian firms' share was down to 22% while the Americans controlled 26%. Fire insurance was the only major financial intermediary activity in which the Canadian relative share fell over the period. The critical point came in the 1890-1895 period. In 1890, Canadian fire companies did well more than double the premium business of the American firms, but for the next nine years their premium business fell absolutely while that of the American companies doubled between 1890 and 1895. Not until 1912, however, did the American firms finally overtake the Canadian. British firms also grew quickly in this period, attracted no doubt by the fact that Canadian insurance rates were among the world's highest.[5]

That the rates were so high must be credited to the success of the firms in organizing their cartel. It had begun in 1872 as the Canadian Fire Underwriters' Association, including all of the joint stock companies in Canada. The progress of the cartel was assisted by the Mackenzie administration's insurance legislation. In 1874, George Brown organized the Isolated Risk Insurance Company in Toronto to try to secure the business of the Tory-controlled Beaver and Toronto Mutual Fire Insurance Co., and placed Alexander Mackenzie in the presidency.[6] In 1875, a bill was passed requiring all mutuals operating in more than one province to make the same mandatory deposit of securities as the joint stock companies.[7] Richard Cartwright, in introducing the bill, assured the Commons that the Ontario mutuals doing business only in Ontario would be unaffected, though he suggested that circumstances might arise when the requirements of security deposit might have to be extended to them.[8] Beaver Mutual was then declared to be within the jurisdiction of the bill, and a $50,000 deposit required. Beaver petitioned for an extension of time, for up to three years to pay the deposit. This was refused, and the company wound up in 1877.[9]

Perhaps even more conducive to cartelization were the results of the great St. John fire of 1877, which followed a year of intensive rate cutting by the fire companies. The ratio of losses paid to premiums received topped 225%. Property loss reached $20 million, with two-thirds of the city destroyed, and insurance liabilities came to over six-and-one-half million dollars. Two small New Brunswick companies failed; one Ontario-based company also failed; several suspended and reduced their capital; and the Royal Canadian, a pioneer among Canadian fire insurance companies in doing business abroad, had its New York license revoked because of the extent to which its capital had been impaired by its losses in the fire.[10]

After 1885, a year of exceptionally low payments for fire losses, the cartel tightened its grip, and agents were forbidden to

deal with other firms that were not members of the cartel. Rates
went up 40% immediately; and were raised another 20% shortly
after.[11] The result was the formation in 1885 of the Millers and
Manufacturers' Fire Insurance Co. by a group of industrialists
headed by James Goldie, the Guelph miller, to try to cut fire
premiums for mills and factories.[12] Other Canadian industries
began to step up the rate at which they insured with "underground" fire companies, American mutuals not licensed to solicit
business in Canada. It was the beginning of open economic war-
fare that continued to rage unabated between the manufacturers
and the fire cartel. The protected manufacturers called for free
trade in insurance, while, in their efforts to cut off the flow of
business to the U.S. undergrounds or destroy the independents,
the fire cartel insisted that they too were entitled to protection.

Neither of the manufacturers' responses to the cartel proved
adequate. While the Millers' and Manufacturers' tariff averaged
25% below the cartel rate, and varied according to risk while the
cartel tariff was uniform, the new firm was too small to carry the
insurance load of any sizable industrial company. It was therefore rendered relatively powerless by the cartel's refusal to
permit any of its members to engage with it in joint
underwriting.[13] This was a serious problem, for joint action by
the small companies was essential. In 1894, for example, J. R.
Booth's Ottawa sawmill required its fire insurance to be
underwritten by 20 British, five American, and three Canadian
companies.[14] The British firms too were several times larger than
the Canadian firms in general, and certainly larger than the
independents. And the British firms were all safely ensconced in
the cartel.

The other alternative, the American mutuals, was only of very
limited efficacy, for in insuring with the firms who were not
allowed to operate in Canada, the manufacturers had no guarantee that the policy would be enforcable in court. Under the
circumstances, many manufacturers simply did not bother to
insure, or had only very limited insurance and very shoddy factories.

In 1904, the Canadian Manufacturers' Association called for
collective action against the cartel. Its Insurance Committee, conscious that each manufacturer in isolation was helpless before
the cartel but that jointly they could wield countervailing power,
proposed

> that we organize for the purpose of collecting premiums and
> paying losses, and that we collect on the basis of scientific
> inspection. Our suggestion aims to eliminate commissions,
> reduce expenses, and return profits to policy holders.[15]

There followed a series of efforts to organize their own mutuals, which failed to take hold. Nor was any concept of pooling successful: the fire cartel would deal with firms only on an individual basis.[16] The cartel renewed its efforts to block the flow of business to the undergrounds as well. In 1909 it sponsored a bill before Parliament that would have barred Canadian manufacturers from dealing with the American mutuals. The CMA sent a delegation to Ottawa to fight the bill, and a compromise was arranged restoring the status quo ante bellum: the American mutuals could not solicit in Canada, but the manufacturers could purchase policies in the U.S.[17] Within a year the fight was raging again. The cartel, reorganized as the All Canada Insurance Federation, pledged itself anew to cut off the flow of business to the U.S.[18]

The fact that Canadian manufacturers had a clear preference for the American fire insurance companies, especially the mutuals, over the British and Canadian joint stock cartel, coupled with both the legal hazards of insuring with "underground companies" and the inability of American firms operating from the U.S. to solicit business in Canada, led to the logical solution — the migration of U.S. fire insurance companies to Canada where they took over an increasing share of the available business.

The manufacturers were not alone in their differences with the cartel. Municipalities across Canada, but especially in Ontario, regarded it with ill-disguised animosity. For the cartel frequently would arbitrarily order a municipality to make sweeping changes in its fire equipment or its waterworks or face massive increases in rates on all establishments in the town. After Welland in 1896 was ordered to install a $50,000 waterworks system or face a 50% rise,[19] and Hamilton and Guelph, who did not give the cartel satisfaction, had their rates increased in 1897, the municipalities began to call for a switch to mutuals or else to a system of municipal fire insurance.[20] This last was a most unfortunate idea, for in a bizarre way it did come to·pass. Municipalities often were called upon to grant loans or gifts of cash to rebuild factories and mills gutted by fire and without any insurance.

The use made by the companies of the funds derived from the extorted premiums is rather curious. Part of them, of course, went simply to enrich a few financiers, of which the Standard Fire Insurance Co. provides a good illustration. This firm was organized in 1877 and grew quickly through mergers. In 1883 it failed, due to the efforts of its president, D. B. Chisholm, who absconded, and its inspector. Between them, in the words of the new president, they "unsparingly plundered those unlucky enough to be cajoled into investing their capital therein or insuring their property therein whenever losses occurred."[21] The firm was kept afloat for a while by heavy loans from the Federal and Exchange Banks (much of which was promptly reborrowed by Chisholm), and finally expired.

In terms of their asset portfolios, fire insurance companies did hold very significant amounts of stocks, bonds, and debentures at the same time that their liquidity preference was very high. British companies very early took the lead in real estate lending, and over the 1900-1914 period, Canadian and British companies shifted heavily into that field.

## TABLE VI (2)

**Fire Insurance Company Assets**

| Year | | Total Assets | % Stocks Bonds Debentures | % Real Estate Loans | % Cash Items and Bills Receivable |
|------|------|-------------|---------------------------|---------------------|-----------------------------------|
| 1900 | Can. | 6,029,107 | 58 | 0.6 | 33 |
| | U.S. | 16,480,531 | 87 | 0.0 | 13 |
| | Brit. | 1,501,932 | 56 | 23.0 | 6 |
| | | | | | |
| 1914 | Can. | 17,501,179 | 51 | 18.0 | 21 |
| | U.S. | 35,852,077 | 81 | 0.1 | 14 |
| | Brit. | 10,467,422 | 39 | 42.0 | 18 |

Source: Superintendent of Insurance, *Reports* 1901, 1915.

## Life Companies

Life companies, by contrast to fire, are expected to accumulate great amounts of funds suitable for long-term investments. During the pre-war period the Canadian insurance tariff was one of the highest in the world, while life insurance holdings among the working class were widespread[22] — except for the black population of southern Ontario and the Maritimes who were regarded as bad life insurance risks.[23]

In terms of their investment activities, life companies in Canada were initially heavy holders of municipal bonds. In 1880, these were over 40% of their total investments. But over time these holdings were decreased substantially, with a shift into corporate stocks and bonds and foreign securities. Mortgages too, dipped sharply after 1891 down to 24% in 1904,[24] but thereafter rising. Canadian companies gradually increased their hold on the Canadian life business, until by 1914 they accounted for over 70% of the total assets of life companies in Canada, precisely the opposite pattern to fire insurance.

## TABLE VI (3)

### Life Company Investments

| Class | 1881 | %<br>1891 | 1901 | 1911 |
|---|---|---|---|---|
| Real Estate Loans | 30.68 | 42.96 | 28.94 | 35.57 |
| Policy Loans | 9.07 | 8.46 | 9.77 | 12.11 |
| Government Bonds | | | | |
| — Canada | 0.06 | 0.23 | 0.41 | 0.8 |
| — Provinces | 0.08 | 0.22 | 0.65 | 0.34 |
| — British and colonial | — | 0.22 | 0.25 | 0.26 |
| — Other | — | 0.55 | 0.18 | 0.21 |
| Municipal Bonds | 40.64 | 14.51 | 15.29 | 11.89 |
| Railway and Corporate Bonds | | | | |
| — Canada | 1.02 | 2.91 | 13.05 | 11.79 |
| — U.S. | — | — | 3.13 | 10.22 |
| — Other | — | — | 0.29 | 0.65 |
| Stocks | | | | |
| — Canada | 2.24 | 3.19 | 5.91 | 4.89 |
| — U.S. | — | — | 0.88 | 2.45 |
| — Other | — | — | — | 0.4 |
| Cash | 2.51 | 1.89 | 1.64 | 1.30 |
| Total  $ | $7m | $23m | $66m | $189m |

Source: Superintendent of Insurance, *Report*. Vol. II, 1929, p. xxxii.

Over all, the foreign life companies invested much more in long-term finance to industry and government than the Canadian ones did. And as the Canadian firms increased their share of the life insurance field, this problem was accentuated, especially in light of the Canadian companies' strong and growing infatuation with long-term investments abroad.

The Royal Commission on Insurance charged that the Canadian life companies "tend to become powerful aggregations of money with financial rather than insurance aims" and vehicles for speculation.[25] The problem was not the aggregate of investments in long-term securities but the type of security held, and especially the amount of equity, which could, and often did, represent pure water. In addition to their activities at home, which were so deeply involved with mortgage lending, the insurance companies were actively engaged in speculative promotions abroad both in investments and by the provision of interim finance. And to the

**TABLE VI (4)**

**Life Insurance Company Asset Items**

|            |    | % Total Assets |      |      |      |      |      |
|------------|----|------|------|------|------|------|------|
| Companies  |    | 1890 | 1895 | 1900 | 1905 | 1910 | 1914 |
| Canadian   |    |      |      |      |      |      |      |
| s.b.d.     | %  | 24   | 27   | 39   | 49   | 37   | 30   |
| r.e.l.     | %  | 45   | 38   | 49   | 26   | 31   | 36   |
| British    |    |      |      |      |      |      |      |
| s.b.d.     | %  | 55   | 55   | 53   | 60   | 56   | 39   |
| r.e.l.     | %  | 33   | 36   | 36   | 29   | 33   | 47   |
| American   |    |      |      |      |      |      |      |
| s.b.d.     | %  | 85   | 79   | 86   | 85   | 78   | 69   |
| r.e.l.     | %  | 1.5  | 1.7  | 3.0  | 2.5  | 5.8  | 13   |

s.b.d. = stocks, bonds, debentures
r.e.l. = real estate loans

Source: Superintendent of Insurance, *Reports,* Vol. II, various
    years.

extensive degree that these companies were vehicles for the
personal and particular promotional activities of a few financiers
rather than a stable source of long-term finance for business and
government in general, their contributions to the development of
a Canadian bond market was that much the weaker. Large
amounts of funds were locked up in a few interconnected financial webs based on the alliance of railway companies with banks
and life companies, rather than being made available to the capital market as a whole.

Ignoring Sun Life, the largest Canadian company and the
worst offender, whose promotional activities were largely in the
U.S., the best example of this use of the insurance funds is provided by Canada Life, the central institution in the Cox empire.
George Cox had begun his career in Peterborough as a telegraph
company official and local agent for Canada Life. In 1877 he
was an organizer and the first vice-president of the Peterborough
Board of Trade.[26] In the next few years, his activities included
railway promotions, real estate speculations, and the promotion
and operation of financial institutions— accident insurance, fire
insurance, and mortgage loan companies. His railway connections grew rapidly, bringing him into close relations with the
Grand Trunk through his presidency of the Midland Railway,
whose London board was headed by Sir Henry Tyler, president
of the Grand Trunk. The year 1884 saw the creation of Central
Canada Savings and Loan Company, which thereafter played a

major role in the Cox empire. The next year Cox's political rise began with his election as Mayor of Peterborough. During all this time he had been surreptitiously buying up equity in Canada Life, and much to the disgust of the existing board, by 1892 he was in a position to elect himself director. He became vice-president in 1900. His two sons joined the firm in various positions and consolidated the empire.[27]

Cox was active in politics as well. After George Brown's death, strenuous efforts were made by Sir Donald Smith to secure control of the *Globe* to silence its criticisms of the CPR. Cox, with Robert Jaffray, headed the list of eminent Liberals who saved the paper. Fund raiser and organizer of the operation was the Ontario Liberal Party bag-man, W. T. R. Preston.[28] In 1896, both Jaffray and Cox were rewarded with Senate seats. They apparently got them for free at a time when W. T. R. Preston was in charge of selling Senate seats for $10,000 each to raise funds for the party.[29]

Cox made good use of Canada Life for his various adventures. In 1899 a writ was issued against him at the insistance of a group of policy holders to compel him to repay all sums he had illegally pilfered from the company, estimated to run up to $50,000 per year.[30] And huge sums were poured directly through the company into firms in which Cox was interested. The company was especially fond of trafficking in the equity of financial, railway, and utility companies. Electric utilities were especially popular until about 1907, when the movement of life funds into real estate speculation on a vast scale began. Dominion Coal was another firm in which the equity dealings returned great profits to Cox and his Dominion Securities Company.[31]

The investment behaviour of Canada Life is of critical importance, both because it was the second largest in Canada, and because its behaviour was typical of the other firms, though the smaller were often not so speculative in their preferences. In 1900 it made loans on security of stocks, bonds and debentures of three million dollars, of which industrial equity represented only about $90,000. Out of nearly $4.5 million in stocks and bonds owned, only 10% were industrial. These were one rolling stock company, directly linked to railroad operations, and Dominion Cotton Co., a merger of some of the holdings of the Montreal commercial capitalist community. In 1905 out of $18.3 million, less than five per cent went into industrials, of which the great majority was in rolling stock firms again, the rest in cotton and primary iron and steel. In 1910, stocks, bonds, and debentures were down to $14.8 million reflecting the movement into mortgages: some seven per cent was industrial, and of this the same firms as in 1905 got the benefit, except for a small holding of the bonds of Patrick Burns and Co., the new Calgary meat packing firm.

Cox also controlled Imperial Life with the assistance of Joseph Flavelle, who fronted for Cox in National Trust, and A. E. Ames, whose brokerage firm was kept solvent only by secret loans from Canada Life. At one point he tried to secure Manufacturers Life as well. But this firm remained in the control of William Mackenzie and Donald Mann as a vehicle for their utility and railway promotions, and as a source of funds to support Henry Pellatt's stock speculations.[32] The investment portfolio of Manufacturers Life was roughly the same as Cox's with a slightly greater penchant for foreign investments and no industrial investments at all. Mackenzie and Mann's various operations were well financed, however.

The Independent Order of Foresters was one of the leading insurance operations in Canada. It was also a source of considerable material well-being for its president, Dr. Oronhyatekha, who made ever-increasing salary and expense account demands upon it during its early years.[33] Its investments were hidden by working through the Union Trust Co., which it had promoted out of an old moribund Ontario trust company. The IOF held all the shares in Union Trust except for a few which went to George Foster and two others as qualifying shares.[34] Foster then became managing director. All of the uninvested surplus of the IOF was turned over to Union Trust at a guaranteed rate of return of four per cent. Foster poured the funds into timber limit and land speculations, some of which involved deals with the property of the Hon. Rodmond Roblin, Premier of Manitoba, into U.S. railroad securities, and into helping officers of the company with their personal speculations. In return, Foster got a share of the profits.[35]

The tendency for one financial intermediary to be interlocked with the promotion and operation of another is very pronounced in Canadian financial history, as the Canada Life and IOF cases demonstrate. One of the most complex, and therefore illuminating instances concerned the activities surrounding Continental Life.

The operations tended to revolve about Gabriel Somers, the former Beeton private banker and grain dealer. Continental Life grew out of an old Ontario life and accident company. Among its assets were $25,000 of Atlas Loan Co. debentures which passed on to Continental Life. In 1902 they matured and were paid off, but the manager of the Atlas, who was a director of the Continental, got the life company to repurchase the debentures.

Atlas failed in 1903, and there was a loss to Continental. To hide it, the debentures were then "sold" to Somers. In return, the Continental was to pay Somers two-and-one-half per cent of its premium income to cover any losses on the debentures. The funds for this deal were borrowed from the Traders Bank, the rather shady operation promoted by H. S. Strathy, the broker who had helped wreck two other banks; the Traders' was also the bank to whom Somers had sold his private bank. In 1903, Continental's directors promoted the Ontario Securities Corporation, with Somers as president, and the security firm subscribed for all the unsubscribed stock of Continental. It was then used to divert all sorts of profitable security deals away from Continental Life and into the pockets of the directors, financed with funds from the life firm which made big "loans" to the security company, some of them secured by equity of the Sterling Bank which the directors were busy promoting. To get the $250,000 deposit necessary to commence operations of the bank, the security company was given securities from Continental Life's portfolio, disguised as a sale, to pledge to another bank for a loan. The rest of the required deposit was acquired by the security company subscribing for stock at a large premium in the same Sterling Bank whose flotation was the object of the exercise, and using the stock, whose value was thus inflated as security for further borrowings from Continental Life.[36] Even George Cox had never managed to pull off an operation like that.

# The Bond Market

The changes in insurance company investment behaviour parallelled those of the banks. Both institutions showed an increase in interest in the bond market until about 1905, and thereafter a movement away, in relative terms, from long-term bond investments. In light of the enormous share of intermediary assets accounted for by the two institutions, their behaviour had great repercussions on the development, and later the underdevelopment of the bond market in Canada, and hence on the ability of governments, railroad companies and industry to secure financing within Canada.

In 1870, only 9.3% of the funded debt of the Dominion government was held within Canada, and by 1900 it was down to 3.7%. Thereafter it held steady, until it began to decline in 1909, reaching 0.4% in 1914. Yet the absolute growth of the funded debt from 1895 to 1913 was only about 15%. At the same time that the relative share held in Canada declined, Canadian holdings fell *absolutely*. In 1885 nearly $20 million had been payable in Canada; by 1914 $700,000.[37]

From the over-all figures for public issues by all levels of government and corporations, the deterioration in Canada's ability to absorb its own funded debt is very striking. In 1906, Canada absorbed 43% of its public issues. By 1908 it was down to 12%. While some recovery occurred, the growth in the reliance on foreign, especially British, portfolio capital was pronounced.

While exact figures are not available, it seems that the reliance on British capital began to be strongest in 1905, when $30 million issues were floated by each of the Canadian Northern and the Grand Trunk Pacific railways in conjunction with the new transcontinental drive, and taken up largely in Britain.[38] In 1906, total borrowings declined greatly. At the same time, large amounts of Canadian capital were drawn off into the Cobalt mining speculation and away from the bond market, which served to make the percentage of bond issues taken up in Canada inordinately low. While this was a once-for-all shift in the flow of funds, the essential trend away from bonds by institutional lenders remained. In 1907, the crisis adversely affected municipal debenture sales, with one estimate of the amount "undigested" running as high as $25 million. It also reflected the westward shift in the flows of economic activity: of the successful

## TABLE VI (5)

### Canadian Bond Issues

| Year | In % Canada | In % U.S. | In % Britain | $ Total |
|------|-------------|-----------|--------------|---------|
| 1904 | n.a. | n.a. | n.a. | 34,249,247 |
| 1905 | n.a. | n.a. | n.a. | 134,874,531 |
| 1906 | 43 | 8 | 49 | 53,987,008 |
| 1907 | 18 | 6 | 76 | 86,635,740 |
| 1908 | 12 | 4 | 84 | 196,357,411 |
| 1909 | 22 | 4 | 74 | 265,158,252 |
| 1910 | 17 | 2 | 81 | 225,100,590 |
| 1911 | 19 | 7 | 74 | 239,992,988 |
| 1912 | 16 | 12 | 72 | 230,782,982 |
| 1913 | 14 | 13 | 73 | 351,408,629 |
| 1914 | 20 | 12 | 68 | 188,900,000 |

Sources: calculated from E. R. Wood, *Review of the Bond Markets of Canada 1906 - 1910* and *CLRII,* p. 910, with adjustments. *MT,* Oct. 27, 1916 gives slightly different estimates.

issues that year, 99 eastern municipalities accounted for about six million, while 39 western towns accounted for eight million.[39] The municipal issues were hardest hit of all during the stringency, because they tended to rely most heavily on Canadian markets, the level of Canadian absorption of municipals being usually 80 to 85%.

In terms of access to the British market, railways and utilities tended to be most favoured. In 1907, for example, they accounted for 43 million of 52 million corporate issues, leaving less than nine million for industrial and navigation companies. By 1909, however, Canadian industrials too were welcomed in London.

In the absence of the insurance companies and banks there was little to take up the slack in the Canadian bond market. The two large Quebec savings banks tended to invest up to 50% of their deposits in bonds, but in 1910 the total came to only about $17 million. And little could be hoped for from government savings banks. Wealthy individual investors tended to favour real estate mortgages, bank and intermediary equity, and railway and utility equity to bonds. The trust and loan companies, too, preferred mortgage lending.[40] The attraction to mortgages reflects the linkage of the big financial institutions to the growth of staple industry in the West, that is, the impact the "wheat economy" had on the direction of the flow of funds in the Canadian capital market.

# The Mortgage Market

Despite the interest of life insurance and trust companies in mortgage lending, the field remained dominated for a long time by the mortgage loan companies. The mortgage loan companies differed sharply from the insurance companies with respect to their liability instruments, and to some extent in their asset structures as well. The insurance companies generated their funds largely within Canada from policies, and were active exporters of capital in addition to their mortgage lending. The mortgage companies did not export capital, but imported large amounts from Britain by the sale of debentures there.

One of the earliest companies to make extensive use of the sterling debenture was the Canada Permanent Loan Company. Its first effort to issue them came in 1862, but was unsuccessful. Legal problems existed at that time, for the validity of the use of the debenture by a loan company under existing legislation was open to doubt. More important, for it was much more difficult to change, was the reluctance of British capital to move into Canada after the railway debacles. By 1875, the Canada Permanent's capital was three times its 1862 level, its reserve fifteen times as great, and it had paid an unbroken string of dividends of 10-12% per annum. Under these circumstances a debenture issue of $334,000 was floated in Britain, the first of a stream that continued for forty years. [41]

Initially their domestic deposit business was of considerable significance, much to the chagrin of the chartered banks who, blocked from mortgage lending, argued that the mortgage companies therefore should stay out of the deposit business.[42] As the U.K. market for their five-year debentures widened, the deposit business was increasingly ceded to the chartered banks. Deposits as a percentage of total liabilities fell from 25.7% in 1870 to 11.3% in 1915.[43] By 1893, of $115 million worth of current loans, $110 million was secured by real estate, and of their deposits and debentures of $80 million, $50 million was borrowed in Scotland.[44] Britain, as a nation characterized by old wealth, was an ideal source of funds, and the landed gentry were the principal holders of the debentures.[45]

The mortgage market underwent a great burst of activity during the boom years of 1879 to 1883, and the after-effects lasted for several years. Profits from real estate were very substantial, and rendered even more so by the all-pervasive practice of cheating the farmers by compounding the interest. Sometimes payments were required on a monthly basis while interest was calculated on the entire principal. New laws were enacted to force them to stipulate the real rate of interest. [46]

Funds poured first into investments in the old provinces, but as the surplus of funds relative to demand began to make itself felt on their earnings position, companies began to switch to Manitoba, where rates of return were higher.[47] Canada Permanent alone put more than a million dollars into speculation there between 1881 and 1883, and the collapse nearly brought down the company with it.[48] Other outlets were found for the surplus funds in Ontario by encroaching on the banks' business. This, in fact, was a fairly old practice. As early as 1869 the Colonial Securities Company went into short-term lending with its mortgage funds.[49] But by the early 1880's the loan companies were even discounting notes illegally, following a big drop in their mortgage business.[50] By 1885, the pressure on their earnings position from a fall in mortgage rates and a rise in the cost of sterling borrowings was severe enough to force mergers of several institutions in an effort to reduce competition. But the squeeze continued, and by 1887 the former spread between debenture and deposit rates was gone.[51]

It was a time of generally falling interest rates, and the rise in the cost of sterling debenture borrowing requires some explanation. Part of it no doubt lay in the fact that, though there were no losses to debenture holders, British investors may have been frightened by the orgy of speculation, and the ensuing liquidation, and by the behaviour of a few of the companies involved.

Notable among these companies was the Ontario Investment Association which was active in the field of sterling borrowings during the land boom.[52] This company was promoted in 1880 by a London group including Henry Taylor of the Bank of London. And its first board included the manager of the Federal Bank, the president of Imperial Oil, the broker H.S. Strathy, and the private banker J. A. Mahon, along with William Meredith and John Labatt.[53] It was not the best set of credentials with which to begin, and the company lived up to them in the full. The company had a meteoric career, absorbing three other mortgage firms in its first few years before it crashed dramatically.

In early 1883, the company's portfolio of assets included mortgages of about one million dollars, and also loans on stocks, bonds, and debentures of over $800,000 at a time when mortgage companies in general were putting well over 80% of their assets into mortgages. While a lot of the companies were trying to develop business supplemental to mortgage lending, none did it on the scale of the Ontario Investment Association. Difficulties began when the English agents of the company stole some £10,000 from it. The company then decided to replace the loss with a subscription of one dollar from each shareholder instead of taking the funds from the reserve.[54] It was an interesting innovation in finance; the real rationale did not come clear for some time.

By 1885 Henry Taylor was the general manager of the company, and within two years the company had failed. An ingenious system had been worked out between its president and solicitor whereby cheques were issued under the signature of the president payable to the solicitor for certain of the company's transactions; and in fact the funds were diverted into speculation. Both president and solicitor absconded, and the failure led to a run on the Bank of London, which collapsed under Taylor's management soon after. [55] In the ensuing liquidation it was discovered that the reserve of $500,000 had been completely lost and its English agents had continued their systematic robbery.[56] The firm had made huge loans on a series of unauthorized securities, including loans on its own stock. The loans on the stock of the company were over $660,000, one-third more than the entire nominal (and non-existent) reserve. Most of the loans had been made in the names of persons who really did not receive the funds; the money in fact went into Taylor's pocket, or to the solicitor and president. In light of the fact that sterling debentures accounted for $1,561,476 of a total of $1,816,505 in liabilities,[57] the failure must have had some impact on the feelings of British investors about Canadian mortgage investments.

Another victim of the end of the Winnipeg land boom was the Montreal Loan and Mortgage Company, which failed in 1884. Over half a million dollars in real estate reverted to it through advances that went into default. In 1883, this land produced a net revenue of only $12,000. Mortgages were yielding 4¾% while the company had $500,000 in debentures outstanding on which it paid five per cent. Moreover, the late manager, George Craig, was always short on his cash, and had given no bond or security. The president, auditor, and directors all "borrowed" from it, but Craig was the chief beneficiary.[58] In 1884, following the issue of a warrant, he took a quick trip to New York where he had a joyful reunion with his brother, Thomas Craig, the Exchange Bank robber who had also found it convenient to emigrate.[59]

These were not the only casualties of the collapse of the period. The Canadian Banking & Loan Co. of Hamilton folded up after its manager, D. B. Chisolm, of Standard Fire Insurance fame, absconded.[60] Then, too, there were the mergers. In 1883 under Frank Smith's presidency the English & Scottish Investment Company of Canada merged into the London & Ontario Investment Co. In 1885 Western Canada Loan & Savings was taken over by an English firm, Omnium Securities Co. Both of these mergers were prompted by downward pressures on interest rates.[61] And there were a series of other liquidations, in 1887 and 1888, some three besides the Ontario Investment Association.[62] The condition of many of these companies had been hidden by falsified returns. In fact, this problem of fraudulent returns was a widespread one among institutions who had less to hide than the Ontario Investment Association. The Lampton Loan and Investment Co. made a point of falsifying to disguise the fact that it regularly exceeded the legal limit on its deposits with impunity.[63]

Another outgrowth of the real estate boom years of the early eighties was the Credit Foncier Franco-Canadien. It was projected to be the largest loan company in Canada.[64] The promotion of the company dated back to 1877 when an envoy was sent to France by a group around E. T. Paquet, the Provincial Secretary of Quebec, to sound out members of the Bourse and the Banque de Paris et des Pays Bas on the project. The same group were interested in trying to float a provincial loan there at the same time, but both projects failed. In 1880 the effort was renewed when Jonathan S. Würtele arrived in Paris on behalf of the Chapleau Government to try to arrange a provincial loan. Both Adolphe Chapleau, the Premier of Quebec, and Würtele were directors of the Credit-Foncier du Bas-Canada which sought a loan in Europe to extend its operations in Canada. Würtele was to negotiate on their behalf, and the company later decided to proceed with the more grandiose project of the Quebec-France joint venture. A new charter was secured, as the one for the Bas-Canada prohibited foreign directors and imposed a series of other restrictions uncongenial to French promoters.[65]

The charter carried with it a series of special concessions including one clause that stated,

> A privilege of 50 years, dating from the day of its final constitution is granted to the Company. The said privilege consists in the fact that the Government of the Province binds itself not to authorize within its territory the formation of any other Credit Foncier in any way represented in France.[66]

Why the government of Quebec should have been so eager to grant a monopoly of access to French mortgage money for 50 years is a moot point, but it would be surprising if it had nothing to do with the personnel of the Canadian promotion team. The Lieutenant Governor of the province had been president of the Canadian syndicate that produced the scheme, and the six syndicate members who became the local directors consisted of Chapleau himself; Würtele, soon to become Treasurer of the province; the provincial secretary, the Hon. E. T. Paquet; the Hon. I. Thibodeau, former president of the Executive Council, former legislative councillor, and president of the Banque Nationale which functioned as Canadian bankers to the operation; another member of the Quebec legislature, who was also a director of the bank; and the president of Molson's Bank.[67] To make doubly sure, it was alleged that bribes of $30,000 had been distributed to members of the legislature.[68]

The floatation of the company was an equally interesting operation. All of the equity except some 300 shares to qualify the Canadian directors was marketed by the French bankers in France, with the Canadian promoters slated to get a share of the profits.[69] And the profits were substantial. The first issue of stock brought a premium of 750,000 francs, which was treated as profit and divided amongst the Canadian and French promoters. A second issue brought a premium of 15-20% which accrued to

Würtele and Chapleau. The shareholders thus paid 15-20% for a chance at dividends when in Quebec the year before only two, or at most three of the 26 loan companies operating therein declared a dividend.[70]

The charter of the company had stipulated that the maximum rate it could charge on loans was six per cent, and the monopoly powers were justified on the grounds that the company would lower mortgage rates in Quebec. In the provincial election, the Chapleau campaign in the rural districts was based on the claim that he had brought the company to Canada and eased the mortgage situation. After Chapleau was returned with a majority unprecedented in Quebec history, the company immediately began to lobby to have the ceiling raised to seven per cent.[71] The Credit Foncier claimed that a financial crisis in France was impeding its operations and that it could not float its debentures in Paris while hampered with the six per cent ceiling. In fact, the real reason for the inability to float the issue was the stock manipulation that had accompanied its promotion and which had undermined its credibility. French investors were also frightened off by the fact that since the company was authorized to issue debentures of an amount up to five times its paid up capital, there was little security for the debenture holder.[72]

The company had also secured a Dominion charter to operate elsewhere in Canada. In eastern Canada its interest rate was limited to six per cent, but west of Ontario it could charge up to seven.[73] Soon, following the decrease in the field for mortgage lending, it was demanding additional powers like the ability to lend on securities as well as land.[74] Efforts to get the interest rate ceiling lifted were fought in the Commons. At that time Quebec's depopulation was being powerfully assisted by mortgage companies whose claims drove many farmers and their families to New England for part-time work in the mills to help pay off the debts. At the same time, lands forfeited or sold because of debts passed into the hands of big land envelopers who held them for speculation.[75] Not only was the requested rate increase granted, but by 1883 it was up to eight per cent.[76] Three years later, the Credit Foncier claimed it had floated a $1,200,000 debenture issue in Switzerland at four per cent.[77]

The progress of the company was rapid. In 1888 Sir Adolphe Chapleau became president of the company,[78] replaced on his death in 1898 by the Hon. Mr. Justice Jonathan Würtele.[79] The Credit Foncier began operating in British Columbia as early as 1893, one of the first eastern-based mortgage companies to do so.[89]

By the time the Credit Foncier began its operation in the far

West, conditions in the Canadian mortgage market were changing. By 1894, the use of sterling debentures reached a peak and began to fall absolutely as borrowing rates continued to rise and lending rates fell. Slow growth of the mortgage companies in terms of relative share of intermediary assets coincided with the slowing of sterling borrowings, and at the same time the chartered banks made a strong move into the savings deposit business. By 1893, the tendency was already strong for the mortgage companies in Ontario to shift to urban lending for factories, houses, and warehouses, with less money going to the Ontario farms. There were two factors involved in determining this reallocation. Individual lenders as well as the newly emerging trust companies were tending to increase the competition in the field of farm lending,[81] a competition already rife from the 69 mortgage loan companies operating in Canada in 1896. By 1898 the former practice of paying a commission on loan business brought to the companies was abandoned in the continuing profit squeeze.[82] Moreover, many farmers were able to settle their debts, especially after agricultural product prices rose after 1896 — mortgage debts were fixed in nominal terms while farmers' money incomes were rising. The shift to urban mortgages was a natural one to make, considering the virtual absence of new farm land in Ontario, the generally improved conditions that followed the move into mixed farming in the 1890's in the face of sagging grain prices, and the surge in home ownership in Toronto and other big Ontario cities. In 1900, farmers in Ontario not only met all their interest due, but that year alone settled one-sixth of the principal outstanding.[83] Wealthy farmers soon became mortgage lenders in their own right.[84] And as the early years of prosperity unfolded, the progress of manufacturing attracted more and more funds into urban real estate. Funds locked up for years in the wake of collapse of earlier bubbles were freed, leading to sharp competition and rate cutting.[85]

In addition to urban speculation, the deluge of funds in the hands of the mortgage companies made its way into other outlets. Loans on securities became more common. The Credit Foncier received an amendment to its Quebec charter permitting it to move into stock, bond, and debenture loans to use up the big flow of funds coming into its treasury.[86] The cashier of the Freehold Loan & Saving Co. helped himself to its funds to speculate in New York, and was jailed for his efforts.[87]

The new patterns produced their share of disasters too. The first was the Homestead Loan and Savings Society of Hamilton in 1897. It was one of the old style of "terminating building societies," whose termination in fact came as a surprise to everyone but its secretary, who had been busy inflating the value of its mortgages to make the firm look solvent and therefore justify the continuation of his salary.[88]

That same year came the failure of the misnamed Farmers Loan and Savings Co. which poured all of its funds into speculation in Toronto suburban land, much of it vacant and unproductive. When the bubble burst, it was left with nearly $1.4 million in unpaid mortgages. Its condition was hidden for a while by systematic falsification by the directors. Profits were assiduously calculated by taking the capital stock, reserve, and borrowings, adding seven percent, and entering this as part of the investment account.[89] Its creditors received 55¢ on the dollar, and it had the distinction of being the first mortgage company to produce losses for sterling debenture holders.[90]

Not learning from the experiences of the Farmers, the York County Loan Co. also invested heavily in Toronto suburbs. It invested in a number of other things as well. Its president, a former preacher from England who ran a life insurance business as well, put the money of the company into a magazine that he published, a grocery store and even a piano factory, which must make the York County the only case in financial history of a mortgage loan company involved in industrial promotions.[91] Most of the funds, however, seem to have been diverted into urban real estate speculation through a real estate company he also owned.[92] These funds were drawn to a large extent from rural savings, for the company had scores of glib and smooth-talking agents roaming Ontario and conning "servant girls and country bumpkins."[93] Efforts were made to sell it to another loan company, but the deal did not materialize, the company was ordered into liquidation by the court, and its president charged with conspiracy to defraud.[94]

In addition to urban real estate speculation, the mortgage companies had become increasingly involved in loans on securities, and this too took its toll. In 1903 came the rather predictable suspension of the Atlas Loan and Savings Company of St. Thomas in the wake of the failure of A. E. Ames and Co. The president of the Atlas was a partner in the brokerage firm. Until 1898, the business of the Atlas was orthodox enough, borrowing on deposit and debenture at 3.75 to 4.25% and loaning on mortgage at 5.5 to 6.1%. Then, however, it shifted its portfolio into stocks and bonds, and raised its interest rates from 3.4% in 1900 to 4.7% in 1901 at a time when other companies were offering 3.5%. In 1903 it reached 5.0%, and later climbed to 6.0%. The bulk of the savings of the people of St. Thomas were secured by the company and put to work in the type of stock operation that wrecked A. E. Ames and Co.[95]

In addition to urban speculation and stock deals, the Ontario companies began to look west well in advance of the rush of settlement. For the rates and market conditions in Manitoba and the Northwest improved as grain prices moved upward and the existing small settler community found its condition somewhat more solvent.[96] Few of the companies active in the West were local promotions, such as the Land and Investment Company of Manitoba, a creation of the former Premier Thomas Greenway with a cabinet minister and other notables.[97] The great majority were eastern companies. While the Manitoba North West Loan Co., for example, was headquartered in Winnipeg and did almost all its business in the Northwest, most of its capital was controlled in Toronto, and its headquarters moved there shortly.[98]

A series of mergers resulted from the squeeze on loan company earnings during the period. The first was the absorption in 1898 of the Manitoba North West by the Canada Landed and National Investment Co., a firm in which George Cox figured along with former Prime Minister of Canada Mackenzie Bowell. Some of the assets of the Manitoba firm went to Cox's Central Canada Loan and Savings. Only a year later, there was another merger of firms active in Manitoba: Canada Permanent absorbed three other firms including the London and Ontario, itself an earlier merger.[99] That same year, Sir Casimir Gzowski and George Cockburn promoted a merger of three firms into the Toronto Mortgage Co., to cut competition in the Toronto area.[100]

No further large-scale mergers occurred until 1906, when two further amalgamations occurred around the Huron and Erie Loan and Savings Co. and the Lambton Loan and Investment Co.[101] But by then the mortgage market was on the verge of another major transformation.

As late as 1905 and 1906 the mortgage market was reported badly overcrowded.[102] Insurance companies were still in the process of shedding their mortgage portfolios. Sun Life moved more funds into utilities, while Canada Life reported more losses on mortgage lending than in any other investment.[103] But by 1904 the downward trend of mortgage rates had begun to change in Ontario, although not until 1907 did Saskatchewan mortgage rates begin to climb, and then very modestly. By 1904 the decline in the level of foreign debenture liabilities of the mortgage companies was arrested, and foreign, especially British investment grew steadily. By 1907 the great influx of population into the new wheat areas made itself felt, and new wheat production began to flow. By 1908 the relative rates of return to mortgage companies on mortgage lending (as opposed to other securities) was reversed, with mortgages taking the lead once more. In addition to the new inflow of sterling debenture funds, Ontario farmers' savings were becoming available for western loans.[104] The new surge in mortgage lending was based in part on a drainage of funds from the mixed farming areas of Ontario and Quebec, to sustain the loans to the wheat-growing regions of the prairies.

Throughout the period 1896 to 1913, four trends stand out in the mortgage rate structure.[105] Rural rates were consistently higher than urban; the smaller the urban centre the higher the rate; western rates were highest, Maritime second highest and central Canadian lowest; and within the West the rates were highest in the areas of most recent settlement. The east-west flow of funds parallelled that of the banking system, with insurance company policy funds and mortgage company deposits raised in the East and shipped west along with the debenture money borrowed in Britain. Furthermore, ownership and control of the insurance and mortgage companies, like that of the banks, remained vested in central Canada — a development quite unlike the American pattern where mortgage companies grew up in the West to service the West.[106]

Saskatchewan, while paying the highest rates, received the greatest amount of eastern funds. By 1913 over and above debts of about $40 million to implement dealers and $55 million to land companies and eastern retail outlets, there was $65 million in mortgage money invested in the province. Total debt charges topped twelve million per annum, payable to central Canadian business.[107] Over 80% of Saskatchewan farms were mortgaged, and it was in precisely those districts where farm prospects were poorest that the mortgage load was heaviest. Nominal rates ran as high as 15%, with the real rate raised above this by the frequent device of subtracting a preliminary "fee." Average indebtedness in the province on mortgages was $1,500 per farm or five dollars an acre. In the seven American prairie states immediately to the south, only 45% of the farms were mortgaged. In the 15 months between June, 1912 and August, 1913 there had been 1,723 sales and proceedings for mortgages in Saskatchewan, while in the State of Victoria, with an Australian state government farm finance plan in operation, there were a total of 28 farms sold in the fifteen years from 1898 to 1913.[108]

But the burden went deeper than "excessive and extortionate" rates, even with the secular upward trend of the nominal rate

**TABLE VI (6)**

**Mortgage Market Conditions**

| Year | Sterling Debentures (1) Liabilities ($ million) | Ont. rural | Ont. urban | Sask. rural | Yield Indices (2) Loan Companies Mortgages | Average Yields On Other Securities |
|---|---|---|---|---|---|---|
| 1896 | 44.7 | 105.7 | 96.4 | 100.0 | | |
| 1897 | 40.4 | 105.6 | 101.1 | 100.0 | | |
| 1898 | 40.4 | 103.7 | 100.7 | 100.0 | | |
| 1899 | 37.4 | 101.1 | 100.5 | 100.0 | | |
| 1900 | 35.7 | 100.0 | 100.0 | 100.0 | 100.0 | 100.0 |
| 1901 | 34.9 | 99.1 | 99.7 | 100.0 | 99.4 | 100.3 |
| 1902 | 34.3 | 98.6 | 99.6 | 100.0 | 98.7 | 100.7 |
| 1903 | 35.1 | 98.4 | 100.7 | 100.0 | 99.7 | 99.4 |
| 1904 | 35.1 | 100.3 | 102.8 | 100.0 | 99.7 | 98.6 |
| 1905 | 43.6 | 101.1 | 102.9 | 100.0 | 100.5 | 100.4 |
| 1906 | 46.9 | 102.0 | 105.7 | 100.0 | 101.7 | 102.2 |
| 1907 | 49.9 | 105.3 | 110.5 | 101.7 | 104.9 | 108.5 |
| 1908 | 55.3 | 108.7 | 111.3 | 101.5 | 106.6 | 105.7 |
| 1909 | 43.8 | 106.5 | 108.1 | 101.8 | 107.4 | 105.4 |
| 1910 | 69.3 | 106.7 | 109.5 | 100.9 | 108.1 | 106.2 |
| 1911 | 72.2 | 108.3 | 110.0 | 100.9 | 110.2 | 107.9 |
| 1912 | 49.2 | 111.1 | 112.4 | 101.9 | 110.6 | 112.8 |
| 1913 | 56.7 | 118.5 | 122.2 | 104.4 | | |

Sources: (1) *SYB, CYB* various years.
(2) *CLR II*, pp. 713, 735.

and tricks like the preliminary fee. For the structure of mortgage credit was squarely inappropriate for the farmer's needs. Under the prevailing system there was little chance to pay off: the final payment was set so high that the borrower would have little possibility of being able to meet it out of his current year's income. The mortgages were for a term of about *five years,* and renewal was almost inevitably necessary under new terms.[109] It was a structure closely related to that of the bank accommodation system — with preliminary fees and discounts, and short terms to force renewal under new and more onerous terms, compounding the interest in the process.

# The Stock Exchanges, the Bucket Shops, and the Money Market

Organized security dealings in Canada grew out of the staple export trades. The Toronto Stock Exchange was established in 1852 by grain millers, merchants, and bill brokers, in part to deal with wheat and flour for export,[110] and in part to facilitate the inflow of capital from Britain at a time when interest rates there were low, and the Grand Trunk project was in full blossom. It was not established primarily with a view to facilitating domestic capital accumulation. Regular meetings began in 1861, though it was not incorporated until 1879.[111] In 1882 Henry Pellatt, partner in one of Toronto's oldest brokerage and private banking firms, Pellatt and Osler (with E. B. Osler), was elected president.[112]

Similarly, the Montreal Exchange had very early roots in commodity trade. Organized trading in Montreal seems to date from 1832, when an issue of £50,000 of equity in the Champlain and St. Lawrence Railroad was subscribed in Montreal through a stock book opened in the Exchange Coffee House.[113] But the origins of the exchange really lie in the weekly meetings of bill brokers to draw up price lists in the 1850s. A Board of Brokers was formed in 1863, becoming the Montreal Stock Exchange in 1872, and incorporated in 1874. D. Lorne MacDougall, one of the original members of the Board of Brokers, became its first chairman, and he is credited with being the virtual founder of the exchange. [114] Growth was very slow. There were originally 40 seats on the Montreal exchange, all of which were not filled until 1901, when the number was raised to 55.[115] In 1876 a seat cost $2,500. In 1897 the seats sold for even less, sometimes as little as

$1,800. But with the great surge of speculation that began in that period the demand for seats skyrocketed. By 1900, on the retirement of J. A. L. Strathy, his seat sold for $10,250. [116] By 1902 a Toronto Stock Exchange seat cost $14,500. [117] And by 1908 the Montreal seats sold for $25,000. [118]

The domestic intermediary function of the exchanges was virtually non-existent until after 1870 when Canadian money for the first time became available cheaply for investment in infrastructure.[119] And the financial and transportation companies were the only ones at first to make any real use of the exchanges. This reflected the social gap between manufacturers and the mercantile community that controlled organized finance and the transportation networks. While the first joint stock industrial company in Canada was A. T. Galt's Sherbrooke Cotton Mill established in 1844,[120] the corporate form in industry remained rare until near the turn of the century. The heaviest users, the cotton and sugar mills, were in fact created by commercial capital. In 1873 the Toronto exchange listed banks, insurance companies, building and loan societies, and one gas company. Its bond listings were all railway or city debentures and those of Dominion Telegraph. Ten years later its listing was essentially the same, with still not a single industrial. [121] And over two-thirds of the business in 1883 was accounted for by bank shares, with most of the rest insurance and loan companies.[122] In Montreal the same year, the exchange listed 22 bank shares, 17 loan and building society shares, 2 telegraphs, 2 gas companies, a few railroad and government bonds, 10 insurance companies, and the equity of four cotton mills,[123] these being the only industrials.

These patterns of stock dealing were of course the creation of the brokerage firms then active. Although in theory the dealings in financial and transportation company stocks should have been more stable than speculation in industrials, the record is otherwise. It was a standard technique of the brokerage firms of the day when manipulating bank stock to get together and sell large amounts of a particular stock which they did not own in the expectation that the effect would be to depress its value, at which point the brokers would buy cheap and fill the sales orders they had already contracted to fulfil.[124] These practices took their toll of brokerage firms. C. Dorwin and Co. suspended in 1869 in Montreal, its principal leaving Canada in a hurry with some of the cash, the other partner, one of the Gault brothers, remaining behind.[125]

More significant was the collapse of the Bond Bros. in 1876, for it illustrates that the practice of "kiting" was already a fine art among Canadian brokers. Louis Forget, Strathy and Strathy

(H. S. and J. A. L.), and Messrs. Bond Bros., the cream of Montreal's brokerage community, established a phony system of mutual credit for their gambling. Forget drew a cheque for $54,000 on the Exchange Bank in favour of Strathy, and one for the Bond Bros. who were to delay cashing it. But in fact they broke the agreement and cashed it immediately, so that when Strathy presented his cheque to Forget's bank there were no funds to cover it. The objective of the exercise was to try to get control of the Montreal Telegraph Co. by buying the equity on margin.[126] In fact the end result was the suspension and failure of the Bond Bros. who found themselves with $2,200 to meet liabilities of about one million. Their creditors included eight banks, two building societies, and nearly $400,000 to Sir Hugh Allan.[127]

In addition to dealing in bank, utility, and transportation company stock from the beginning, Canadian brokers were enthusiasts for American equity, and by 1876 their New York dealings were as heavy as their Canadian ones,[128] a situation which remained roughly constant until World War I.

Concomitant with the rise of organized exchanges came the inevitable efforts to suppress competition. This took the form of a vendetta against the "bucket shops." These bucket shops were widespread, for one attribute of the Canadian population of the period was its fondness for gambling in stocks and even in commodity futures. One bucket shop in Napanee thrived on pork futures until taken to court in 1886. The judge referred to the operation as "dealing in pork without any pigs."[129] The bucket shops, like the brokers from whom they differed only by social class, operated on a branch basis. One of the largest in the 1880's was E. S. Cox and Co., which had small offices in virtually every town in Ontario and used telegraph instruments rented from the Great North Western Telegraph Company as well as having the co-operation of Canadian Pacific's telegraph facilities.[130] Some operated across Canada: Hanaran and Co. of Toronto had Montreal branches, while one Montreal bucket shop in 1886 opened a Halifax branch.[131]

In 1888, the orthodox brokers pressed for legislation to classify the bucket shops as ordinary gaining houses. But complications resulted. For it proved exceedingly difficult to define the bucket shop operation in such a way as not to include the activities of virtually every established broker in the country. Their business was, after all, precisely the same, and the sole objective of the bill was to open up the business formerly done by the bucket shops for takeover by the established brokers. Amidst a spate of self-righteous denunciations of their godless behaviour, the Bucket Shop Act was passed, sponsored by J. J. C. Abbott, who had won his spurs as Sir Hugh Allan's chief bargaining agent in the Pacific Scandal contract. The criterion by which the bucket shop was distinguished from the orthodox broker or commodity dealer was that the transactions of a bucket shop were simply speculation on the course of prices and did not imply there would be any delivery of the merchandise.

On its passage in 1888, the Act led immediately to a wave of arrests of bucket shop operators in Montreal and Toronto. Hanaran and Co. had both its Montreal and Toronto offices raided and it was selected for a test case. Convicted in respect to dealing in American railway stock, the principal of the firm appealed and the conviction was overruled on a technicality.[132] The Act itself was still untested. That same year, E. S. Cox was acquitted of all charges with respect to his destruction of the Central Bank.[133] For his role in wrecking the Federal, the private banking and brokerage firm of Forbes and Lownsborough, and the private Guelph Banking Company, he was never even tried.

The bucket shop operators very quickly evolved a possible means of escape from the impact of the new law by claiming to be acting as the agents for parties in foreign countries, which would help circumvent the delivery criterion,[134] but not for several years was the new technique tested in court.

After 1895 came a new bout of suppression, probably prompted by the beginnings of a mining stock boom. Following an evangelist revival in St. John, New Brunswick, in which the bucket shop was denounced as immoral, the Baldwin Bros. were raided by the city police leading to the arrest of "the manager, the telegraph operator, and a prominent citizen who happened to be the only customer."[135]

In 1896, the new system of evading the law was aired in court in a grain dealing case. A Toronto broker bought grain in Chicago for a Chicago buyer, lost money on the deal, and claimed that his Chicago client had promised to indemnify him. The Chicago client tried to avoid payment by declaring that the sale and delivery were purely fictional, and that the deal was solely for the purposes of price speculation. The judge found with the plaintiff, though he denounced both parties.[136] It is interesting to note that the Toronto broker whose activities were denounced was charging one-eighth of a cent a bushel commission on wheat futures at the same time the organized brokers in the Winnipeg Grain Exchange charged one cent. The decision in the case may well have been a factor in London in 1897, when four bucket shops were raided but no arrests made. The custodians, accused of keeping a common gaming house, were let off with a warning.[137]

Not so fortunate was the manager of the Montreal Investors' Guarantee Co. in 1899. This company attracted a lot of funds on deposit with promises of three per cent per month return. Its manager closed up and absconded when the threat of arrest was made.[138]

While the Investors' Guarantee seemed a fringe operation, many of the Montreal bucket shops were so indistinguishable from the orthodox broker that often the same people ran both operations.[139] One illustration was the tangle of brokerage operations surrounding the Banque Ville Marie debacle. Most of the funds stolen by the clerk J. J. Herbert went into the bucket shops through an established broker James Baxter, as did some of the borrowings of the president William Weir, who ran a brokerage firm along with the chartered bank. The bucket shop into which the money went dealt in both equity and commodities. When the crash came, Herbert called upon Baxter to assist him in leaving Canada, and he was hidden away for sometime, going out only at night dressed in women's clothing. Baxter went to prison along with Weir and other officers of the bank.[140]

Further efforts were made in subsequent years by the brokers to stamp out their competition, but the shops continued to thrive, especially in Montreal. By 1907 some of the large ones were doing up to 20,000 shares a day in business and contributing up to $7,000 per year to government revenue by stamp purchases.[141] Moreover, as the Canadian stock market evolved, the big established brokers were so openly involved in precisely the same type of speculation for which the bucket shops were condemned that it became increasingly difficult to justify the suppression.[142]

The exchanges changed a great deal over time, especially after the new era of prosperity led to easy money and rising security prices.[143] With the Klondike gold rush and the flood of mining promotions in B.C., mining equity for the first time became a widely accepted investment among the Canadian middle class. Most of the funds for speculation from Canadian sources and even from abroad were channelled through Toronto brokers who played an active part in the mining promotions. During 1896, three to four times as many telegraphic messages concerning the B.C. mining speculation emanated from Toronto as from Montreal.[144] Mackenzie and Mann, Pellatt, George Cox, Robert Jaffray, and other Toronto notables were early entrants.[145]

New exchanges were formed to handle the mining equity. In 1898 fifteen Toronto brokers formed the Mining Stock Exchange, and closed it to further entrants,[146] a fact which may have contributed to the creation of a rival Toronto Mining and Industrial Exchange. These two merged in 1900 under the esteemed presidency of E. S. Cox,[147] and in 1902 became incorporated as the Standard Stock and Mining Exchange of Toronto, with additional powers and new listings of railway, utility, and iron and steel shares.[148] Montreal also felt a round of speculation, which culminated in 1899 with the formation of a mining exchange, but even then most of the trading during the speculative wave was bank and railroad stocks.[149]

It was mining stock and other securities connected with the new prosperity in the staple industries that led to the formation of exchanges in western cities. While the first effort to form a stock exchange in Winnipeg to deal with bank equity, railway and mining shares, and wheat came during the Winnipeg land boom in 1882,[150] the exchange was in fact never established until 1903, and did no business until 1907.[151]

In B.C., some seventy brokers in Rossland formed the first mining exchange in 1897,[152] but it did not last long. Most of the B.C. stocks were dealt in in Spokane, and the need for local flotation facilities with the growth of mining led to the creation of the Vancouver Stock Exchange in 1907. By 1908, the new exchange was listing shares of the Cobalt, Ontario, mining companies once the silver boom began there.[153] Finally, in 1914, the opening round of the Calgary oil rush led to a great wave of speculation and an inflow of venture capital that culminated in the establishment of the Calgary Stock Exchange to trade in petroleum and gas equity, thus completing the roster of Canadian stock exchanges.[154]

Many of the new promotions had their shady side. In 1897, fifteen Toronto brokers were hauled into court and charged with falsely advertising the capital of the companies they represented in an effort to attract new subscribers. These brokers represented all of the large houses in Toronto, and all charges were duly dismissed.[155] In addition, brokers did a great deal of open swindling in their stock dealings, publicizing fraudulent quotations so they could bull or bear the stock at will, a process abetted by the periodic flooding of markets with promoters' stock.[156] Once the Cobalt boom started, the brokers and promoters took the government certificates stating there was ore in the claim and used them to dupe British investors into thinking the mine had government backing.[157]

Industrials slowly made their appearance on the exchanges, but remained very weak. Over the course of 1899 Toronto traded four major industrials — CCM, Commercial Cable, Carter-Crume, and Dunlop Tire, all of them licensees of American firms and all connected to George Cox or his immediate associates. The great bulk of trading remained in banking and loan company equity, utilities, or mines.[158] Despite the steady inflation which should have made them buoyant, industrials over the 1900-1913 period were the weakest shares on the exchanges, except for telegraph companies and similar utilities.[159] Bonds traded rose about two-and-one-half times on both exchanges. Stocks on the Montreal exchange rose nearly seven-fold, but in Toronto they dropped absolutely. And in both, industrials were only a small percentage of total shares traded, in Montreal falling from 3.5% in 1901 to two per cent in 1913. In both exchanges the only exception was 1909, when because of a wave of merger activity the volume of industrials traded rose substantially.[160] The industrial merger movement had the effect of introducing widespread industrial stockholding in Canada for the first time,[161] very much as the gold rush of 1896 had for mining stocks.

The nature of the equity changed, but much of the brokers' activity remained constant, included the usual series of failures. In 1898 Thomas Lownsborough (formerly of the failed firm of Forbes and Lownsborough), who had got back into broking, collapsed again after clients failed to keep up their margins.[162]

The traffic in American stocks remained abundant. In fact, before the war the business in American equity done by Toronto and Montreal brokers exceeded that done in Canadian shares.[163] And it was this trafficking in American shares that brought down A. E. Ames and Co. in 1903.[164] Ames had been kept afloat for a while by secret loans from Canada Life,[165] but a sharp contraction in the money market in 1902 precipitated failure. In the final analysis, Ames could only pay off 25% of his debts. He asked his creditors to accept the rest in the form of equity in a new joint stock brokerage house, and thus A. E. Ames and Co. Ltd. was created.[166]

The links to the U.S. stock market went deeper than simply trafficking in American equity. New York bucket shops and brokers maintained offices in Canada. One large New York bucket shop, M.J. Sage and Co., failed in 1906 and caused severe losses in Montreal.[167] And late in 1908 and early in 1909 a series of four American brokerage failures all involved Canadian losses.[168] But it was above all through money market conditions that the linkage was forged.

Money market conditions were extremely important in explaining the course of stock trading, since the great majority was done on borrowed money. The rate of interest on short-term loans varied inversely with stock prices. For example, when funds were diverted to moving the crops and the money market tightened, stock prices would be adversely affected, and so too would the volume of trading and the ease of raising funds for new enterprises. Thus, once again the requirements of a staple-extracting economy and the banks' concomitant involvement with commodity movements conflicted with the requirements of a modern industrial economy, indirectly via the stock market as well as directly through the banks' asset portfolios. But in addition the banks' call money operations were centred in New York, where call and short loans as a percentage of banks' total assets exceeded call and short loans in Canada. And the banks' figures badly overestimated the amount of a "call market" in Canada, for the loans in Canada were not nearly as callable as in New York, and bore much higher rates.[169] In fact, the Bank of Montreal, the largest bank in Canada, refused to make call loans in Canada at all on the grounds that Canadian equity had no outside market which reduced the callability of loans. [170] And of course, the resulting absence of call money helped create the thinness of the equity market that justified the refusal to advance on call.

## TABLE VI (7)

### Call Money Market Conditions, 1901-1913

| Call Loans as % Total Assets of Banks | | | | | | |
|---|---|---|---|---|---|---|
| | 1901 | 1902 | 1903 | 1904 | 1905 | 1906 | 1907 |
| In Canada | 6.6 | 7.1 | 6.8 | 5.3 | 5.5 | 6.4 | 5.1 |
| Abroad | 7.9 | 8.0 | 6.0 | 6.1 | 6.7 | 6.7 | 6.2 |
| | 1908 | 1909 | 1910 | 1911 | 1912 | 1913 | |
| In Canada | 4.5 | 5.0 | 5.1 | 4.9 | 4.9 | 4.6 | |
| Abroad | 6.1 | 11.1 | 9.2 | 7.2 | 7.1 | 6.3 | |

| Call Money Rates | | | | | | |
|---|---|---|---|---|---|---|
| | 1901 | 1902 | 1903 | 1904 | 1905 | 1906 | 1907 |
| Montreal | 4.96 | 5.28 | 5.70 | 5.07 | 4.76 | 5.57 | 6.00 |
| New York | 3.69 | 4.39 | 3.64 | 1.82 | 4.15 | 6.78 | 5.89 |
| London | 2.45 | 2.63 | 2.93 | 2.29 | 2.25 | 3.47 | 3.49 |
| | 1908 | 1909 | 1910 | 1911 | 1912 | 1913 | |
| Montreal | 5.47 | 4.21 | 5.25 | 5.48 | 5.39 | 6.26 | |
| New York | 1.90 | 2.72 | 2.87 | 2.55 | 3.75 | 3.28 | |
| London | 2.01 | 1.98 | 2.55 | 2.10 | 2.85 | 3.50 | |

Sources: CLR II, pp. 739 - 41; C.A. Curtis, Statistical Contributions, p. 67.

The avowed objective of the chartered banks' maintenance of call loans in New York was to create a buffer system to insulate Canadian credit conditions from world stringencies. The result was precisely the reverse. In 1902, at a time when call loans in New York were rising, Canadian brokers complained of a shortage of money. A collapse of the speculative boom resulted directly from the banks' calling loans in Canada following an American crisis in addition to the usual problem of the diversion of funds to crop movement.[171] The same problem emerged in 1907, when Canadian loans were called and funds diverted to commercial loans and discounts.[172]

Faced with these gaps in the Canadian capital market, Sir Rodolphe Forget, a Montreal financier and nephew of Sir Louis Forget, attempted in conjunction with French capital to float La Banque Internationale in Montreal, with the express purpose of using the bank funds to make loans to Canadian stockbrokers, underwriters and promoters, notably himself. The bank was beset by difficulties both within Canada and without. First came the refusal of the Ministry of Finance to issue it a certificate because it had hidden the double liability from the French shareholders who subscribed for 80% of the equity. An additional factor was that Rodolphe Forget had declared for the Tory cause in the 1911 election and was running against the Mayor of Quebec, who was a close friend of Laurier.[173] After the Tory victory the certificate was issued. For the French shareholders the result was disastrous. The Canadian directors engaged in a spate of deals aiming to enrich their friends and associates, and when the French directors sent representatives to Canada to investigate, they were physically barred from the directors' meeting. A French government investigation ensued.[174] The bank tottered and verged on collapse. Henry Pellatt secured control late in 1912 and merged the institution into the Home Bank, with heavy losses to the shareholders of La Banque Internationale.[175]

In addition to simply performing illicit activities, the bank had hidden them by falsifying returns to the federal government. As a reward, Sir Rodolphe was appointed by the Tory government to the parliamentary banking and commerce committee, which was responsible for shaping legislation regulating the operation of financial institutions and otherwise standing on guard for the monetary morality of Canada.

# Miscellaneous Sources of Funds and the Distribution of Income

One much neglected intermediary of considerable importance was the Catholic Church in Quebec, which absorbed large amounts of wealth, helping to impoverish its followers and precipitate that very flight of population from the Province which it so vocally deplored. By encouraging population growth too, it contributed to the subdivision of land and soil exhaustion. It also engaged in mortgage lending to French farmers to buy out the English in the Eastern Townships, for the French were subject to the tithe while the English were not.[176] Money raised by rents, tithes, or borrowed at zero interest was ploughed into steamships, railways, banking, and finance.[177] The earliest incidents of such transfers sanctioned by law involved the St. Lawrence and Atlantic Railroad Charter, in which the Sulpicians and other bodies were given authority to subscribe stock and to lend money to the company. All of the parishes along its main line as well as several Montreal orders subscribed.[178] There were even cases of parishes subscribing stock in industrial firms locating nearby.[179] But no public accounting was ever made of the Church's investments, and hence there is no way of estimating its importance to the intermediary process.

There were many instances where organized capital markets, such as they were, were bypassed by investors. Town councils subscribed stock in firms, and so would groups of citizens of a particular locality. The city of Kingston was especially zealous in this respect. In another case, in 1882, the woollen mill in Woodstock, New Brunswick, was erected by the stock subscriptions of the farmers of the area.[180]

Individual stock subscription depended, of course, on the degree of inequality in the income distribution. In a pioneer economy with relatively equal distribution of income, the great bulk of income is consumed. But with the progress of social differentiation increasing amounts became available for capital formation through the savings of the rich.[181] By 1889, the hardening of class lines and the concentration of capital had proceeded to such a degree that complaints over the closing of the Canadian frontier were heard, and immigration agents were urging new men to head west where more opportunity existed.[182]

Despite the accumulation, there was a trend to increased American direct investment in resources and manufacturing. The problem again lay in the tying-up of funds in certain fixed patterns of investment. As with institutional investments, which tended to remain and reproduce in the same sector in which they were initially accumulated, so too with individual wealth, which tended to stay in the same general fields in which the fortunes were made. In 1893, the five richest men in Canada were all railwaymen: D. McIntyre, Sir Donald A. Smith, R.B. Angus, and William Van Horne of the Canadian Pacific Railway; and J. Hickson of the Grand Trunk.[183] Twenty years earlier, the richest had been George Stephen and Sir Hugh Allan, also railwaymen and Montreal financial magnates. Twenty years later, in 1913, railwaymen again tended to top the list. Of the 42 richest men in Canada and those who controlled the greatest aggregations of funds, in terms of their principal preoccupations, ten were in railroads, seven in banks, nine in insurance and other finance, eight in utilities, four in grain mills and only four whose chief

## TABLE VI (8)

### Real Income 1900 - 1913

| Year | (1) Wages Index | (2) Index of 15 Foods | (3) Workman's Rent Index | (4) Family Budget Index | (5) G.N.P. per capita Index-current |
|------|-------|-------|-------|-------|-------|
| 1900 | 100.0 | 100.0 | 100.0 | 100.0 | 100.0 |
| 1901 | 102.0 | 107.0 |       |       |       |
| 1902 | 104.3 | 104.0 |       |       |       |
| 1903 | 106.1 | 107.0 |       |       |       |
| 1904 | 108.1 | 107.0 |       |       |       |
| 1905 | 111.6 | 117.0 | 112.3 | 108.7 |       |
| 1906 | 114.5 | 120.0 |       |       |       |
| 1907 | 119.2 | 130.0 |       |       |       |
| 1908 | 121.1 | 135.0 |       |       |       |
| 1909 | 125.4 | 143.0 | 140.0 | 122.4 |       |
| 1910 | 129.7 | 141.0 | 150.0 | 127.3 | 160.0 |
| 1911 | 133.1 | 135.0 | 154.7 | 131.5 |       |
| 1912 | 139.3 | 155.0 | 135.6 | 137.8 |       |
| 1913 | 142.9 | 146.0 | 149.6 | 138.8 |       |

Sources: (1) *CLR II*, p. 427.
        (2) K. Taylor and H. Mitchell, *Statistical Contributions*, p. 55.
        (3) *CLR II*, p. 379.
        (4) *CLR II*, p. 76.
        (5) Calculated from O.J. Firestone, *Canada's Economic Development*, p. 74.

interests were industrial. Of these, men linked to the Canadian Northern and Grand Trunk railways abounded. And of the top ten in terms of corporate assets controlled, six were railwaymen, two were financiers, one was a banker and one in utilities.[184]

But at the same time that great fortunes were being consolidated, living standards for the working class were deteriorating: real wages fell during the great expansion after 1896. Even for a select group of highly skilled, well organized workers, money wage rates barely kept ahead of the cost of living. Rents rose more quickly than money wages, and the share of rent in total expenditures tended to rise.[185] Food costs rose very quickly, and between 1900 and 1910 while per-capita GNP rose 60% in nominal terms, money wages for the selected group rose only 30%.

Moreover, any attempt to gauge the course of real income and its distribution must take account of the highly regressive structure of taxes prevailing. Government revenue per head of population rose from $9.78 in 1901 to $21.74 in 1913, while over the same period the proportion of total taxes accounted for by the steeply regressive customs tariff rose from 73% to 82%.[186] It is also noteworthy that during this period of rapid inflation, money wage reductions were one of the most common causes of strikes, and that in such disputes employers won three times as often as employees.[187] Such a deterioration in living standards of the mass of wage earners was the precondition of the accumulation and concentration of the great fortunes that sustained the development of Canadian financial institutions of the era.

# Notes to Chapter VI

1. E. P. Neufeld, *Financial System,* p. 282.
2. *RCRLC, Report* 1889, pp. 20-22.
3. *Ec,* April 25, 1903, p. 735.
4. Data from Department of Trade and Commerce, *Annual Report Part IV,* Sessional Papers 1914, pp. 37-8.
5. *Ec,* May 7, 1904, p. 779.
6. S. Thompson, *Reminiscences,* pp. 235-41.
7. *Statutes of Canada,* 1875, 38 Vic. Chapter 20.
8. *HCD,* March 3, 1875, p. 452.
9. *MT,* August 25, 1875, p. 215; March 9, 1877, p. 1029; March 30, 1877, p. 114.
10. Superintendent of Insurance, *Report* 1877, *MT,* July 6, 1877, p. 41; July 31, 1877, p. 70.
11. *SCC, Evidence,* pp. 470-1.
12. *MT,* Aug. 28, 1885, p. 240.
13. *SCC, Evidence,* pp. 485, 491.
14. *MT,* June 29, 1894, p. 1635.
15. *IC,* Oct. 1904, p. 189.

16.   *IC,* Oct. 1906, p. 220; Oct. 1907, p. 221.
17.   *IC,* April 1909, p. 748.
18.   *IC,* Oct. 1910, p. 310.
19.   *CE,* Oct. 1896, p. 179.
20.   *MT,* April 23, 1897, p. 1408.
21.   *MT,* Nov. 3, 1883, pp. 602-3.
22.   *RCRLC, Report* 1889, p. 24.
23:   *MT,* Aug. 17, 1894, pp. 206-7.
24.   *MT,* Dec. 1, 1906, p. 729.
25.   *RCLI, Report,* p. 167.
26.   *MT,* Jan. 5, 1877, p. 754; July 29, 1881, p. 127; May 13, 1881, p. 1316; May
      26, 1882, p. 1442; Oct. 5, 1883, p. 378; Aug. 28, 1882, p. 1322; Nov. 2, 1883,
      p. 484; July 27, 1883, p. 91; Aug. 17, 1883, p. 176; Feb. 20, 1885, p. 941;
      April 17, 1885, p. 1179; June 5, 1885, p. 1368.
27.   *RCLI, Report,* p. 10, *Evidence,* p. 948 *et passim.*
28.   W. T. R. Preston, *Lord Strathcona,* pp. 171-4.
29.   Senate, Special Committee...Allegations made by Mr. Herman Henry
      Cook, *Senate Journal 1901,* Appendix I.
30.   *MT,* May 19, 1899, p. 1508.
31.   *RCLI, Report,* p. 16, *Evidence,* pp. 973, 1638.
32.   *RCLI, Report,* p. 53.
33.   *MT,* Oct. 9, 1891, p. 431.
34.   *Globe,* Oct. 4, 1906; Oct. 5, 1906; Oct. 11, 1906.
35.   *RCLI, Report,* pp. 133, 135-6.
36.   *RCLI, Report,* pp. 94-7, *Evidence,* p. 1416.
37.   See Dept. of Finance, *Public Accounts,* 1915, p. 75.
38.   E. R. Wood, *Annual Review of the Bond Markets of Canada* 1906, p. 6.
39.   *CAR,* 1907, pp. 46-7.
40.   E. R. Wood, *Annual Review of the Bond Markets of Canada* 1910, pp. 10-
      11.
41.   G. R. Stevens, *The Canada Permanent Story,* pp. 17, 19.
42.   B. E. Walker, *History of Banking in Canada,* p. 91.
43.   E. P. Neufeld, *Financial System,* p. 206.
44.   B. E. Walker, *History of Banking in Canada,* pp. 90-1.
45.   M. Morris "The Mortgage Loan Companies...", p. 243.
46.   *MT,* Nov. 6, 1880, p. 614.
47.   *MT,* Jan. 30, 1882, p. 387.
48.   G. R. Stevens, *Canada Permanent, p. 24.*
49.   *MT,* Aug. 27, 1869, p. 25.
50.   *MT,* Jan. 5, 1883, p. 739; April 13, 1883, p. 1147.
51.   *MT,* Oct. 21, 1885, p. 301; March 12, 1886, p. 1037; Feb. 18, 1887, p. 958.
52.   *MT,* Sept. 8, 1882, p. 260; Aug. 28, 1885, p. 229.
53.   *MT,* Feb. 27, 1880, p. 1014; April 21, 1882, p. 1285.
54.   *MT,* Feb. 16, 1883, p. 913; Feb. 23, 1883, p. 940.
55.   *MT,* July 24, 1887, p. 136.
56.   *MT,* Aug. 5, 1887, p. 168.
57.   *MT,* Oct. 14, 1887, pp. 491, 496.
58.   *MT,* March 14, 1884, p. 1038.
59.   *MT,* March 21, 1884, p. 1058.
60.   *MT,* Dec. 28, 1883, p. 705.
61.   *MT,* Oct. 2, 1885, p. 381.
62.   *MT,* July 20, 1888, p. 68.
63.   *MT,* Aug. 19, 1887, p. 231.
64.   *MT,* July 9, 1880, p. 39; July 16, 1880, p. 70.
65.   Quebec, *Rapport Sur...Le Credit Foncier,* pp. 5, 12, 43.

66. *HCD,* Feb. 11, 1881, p. 944.
67. Quebec, *Rapport Sur...Le Credit Foncier,* p. 86.
68. *MT,* May 6, 1881, p. 1292.
69. Quebec, *Rapport Sur...Le Credit Foncier,* p. 63.
70. *MT,* July 8, 1881, p. 40.
71. *MT,* Dec. 30, 1881, p. 793.
72. *MT,* Sept. 1, 1882, p. 239.
73. *HCD,* Feb. 11, 1881, p. 1288.
74. *HCD,* Feb. 11, 1881, p. 942.
75. *HCD,* March 20, 1882, p. 439.
76. *MT,* March 16, 1883, p. 1034.
77. *MT,* Nov. 5, 1886, p. 523.
78. *MT,* June 24, 1898, p. 1676.
79. *MT,* Oct. 8, 1897, p. 469.
80. *MT,* Nov. 10, 1893, p. 568.
81. *MT,* Feb. 22, 1889, p. 970.
82. *MT,* Nov. 25, 1898, p. 702.
83. *MT,* Feb. 22, 1901, p. 1089.
84. Wm. Drummond, *Financing of Land Purchases in Canada,* p. 383.
85. *MT,* Feb. 20, 1903, p. 1128.
86. *Statutes of Quebec,* 1900, 63 Vic. Chapter 74.
87. *MT,* Aug. 11, 1899, p. 211; Sept. 1, 1899, p. 275.
88. *MT,* May 14, 1897, p. 1536; May 28, 1897, p. 1568.
89. *MT,* Dec. 10, 1897, p. 760; Dec. 17, 1897, p. 791; Feb. 18, 1898, p. 1090.
90. *MT,* July 28, 1899, p. 111; Sept. 1, 1899, p. 270.
91. *MT,* Oct. 21, 1904, p. 515-6.
92. *MT,* April 6, 1906, p. 1338.
93. *MT,* Dec. 24, 1905, p. 823.
94. *MT,* Dec. 1, 1905, p. 695; Jan. 12, 1906, p. 900.
95. *MT,* June 12, 1903, p. 1682.
96. *MT,* Feb. 23, 1900, p. 1110.
97. *MT,* July 1, 1898, p. 8.
98. *MT,* Jan. 21, 1898, p. 957.
99. *MT,* Jan. 5, 1899, p. 898; G. R. Stevens, *Canada Permanent,* p. 31.
100. *MT,* March 10, 1899, p. 1193; Oct. 6, 1899, p. 433; Nov. 17, 1899, p. 651.
101. *MT,* Feb. 23, 1906, p. 1111; Nov. 3, 1906, p. 636.
102. B. E. Walker to W. C. Ward, April 14, 1905, *Walker Papers.*
103. *RCLI, Evidence,* pp. 1039, 2890.
104. B. E. Walker to W. G. Macfarlane, Nov. 23, 1908, *Walker Papers.*
105. *CLRII,* pp. 721-2, 730-4.
106. M. Morris, "The Mortgage Loan Companies...", p. 247.
107. *SACC,* p. 846.
108. *SACC,* p. 831.
109. *SACC,* p. 844.
110. R. L. Jones, *History of Agriculture in Ontario,* p. 236.
111. *MT,* Nov. 18, 1913, p. 747.
112. *MT,* June 16, 1882, p. 1545.
113. Carl Bergithon, *The Stock Exchange,* p. 11.
114. *MT,* May 20, 1886.
115. *MT,* Aug. 18, 1908, p. 241.
116. *MT,* Feb. 16, 1900, p. 1070.
117. *MT,* April 4, 1902, p. 1286.
118. *MT,* Nov. 28, 1908, p. 883.
119. A. Trigge, *Bank of Commerce III,* p. 60.
120. Royal Commission...Textiles *(RCT) Report,* p. 32.

121.  Toronto Board of Trade, *Annual Report,* 1883.
122.  *MT,* Jan. 4, 1884, p. 739.
123.  *MT,* May 26, 1899, pp. 1544-5.
124.  *MT,* March 26, 1880, p. 1143.
125.  *MT,* March 18, 1869, p. 492.
126.  *MT,* Nov. 24, 1876, p. 586.
127.  *MT,* Dec. 1, 1876, p. 613; Aug. 23, 1878, p. 241.
128.  *MT,* Dec. 1, 1876, p. 616.
129.  *MT,* Oct. 15, 1886, p. 436.
130.  *HCD,* May 14, 1888, pp. 1405-1412.
131.  *MT,* Oct. 1, 1886, p. 380.
132.  *MT,* July 27, 1888, p. 96; Aug. 10, 1888, p. 151; Sept. 7, 1888, p. 268; Sept. 28, 1888, p. 357.
133.  *MT,* Oct. 5, 1888, p. 835; Oct. 12, 1888, p. 413.
134.  *MT,* July 13, 1888, p. 39.
135.  *MT,* April 12, 1895, p. 1318.
136.  *MT,* May 15, 1896, p. 1471.
137.  *MT,* May 14, 1897, p. 1499.
138.  *MT,* Sept. 15, 1899, p. 331.
139.  *MT,* Oct. 4, 1895, p. 428.
140.  *MT,* Jan. 5, 1900, p. 874; Jan. 12, 1900, p. 916; Aug. 17, 1900, p. 202.
141.  *MT,* Feb. 16, 1907, p. 1267.
142.  *HCD,* July 21, 1903, pp. 7006-7010.
143.  B.E. Walker to T.C. Higgins, Jan. 21, 1896, *Walker Papers.*
144.  *MT,* Oct. 9, 1896, p. 486.
145.  *MT,* Jan. 5, 1899, p. 888.
146.  *MT,* Jan. 21, 1898, p. 958.
147.  *MT,* June 29, 1900, p. 1712.
148.  *MT,* Feb. 7, 1902, p. 1010.
149.  *MT,* March 31, 1899, p. 1284.
150.  *MT,* Oct. 20, 1882, p. 428.
151.  R.C. Bellan, *The Growth of Winnipeg,* p. 156.
152.  *MT,* March 26, 1897, p. 1275.
153.  *MT,* March 23, 1907, p. 1493; June 29, 1907, p. 2069; Oct. 24, 1908, p. 671.
154.  *Ec,* May 30, 1914, p. 1330.
155.  *MT,* Jan. 22, 1897, p. 976; Feb. 5, 1897, p. 1045.
156.  *MT,* March 26, 1897, p. 1281.
157.  *MT,* July 20, 1907, p. 93.
158.  *MT,* Jan. 5, 1900, p. 880.
159.  *CLRII,* p. 625.
160.  *CLRII,* pp. 686-7.
161.  *Globe,* April 13, 1910; July 4, 1911.
162.  *MT,* Sept. 9, 1898, p. 329.
163.  *MT,* May 3, 1918, p. 9.
164.  *MT,* June 5, 1903, p. 1646.
165.  *RCLI, Report,* p. 17.
166.  *MT,* Jan. 15, 1904, p. 912.
167.  *MT,* April 24, 1906, p. 257.
168.  *MT,* April 17, 1909, p. 1854.
169.  *CBC,* 1913, p. 310; *CLRII,* pp. 739-741.
170.  *FP,* April 6, 1907.
171.  *MT,* Oct. 11, 1902, pp. 1569-70; Dec. 19, 1902, p. 791.
172.  *FP,* March 23, 1907.
173.  *MT,* Feb. 1, 1913, p. 273.
174.  *HCD,* Jan. 27, 1913, p. 2208; *MT,* Jan. 25, 1913, p. 241.

175. *MT*, Dec. 14, 1912, p. 886.
176. Goldwyn Smith, *Canada and the Canadian Question*, pp. 20-21.
177. G. Myers, *History of Canadian Wealth*, p. 17.
178. *Ibid.*, p. 166.
179. *JC*, Jan. 9, 1880, p. 671.
180. *CM*, April 28, 1882, p. 159.
181. J.S. Mill, *Principles of Political Economy*, p. 69.
182. *RCRLC, Ontario Evidence*, p. 759.
183. *JC*, March 17, 1893, p. 419.
184. *GGG*, June 25, 1913.
185. *CLRII*, p. 1016.
186. *CYB*, 1916, pp. 538, 547.
187. Dept. of Labour, *Report on Strikes and Lockouts in Canada 1901-1916*, p. 106.

*If Caesar were to reappear upon earth...Rothschild would open and shut the Temple of Janus; Thomas Baring...would probably command the Tenth Legion, and the soldiers would march into battle with loud cries of Scrip and Omnium reduced, Consols and Caesar.*

Reverend Sydney Smith,
*Letters on American Debt,* 1844

# CHAPTER VII
# Canada and the International Flow of Finance Capital

## Patterns of Foreign Portfolio Investment

To a substantial degree, the terms of Confederation were designed explicitly to placate British investors after the Grand Trunk debacles of the 1850's and 1860's, and to restore the Province of Canada's sagging credit. Yet despite the efforts of the Canadian politicians British confidence did not return on a great scale until after the great expansion began at the end of the century, though there was, of course, substantial foreign and British investment in Canada before that date.

In 1881 in London there existed a chain of debts, the structure of which reflected the financial hierarchy envisaged in the Confederation arrangements. At the top were £6.3 million of imperially guaranteed Canada four per cent bonds, a total of £19,233,840 in unguaranteed Dominion debt at four, five, and six per cent, plus a range of other bonds: B.C., P.E.I., New Brunswick, and Quebec, mostly carrying Government of Canada guarantees, totalled £3,319,600, while the borrowings of municipal governments came to £3,340,497. In addition, a Canada Central Railway loan of £500,000 carried a Government of Canada guarantee. Unguaranteed railway debts whose nominal value came to £47 million also existed. Part of these were not bonds and debentures but preference stock. At that time, then, Canada's funded debt in Britain came to about £70 million, on which interest and dividend remittances were about £3,150,000 per annum. However, the total is deceptive. Much of it represented the cumulation of loans over a long period. The rate of return at that time was lower on Canadian securities than that available on British bank loans and mortgages[1] which restricted the flow of British money to Canada.

By 1896, foreign capital of all types in Canada was estimated to have reached a cumulative total of $1.2 billion, of which nearly one billion had been British and the great majority in railroad and government securities.[2] Of this, Dominion-Government-funded debt payable in London was $218 million in 1896. The provinces had been active in London since well before Confederation, and their borrowing continued whenever possible. The Bank of Montreal after Confederation began developing a substantial business in underwriting Quebec government issues in London[3] and even a few issues in the United States,[4] the 1874 London issue being done in conjunction with the British-Canadian private bankers, Morton, Rose and Company.

For both the provinces and the Dominion a great upsurge in borrowings in London occurred at the end of the century, especially after 1907. Two provincial government issues in 1899 were placed there, by British Columbia and by Nova Scotia. From 1907, all the issues of the federal government were placed in London, as were those of Quebec, Nova Scotia, P.E.I. and B.C. From 1909 on, Saskatchewan floated issues in London. Manitoba, which had earlier placed issues in Montreal and Chicago, switched to London in 1910, and Alberta, except for one 1913 New York issue, negotiated all of its loans there.[5] Much of the prairie provinces' borrowings, in addition to local railroads, was in conjunction with their takeovers of the Bell Telephone network in those provinces.[6]

British funds flowed into many fields, especially after 1905, in addition to government borrowings. The largest share went to railroads (to build two new transcontinentals); government finance, including some municipal debentures, came second; and after 1908 the flow into industrial bonds began to rise to support a merger wave. Utilities, with their monopoly position and links to the state structure, were also popular. And there was substantial investment in the purchase of land through land companies, although mortgage lending remained largely the prerogative of Canadian institutions, aided, of course, by British purchases of mortgage loan company debentures. Nor was there any significant share of "mercantile" debt of the sort that in earlier periods accounted for such a large share of Canadian borrowings in Britain, for the Canadian chartered banks had taken over this function.

There were also some investments by other than public issue. British investments directly in branch plants did occur, though they were rare, while British purchase of industrial bonds was substantial — precisely the opposite pattern to that of American investments. There were some holdings of British insurance companies, but these cannot be regarded as an inflow of capital since most, if not all, of the policy funds with which they were made were generated inside Canada. And there were of course a number of private investments or individual holdings of bonds and equity in financial institutions, private debenture sales, and direct purchase of real estate by individuals. By 1914 these items could not have totalled more than $200 million, while total British investments in Canada were close to three billion dollars.[7] A number of estimates of British capital invested in Canada from 1896 to 1914 exist, of various degrees of credibility. While it is generally regarded as an underestimate, *The Economist's* data yield the best breakdown by classification of investment for new public issues in London over the period.

The opening years of the boom saw the level of new public issues in London actually fall; Canada's balance of trade was in surplus over-all and there was a great deal of retirement of existing debt. Mining issues in conjunction with the Klondike and B.C. gold, lead, copper, and silver rushes were the most noticeable change in the early period. Over the next few years, railway issues tended to dominate. Then, with the commencement of the wheat boom proper after 1907, major changes in the structure of debt occurred. Insurance companies switched out of bonds and municipal debentures into mortgage lending, the banks tended to reduce their security holdings as a share of total assets, and as a result municipalities turned increasingly to London. Government expenditures on infrastructure rose sharply in this period, as did the amount of railway investment, sending both to the London capital market with ever-growing demands. In addition, from 1909 to 1912 there occurred a rush of industrial bond floatations in conjunction with the Canadian merger movement.

# Policy Towards Portfolio Investment

The slow flow of British investment to Canada after Confederation was the object of considerable consternation, and policymakers' efforts were directed energetically towards encouraging the stream. Macdonald at one point tried to instil some enthusiasm for Canadian investments into Baron Rothschild by promising land for the establishment of a Zionist colony in the Northwest.[8] Once the flow began, efforts were redirected towards keeping it coming. Even before the National Policy, the prize

## TABLE VII (1)

### Canadian Public Issues in London, 1896-1913

(new issues net of refunding)
£ 1,000's

| Year | Federal and Provincial | Municipal | Railway | Utility | Mining | Misc., Including Industrial | Total |
|---|---|---|---|---|---|---|---|
| 1896 | | | 54 | | | | 508 |
| 1897 | 2,381 | | 305 | | 1,125 | 1,000 | 4,811 |
| 1898 | | 213 | | | 1,328 | 120 | 1,661 |
| 1899 | 481 | | | | 130 | 200 | 861 |
| 1900 | | | 630 | | | | 630 |
| 1901 | | 499 | 1,153 | | | | 1,652 |
| 1902 | | 411 | 255 | 60 | | 2,270 | 953 |
| 1903 | | | 4,065 | 67 | | 315 | 4,447 |
| 1904 | | | 4,087 | 53 | | 364 | 4,504 |
| 1905 | | 73 | 9,636 | 253 | | 605 | 10,567 |
| 1906 | 1,182 | | 6,874 | 62 | | 642 | 8,759 |
| 1907 | 1,500 | 690 | 2,020 | 511 | 150 | 215 | 5,186 |
| 1908 | 5,629 | 5,000 | 12,453 | 2,080 | | 1,361 | 27,504 |
| 1909 | 9,903 | 2,150 | 8,061 | 2,124 | 20 | 4,555 | 26,403 |
| 1910 | 11,755 | 3,350 | 6,426 | 1,619 | 145 | 13,094 | 36,343 |
| 1911 | 505 | 4,152 | 19,608 | na | na | na | 41,215 |
| 1912 | 970 | 5,286 | 29,347 | na | na | na | 46,983 |
| 1913 | 7,877 | 13,612 | 11,431 | na | na | na | 44,119 |

Sources: *Ec*, July 8, 1911, p. 62; June 13, 1914, p. 1431.

point of contention between the financial spokesmen of the two political parties was their respective ability to lower the rate of interest at which Canadian issues were floated in London.[9] Also important were the links between the high tariff and the relative attractiveness of the country for portfolio as well as direct investment. In 1878, New South Wales' securities were the highest of colonials in London, selling at four to five per cent more than Canadian. But after the 1879 Tilley Budget speech, Canada's securities rose quickly: by 1881 they were two per cent above New South Wales and second only to British consols.[10] From 1878 to 1882, mortgage rates inside Canada fell from four to two per cent and many old mortgages were paid off.[11] The federal government advanced the propagandistic claim that this and the accompanying interest rate decreases were due to the National Policy, in a vain effort to convince farmers that they too had a great stake in the protective system.[12] But it was exactly at the time of the National Policy that the great flow of British funds into mortgage company debentures began, and these two events, while occurring roughly simultaneously, were due to totally different causes.

Federal control over banking and currency, and the additional security resulting from the federal assumption of provincial debts, were both reinforced by the disallowance power, which was used as an instrument in the effort to secure high credit ratings abroad. In 1888, a Quebec act designed to enable the province to issue new debentures in a roll-over operation with respect to some outstanding debt was disallowed on the grounds that it would affect the provincial credit adversely, and hence reflect badly on the credit of the other provinces and the Dominion as well. The following year, a New Brunswick mining act was disallowed because it "invades the rights of property which are so important to preserve for the credit of the whole country," and in 1893 an Ontario statute was disallowed on similar grounds.[13] Then too, the myriad of federal disallowances of provincial railway charters from 1871, especially those of Manitoba, were prompted in part by the need to secure the CPR monopoly as a defence of its power to raise bond capital in Britain on the security of its earnings.

Once the inflow of British capital got underway in sizeable proportions, any and all threats to its security, real or imagined, were denounced and avoided, anything from labour unrest to "socialist" legislation. Industrial peace was regarded as essential to preserve the influx. The *Monetary Times* therefore suggested a simple solution to industrial disputes:

Canada wants capital. Extremists of any variety will scare it away. Capital and labour will not always be bitterly grappling. . . . Differences should be balanced by a little thinking. To direct capital to Canada, it is necessary that employers and employees be reasonable beings.[14]

The flow of British capital depended upon high credit ratings which, in the opinion of Sir Edmund Walker, depended in turn upon (1) the enormous natural resources of Canada, (2) "the agricultural and pastoral basis of our industrial life," i.e. the production of staples to provide cheap food for Britain, and (3) "respect for law and order." The flow was threatened by the irresponsibility of the press, by the spread of "democratic sentiment" with concomitant "hatred of success," as well as by labour strife.[15] And without capital there could be no immigration.

Our power to receive . . . immigrants depends on our credit with England. We enjoy at her hand the best credit of any country in the world. Every foolish operation in Canadian finance imperils that credit.[16]

The greatest of these "foolish operations" was the Ontario Hydro operation, whereby the municipalities and manufacturers forced the nationalization of private power monopolies. Strenuous efforts were made to secure federal disallowance on the familiar grounds that the power operation injured Canadian credit in Britain, for the province entered the field of power transmission and distribution, and later production, in competition with a number of utility firms of the Mackenzie-Mann group supported by large investments of British funds.[17]

The British financial interests and the Canadian power magnates mounted a strong campaign against Hydro. British opinion was led by Professor A. V. Dicey who contributed his view that the legislation was unconstitutional. Lord Ridley of the so-called "Tariff Reform League" claimed it would ruin Canadian credit, as did many other British bankers and brokers who flooded the Minister of Finance, W. S. Fielding, and Lord Strathcona (then High Commissioner in London) with cries of discrimination, "unBritish behaviour," despotism even beneath the dignity of central American republics, and even the opinion of the *Financial Times* that likened the nationalization to the repeal of the Magna Carta.[18]

The agitation failed to force disallowance, and the British funds continued to flow to Canada — with one exception. In 1909 Ontario attempted to float a power loan in Britain of $3,-500,000. The issue was boycotted, the Canadian banks lining up with those in Britain to prevent it being taken up.

A few years later, very similar vituperations were heard from

the president of the Grand Trunk Railway to try to exact more
public support and ward off nationalization:

> The repudiation of this legitimate indebtedness in any
> arrangement made with the government would not only injure
> the Grand Trunk Company's credit but might induce a spirit
> of hostile criticism on the part of the investor in Grand Trunk
> securities in London and New York that might easily react
> upon the credit of the country.[19]

# The Colonial Stocks Acts

No sooner had Confederation granted a modicum of nominal
financial autonomy to Canada, than its politicians were anx-
iously attempting to subvert it by restoring to Britain a substantial financial control through the Colonial Stocks Acts. These
acts were designed to facilitate the integration of the colonial
capital markets with those of the imperium, and narrow the
interest rate differential between British and colonial securities.
British investors had to be convinced that colonial securities were
as safe as British, and this required a tightening of British control
over colonial finances.[20]

The first Colonial Stocks Act was unsatisfactory to the colonies. Sir Julius Vogel, Prime Minister of New Zealand, who led
the new colonial dependence movement, had sought to have
colonial securities admitted to the Trustee List. But all the Act
gave the colonies was a specially low composition stamp duty on
the transfers of their inscribed stock in London.[21]

Canadian inscribed stock gained admission to the Scottish
Trustee List in 1884,[22] but not to the English list. The reasons for
the Scottish inclusion probably had to do with the large amount
of Scottish investment in Canadian mortgage, loan, and building
societies' debentures, and the large number of Scottish firms
operating in Canada under imperial charter. An attempt was
made in 1888 to secure admission to the English list, the Lords
approving but the Commons rejecting. In England the yields on
colonial inscribed stock by the mid-1890's were higher than on
consols or British corporate bonds, the differential being imputed
there directly to the absence of trustee status.[23] Yet, despite the
lack of admission, Canadian securities continued to do better
than those of any other self-governing colony,[24] a credit to its
many other policies to court favour among London money-mag-
nates.

In 1900, a new Colonial Stocks Act set out the conditions for
admission of the colonies' inscribed stock:

1. The colony shall provide by legislation for the payment out of the revenues of the Colony of any sums which may become payable to the stockholders under any judgement, decree, rule or order of a Court in the United Kingdom.

2. The colony shall satisfy the Treasury that adequate funds (as and when required) will be made available in the United Kingdom to meet any such judgement, decree, rule or order.

3. The colonial government shall place on record a formal expression of their opinion, that any Colonial legislation which appears to the Imperial Government to alter any of the provisions affecting the Stock to the injury of the stock-holders, or to involve a departure from the original contract in regard to stock would properly be disallowed.

In addition, to protect existing British investments in Canada, a further pledge was required that only Canadian revenues would be liable for the stock and dividends, and that no claim directly or indirectly against British revenue would be permitted.

Provincial securities, despite constant efforts,[25] were not admitted to the list, although Australian state securities were. In Canada, the constitution barred the individual provinces from bringing their legislation directly under the scrutiny of the Imperial Government for approval or disallowance. The Australian states, too, had gained admission while still individual states.[26] Moreover, under the terms of the Commonwealth of Australia Act, the Australian states remained nominally the dominant economic units, while the Canadian provinces had been totally subordinated to the federal government. The Canadian provinces, therefore, lacked the revenue sources that Australian states could command, with a resulting decline in their security.

W. S. Fielding predicted great benefits to Canada from the Act. He foresaw a reduction of two percentage points in the interest rate on the inscribed stocks, which over ten years would sum to a net saving of two-and-one-half million dollars.

There are vast sums of money in England in the hands of trustees who have to invest it in the best class of securities. . . . The gain that we shall make by this action of the British government in coming to the assistance of Canada will be in actual cash equal to every penny we spend for the sending of the Canadian soldiers to South Africa.[27]

A more candid confession of the rationale behind the war policy would be hard to find. Canada, he predicted, would soon add two million a year to its debts and actually pay less interest than it did in 1900.[28]

The actual effects of the Act are difficult to unravel.[29] The yields on colonial stocks in fact rose rather than fell. It is conceivable that the colonies lost some of the benefits of the Act by swamping the market in 1900.[30] And in colonial securities in general, the gap between their average yield and that of British widened after 1900, until 1907.

**TABLE VII (2)**

**Average Rates of Return on Securities**

| Year | U.K.[1] | Colonial[1] | Foreign[1] | Canada Funded Debt[2] |
|------|------|----------|---------|----------------------|
| 1888 | 4.35 | 3.43 | 5.61 | 3.94 |
| 1893 | 2.92 | 4.09 | 5.53 | 3.79 |
| 1898 | 2.81 | 3.07 | 3.97 | 3.67 |
| 1899 | 3.44 | 3.27 | 5.11 | 3.67 |
| 1900 | 3.35 | 3.20 | 4.05 | 3.67 |
| 1901 | 3.00 | 3.40 | 5.34 | 3.67 |
| 1902 | 3.12 | 3.21 | 4.94 | 3.67 |
| 1903 | 3.44 | 3.21 | 5.77 | 3.67 |
| 1904 | 3.46 | 3.78 | 5.83 | 3.63 |
| 1905 | 3.39 | 3.78 | 4.99 | 3.63 |
| 1906 | 3.37 | 3.85 | 5.14 | 3.66 |
| 1907 | 3.61 | 3.99 | 4.90 | 3.57 |
| 1908 | 4.00 | 4.04 | 4.95 | 3.56 |
| 1909 | 3.60 | 3.96 | 4.88 | 3.56 |
| 1910 | 3.72 | 4.19 | 4.85 | 3.53 |
| 1911 | 4.01 | 4.03 | 4.85 | 3.44 |

Sources: (1) R.A. Lenfeldt, "The Rate of Interest on British and Foreign Investment"; (2) Dept. of Finance, *Public Accounts,* 1915, p. 75.

Canada, in fact, made relatively little use of the Act. Of all the four Dominions its borrowings were the least, amounting by 1910 to $42 million at the same time its borrowings in Britain in all classes of securities were the greatest of all the colonies.

# Dominion Government Finance

By the time of the advent to power of Alexander Mackenzie's government in 1873, Canadian finances were in a chaotic state.[31] Excessive public spending in the dying days of the Macdonald government had occurred in a frantic effort to buy its way out of the opprobrium that resulted from the Pacific Scandal. After Sir Richard Cartwright's tariff adjustments the situation improved somewhat, but by 1876 the budget deficit was again acute,[32] and foreign investors remained anxious, until the "protective" tariff of 1879. The National Policy was initially a great success as a revenue source, budgetary surplus in conjunction with government savings bank deposits sufficing to pay for public works. And the new revenues restored investors' confidence, placing Canadian securities at the top of the colonial list.[33] By late 1883, however, the budget surplus disappeared in the face of economic collapse.

With the loss of revenue, Tilley was forced to try to place a four million dollar loan in Canada late in 1883.[34] It was almost a total failure. Tenders were received for only $1,177,000, of which only $977,000 was acceptable. The spring of 1884 saw Sir Leonard off to London to try to raise $50 million, $29 million to pay off maturing debentures and $21 million to be given to the CPR[35] as a reward for its role in the 1882 election.

At that time London was not very receptive to Canadian securities. A loan of five million pounds was placed at 3.5% but at a discount of nearly ten per cent. This loan for the CPR by Tilley's own admission was necessary only for political purposes, that is, to buy seats by generating patronage along the route; and Tilley affirmed that if the CPR were built slowly it could finish the line within the contract time on its own resources.[36] In early 1885, Tilley was back in London seeking another loan, which, while it was taken up a little above par, bore an interest rate half a per cent higher than its predecessor.[37]

Once the immediate demands of the CPR were met, little new Dominion borrowing except to meet maturing issues occurred until after 1896. It was a time of generally falling interest rates.[38] In 1892 a Canadian loan was placed at three per cent, though it sold at a large discount. But by 1894 Canadian three per cent debentures were quoted at par, and a new loan bearing that rate sold at a much lower discount.[39]

When Laurier took office, the state of Canadian credit was as much a Liberal as it had been a Tory preoccupation. Prominent Liberals immediately began to press for the recall of Sir Donald A. Smith (Strathcona) from his lofty position as High Commissioner on the grounds that he would use his position to divert British funds into his own enterprises.[40] Laurier at one point planned to replace Smith with Sir Richard Cartwright,[41] a move that would have effectively rid domestic politics and the Liberals of Cartwright's embarrassing presence in the face of the distrust he engendered among big business, would have at least partially placated Cartwright after the chartered banks refused his application for the post of Minister of Finance, and would have taken care of the problem posed by Smith all in one stroke. But Smith was judged to be more dangerous in Canada than in London and left at his post.[42] And in fact Fielding's 1897 50-year loan was easily raised at 2.75%, most of it earmarked for railways,[43] especially the CPR, and so there was little need for Smith to exercise any diversionary tactics for the time being.

Between 1897 and 1902, no federal loans were floated in London, for by 1898 buoyant tariff revenues produced large and growing budgetary surpluses sufficient to pay for the public works.[44] But by 1903 the extravagant development schemes of the Laurier administration in response to corporate greed and the insatiable appetites of the new railroad lines forced the federal government to turn to London again[45] as a prelude to the great rush of borrowings after 1907.

# Provincial Finance

Under the Confederation terms, those provinces whose debts were relatively heavy had to pay interest on the amount by which their debts exceeded a certain level, while the others got a sum for interest on the amount by which their debts fell short of what was judged their fair quota. In total the Dominion assumed $125,645,148 on behalf of the provinces, and at the same time secured all the major revenue sources. In turn the provinces received a subsidy, partly in the form of a small specific grant of between $100,000 and $240,000 depending on population, plus a variable subsidy of 80¢ per head of population up to two-and-one-half million, and 60¢ per head thereafter.

There were a few special alterations. P.E.I. was given extra because of its absence of crown land. New Brunswick later got an increase in subsidy in return for surrendering the rights to impose certain timber export duties to the federal government. And the prairies, whose land was seized by the federal government to give away to eastern big business, received a few special grants. There were some additional revenue sources — stumpage fees on timber, royalties from minerals, crown land sales, except for the prairies, and liquor licenses for all the provinces. In addition, all provinces imposed succession duties and taxes on financial and transportation companies by number of branches or paid-up capital in the first case, and mileage, gross earnings, or real estate in the province in the second case. B.C. and Quebec intermittently taxed other corporations, while B.C. and P.E.I. experimented with income taxes. For most provinces, however, the subsidy from the federal government remained a very important source of funds.

The paltry subsidy of 80¢ per head from the federal government, together with its usurpation of most of the politically feasible revenue sources, left the provincial governments, as it was intended to do, in tight financial straits.[46] Pressures for alteration of the terms of federation began almost immediately, especially from Quebec and Nova Scotia. For the latter, the minor adjustments of 1868 that followed the open purchase of its champion Joseph Howe relieved the dissatisfaction to some degree, but only temporarily.

In Quebec during the Chapleau administration the clergy stepped up their agitation for a system of colonization railroads within the province to help fight the outflow of population. And this led directly to demands for an enlarged subsidy from the federal government.[47] In the absence of increased federal aid, recourse was had to external borrowings. In 1879 Quebec placed a loan in New York through the Bank of Montreal and two New York banks.[48] The following year it announced the "success" of a loan in Paris.

This was the loan that Chapleau's comrade-in-arms and eminent frontbencher Jonathan S. Würtele was supposed to have negotiated for the province while in France on the Credit Foncier promotion job. The purpose was to acquire funds for the colonization railway schemes; the loan of £800,000, payable in either London or Paris, was sold at 98 bearing five per cent interest. The brokers in Canada for the issue were two Montreal firms, Louis Forget and Co., and Jonathan S. Würtele and Co.[49] The spectacle of the Treasurer of the province underwriting and handling the very loans he was responsible for on behalf of the province went unchallenged, a comment not on Würtele's reputation for honesty so much as on the astounding degree of corruption which was then the norm of Canadian public life. The brokers in Paris turned out to be the same group of bankers who were busy with Würtele and Chapleau in the Credit Foncier stock manipulation. And in the final analysis, far from being an innovation in Canadian public finance, the so-called French loan turned out to be a fraud. The funds for the loan were actually British, and the sole effect of the French front, apart from the obvious public relations, was to add an extra layer of brokers with claims to a commission.[50]

The Chapleau government also sought new internal revenue sources from Quebec's natural resource endowment. But the effort to restore some semblance of provincial control over timber limits led in 1882 to the formation of the Timber Limit Holders' Association, which included all of the banks who had made large loans on security of the limits. The Bank of Montreal, the Bank of British North America, Molson's, La Banque Nationale, George Hague representing the Merchants, and John MacDougall of the Quebec Bank were all involved with the leading timber firms in the successful fight to secure their tenure and keep Chapleau from increasing their payments to the province.[51]

It was under the Mercier administration that the agitation from Quebec for more federal money became most acute. In 1887, Mercier called an Interprovincial Conference at Quebec in order that the provinces could collectively push for better terms. Out of the Conference came a call for repeal of the federal disallowance power, for the establishment of the provinces' right to levy excise taxes, a request for the federal government to stay out of provincial public works, and opposition to the federal government's interference with Manitoba's railway projects which threatened the CPR's monopoly.[52]

Behind Mercier stood a bizarre alliance maintaining him in power. On the one hand were the railway promoters to whom he virtually presented the keys to the provincial strongbox; on the other were a few highly placed ultramontanes in the hierarchy who were pressuring for re-endowment of the Jesuit order under the guise of compensation for the earlier seizure of their estates. Mercier needed money to satisfy the demands of both groups. In 1887, Quebec's deficit reached three million, and that year he tried unsuccessfully to float a loan for that sum in New York.[53]

His inability to fund the debt led the next year to an effort at a forced conversion loan. If the bondholders refused to accept the new loan, Mercier decreed that the interest rate on outstanding bonds would be lowered to four per cent. The Quebec Legislative Council, the citadel of Montreal finance in the Quebec Legislature, forced Mercier to back down and agree that the compulsion clause would not be enforced.[54] Demands from London bondholders that the Act itself be repealed brought an ever-pliant Macdonald government into action, and disallowance followed.[55]

The Mercier government was forced into a number of fiscal expediencies, including direct taxes on commercial companies, which led to howls of outrage from the downtrodden merchants and manufacturers of the province. Taxes placed on mining companies resulted in the mining promoters threatening to leave the province — the Huntingdon copper mines actually staged a short-lived shutdown — and led to the creation of a special mining lobby to press for the abolition of the tax. Canadian promoters and British capitalists involved in Quebec railway ventures were alienated by his imposition of a tax on their earnings and his insistence on the right of the province to appoint two directors on every line receiving a provincial subsidy. In 1891, his efforts to raise foreign loans were even further impeded by the Baring Crisis. While an attempt to float a ten million dollar loan in Belgium failed that year, a temporary loan of four million was underwritten and partially taken up by the Banque de Paris, the Credit Lyonnais, and by their offspring, the Credit Foncier,[56] a rather strange realm of financial activity for a mortgage loan company to be pursuing.

It was during the 1891 financial difficulties that Honoré Mercier made a fiscal manoeuvre that eventually proved his undoing. That year in the federal election campaign Laurier promised Mercier an additional $400,000 per year of federal money if the Liberals won in return for Mercier's moral and financial support.[57] It seemed like a good investment, but the provincial treasury was empty. To generate the needed money, a scheme was concocted whereby the Quebec stationer claimed to be short of the means to fulfill his contract for the provision of paper to public offices, and applied for an "advance". The immediate "advance" was $30,000, with another $30,000 promised, while the total requirements of the stationery department were only $20,000 a year. A letter of credit for the sum advanced was cashed at one of the Quebec savings banks and the funds diverted into Liberal Party coffers.[58] In fact, the move was not unique in the 1891 campaign, for the Secretary of the Government Printing Bureau in Ottawa was likewise busy diverting federal public money into the Tory election fund.[59] In addition, Liberal funds came from money earmarked for the Quebec government's subsidy to the Baie des Chaleurs railway. A lot of the remaining funds for the Baie des Chaleurs line went into settling the personal debts of some of Mercier's ministers, some of it to build a new house for a member of the government.[60]

Provincial elections in Quebec were financed by a somewhat different arrangement. For example, Mercier's administration blackmailed a contractor on the Quebec Court House to inflate his charges from $200,000, the original tender, to $800,000, the difference being siphoned off largely into election funds. If the contractor had refused to inflate the expenses, the government threatened to strike out all the sums due him from the estimates. After these operations were unveiled in the *Globe*, the Mercier government charged seditious libel and took out warrants against all newspaper proprietors who published the charges. The choice of seditious libel was an extremely astute move politically. A charge of criminal libel would have involved a trial to determine the truth or falsehood of the allegations. But to make seditious libel stick, all that was required was that the publication of the charges tended to bring the government into disrepute, with no necessary reference to the veracity of the claims.

The very narrow Macdonald victory in 1891 was also the defeat of Mercier. His cabinet was dismissed from office by the Lieutenant Governor[61] at the request of the Tory government on charges of corruption. It was a classic case of Satan denouncing Sin. An appeal to "the people" followed, which permitted the bond holders to add their forces to those of the federal government to ensure his defeat. The new government repudiated some of his political debts and reclaimed some of the lavish railway bonuses. Mercier himself faced charges, but selective use of bribes allegedly ensured his acquittal.[62] The jury was thus bribed to find Mercier not guilty of corruption. In 1895 the new government repealed the taxes on commercial companies,[63] though some corporation taxes were later imposed.

Despite the fact that the chief *raison d'être* of the government that succeeded Mercier was to stabilize the provincial budget and thus reassure foreign investors, the credit of the province remained suspect for some time. During the years between the fall of Mercier and the inauguration of Laurier, two new overseas loans were effected, one in England via Montreal's Hanson Bros. brokerage firm, the other in France through the Banque de Paris-Credit Lyonnais group. Although this five million dollar loan bore only three per cent, it sold at a huge discount at 77 at a time when Dominion three per cents were being placed at or near par.[64] For the French investors, notably the banking clique, it was a fine gift.

The other provinces had far less exciting fiscal histories. Nova Scotia was the second major source of discontent over the terms of federation and, with P.E.I., the first to join Mercier in his campaign for better terms.[65] During the boom years of 1879-1883 its revenues were adequate. And in 1884 its extra revenue needs were met by floating a $400,000 loan at five per cent within the province itself. The loan was taken up at a premium, and English tenders were unable to match local offers.[66] But the province's deficits started to mount and the search for new revenue sources began. In 1892 it placed its first loan since Confederation in London at 3.5%. That year, too, it raised the royalty on coal mined within the province by 25% to 12.5c per ton over the strenuous objections of the small mine owners.[67]

Nova Scotia's share of the federal purse increased after Laurier's victory when W. S. Fielding, the former secessionist Premier of the province, joined the federal cabinet as Minister of Finance. The result was the creation of a system of iron and steel subsidies, the immediate beneficiary of which was Nova Scotia. It also led to the upward revision of the coal duties in 1897 to try to increase the Canadian market for Nova Scotian bituminous, and with it the provincial revenue. After the new cabinet was formed, a bill passed the Nova Scotia Legislature declaring July the first a public holiday for the first time. In spite of these changes, Nova Scotia's revenues were still inadequate. In 1899 it had to resort to the London capital market once more.[68]

All of the western provinces were heavy borrowers, mostly in direct relationship to railway development schemes. The result was to make provincial politics little more than a struggle among railway promoters for shares in the spoils. In some cases it also led to provinces being chained financially to conditions imposed by outside financiers. In 1896, B.C. was unable to help build rival roads to the Rossland gold diggings to break the CPR monopoly, because it had pledged not to increase its debt for two years as a condition for prior loans in London.[69] And when it did subsequently borrow, its success was varied. An 1899 loan at three per cent through the Bank of British Columbia (which operated as its fiscal agent) succeeded, while with a 1902 three per cent loan the underwriters ended up absorbing 80% of the total.[70]

# Municipal Finance

The need for municipal borrowing abroad in relative terms was until 1907 lessened by the fact that banks and insurance companies held sizeable portfolios of their debentures. But on the other hand their absolute revenue requirements and consequent need for borrowing were raised considerably by the results of the "bonusing system" whereby municipalities on a fiercely competitive basis offered sweeping tax concessions or cash handouts to tempt industry into their sphere of authority. Even where bonusing was absent, manufacturers could be safely counted on to use their political power to reduce their share of the tax burden and shift the revenue raising activities to borrowing. Montreal's efforts to extend its tax base by putting more of a load on manufacturers led in 1899 to a protest meeting of manufacturers headed by the Hon. George Drummond. Out of it grew a new Montreal Manufacturers' Association to replace the dormant one formed in the 1870's to agitate for the National Policy. The Association's successful campaign to avoid taxation was ably assisted by its legislative arm, the Legislative Council of Quebec.[71]

Municipal borrowings abroad, when necessary, were until well into the first decade of the twentieth century not very easy to effect for most eastern towns and even more difficult for the West. The West was particularly burdened by the result of federal government development policy, both in the loss of revenue from Crown lands and in the tax exemption granted the CPR. As a result, the entire burden of financing the building of necessary infrastructure fell on the settlers at the time when they were most in need of all available cash to establish themselves on their farms.[72] Thus the tendency to seek funds through outside borrowing was all the greater at the same time the security to be offered the potential buyer of debentures was reduced by the loss of revenue.

Manitoba from an early date had difficulty keeping its municipalities solvent. The towns overextended their borrowing, much of it in England, during the years of the land boom when money was easy to get. The deflation of land values that accompanied the end of rapid growth led to the collapse of revenues. Portage la Prairie was the first to go into default. It attempted without success to negotiate with its English creditors through W. Boyle Lewis, one of the partners in Duncan MacArthur's private bank that negotiated some of the loans, to cut down the burden of interest.[73] Emerson followed it into default, and then a string of municipalities — Neepawee, Gladstone, Minnodosa, East Selkirk, Morris, West Lynne, and Rapid City — did likewise. A Manitoba commission was established to scale down the debts to a level the towns could repay, the difference assumed by the province. Portage la Prairie, for example, was found capable of meeting only 40% of its total debt.[74] Manitoba's problems did not end there. Brandon went into default a decade later.[75] And although no losses to debenture holders occurred, the legacy of western difficulties made their securities suspect in Britain for a long time thereafter.[76]

Nor were Eastern municipalities free from the problem of jittery foreign investors. This sensitivity showed itself strongly in 1890-1891 when the Baring crisis prevented Toronto from raising a loan on the open market and it had to rely on temporary borrowings from banks to tide it over.[77]

The Baring Crisis resulted from the degree to which the then senior partner of the house, Lord Revelstoke, involved its assets in the Argentine. By one account, he had bought the Buenos Aires water works for $24 million, of which $21 million went into the actual purchase and the other three million into bribes. The return on the investment was to come from the exploitation of its monopoly in the rates charged to houses supplied. Revelstoke also put large sums into a thoroughly shady deal in land grant and irrigation bonds of one of the Argentinian provinces that were not worth a third of their face value, and took ten million of bonds of another province, of whose total revenue of $4.8 million the year before, four million was already spoken for in interest claims on past debts. There was also a large investment in Argentinian railways. An ill-timed revolution cost Toronto its financial agent and resulted in difficulties in marketing its debentures.[78]

The Baring Crisis affected Montreal as well. The city's administration rivalled that of the province of Quebec in both extravagance and corruption. In 1888, its credit was already so low that a £840,000 issue sold in England via the Barings at 83 and contained as well a commitment by the city to limit its borrowings to a maximum of fifteen per cent of its assessment. By 1890, the original loan was exhausted and the city was forced to rely on interim borrowings until a new long-term loan was possible.

The difficulties of Canadian municipalities in floating their loans abroad were protracted. In 1902 the second annual meeting of the Union of Canadian Municipalities, a municipal congress formed to co-ordinate certain activities with regard to public utilities, considered the possibility of municipalities combining to cut down their borrowing costs. It was further hoped that by borrowing on a united basis they might secure a provincial or Dominion guarantee.[79] The similarity of these proposals to the old Municipal Loan Fund pork barrel was striking, and in light of the fact that the Grand Trunk Railway was about to launch its second great assault on the financial resources of Canada, it is fortunate that nothing concrete materialized from these plans.

Even as late as 1905, problems of floating loans abroad remained. That year, western towns issued $4.6 million, eastern $4.4 million; and of the total, 80% was absorbed in Canada, 15% in the U.S. and only 5% in Britain. British municipal debenture yields were as high as Canadian, thereby curtailing the demand, while the only U.S. demand came from American insurance companies who had to make a deposit of securities with the Canadian government in order to do business in Canada. While the flow of British funds began to pick up in 1906, not until 1913 were all the barriers down and Canadian municipal debentures, especially western, readily acceptable. The result was a great flood of municipal borrowing.[81]

Undoubtedly part of the reason why Saskatchewan and B.C. appointed official boards to control and limit municipal debts, and Nova Scotia adopted a similar constraining policy, was the tendency of the towns to overload themselves with obligations whenever external capital was easily had.

# Public Utilities Investment

Electric utilities and gas and waterworks were popular investments for Canadian financial institutions and for British and foreign investors, because their monopoly position in the communities they serviced guaranteed a rate of return in proportion to the level of rates that could be extorted from consumers. The financing of electric utilities in particular, power plants and street railways, underwent a rapid transformation as electricity's role in the economy grew in importance. Once electricity came to be accepted generally as a source of power or light, and the geo-economic advantages of Quebec and Ontario in its large-scale production were appreciated, then the mode of production underwent a major change as the small local power plants became the targets of promoters who merged and integrated electrical systems to extract higher rates from industrial users in particular. Transportation and financial magnates took control of the systems, and manufacturing interests along with municipalities fought back.

Initially many of the little municipal electrical plants were owned by local entrepreneurs and built by them with their own capital plus substantial grants and other assistance from the municipalities concerned. The plant itself would be built by one of the large electrical companies like Royal Electric or Canadian General Electric. Municipalities gave cash gifts, bond guarantees, free sites, etc., to the electric companies — and to gas and waterworks systems as well. A guarantee of monopoly was often a precondition of operation.[82] Monopoly may well have been encouraged by the municipalities themselves, for the municipal share of the receipts from the utility operations was one of the most important sources of municipal revenue.

When monopoly was not granted, it could often be secured by merger. As early as 1884, Toronto's two electric utilities merged under the auspices of Henry Pellatt and E. S. Cox, the numbers racketeer.[83] Three operating in Ottawa were merged in 1894.

Mergers in St. John, N.B., followed the absorption in 1894 of local utilities by a CPR group, Van Horne, R. B. Angus, and T. Shaughnessy.[84] That year, too, Sydney, Nova Scotia, had its two light companies consolidated and in turn in 1901 the merger was further amalgamated with all the other utilities in the city by the Halifax promoter B. F. Pearson.[85] Maritime Telegraph and Telephone, one of the largest Atlantic utility operations, combined several Nova Scotia firms in 1910, and added another dozen by 1913, including control of P.E.I.'s telephone system.

As electrification spread, so did outside promotion and the use of Canadian financial institutions, especially life insurance companies, as both underwriters and sources of investment funds. Until 1907, of the bond holdings in utility companies of the insurance firms of the George Cox empire, some 80% were in utility promotions in which he had a direct interest.[86] After 1907, the structure of life company assets shifted in favour of mortgages, and British funds, while present in some measure before 1907, began to move into Canadian utilities on a greatly expanded scale.

**TABLE VII (3)**

**New Public Issues of Canadian Utilities in London, 1902-1910**

*(£1000's)*

| Year | Electric Power | Gas and Water | Tramways |
|------|----------------|---------------|----------|
| 1902 | — | — | 60.0 |
| 1903 | — | 66.5 | — |
| 1904 | 53.0 | — | — |
| 1905 | 138.0 | — | 115.0 |
| 1906 | 62.0 | — | — |
| 1907 | 411.0 | — | 100.0 |
| 1908 | 754.0 | 79.3 | 1,146.6 |
| 1909 | 291.0 | 94.0 | 530.0 |
| 1910 | 429.0 | — | 1,190.0 |

Source: *Ec*, July 8, 1911, p. 62

There were cases of British direct investment in Canadian utilities, especially in B.C. As early as 1891, a British syndicate under the Presidency of Sir Charles Tupper, then High Commissioner in London, was formed to attempt to secure control of Canadian gas and waterworks.[87] The B.C. Electric Railway Company and the Vancouver Power Co. were both controlled by a British firm.[88] And reversing the normal procedure, British arms manufacturer Sir Charles Ross promoted the West Kootenay

Power and Light Co. to furnish power for mines, smelters and refiners while Charles Hosmer, head of the CPR telegraph system, formed a Montreal syndicate to put up the money for Ross's project.[89] But British direct ownership was very marginal compared to the flow of British bond investment after 1908. And the great Canadian electrical monopolies were formed before the inflow of British funds, using the services of the Canadian insurance companies.

In Ontario, a long series of unsuccessful attempts had been made by the Legislature to get private capital to harness Niagara Falls for the generation of cheap power before a charter was granted in 1902 to a syndicate headed by William Mackenzie. With the Canadian Northern magnate was an illustrious band — Sir Henry Pellatt, and Senator Frederick Nicholls of Canadian General Electric, with Senator George Cox and Sir Edmund Walker in the wings. Since the syndicate's members already controlled distribution in Toronto and other localities, their project met with immediate opposition from manufacturing interests throughout the province. In the Ontario Legislature the Tory opposition disapproved of the deal, given the fact that all the beneficiaries were leading Liberals, and some Liberal members joined in opposition, including W. Beattie Nesbitt, who was one of the first advocates of public ownership[90] before he won fame for the Farmers' Bank disaster.

In Quebec, the fact that several suitable power generation sites existed prevented the issue from producing the polarization which Niagara introduced in Ontario.[91] In 1901, however, Royal Electric and two other firms under the control of Rodolphe Forget were merged with Sir Herbert Holt's gas monopoly into the Montreal, Light, Heat and Power Co., the infamous "Octopus of Montreal," under Holt's presidency. With him on the board were Louis and Rodolphe Forget, Sir Hugh Montagu Allan, and Senator Robert Mackay.[92] The merger subsequently absorbed its rivals by buying them out at inflated prices covered by bond issues in Canada and in Britain. Enormous amounts of water too were introduced into the equity. At the time of union the shares of both Royal Electric and the gas company were at 250 and paying dividends of ten per cent. Afterwards the stock never got above 105, and while it paid four per cent the dividends in the early period at least were not justified and hence came in part out of capital.[93] The principal rival that it did not absorb, Shawinigan Water and Power Co., was locked into a long-term supply contract, and the Octopus was then in a position to ruthlessly exploit its monopoly to secure the earnings to pay for the bond issues that had been used to buy out its rivals.

During 1908 it was selling power for $80.00 per unit that it had obtained from the generating company for $14.00 per unit.[94] Objections grew stronger.

In 1906, the Montreal city council had obligingly added 30 years to the lease of the gas franchise to the firm, a monopoly of the gas mains, and a guaranteee of the monopoly of the electric power supply. The Executive Committee of the Montreal branch of the Canadian Manufacturers' Association recommended expropriation,[95] and its legal counsel contended that the city had no power to grant an exclusive franchise to any company to use the streets of the city.[96]

Along with the protests of manufacturers, many of whom continued to use steam power in their Montreal factories because of the costs of electric power,[97] there emerged the Union of Canadian Municipalities, pledged to fight the privately owned utility companies in general and Herbert Holt's Octopus in particular by using the municipalities' collective strength against their utility overlords. Its oracle, the *Canadian Municipal Journal*, contended that

> no municipality, however large and powerful, could hold its own against the lobbies which secured legislation which overrode municipal rights. The only escape from such tyranny was an alliance of the interested victims.[98]

Although its efforts against Holt met with little success, the Union did provide powerful assistance to a number of towns struggling with transportation and utility companies: Halifax against the Grand Trunk Railway; Montreal against the attempt by the Terminal Railway to secure a free perpetual monopoly of the use of the streets; Fort William, Winnipeg, Toronto, and other cities against their electric utility or street railway companies. In the case of Ottawa versus its electrical company, the result was a drastic rate reduction that cut costs to the town and its consumers by nearly $300,000 a year. The Union helped force a rate reduction on Bell Telephone, whose rapacity had incurred the ire of several municipalities as well as the Toronto Board of Trade.[99] But its most important role was in preparing the ground for the assault of municipalities and manufacturers on the Pellatt-Cox-Mackenzie-Walker syndicate that had Ontario's electrical supply under lock and key.

Once begun, the movement for public ownership of utilities spread quickly. By the end of 1903, 37 cities and towns in Ontario had taken control of their electric light plants, and 78 of their waterworks.[100] But municipal ownership of little local utilities and provincial ownership of a huge system of generation, transmission, and distribution were two different matters. In 1902 the Canadian Manufacturers' Association declared its adherence to the principle of public ownership, and that body was the key instrument in toppling the Liberal Party in Ontario and installing a pro-nationalization Tory administration. Helpful in securing the CMA's adherence was the example of the U.S., where about 50% of the commercial hydro power was at that time controlled by J. P. Morgan and General Electric. The fact that Senator Fred Nicholls, head of Canadian General Electric, was a leading figure in the private power syndicate must have been thus doubly threatening, despite his having been formerly president of the CMA. And the example of Hamilton, the most industrialized city in Ontario, which had used cheap power as a drawing card for migrant industry, was a powerful influence on the policy of the new Tory administration bent on effecting widespread industrialization in Ontario.[101]

The importance of securing access to cheap power for industrial development was underlined by other factors in the markets for energy in the late 1890's and beyond. The danger of reliance on water power became clear in 1895, when drought forced the closure of many mills in Ontario and Quebec. Some began to switch to steam to prevent a recurrence.[102] Steam, however, was a relatively costly source of energy, especially in the absence of the huge, accessible timber stands for fuel typical of earlier decades.

By 1899, oil was a sensitive issue. The huge Standard Oil trust had secured a virtual monopoly of the refining industry in Ontario, and it began immediately to exact higher prices. Pressure from Ontario manufacturers led to some countervailing adjustments in the tariff,[103] but there remained an ever-present threat. In addition, by 1900 the natural gas fields of southern Essex county were becoming exhausted, and some factories began searching for another fuel.[104] A further complication lay in the fact that the gas fields were for the most part controlled by American companies, especially United States Gas and Oil, which supplied Detroit consumers by diverting supplies away from Ontario factories. A Dominion Government order-in-council was passed, demanding that the company supply gas at any point on its pipeline to all companies and persons at a rate ten per cent below the American rate.[105] In addition it had export quotas which it generally exceeded. It announced it would accede to Ottawa's demands, and surreptitiously continued to export. A sheriff in Essex tried to seize the pipes to stop the export, but was blocked by an injunction. However, the company finally agreed to cease exporting.[106]

It was only a few months after the Essex gas war that a coal famine hit Ontario factories, forcing some to close. The famine resulted from a strike of Pennsylvania miners.[107] The alternative source of coal was the much more expensive Nova Scotia bituminous. It was in the midst of this energy crisis that the Ontario power syndicate began to face the ire of the manufacturing interests, culminating in the nationalization. Ontario's power production, already growing quickly under private ownership, in short order outstripped Quebec, which still suffered under the grasp of the Octopus.

**TABLE VII (4)**

**Hydro Power Production**

| Year | Quebec | Ontario | Canada |
|------|--------|---------|--------|
| 1900 | 83 | 54 | 173 |
| 1905 | 184 | 203 | 355 |
| 1910 | 335 | 491 | 977 |
| 1914 | 664 | 859 | 1951 |

*(millions of horsepower)*

Source: *CYB,* 1936, p. 361.

The street railway systems which became a mania about the turn of the century followed the same pattern of evolution as the other electrical utilities. The electric railway systems of small towns tended to be locally owned and financed in part by assistance from the municipality in various forms. Municipalities would pool funds to build some of the interurban lines, for example the towns served by the Galt and Preston Electric Railway, including Berlin and Waterloo, or the Hamilton, Guelph, and Galt line.[108] St. Thomas in 1897 supported the establishment of a tramway by guaranteeing the company's bonds.[109] Some of the lines were owned by outsiders: Canadian General Electric owned the London system, with the assistance of Canada Life's underwriting,[110] and it built the Brantford system and later seized it for nonpayment of its construction account.[111]

In the larger cities across Canada, railway promoters and financiers figured largely in the system. William Mackenzie, for example, secured control of the Winnipeg system and subsequently, in conjunction with a New York group, of the Toronto Electric Railway. The first system in Toronto was built by the Edison Electric Co., who bribed several aldermen to secure their support for the establishment of the trolley system.[112] In 1895 the company passed into the hands of a new syndicate headed by William Mackenzie and including George Cox and the CPR contractor, James Ross. Further bribes were necessary to secure the assent of the city council to the new 30-year monopoly.[113]

The syndicate's next problem was a piece of legislation that limited their capital to one million in equity. A new syndicate was then formed, consisting of the same group as the old, to "buy" the system in order to swell the stock to six million.[114] The only real investment was a bond issue of $2.2 million: the stock itself was pure water, and within a short time its market value had fallen drastically — but not before its promoters, affectionately dubbed "the Toronto railway gang" by the *Monetary Times,* had reaped substantial profits. The gang then sought a charter for a London and western Ontario line but were refused by the Ontario Legislature, which passed a new electric railway act to prevent any repetition of the Toronto stock-water job.[115]

Toronto's utility woes were not confined to the consequences of the Mackenzie-Cox-Pellatt power syndicate or the tramway group. The city and its citizens also engaged in a series of legal battles with Sir Frank Smith's Consumers' Gas Company monopoly to reduce its exactions.[116] One lawsuit in 1894 tried in vain to recover one-and-one-half million dollars of payments that had been secured in excess of the legal maximum charges.[117]

In Quebec, the Forgets and their associates were key figures in several of the largest street railway systems. Montreal had two systems in the early 1890's, one controlled by the Forgets and William Mackenzie, the other under the wholesale merchants J. R. Thibodeau, J. S. Bousquet, R. L. Gault, and David Morrice.[118] The Forget's Montreal Street Railway Co. had the city council well in hand, and the council offered it unlimited merger power plus sweeping rights to expropriate real estate. Though these clauses were struck out of its charter by the Quebec legislature in 1894, that did not impede its expansion.[119] Local lines were quickly acquired, and in 1901 it absorbed the other major Montreal system, Sir Louis Forget becoming president and James Ross vice-president of the new operation.[120]

The improved access to foreign capital after the turn of the century permitted far more grandiose schemes, notably Sir Rodolphe Forget's Quebec City adventures. In 1909 he launched in France the Quebec Railway, Light, Heat and Power system, a holding company controlling all the gas, electricity, and tramway facilities in the city. In addition, a number of subsidiary railway and utility operations were launched in other areas, with capital subscribed both in France and Belgium. These operations were assisted by the fact that the federal Postmaster General, Hon. Louis Pelletier, put his name on the prospectus as an assurance to the investors.

For the French investors the result was another Forget catastrophe. The prospectus was a collection of lies. Great claims were made about pulpwood carrying traffic available to the railroad subsidiaries. The pulp traffic was supposedly generated by three companies: one of these was bankrupt at the time the prospectus was issued, another had no operating plant at all, and the third was a lumber company rather than a pulpmill. The prospectus was worded to deceive the investors into thinking the subsidiaries' bonds were guaranteed by the utility company, and the holding company itself was presented as a merger — thereby deceiving the French investors into thinking they had first claim on the assets when in fact they ranked second.

By 1913 the stock was almost valueless and French bondholders had lost about 17,860,000 francs. Part of their loss was due to the diversion of their money into private speculations by the promoters, and part went to pay unearned dividends on the promoters' stock before the crash came. The French bondholders referred the issue to the National Association for the Protection of French Investors in Foreign Securities, a body which, in conjunction with a similar British group, acted as an international financial policeman. After Forget's plundering in this and in the Banque Internationale affair, Canadian securities were not exactly a popular investment in France.[121]

# British Industrial Bond Investments

After 1908, British funds flowed freely into industrial bonds to support a great merger wave. This merger wave occurred as a result of a particular confluence of events. The 1907 upward tariff revision assured higher prices for the mergered firms which were chronically overcapitalized, and hence permitted them to pay dividends on their severely watered stock. The new merger wave was not industrial in origin, but the work of a handful of Montreal, and to a lesser degree, Toronto financiers who organized the combines on a grab-and-run basis. The year 1909, when the wave began, was a particularly appropriate one. Industrial share prices, always weak, reached a new low, call money rates were at their lowest point for the period, and, of course, British funds were available for the first time.

The costs of the merger wave fell on the consumer. An enormous amount of monopoly power was achieved by the combines formed, and the resulting price increases fed the inflation of the period. It also introduced chronic inefficiency into Canada's industrial structure, making the new water-logged firms totally dependent on the tariff to maintain their prices and pay interest to British bond holders or dividends to promoters. As with railway finance during the period, much of the British investment was a complete waste from the point of view of contributing to Canadian economic growth. But the costs were not realized until after the war, when a great wave of liquidations afflicted the industrial mergers and the railways.

# Conclusions

Canadian governments historically showed an almost paranoid sensitivity to the state of Canadian credit in London. Confederation itself was little more than an elaborate exercise in public finance. And subsequent government policy was directed at maintaining and improving the state of confidence Confederation had introduced into the minds and pockets of British financiers.

These conciliatory policies took many forms. Beginning at least as early as the Galt tariff of 1859, Canadian fiscal policy had as its primary objective the raising of revenue to bolster the saleability of Canadian government securities abroad. This objective lay in part at least behind the National Policy tariff of 1879. The centralization of fiscal power in the hands of the federal government was accompanied by its close control over banking and finance, again with a view to stabilizing the overseas market for its debentures. The federal power of disallowance was used against provincial statutes that threatened to invoke the ire of British financiers. And the federal government even proved willing to place its legislation directly under the purview of the Imperial Government to gain admission to the much-desired Trustee List. The most important function played by the Dominion's High Commissioner in London was precisely that of maintaining friendly relations with Lombard Street.

The result of the usurpation of all feasible tax sources by the Dominion with a view to bolstering its credit led to a squeeze on the revenue resources of the provinces. As a result, provincial governments were forced into a policy of rapid resource alienation to generate royalties to finance their fiscal responsibilities. When these proved inadequate, bonds had to be sold abroad and pitched political battles for "better terms" fought with the Dominion government. For the municipalities, too, fiscal crisis was always on the horizon, and the opening up of the London market for municipal debentures led to a scramble for access.

British capital flowed into other fields beside government debt. Public utility bonds, with the generally guaranteed monopoly returns the utility companies enjoyed, were a popular investment. And the attitudes of British finance to the nationalization struggle were an important part of the campaigns conducted for state takeover of the larger utility operations. For a brief time, industrial bonds issued by the great mergers formed in Canada in the first decade of the twentieth century also attracted British money. But more than any other category, it was in railway finance that the flow of capital was most critical.

# Notes to Chapter VII

1. *Ec,* Oct. 8, 1881, p. 1245.
2. S. Bates, *Financial History of Canadian Governments,* p. 32.
3. M. Denison, *Canada's First Bank,* p. 184.
4. H. Marshall, F. Southard and K. Taylor, *Canadian-American Industry,* p. 15; *MT,* June 25, 1880.
5. *CLR II,* p. 735.
6. S. Bates, *Financial History,* pp. 212, 235, 259.
7. Cf. *MT,* Oct. 27, 1916, pp. 5-7; J.Viner, *Canada's Balance of International Indebtedness,* p. 126.
8. John A. Macdonald to A. T. Galt, Feb. 26, 1882, *Macdonald Papers.*
9. See esp. the Richard Cartwright-Dalton McCarthy exchange in *HCD,* Feb. 26, 1878, pp. 540-5., and that of Cartright and Tilley, *HCD,* March 14, 1879, pp. 435-440.
10. J. C. Hurlbert, *Protection and Free Trade,* p. 158.
11. Anon., *Canada Under the National Policy,* p. 9.
12. Select Committee . . . Tariff . . . Agriculture, *(SCTA), Report,* 1882, p. 14.
13. Department of Justice, *Memorandum on Dominion Power of Disallowance,* p. 16.
14. *MT,* July 20, 1907, p. 92.
15. B. E. Walker, "The Dangers of Democracy," Address to the Canadian Club of Halifax; *MT,* March 28, 1908, p. 1632.
16. B. E. Walker, address to the Canadian Club of Montreal, Jan. 29, 1912, p. 6, *Walker Papers.*
17. Dept. of Justice, *Memorandum on Disallowance,* p. 23.
18. See esp. R. V. Dicey et al., *The Credit of Canada: How it is Affected by the Ontario Power Legislation,* pp. 1-4, 5-8, 12-13, 30, 32, 55.
19. Royal Commission to Inquire into Railways and Transportation in Canada *(RCRTC), Report,* 1917, p. xxxix.
20. See especially R. G. Hawtrey, *The Economic Problem,* p. 271: "The economic advantages to a country of gaining sovereignty over new possessions are found especially in the investment market." See also J. Viner, "Political Aspects of International Finance."
21. A. Baster, "A Note on the Colonial Stock Acts and Dominion Borrowing," p. 602.
22. "Correspondence Relating to the Admission of Canadian Securities to the British Trustee List," p. 1.
23. *Ec,* Oct. 8, 1897, p. 470.

24.  "Correspondence . . . Trustee List," p. 3.
25.  *CF,* April 5, 1911, p. 299.
26.  *SACC,* p. 862.
27.  *HCD,* March 23, 1900, pp. 2602-3.
28.  *HCD,* March 23, 1900, pp. 2573.
29.  A. Baster, "A Note . . .," p. 607, asserts the impact of the Act on Dominion borrowings was negligible. J. A. Schumpeter, *Business Cycles,* I, p. 430, claimed it was important and substantial diversion of funds occurred, a view seconded by H. Feis, *Europe, The World's Banker,* pp. 93-95.
30.  A. Baster, "A Note . . .," pp. 604-605.
31.  *Ec,* May 23, 1874, pp. 620-1.
32.  *Ec,* March 4, 1876, p. 278.
33.  *MT,* Sept. 22, 1882, p. 319; *Ec,* Aug. 6, 1883, p. 1114.
34.  *MT,* Oct. 19, 1883, p. 431.
35.  *MT,* Nov. 2, 1883, p. 488; March 28, 1884, p. 1093.
36.  *MT,* June 20, 1884, p. 1427; Feb. 6, 1885, p. 885.
37.  *MT,* May 15, 1885, p. 121; June 17, 1885, p. 70.
38.  *MT,* Aug. 29, 1892, p. 99; Oct. 14, 1892, p. 420.
39.  *MT,* Oct. 26, 1894, p. 541.
40.  *MT,* Sept. 18, 1896, p. 389.
41.  Laurier to John Willison, June 29, 1896, *Willison Papers;* I am indebted to Professor J. T. McLeod of the University of Toronto for this and several other references.
42.  *W.T.R.;* Preston, *Strathcona.*
43.  *MT,* Oct. 22, 1897, p. 533.
44.  *Ec,* May 3, 1902, p. 864.
45.  *Ec,* May 16, 1903, p. 880.
46.  *Confederation Debates,* Feb. 7, 1865, pp. 63-7.
47.  *MT,* Aug. 25, 1882, p. 204; Aug. 6, 1883, p. 1122.
48.  *MT,* March 14, 1879, p. 1146.
49.  *MT,* Nov. 10, 1882, p. 519.
50.  *MT,* Sept. 30, 1887, p. 428.
51.  *MT,* June 16, 1882, p. 1544.
52.  Department of Justice, *Dominion-Provincial and Interprovincial Conferences,* pp. 20-27.
53.  *MT,* April 15, 1887, p. 1219; May 27, 1887, p. 1405.
54.  *MT,* July 20, 1888, p. 68; *MT,* Aug. 17, 1888, p. 179; Feb. 8, 1879, p. 907.
55.  Montreal *Gazette,* Jan. 15, 1891.
56.  *MT,* Jan. 30, 1891, p. 928; March 27, 1891, p. 1179; July 24, 1891, p. 101.
57.  *MT,* Feb. 13, 1891, p. 993.
58.  *MT,* Jan. 29, 1892, pp. 902-3.
59.  *MT,* Oct. 9, 1891, p. 427.
60.  *MT,* Aug. 21, 1891, p. 219; Oct. 30, 1891, p. 519.
61.  *Globe,* Nov. 14, 1891; *New York Times,* Nov. 15, 1891; *MT,* Dec. 18, 1891, p. 721.
62.  *MT,* Jan. 22, 1892, p. 66; Sept. 8, 1893, p. 297; Oct. 21, 1893, p. 459.
63.  *MT,* Oct. 4, 1895, p. 434.
64.  Quebec, *Correspondence Re the Resignation of the Provincial Treasurer,* pp. 3-4.
65.  *MT,* April 15, 1887, p. 1219.
66.  *MT,* Nov. 28, 1884, p. 610.
67.  *MT,* July 28, 1892, p. 16; May 6, 1892, p. 1337.
68.  *MT,* July 21, 1899, p. 84.
69.  *MT,* Nov. 26, 1896, p. 717.
70.  *MT,* July 14, 1899, p. 41; *Ec,* Nov. 22, 1902, p. 1798.

71. *MT,* March 31, 1899, p. 1285; *MT,* April 20, 1900, p. 1383.
72. A. S. Morton, *History of Prairie Settlement,* p. 66.
73. *MT,* Aug. 13, 1886, p. 174; Aug. 27, 1886, p. 236; Sept. 17, 1886, p. 331; Dec. 24, 1886, p. 724.
74. *MT,* July 1, 1887, p. 11; Dec. 23, 1887, p. 785.
75. *MT,* Dec. 2, 1898, p. 732.
76. *Globe,* Jan. 1, 1911.
77. *MT,* Dec. 12, 1890, p. 715.
78. *Brad,* April 11, 1893, p. 199; *MT,* June 26, 1891, pp. 1584-5.
79. *MT,* Sept. 19, 1902, p. 372.
80. Montreal *Gazette,* Jan. 14, 1891.
81. *Ec,* Sept. 27, 1913, p. 587; *MT,* Jan. 19, 1906, p. 936.
82. See for example *MT,* Dec. 30, 1892, p. 754; Jan. 19, 1894, p. 884; *CE,* Feb. 1894, p. 287.
83. *MT,* Nov. 18, 1884, p. 605.
84. *CE,* April 1894, p. 349; Nov. 1894, p. 248; May 1894, p. 14.
85. *CE,* Sept. 1894, p. 146; MT, April 12, 1901, p. 1337; A. G. Brown and P. H. Morres, *Twentieth Century Impressions,* p. 852.
86. C.A. Hall, *Electric Utilities In Ontario,* pp. 159-161.
87. *MT,* May 8, 1891, p. 1361.
88. *MT,* May 9, 1902, p. 1448.
89. *MT,* Aug. 13, 1897, p. 206.
90. W. Plewman, *Adam Beck and Ontario Hydro,* p. 31.
91. J. H. Dales, *Hydroelectricity and Industrial Development,* p. 23.
92. *MT,* April 12, 1901, p. 1337.
93. *FP,* April 13, 1907.
94. *CMJ,* Jan. 1909, p. 6.
95. *IC,* Dec. 1906, p. 486.
96. *IC,* Feb. 1907, p. 621.
97. W. Plewman, *Adam Beck and Ontario Hydro,* p. 46.
98. *CMJ,* June 1909, p. 243.
99. Toronto Board of Trade, *Annual Report,* 1902, p. 15.
100. *CAR,* 1904, pp. 59-60.
101. See especially V. Nelles, *The Politics of Development.*
102. *CE,* Aug. 1895, p. 100.
103. *MT,* March 17, 1899, p. 1227.
104. *MT,* Dec. 28, 1900, p. 815.
105. *MT,* Jan. 4, 1901, p. 849.
106. *MT,* Aug. 9, 1901, p. 176; Dec. 13, 1901, p. 746.
107. *CE,* Nov. 1902, pp. 307-9; *MT,* Feb. 21, 1902, p. 1075.
108. *MT,* June 17, 1898, p. 1640; Sept. 28, 1900, p. 392.
109. *MT,* Nov. 5, 1897, p. 592.
110. *RCLI, Evidence,* p. 973.
111. *MT,* Dec. 10, 1897, p. 757.
112. *MT,* March 15, 1895, p. 1194.
113. *MT,* May 17, 1895, p. 1489.
114. *MT,* March 22, 1895, p. 1226; March 29, 1895, p. 1261.
115. *MT,* April 12, 1895, p. 1322; April 26, 1895, p. 1387.
116. *MT,* Jan. 19, 1900, p. 944.
117. *CE,* March 1894, p. 325.
118. *CE,* April 1894, p. 350.
119. *CE,* Jan. 1894, p. 250.
120. *MT,* Aug. 9, 1901, p. 167.
121. *HCD,* Jan. 27, 1913, pp. 2180-2198.

*It costs the Candian people more to maintain and operate Sir William Mackenzie and Sir Donald Mann as public burdens that it does to maintain our entire military and naval forces. William and Donald are certainly expensive playthings. But then they do have such a winning way.*

*Grain Growers' Guide,* June 11, 1913

# CHAPTER VIII
# High Finance and the Canadian Railways

## Early Ventures

Sir Henry Tyler, long head of the London board of the Grand Trunk, once claimed that "the prosperity of Canada is the prosperity of the Grand Trunk Railway."[1] It was no idle boast, for at the time of Confederation and for a few years after both verged on bankruptcy simultaneously. But soon rival schemes to drain the coffers of the Dominion, provinces, and municipalities were afoot. And essential to the success of any railway enterprise was the ability to float bond issues in London.

Dominion government borrowings for railway building began in 1868 with an Intercolonial Railway Loan of £1.5 million, carrying an Imperial Government guarantee and another half million unguaranteed. So responsive were British investors to the financial prospects of the new Dominion — and of course the Imperial guarantee — that the tenders totalled over eight million pounds, and the loan was ultimately taken up entirely by the Rothschilds at a six per cent premium. Thereafter railway finance became a complex business, and the first prerequisite to its success was the appropriate Minister of Finance.

In 1854, John A. Macdonald had described Francis Hincks as a man "steeped in corruption to his lips." With such qualifications Hincks was a natural choice for the finance post, and after he was secured a safe seat in Ontario in 1869, his talents were zealously applied to finding the funds for a new wave of railway building that would far eclipse his work in the 1850's. His first task was the readjustment of the provincial debt allowance. Nova Scotia had been overloaded with railway debts in the last moments of Charles Tupper's rule, and the "better terms" campaign launched by Joseph Howe turned in large measure on the desire to have the federal government assume the burden of Tupper's profligate patronage. Hincks's consolidation and rationalization of the Canadian debt structure drew fire from the Lords of the Treasury: the funds from the 1869 loan, instead of going into public works, were diverted into paying off the large floating debts to the Bank of Montreal and the Barings and Glyn, Mills which had figured so large in these institutions' pressure on behalf of Confederation.

Nor were Hincks's other financial operations better received. In 1870, a set of duties on articles of ordinary consumption — grain, coal, flour, and salt — were introduced, in large measure with a view to raising revenue for public works. The outrage that followed forced their withdrawal in 1871, but by then another source of cash had come to light. Deliberations between the United States and Britain had begun with a view to settling outstanding grievances, and, among other matters, the fate of the Nova Scotia fisheries hung in the balance. Sir John Rose, formerly delegated as Canada's chief representative, was disqualified. At that time his banking firm, Morton, Rose and Co., acted as agents for the sale of U.S. government bonds in Britain, while his American affiliate, Morton, Bliss and Co., was threatened with legal action by the American government. The fear that Rose would sell out Canadian fishing interests to stabilize relations with the American government led to Hincks being delegated to Washington. Hincks pushed hard for the sale of the fisheries for cash to distribute to railway magnates and for a British bond guarantee for the planned transcontinental. Despite the vehement opposition of Joseph Howe, and the consternation it caused in Ontario, John A. Macdonald blithely assented.[2] The Imperial Government ultimately granted a guarantee of up to £2.5 million for the transcontinental in addition to the Intercolonial Railway guarantees still outstanding.

In 1873, another Intercolonial loan bearing an Imperial guarantee for £1.5 million plus a £300,000 loan to buy up the Hudson's Bay Company charter rights were taken at a 1½ per cent premium through the Barings and Glyn, Mills. While the Tory government publicly congratulated itself on the state of Canada's credit and the financial genius of the new Finance Minister, Sir Leonard Tilley, the loan in fact reflected the British government's credit through the guarantee more than Canada's; and compared to the 1868 loan, part of which was unguaranteed, the results were less favourable.[3] It was clear that the investors' euphoria that followed the creation of the new Dominion had begun to wear off by the time the Pacific railroad project was slated to begin.

# The Pacific Project: I

It had been confidently expected that the Grand Trunk would assume the task of building the Pacific railway, but a stock-holders' coup in 1869 resulted in a new set of officers pledged to a policy of retrenchment and maximum dividends. By 1869, the Grand Trunk was again on the brink of insolvency, and the Bar-ings and Glyn, Mills had once more secured writs of attachment to protect it from its other creditors in order to defend the pri-ority of their claims. The government had to look elsewhere, and was immediately presented with a major quandary — satisfying two competing syndicates of highly placed Tories, one repre-senting Toronto, the other Montreal, for without the ability to hold a reasonably strong position in both Ontario and Quebec, Macdonald's tenure in office would be short. The problem was further exacerbated by the equally compelling claims each group had for Macdonald's favour. The Toronto group, headed by Senator David Macpherson, sported eight Senators and M.P.s, plus leading Toronto and Ontario business figures including Mayor John Walker of London, Sir William Howland, Casimir Gzowski, and Frank Smith. It was a syndicate with excellent Grand Trunk connections as well as considerable political power. It was under Macpherson's direction that funds had been embezzled from the Northern Railway in 1869 and 1872 to pour into Conservative election coffers including those of Francis Hincks, as well as being siphoned off into a testimonial fund for John A. Macdonald — funds which Macdonald very properly refused to touch, turning them over instead to his wife's trustees for handling. In return the Conservative government offered to discharge all of the Northern's £500,000 debt to the public for a mere £100,000.[4] Well might Sir Richard Cartwright remark on the antics of the Highland Scots, Macdonald and Macpherson, that

> The ancestors of these gentlemen, in times gone by, stole many a head of black cattle, and if they got caught they were sometimes hanged for it. Their descendants milk the Northern Railway cow on the sly, and get presented with a testimonial.

In the case of the rival syndicate, Sir Hugh Allan, Canada's richest capitalist, doyen of Montreal's commercial and transpor-tation community, headed a string of nineteen Senators and legislators plus a long list of other Montreal eminences — Andrew Allan, Victor Hudon, D. McInnes, and Sandford Fleming among others. To tighten his hold, Sir Hugh went to work on the Montreal Tory machine, buying newspapers and their editors, and hiring bushy-tailed young lawyers as organisers and eulogists. Sir George Cartier, the Grand Trunk Railway's solicitor and the kingpin of the Macdonald cabinet, suddenly discovered his 45 moutons had lost their way and could now be found grazing in other pastures. Nor could the fact that Sir Hugh's Merchants Bank of Canada had absorbed a number of Macdonald's debts when it had taken over the defunct Commercial Bank have lessened Sir Hugh's influence in leading Tory circles.[5] In addition a program of stock distribution to Dominion notables was undertaken, Macpherson alone demanding $250,000 of stock in the syndicate and threatening to make trouble if he did not get it. And hundreds of thousands of dollars found their way into the election funds of the Party leaders in 1872.

Allan received his charter under terms negotiated by John Abbott and Francis Hincks. A reshuffle of directors absorbed several of Macpherson's allies; new faces were added; others, especially the offending American financiers who were very active in the project, were dropped.[6] The Grand Trunk was partially mollified by the promise of a gift of the Intercolonial Railway, which would give it effectively an eastern Canadian monopoly.

In 1872 the plans for the new railway were well in hand. Sir Hugh had begun the preparation for an eight million pound bond issue of which £2.5 million received an imperial guarantee, and another £1.1 million carried a guarantee under the Canada Defence Loan Act of 1870.[7] Without the guarantee, prospects of success of the issue were slim. For the Grand Trunk's heavy borrowings continued to absorb a large amount of potential investment funds, as well as undermining the confidence of investors in the ability of Canadian railroads to ever make a return. Even as Sir Hugh was preparing for the issue, the Grand Trunk was making a fresh offering of ten million pounds of equity, with the hope that the new capital would finally suffice to put the line in a condition to pay dividends.[8]

In addition to an enormous subsidy in cash and 50 million acres of land, the government pledged that for 20 years it would never sell its lands for less than $2.50 an acre unless by prior agreement with the company, to avoid having government sales reduce the average price the railway company could extract from its lands. It was further stipulated in the charter that the government would undertake to extinguish Indian title to the lands. The contract was to be supervised by a board of three trustees, one oppointed by the government, one by the shareholders, and one by the bond holders: all decisions were to be made on the majority principle — in other words by the capitalists involved. As was often the case in similar arrangements, the contract inspired the animosity of those left out, who revealed, through Liberal M.P. L. S. Huntingdon, the degree to which the Macdonald ministry had been blatantly bribed with personal and election gifts to secure the charter.

When the Pacific scandal broke, the Macdonald government had already been weakened by losses in Ontario and Quebec. He had retained power largely by virtue of the over-representation accorded to British Columbia and Manitoba.[9] But with the desertion of Donald Smith from the Tory fold, the Macdonald coalition collapsed and thus ended Sir Hugh Allan's Pacific ambitions.

# The Saga of Labrador Smith

Because of his critical importance not only to railway development but to the entire sweep of Canadian history from Confederation to the First World War, a digression on the career of Donald A. Smith (Lord Strathcona) seems in order. This most important Canadian capitalist of the period, like so many other financiers, was a Scot by origin, born in Forres, Morayshire, appropriately enough the place where Macbeth first met the witches. In 1838, in a classic example of unequal exchange in operation, Smith came to Canada — the steamer bearing him up the St. Lawrence passing on the way the ship carrying the last load of *Patriotes* of the 1837 rebellion on their way to exile in Australia. Smith entered the employ of the Hudson's Bay Company and was soon posted to Labrador.

The fur trade was his central preoccupation, for in his capacity as Chief Factor or Chief Trader his income was derived through a share of the profits from the trade. It was a barter trade based on the exchange of commodities such as gunpowder or alcohol, which effectively tied the Indians to their source of supply in return for furs. The Indians were totally dependent upon supplies of gunpowder for survival, and were perpetually in debt to the company. Profits could be increased by the reduction of the quantity of powder offered for a fixed amount of furs.

During the course of Smith's tenure in Labrador, starvation and ensuing murder and cannibalism wiped out half of the Nascopie Indians, and completely eliminated the Eskimo from the south shore;[10] this famine had resulted from the Indians' not having obtained sufficient supplies of gunpowder from the company's servants.[11]

In addition to his share of the profits from the fur trade and from the private banking business he conducted in competition with the company, Smith also pioneered a salmon fishery. The men working the fishery had to give half their catch to the company as rent for nets and for the use of the ports, which were situated in the best fishing areas and directly under the control of the company.[12] Although the cannery he established was abandoned after the area around it was completely depleted of salmon, the company remained the largest buyer of salmon on the Labrador coast until well after the turn of the century.[13]

The profits of these various activities flowed to Montreal where, especially after he became head of the Montreal Department in 1869, Smith became increasingly involved with the commercial and financial elite, notably his cousin George Stephen and Sir Hugh Allan.

Smith's connection with the Northwest began in earnest in 1869 when he was sent to Manitoba as Macdonald's emissary to bribe Louis Riel to leave Canada. At that time the transfer of the area from the Hudson's Bay Company to the Dominion Government was in motion, a transfer which would have resulted in the centralization of power in the fur trade in Smith's hands in Montreal. Smith's next step was a visit to England as a representative of the wintering partners of the company to present their claims to a share of the funds being paid to the company by the Dominion for their rights to the area. News of the pending transfer threw the market for HBC stocks into panic, and Smith proceeded to buy up all that were offered at from £9/0/0 to £12/0/0 per share.[14] He returned to Canada as Chief Commissioner of the company, whose prospects for a future increasingly depended upon the terms on which it could sell the huge area of land left in its hands after the transfer.

In 1871, the Macdonald government made its decision to proceed with the Pacific Railway and subsequently granted the charter to Sir Hugh Allan's syndicate, the board of which Smith initially appeared upon. Smith's presence was expected to ensure close co-operation with the Hudson's Bay Company in the matter of land sales and especially to secure its influence among London bankers in marketing Pacific railway securities. Smith's name was dropped from the final syndicate, and although Macdonald and the Tories continued to expect his assistance in Parliament, Smith bolted the Tory cause and brought down the Macdonald government, on Guy Fawkes Day, 1873.

Behind this change of allegiance there was a serious purpose with respect to his western ambitions. Sir Hugh Allan's syndicate linked up to Jay Cooke, who wanted to extend his Northern Pacific into the Canadian prairies.[15] The linkage to an American line was essential to any CPR plan, and a key link would be controlled by whoever secured the charter to build from Pembina in Manitoba to the border. In 1871 and 1872, a series of petitions and applications for such a charter were made, including one from Smith, George Stephen, and some Montreal associates.[16] Nor was this Smith's only Manitoba venture of the year, for also in 1872 he introduced bills in the House to incorporate the Bank of Manitoba and the Manitoba Insurance Company.[17]

Smith's ambitions were thwarted when Sir Hugh Allan was forced to withdraw from the contract. For the Hudson's Bay Company, whose future profitability hinged almost totally on the potential for land sales, and whose equity had shot up after the Allan contract was concluded, it was a major blow.[18] Pressure from pro-government circles began to build for the government itself to construct the railway,[19] and Macdonald apparently assented, though no public statement was made. Macdonald further promised to a visiting representative of the British labour movement that the great tracts of land in the West would be available free of all cost.[20] Faced with the possibility of government construction and therefore no sales of government land at remunerative prices, the Hudson's Bay Company shareholders saw their prospects of recouping their fortunes from land sales vanish. In addition, Montreal in 1873 was alive with rumours that Sir Hugh Allan planned a new Northwest Company to compete with the Hudson's Bay Company for the fur trade. Smith's disenchantment with the Macdonald government is easily comprehensible. So too is the fact that by 1878 he could be back in the Tory fold, pushed by the Mackenzie administration's refusal to budge from the principle of public ownership of the CPR, by the fact that a Tory-controlled Senate spitefully rejected his applications for a Pembina branch charter, and by the fact that his investments in the Montreal textile industry were threatened by British and American competition.

Smith's return to the fold was not an easy one, for few figures in political history apart from Benedict Arnold and Warren Hastings have incurred the opprobrium directed at the Member from Selkirk. The 1878 election in fact saw Tory funds poured into attempting to secure his defeat. While he won the election, the victory was contested on the grounds that the voters had been bribed. A judge investigated, and solemnly decreed it to have been a fair fight, only to have an embarrassing debt of his honour to Donald Smith exposed by less credulous constituents. A new contest saw Smith's money flow liberally into the riding to no avail, and the former member returned to Montreal, reflecting sadly on the public immorality of an electorate that would take his money and still vote against him. Alexander Mackenzie's 1873 decision to introduce the secret ballot may well have been another of Smith's grudges against his former chief.

# The Pacific Project: II

The failure of Sir Hugh's Pacific ambitions was duplicated in other endeavours as the Grand Trunk London board commenced a counter-attack against potential competition. In 1875, Sir Hugh attempted to raise money in London for his Northern Colonization Railway scheme — a project supported by the Quebec government as part of a program to colonize Quebec's forbidding interior to stem the flow of population to New England. The Grand Trunk and its allies in the British financial press fought the loan and were successful in blocking it.[21] In 1875, the president of the London board of the GTR asked the Colonial Office to intervene and disallow any Quebec Act which contravened the 1852 GTR subsidy program, with the potential competition of Allan's North Shore and similar projects specifically in mind. The Colonial Office declared it had no business interfering — though 1875 elsewhere was a turning point in British imperial history, marking as it did the Suez Canal seizure when British foreign policy and foreign investment for the first time became explicitly and mutually reinforcing. Nonetheless the GTR's London antics proved so disturbing to Canadian credit in general that Alexander Mackenzie requested John Rose, then de facto High Commissioner in London, to call on the Barings and Glyn, Mills to have them put pressure on the GTR's president to shut him up[22] — the chain of authority involved was an interesting illustration of the prevailing power structure.

Under the Mackenzie administration, an effort was initially made to continue the policy of subsidizing a private syndicate to build the line. However, the panic of 1873, which saw the failure of Jay Cooke, the bankruptcy of a large part of the American railway system, and the flight of British capital from North

American railway ventures, effectively ended that strategy. Mounting Canadian budget deficits in spite of increased tariffs, together with the limitation of the country's borrowing powers in Britain, led to a policy of slow construction. The road was divided into four sectors for purposes of contracting, with construction to be supervised by the Department of Public Works. Ownership was to remain vested in the Dominion Government. To assure that the contractors were capable of undertaking the work, they were required to have a capital of $4,000 per mile, of which 25% was to be deposited with the Receiver-General. They were to get a guarantee of interest on bonds issued at four per cent for 25 years plus 20,000 acres per mile in alternate sections. To guard against speculation, two-thirds of the land grant was to be sold by the government on behalf of the contractors and the other third delivered directly to them. Cash subsidies of up to $10,000 per mile were also authorized. Under one variant or another of this format the railroad edged forward during the Mackenzie years.

In the interim, a Tory-sponsored secessionist movement sprang up in British Columbia headed by disappointed fortune hunters and the B.C. federal M.P.s who had counted on large gifts of CPR stock to secure their allegiance to the Dominion.[23] The Mackenzie government attempted to placate the province by advocating rapid building of the Esquimault and Nanaimo Railway, but the Tory Senate threw out the bill. The political turmoil in the Pacific province led to a series of shortlived governments, culminating in 1878 in an avowed secessionist group taking office in Victoria.

All of the clamour for faster construction had sent Sandford Fleming to England on behalf of Mackenzie in an unsuccessful effort to tempt British contracting firms to invest their money and energy in the road. Although progress was slow and the line remained in government hands, that did not prevent the construction from creating a fair array of minor fortunes among the Liberal Party faithful before the return of the Macdonald government to federal office in 1878.

The year 1878 was a propitious one in Dominion politics. John A. Macdonald, just five years after being turned out of office as a result of the worse political scandal since that which toppled Francis Hincks in 1854, returned to office with an unprecedented majority. His program of "protection" to some industries and to a lot of British bondholders certainly played a role. A great deal of support too, came from contractors disappointed at the lack of spoils under the Mackenzie regime. And, as it was freely contended in Liberal Party circles, a major reason for Mackenzie's defeat, and ipso facto Macdonald's victory, was the key role of bartenders and saloonkeepers in the election. These men, whose political influence over their clientele was considerable, leaned to the Tory camp because so many owed their licenses to Tory patronage, because of Mackenzie's avowed connections with the Temperance League, and because Sir John A. Macdonald's personal habits were such a splendid advertisement for their trade.[24]

Macdonald appointed Charles Tupper to the Ministry of Railways, and immediately Tupper hatched a plan that involved ceding virtually all the prime land in the Northwest to a railway syndicate; some 100 million acres were to be sold at a minimum price of $2.00 per acre. The land was to be placed in the hands of a commisssion on which it was hoped to have Imperial Government representation. Construction and British colonization could then go hand in hand.[25] The CPR was to be an imperial highway. And along it would be settled the unemployed labourers then threatening the social equilibrium of Victorian England. The scheme, which would have involved the ceding of virtually all of the ungranted lands within 20 miles of each side of the line to the company, had to be changed the next year to an American alternate section plan, for American railroads, notably the Montreal-controlled St. Paul, Minneapolis, and Manitoba, were offering more liberal terms for land and thus diverting the flow of immigrants into the U.S.[26]

For a time Macdonald followed the Mackenzie plan of slow construction in pieces as a public work. The sole major departure from Mackenzie's approach lay in the routing of the line. In 1875, Donald Smith and John Schultz had both requested Mackenzie to run the railway line through Winnipeg, where both held land, instead of 30 miles north through Selkirk. Mackenzie, however, insisted on the shortest possible route and refused. But in 1879 Macdonald rerouted the line through Winnipeg, against the advice of his engineers.

By the end of 1879, with a new high tariff yielding large budget surplus and the gloom long overhanging world money markets dispelled, Macdonald changed policy again, and decreed in favour of a private syndicate again. In 1880 a new syndicate, composed of a group of financiers dripping with the spoils of the St. Paul, Minneapolis and Manitoba railway job, undertook the task. They numbered Smith, Stephen, R. B. Angus, and Duncan McIntyre, all eminent Montreal financial and commercial figures; J. S. Kennedy of New York; together with the Americanized Canadian railway magnate J. J. Hill, and the Canadianized American railway magnate William Van Horne, who joined shortly thereafter. Under the terms of the new contract, huge gifts of cash and completed lines and surveys were supplemented by a land grant of 25 million acres and a variety of tax concessions. Construction and operating materials were exempted from duty; land granted was exempted for 20 years after the grant (an exemption that was extended and even introduced into the acts establishing the new provinces of Alberta and Saskatchewan in 1905); the equity was forever tax exempt; and western monopoly was guaranteed. To assure continuity of control, the transfer of stock to non-shareholders was subjected to a directors' veto until the completion of the contract. Rates charged were exempt from government interference until the profit rate reached ten per cent. Opposition emerged immediately, with a largely Ontario-based group offering to build the line at a lower cost. The new group was led by Sir William Howland and included George Cox, the insurance magnate; James McLaren, an Ottawa lumber baron; Alex Gibson, the New Brunswick cotton magnate; John Walker, the perpetrator of oil swindles; and A. B. MacMaster, a noted banking figure. Curiously enough, this group of Liberal-Party-affiliated financiers offered to build the line specifically without a tariff exemption, while the Conservative group demanded the abeyance of the tariff for purposes of construction. The Liberals would maintain the National Policy: the Conservatives would undermine it. The Liberal Party group clearly could command the resources necessary for the job as well as could the Montreal syndicate, but was obviously hampered by its party connections, and its offer in fact may well have been simply a political manoeuvre.

The project was immediately beset by capital market problems. The suspicion already surrounding Canadian railway investments was exacerbated by the Pacific Scandal and the Grand Trunk's hostility towards competitors. Relations between the Conservative Party and the City of London were far from cordial. During Macdonald's ten-day de facto impeachment in the House in 1873, Lord Rosebery, a member of the Rothschild family, sat in the gallery and observed the proceedings.[27] It was hardly an edifying advertisement for Canadian railway finance. While in opposition during the mid-1870's, the Conservatives had fought back against the GTR's anti-Hugh-Allan campaign by charging the Barings with misleading the Liberal Minister of Finance, Richard Cartwright, for corrupt reasons, and by assailing the very institution of the Canadian financial agents in London. Despite Francis Hincks's intervention on behalf of the Barings and Cartwright, the slight could not have helped Conservative Party relations with the bankers.[28] In 1876, Sir Hugh Allan had spent several months in Britain again trying to raise money for a colonization railroad in Quebec, but the loan was attacked in the financial press even though it was nominally a Quebec government loan, not a railway one.[29] In 1879, Duncan McIntyre's Canada Central did successfully place a £500,000 issue there, but it required a Dominion Government guarantee of five per cent interest for twenty years,[30] and this at a time of very easy money in Britain.[31] Canadian railways' earnings record continued to deteriorate. Over the period 1870-1879 the Grand Trunk paid dividends only in 1879, and then it was restricted to two per cent on its first preference shares. The Great Western paid nothing at all, and was only saved from complete bankruptcy by its through traffic between the two parts of the U.S. via the southwestern Ontario peninsula.[32] Throughout 1880 the stocks of both these lines continued to deteriorate.[33]

The new CPR syndicate adopted the policy of financing by sales of equity, which, together with gargantuan subsidies from various levels of government, especially the federal, in the form of cash gifts, land grants, and gifts of completed lines and surveys, was expected to enable them to avoid fixed interest debt and the concomitant problems that plagued the other lines. In turn, the federal government expected to finance the giveaway program and its other infrastructural requirements from the proceeds of the government savings banks and the "protective" tariff.

While the syndicate has been given a great deal of credit for farsightedness with its "shares only" policy, it is not at all clear that it was a voluntary decision. For initially an imperial bond guarantee was sought, and refused.[34] In 1880 too, Sir John A. Macdonald, Sir Charles Tupper, and the Minister of Railways J. H. Pope made a pilgrimage with McIntyre and Stephen to the London office of the Grand Trunk to beg Tyler to join the project.[35] With his refusal automatically came that of the Barings and the Rothchilds. And, in any event, since the huge cash gifts and government loans to the syndicate had to be covered by federal government bond issues, all that the policy of avoiding bond financing meant was that the federal government, rather than the CPR syndicate, did the borrowing—an index not so much of financial acumen as of political manipulation. Furthermore, the entire rationale of favouring equity financing instead of more readily saleable bonds turns theoretically on the hope of avoiding a burden of fixed interest debt that would drain the cash resources of the line from the outset. For the CPR this explanation makes no sense. From the start it paid dividends of five per cent out of capital, and since the equity on

average yielded but 40% of par value, the real drain on cash
resources from the beginning was of the magnitude of 12.5%,
far higher than would result from bond financing. The real
reason for favouring equity financing probably turned on the
desire to avoid the loss of control of the line to bond holders in
the event of its being unable to cover its interest charges. It was
CPR policy to spread ownership of the equity, apart from the
blocs of stock held by the promoters themselves, among a large
number of small shareholders to assure continuity of control
even after construction was completed.

Sales of equity and of lands were essential to the financial
success of the line. While land grant bonds and lands sold relatively freely until the crash of 1883 — British capitalists being
much more willing to invest on the security of the land grant
than in the equity of the line itself — the equity sales ran into
problems from the start. Throughout Europe, capital markets
were already partly closed to the project by the former Dutch
bond holders of the St. Paul Railway, who had been cheated by
Smith, Hill, Stephen and J. S. Kennedy when the group purchased their road in 1873, and they spread the word about European markets to avoid the new syndicate's securities.[36] Furthermore, after Macdonald unsuccessfully tried to retain its affec-
tions by more promises of government largesse,[37] the GTR
turned all its connections against the CPR to block the marketing of its securities in London.[38] The GTR was successful
enough that it even blocked another colonization railroad loan
sought by Sir Hugh Allan and the Hon. Thomas McGreevy in
1883,[39] while the year before George Cox and Robert Jaffray had
placed an issue of Midland Railway bonds there, bonds which
because of the link between the GTR and the Midland were sold
easily.[40] The announcement made to the GTR shareholders
meeting in London was emphatic:

> Let it be known that the pursestrings of England are closed,
> and then means will be found to bring this wonderfully
> aggressive syndicate to its senses, and you will hear of no
> more competitive schemes.[41]

The result was that the CP syndicate turned increasingly to
New York and Amsterdam to sell its equity.[42] In 1881 New York
had been tested and found receptive to a land grant bond issue
underwritten by the Bank of Montreal and some New York
banks, including J. S. Kennedy and Co,[43] though in 1883 some
trouble resulted from J. J. Hill leaving the CPR and trying to
close New York to it.[44]

By the end of 1883, some $65 million nominal value of stock

had been issued. The first five million had been taken at par by the promoters under the terms of their contract. The next $20 million they also absorbed, at 25% of its par value — for a total of $25 million in stock at an average of 40%. The next $30 million were placed in New York and Amsterdam at 61. Thus a total issue of $55 million yielded $25,300,000 in cash. Another $4,950,000 cash advance was secured from the government in return for a pledge of ten millions in stock. To bolster saleability even during construction, a five per cent dividend was paid out of capital and subsidies — representing for the promoters a 12.5% return on their investment. Nonetheless, by the end of 1883 the prospects of further issues in New York seemed exhausted, partly perhaps because of Hill's active opposition, partly too, in all probability, because the initial watering operation frightened off potential investors in the U.S. who bore some sizeable scars from the antics of their own railway promoters, but chiefly because of the crash of railway financing in the U.S. that year following an orgy of overbuilding of several years duration.

In a futile effort to maintain sales of equity, London and New York financiers advised that a government dividend guarantee system be instituted. Accordingly, a cash deposit was placed with the federal government sufficient to guarantee three per cent dividends on the common stock. It was, if anything, counter-productive, for it froze a large sum of ready cash without yielding any significant new inflow through sales of new stock.[45] In 1885, Liberal leader, Edward Blake pointed out that, omitting the last sale of ten million, the company had raised about $25 million in cash; while, counting the subsequent two dividends, the company would have paid out, or provided for by the deposit with the government, dividends of a larger amount. Of the seven million already paid out in dividends, the syndicate members alone had been repaid $3.6 million on an investment of ten million. Thus, before the road was open for traffic every cent of cash put in by the initial shareholders would have been repaid or set aside for dividends.

Under the circumstances, the company's appeal for government aid after 1883 is readily understandable. The high cost of the CPR in relation to estimates and the rapidity with which it exhausted government aid and its other revenue sources was due to a number of factors, apart from the drainage into dividends, not least of which was the high cost of buying up every Grand Trunk feeder line it could find in an effort to destroy its rival and monopolize Canadian traffic in the East as well as the West. This competition was especially bitter after the 1883 rift between J. J. Hill and Van Horne. Until then, the idea of an all-Canadian route evidently was not taken very seriously by the promoters, for not until then was the issue resolved. And Van Horne's plan to run the line north of Superior in order to generate long-distance through traffic for the CPR in lieu of local western traffic — with its implications of sharp competition for Hill's Great Northern — led to the rift.[46] In addition, the barren section would have to be supported by a concerted invasion of GTR traffic in the east.

Moreover, the construction itself produced opportunities to imitate the behaviour of some of the more notorious American lines, for much of the work was done under contracts made with the North American Construction Company. According to Liberal Party critics who might have been lying, but then again might well have told the truth, the company was formed "for the purposes of vastly increasing the costs of that road, and of putting the increased cost into the pockets of a ring of speculators." Just who this "ring of speculators" were was at first difficult to determine. The construction firm claimed to be headquartered in Walton, New Jersey — which sparked off an unsuccessful hunt on the part of the opposition to ascertain the existence of any such municipality among New Jersey's multitude of havens for fly-by-night firms. However it appeared that of 25,000 shares, some 20,000 were held by the CPR. The nature of the bargains struck between the CPR and its prodigy were a closely guarded secret, the Minister of Railways refusing to divulge them in the Commons.[47] It was charged that the construction firm was paid for its work fully in cash, rather than in cash and stock as had been agreed to earlier, and as a result the cash reserves of the CPR were drained off, forcing it to apply for more government aid.[48]

Financial difficulties, real or concocted, led to new demands for public assistance. In 1884, George Stephen presented himself in Ottawa with a hair-raising tale of the adversity and misfortune that would follow the collapse of his line. The Bank of Montreal and other banks would fail; high unemployment would stalk the land; a long string of wholesale houses, including that of the Honourable Frank Smith, a member of the cabinet, whose credit advances had been an important part of the CPR short-term financing, would go bankrupt; and Canada's credit abroad would be ruined. The government was ready to comply. To keep a modicum of dignity in the proceedings, Tupper in 1884 appointed a government auditor, Edward Miall, to investigate the CPR accounts to see if it merited further aid. Miall, then Deputy Minister of Inland Revenue, was well suited for the task. Described by the surveyor Henry Hind as "an accomplished manipulator of forged figures," Miall had previously been responsible for falsifying fishery statistics on behalf of the Macdonald government for purposes of the Treaty of Washington negotiations.[49]

In 1884, the CPR received a federal loan, part of which was immediately diverted into buying stock in the North West Land Co. to keep up the value of the equity.[50] This land company was set up by the CPR magnates with a view to dealing in CPR lands, and the collapse of the Manitoba land rush hurt it. It subsequently foundered.

The federal loan had been secured by a first mortgage on the line, a first lien that had to be eliminated if the CPR hoped to sell its securities elsewhere. Further federal gifts were forthcoming, some poorly disguised as sales of land back to the federal government at prices bearing no relation to the prevailing depressed value of Manitoba land.[51] This operation, coupled with the pledge of some first mortgage bonds, removed the government's general first lien on the assets of the line and cleared the air for a bond issue. By this time both the Barings and Glyn, Mills had been wooed away from the GTR, and George Carr Glyn, Lord Wolverton, and Alexander Baring, Lord Revelstoke, both appeared as trustees for the loan which the Barings marketed. The Barings acted as agents for all of the CPR's subsequent issues until 1889, when Revelstoke refused any further aid. His plea was that the CPR was sufficiently mature to market its own securities, but his reluctance to undertake any further CPR financial operations probably resulted from his enthusiasm in involving his bank in Argentine railways, utilities, and government bonds, a zeal which culminated in the collapse of the House of Baring in 1890. In any event the 1889 issue of CPR bonds probably had no need of Baring's aid, for it carried a federal government guarantee of interest in exchange for the cancellation of the CPR's monopoly clause.

The "monopoly" clause in the contract was a mandate for the CPR to determine the structure of commercial arteries in Manitoba, with the federal government obligingly disallowing any charters that failed to meet with the company's approval. The most serious effort to find an alternative access route to the American lines was Premier John Norquay's Red River Valley Railroad project. In 1887, Norquay attempted to raise money in both London and New York, but the federal government had disallowed the railway, and his efforts failed in both places.[52] Donald Smith had given instructions to the Manitoba financial agents, Morton, Rose and Co., to block any issues. And John A. Macdonald himself sent word to John Rose's bank to destroy

Manitoba's credit.[53] Norquay attempted to float a $300,000 bond issue, of which $2,000 only was taken up.[54]

Norquay continued to ignore the disallowance, and proceeded to build from his available revenues. Macdonald and Tupper had initially agreed to permit the line to be built, but at the CPR's request they had gome back on the commitment and disallowed the bill. In addition, Donald Smith secured injunctions to block the Red River Road from crossing his properties in the province. And when Norquay tried to have the railroad built under the Public Works Act a judge disallowed it. Ultimately it was the threat of military intervention that blocked progress. As a last resort, the City of Winnipeg had offered to issue municipal debentures to pay for the line, but only if it received a prior guarantee of completion. The possibility of military intervention prevented the contractor from being able to make such a guarantee.[55] Norquay resigned soon after.

While until 1888 lines competitive with the CPR from the south were assiduously fought and defeated, complimentary lines to the north of the CPR in the West or feeders and branches in the East were built at a feverish pace. In the East, a system of subsidies of cash was used to complement those of the provinces and municipalities. Tupper began the new federal subsidy program in 1882 when the provinces and municipalities, nearly exhausted of funds by the demands of the railways, began begging for federal aid. Cash grants of up to $3,200 per mile were made available to a series of "carefully selected" lines. Fresh votes of cash subsidies were made each year, setting off a scramble for charters. The most important principle of "careful selection" was the party affiliation of the promoters. And a long list of Tory M.P.s and their political allies collected their share. The line in the East that received the largest share of federal subsidies, the International Railway running from Maine to Montreal, collected a total of $2,250,000 up to 1886; its president was John Henry Pope, Minister of Railways.[56]

In the West, a different subsidy principle was used. A series of misnamed "colonization" railways based on land grants was initiated in 1884 and discontinued in 1894 for the very good reason that the Conservative government simply ran out of land to give away. Six of these lines were ultimately absorbed into the CPR, and the remaining four into the Canadian Northern system later on. Under the terms of the colonization railway system, the line could buy up to 6,400 acres of selected land anywhere in Manitoba or the Northwest for $1.00 per acre. In addition, several borrowed from the Manitoba government under its 1885 Railway Aid Act; provincial debentures were issued and the funds advanced to the railway secured on the land grant at $1.00 per acre. The regulations were subsequently modified to allow the railroads a free land grant, rather than the nominal charge of $1.00 per acre. The story of the change of regulations seems to be bound up with the history of one of the colonization roads that was shortest on mileage but longest on political connections, the North West Central, later known as the Great North West Central. It was founded in 1885 by a syndicate of M.P.s who took over the charter of a defunct line. While under the presidency of James Beaty, a leading Toronto Tory and M.P., it included on its directorate the Hon. John Norquay, Sir Charles Tupper, and three other federal M.P.s.[57] Initially slated to receive a land concession of up to 6,400 acres per railway mile at $1.00 per acre, its promoters managed to secure a change in the regulations giving them the land as an outright gift. It was charged, with impressive documentation, that $100,000 in cash had been used to bribe the Minister of Interior to secure the land grant, and Beaty admitted to having received free $386,000 worth of equity in the line being reorganized. Upon completion of these preliminaries, plans were laid to complete the line quickly, timing the construction to coincide with harvest time so that big bonuses could be squeezed out of the municipalities en route. Without the bonuses, the railway could then refuse to complete the line and leave the towns with no way of marketing the local harvest. Progress under Herbert Holt's direction was rapid for a while,[58] then it halted in 1887, with the workers in Holt's firm complaining they had not received any wages for a full year. It underwent a series of reorganizations with little result. In 1897, the latest of a series of contractors found himself working as a foreman of a road gang on the railway under orders from its receiver in order to earn a living while awaiting the close of litigation around his and other creditors' claims.[60] Finally in 1898 the CPR absorbed the line, its land grant becoming a source of great profit.

Others of the "colonization" railroads are worthy of note. The Manitoba and North Western, for example, had as its solicitors a law firm comprised of the eldest sons of John A. Macdonald and Charles Tupper. This line, in addition to its federal land grant, received ample assistance from the Manitoba government as well. In 1885 Manitoba loaned it $787,500 on the security of its land grant—which in effect meant Manitoba would be buying back its own land seized from it by the federal government in the Manitoba Act in the event of default. In addition, it issued bonds at a rate of $22,000 per mile, when independent engineering estimates put the cost at which it could be built at $12,000-15,000 per mile. By 1900, not only had it not repaid Manitoba any of the principal, but its arrears of interest totalled $336,500. It was subsequently absorbed by the CPR.[61]

A similar fate awaited several other colonization railroads. The Manitoba South-Western's rocky political career under the leadership of the Lieutenant Governor, John Schultz, also finished with it in the CPR-Tory camp. Alexander Galt's Alberta Railway and Coal Company presented him and a collection of British financiers with untold wealth in coal, timber, and lands in Southern Alberta before being sold to the CPR. The Calgary and Edmonton, promoted by CPR director Edmund Osler, in addition to its land grant of 6,400 acres per mile, got a federal mail subsidy of $80,000 per annum and issued five-and-one-half million dollars in first mortgage bonds. In total, its promoters raised $28,000 per mile on bonds and land while the cost of the road by the company's own figures was but $13,000 per mile, and according to other estimates was as low as $7,000. Yet when it opened, its roadbed had already deteriorated to the point of virtual unusability, and it was quickly absorbed by the CPR.

It is worth noting that the federal mail subsidy of $80,000 per annum was tantamount to a surreptitious guarantee of interest for those lines that received it. The Calgary and Edmonton actually arranged with the federal government that its mail subsidy would be paid directly to the London agents who were trustees for the bond holders. A similar arrangement graced the Qu'Appelle, Long Lake and Saskatchewan Railway and helped it sell $3,500,000 worth of bonds in addition to receiving 1,400,000 acres of land. Its promoters walked off with somewhere between one and two million dollars in profit. This line was then leased rent-free to the CPR.

The investment of Canadian resources represented by the CPR and its affiliates was enormous. By as early as 1888, total investment in Canadian railways was valued at nearly $684 million of which federal and provincial governments had contributed over $150 million and the municipalities another $13 million. Over $190 million was represented by bond issues, virtually all in Britain. Some 12,332 miles of line had been built with another 660 under construction.[62] There was some slowing down of federal government investments, especially after 1891 when the sugar duty remission took a large slice out of customs revenue. But by 1896 the stage was set for a round of creating millionaires out of friends of the Liberal Party to balance those established from public funds by the Tories. That year, Sir Donald Smith made the claim that he would have been $200,000 per annum better off if he had never touched the CPR[63] —

calling to mind Sir John A. Macdonald's earlier assessment that "that fellow Smith is the biggest liar I ever met."[64]

# Railway Policy and Politics

Elections in Canada were often little more than a tug-of-war between the big railway companies. The importance of the railroad companies to the functioning of the democratic process included assisting in economic blackmail, ballot box stuffing, bribery, and all the other standard accoutrements of the Canadian political process of the day. The railroads were the biggest employers of labour, and the employees of the lines, even after the introduction of the secret ballot, could usually be depended upon to vote in a bloc. Moreover, apart from direct election subscriptions, the railways' economic power was enhanced in their links to the rest of the business community.

To try to keep its loyalty, John A. Macdonald had offered the Grand Trunk any public money that the CPR left behind in its periodic raids on the treasury, but to little avail. In 1882 he pleaded with the general manager to "put [his] shoulder to the wheel and help us as of yore in the Elections. In return for such aid I shall endeavour to do all I properly can for the GTR." This assurance, together with his plea that "I have as you know uniformly backed the GTR since 1854 and won't change my course now"[65] contrasts rather sharply to his public statements on the Kingston wharf and Sarnia land jobs in 1860, when he publicly claimed as his main defense that "I opposed the Grand Trunk from its conception."[66]

His appeal for aid in 1882 appears to have succeeded. Both of the big railway companies worked avidly for the Tory cause, ferrying Canadians resident in the U.S. free of charge to their former constituencies to vote Conservative. But as the tension between the CPR and the GTR mounted in Eastern Canada, relations between the GTR and the Conservative Party quickly soured. By the time of the notorious 1891 election, the Grand Trunk, on orders from London, put all its resources into the battle against Macdonald, while Van Horne took the field for the government.[67] Charles Tupper offered to drop the duty on U.S. coal in favour of the GTR, for an estimated saving of £50,000 per annum in exchange for its support in delivering its vote en masse. The offer was respectfully declined. The General Manager of the GTR's Michigan lines announced he was busy rounding up émigré Canadians to carry them free to Canada to vote Liberal. And in the aftermath of the election Macdonald asserted that the GTR had nearly defeated him. The narrow Tory victory was assured by the CPR's returning a Tory in every riding but one through which its main line passed.[68]

The CPR's support was not a labour of love. It was the year of J. J. Hill's big offensive against the CPR's mining and Pacific cargo business in B.C. And in the East the question of control of the Intercolonial Railway was at the fore again. In 1889, the CPR had begun buying up Maritime links. Sir John A. Macdonald had indicated a willingness both to subsidize an Atlantic fleet for the CPR and to give it the Intercolonial. On Sir John A's death just after the 1891 election, John Abbott, Hugh Allan's old bargaining agent and former CPR director, took over the Prime Minister's post. A near-revolt of his chief Quebec lieutenants, Hector Langevin and Adolphe Chapleau, was smoothed over by Van Horne, and plans proceeded for the transfer of the Intercolonial. John Abbott's death brought the Maritimer John Thompson to leadership, and with it a refusal to give the Intercolonial away. His successor Mackenzie Bowell concurred, only to have Sir Charles Tupper's son lead a cabinet revolt against him. Just by the remotest coincidence Sir Charles arrived back in Canada at that opportune moment, and in 1896 he led the Tories triumphantly into electoral disaster. Donald Smith, whom many had favoured for the Tory leadership, was dispatched to London to replace Tupper as High Commissioner, and he immediately began work on a prospectus for a bond issue based on the CPR receiving control of the Intercolonial Railway.[69] But the Liberal victory spelled an end to the CPR's ambitions in the East, and made it inevitable that public funds would be poured into breaking the line's political and economic hegemony of the West.

In the provinces, railway politics were equally intricate. Quebec, despite its periodic fiscal crises, continued its colonization railway project until 1891. In addition to such early eminences as Hugh Allan, Quebec railway promotions owe a large share of the provincial debt to one Christopher N. Armstrong, railway entrepreneur par excellence—meaning simply a remarkable capacity for investing other people's money. His first project was the Montreal and Sorel Railway in 1882, the funds for which all came from London bond sales. After Armstrong had duly examined the tenders and selected himself as contractor, building began—and ceased well short of its objective. When it was discovered that 40% of the funds raised by bond sales never reached the coffers of the company, the bondholders threatened action. Within a year of being issued, the bonds were in default, and although they had been purchased at 97, the British investors turned the bonds over to a Canadian syndicate at one-third their face value. A series of federal, provincial, and municipal grants permitted periodic renewals, and Armstrong managed through one financial trick or another to stay a step ahead of the bailiffs until 1894, when a group of his patchwork promotions were sold off at a sheriff's auction. In the interim, Armstrong's star had continued to rise, and in 1891 he was a central figure in the Baie des Chaleurs Railway scandals that rocked, and ultimately toppled the Quebec provincial administration of Honoré Mercier.

The affair turned on a longstanding project for a railway in the Gaspé. It was a seedy promotion from the start, and hence Armstrong was an appropriate choice of contractor in 1885. Sporadically, pieces of line were tacked down with provincial subsidies. In 1890, Mercier pledged completion to the constituents if a by-election result was favourable. After the electoral victory a new vote of aid was made, including $280,000 to take care of certain old "privileged" debts. As soon as it was voted, Armstrong presented a bill for $298,000 for work that was never done, and $175,000 was approved for payment—of which $100,000 was retransferred to a group of cabinet ministers for sundry electoral and personal expenses. After the Mercier government had been dismissed, Armstrong still kept his $75,000 share.

Mercier's discomfiture failed to dampen Armstrong's enthusiasm, and by 1893 he was in business again, trying to turn his patchwork of bits and pieces into a genuine railroad. A long string of eminent financiers and politicians supported him—J. R. Thibaudeau, J. N. Greenshields, Alphonse Desjardins, and Sandford Fleming—the secret of securing their support being simply to lie. He told them the federal government had agreed to a bond guarantee and a cash grant, though it was all to be a closely guarded secret. His new project, the Atlantic and Lake Superior, was incorporated on April Fool's Day, 1893. The British financial press, which had not forgotten Armstrong's earlier antics, fought the project and blocked its bond sales. In 1894, the sheriff seized a number of his lines. The remaining bits were finally put into receivership in 1900. A complex subsequent history included a reorganization by a syndicate headed by the receiver, a fresh infusion of British money, and periodic appeals for government support which yielded a fund of financial absurdities but little cash and even less railway mileage.[70]

It is clear that Chris Armstrong should have heeded the old adage that entrepreneurs should go west, for British Columbia at

the turn of the century was fertile ground for his type of operation. The return of Macdonald to power in 1878 led to a mysteri-
ously abrupt end to the B.C. secessionist movement, and to a
new charter for the Esquimault and Nanaimo Railway. Robert
Dunsmuir was given a federal subsidy of $750,000 plus 1,900,000
acres of land containing the bulk of the Vancouver Island coal
mines not already in his possession by the terms of a bill sponsored by John Henry Pope in 1884. The railway was to be only
78 miles in length. On Robert's death in 1889, his two sons
James and Alex took over the mining and transportation empire,
and with it British Columbia politics.

British Columbia at the turn of the century, especially after
the new minerals rush, was graced with a remarkably straightfor-
ward and economical political system. Instead of parties, governments were based on factions of no professed political principle
whatsoever, glued together with largesse from the public purse
and periodically bursting assunder in a wild individualistic
scramble for larger shares.[71] Under the regime of John H. Turner
in 1898, the spoils system reached its apogee. The business of
buying and selling railway charters was placed on a scientific
basis with the actual establishment in 1898 of a British firm, the
London and Vancouver Finance and Developing Co., explicitly
to deal in charters. It did a profitable business.[72] Mining companies competed with railway promoters for public favours, and
Turner was happy to oblige. He therefore did not hesitate to
assume the dual role of head of a government overseeing the
administration of mining royalties and the building of infrastructure to service the mines on the one hand, and director of various
mining companies on the other. Under attack by the "opposition" for his divided loyalties, Turner's defense consisted in
claiming that his presence on the boards of the mining companies had been requested by the British financiers who controlled them because of the extra security it gave their investments![73] Turner's defeat led to a series of unstable ministries
called in by an even more unstable Lieutenant Governor who
was notorious for his lack of respect for certain types of private
property, especially that of the CPR and certain coal mining
companies. [74] One of his choices for Premier fell upon a former
Attorney-General of Manitoba who in that previous capacity
had fought the CPR's monopoly clause. Direct intervention both
by the CPR and by leading eastern financiers like George Cox
and Robert Jaffray failed to block the Premier's appointment.
The political contest, however, went in favour of the railways,
the Premier resigned, and the Lieutenant Governor was dismissed by the federal government in order to stabilize business

conditions. [75] The situation found a temporary equilibrium with the advent to power of James Dunsmuir, an open tool of the CPR whose most distinguishing characteristic in his administration of office was the number of gifts to railways and mines he pushed through the provincial Legislature.[76] A few years later, his Finance Minister, Richard McBride, shifted the province's allegiance to a new set of railway promoters.

In Manitoba, the CPR was equally unsuccessful in maintaining power even with the fall of the Norquay government, for the new Premier had divided loyalties. Under an arrangement worked out in 1887, the solicitor of the Manitoba Central Railway had control of certain charters that the St. Paul, Minneapolis and Manitoba Railroad, under J. J. Hill's direction, wanted to acquire, but which required alterations in the Manitoba railway act. In return for election funds, Thomas Greenway pledged to make the required alterations. Greenway lived in fear that the CPR and the Dominion Tory government would spend large sums to ensure his defeat, and his demands for election contributions from Hill's road escalated. The new funds were forthcoming after Greenway signed a document agreeing to make the described changes.[77] These transactions came to light in 1899, when the Greenway government was defeated by the Conservative Party led first by John A. Macdonald's son, and later by Rodmond Roblin, who threatened to nationalize the railways.[78] The "nationalization turned out to be a rate fixing agreement with the new Canadian Northern syndicate.

In Alberta, the relationship of the CPR to provincial politics was circumspect, and it was itself not directly involved in the fall of the government in 1910 when A. L. Sifton, brother of Laurier's first Interior Minister, took power from the Tories. The problem revolved about the curious relations between the government and the Alberta and Great Waterways Railway.[79] The province gave the railway a guarantee of its bonds for up to $20,000 per mile. These bonds were then sold at par to J. S. Morgan and Co. of New York, the banking house of J. P. Morgan's nephew, who in turn immediately disposed of them in London at 110. The resulting profit was $500,000, part of which apparently returned to Alberta as a rake-off to the promoters and to the Premier, who had pushed through the necessary legislation.[80]

# The New Railways: I

The last years of Tory rule in Ottawa were exceedingly unpropitious for railway adventures. The Baring Crisis of 1890-1 followed by the Panic of 1893 deranged the international flow of financial capital. Deep depression did the rest. In 1895 even the CPR passed its dividend. The Canadian patriot, Lord Mount Stephen (George Stephen) was earnestly advising friends to dump their CPR stock, which fell to 35 and would have kept going down had not one of the Dutch financiers who had earlier helped market CPR equity managed to tempt German money into it.[81] When prosperity and Wilfred Laurier arrived simultaneously in 1896, new developments on the railway front were inevitable. The West opened and Van Horne appointed Clifford Sifton as Laurier's Minister of the Interior. But the protest against CPR monopoly could only strengthen as the Dominion's financial capacity to launch a new transcontinental grew.

Developments, however, were slow. In fact in 1899 Laurier announced an end of the system of free cash bonuses to new lines. Henceforth to earn subsidies the lines had to return services like mail carriage to the government. The announcement was greeted with pleasure by the established lines which had been built with subsidies, for it meant that all new competition had to build with its own resources.[82] Sir Edmund Osler, for one, denounced the old system of railway subsidies.

> These railway subsidies . . . are a main source of corruption in elections, such as we are now having exposed. It is from such subsidies that the money is supplied to pay the men who have been engaged in ballot box stuffing and the election frauds which we hear so much about. These men are not committing these crimes for nothing. They are paid with the money of the people.[83]

Sir Edmund's words undoubtedly carried extra weight in light of his first-hand experience in the utilization of railway subsidies from his CPR and Calgary and Edmonton connections.

Though no new transcontinentals were immediately launched, railway development on a more local and specific basis did occur, and with it ample seamy promotions, especially in the far West following the gold and mineral rush. One of the more spectacular operations was the White Mountain Pass Railroad, a British promotion in the Yukon during the gold rush. The syndicate, headed by the Duke of Teck and including an impressive array of parliamentarians, merchants, and bankers in the U.K., noteable among them the Hon. Sydney Carr Glyn, was formed in 1897. Its principal Canadian contact was the Montreal broker Edwin Hanson.[84] In addition to a railway, the company took over a steam barge line and a fleet of steamers and secured virtual monopoly of the route from Skagway to Dawson. Its capital consisted of £7,500,000 in bonds and £1,700,000 of equity which was mainly water.[85] But the return from water was fabulous in the gold rush days, when even the Bank of Commerce, which Laurier had appointed government banker in the Klondike,[86] and the Bank of British North America, were charging 24% on loans.[87] By 1901, White Pass was the richest and most profitable operation in the Yukon, even more so that the big American mining, trading, and transporation conglomerates who literally oozed gold from every pore.[88] In fact, so extortionate were the rates demanded by White Pass that the Dominion government was forced to intervene and impose a new rate schedule on the average only one-third the level of the old; in some items the reductions were 80% and more.[89]

White Pass was a temporary phenomenon; its orientation was exclusively towards exploiting the Yukon gold fields. The minerals boom in the Pacific region that ushered in the new age of prosperity had other, more lasting effects, for it was out of the B. C. mines that the Canadian Northern system took shape. And the prosperity of the period brought in its trail the second round of transcontinental construction.

The mode of financing the second round of transcontinentals had to be very different from the first. Land grant potential was almost exhausted; in the final analysis the CPR got 75% of all railway land grants ceded. And the tariff drawbacks and tax exemptions that had been awarded the CPR were no longer feasible. The second round of building was linked to the decisions to make renewed efforts to foster a Canadian primary iron and steel industry, which greatly escalated construction costs, all of which had to be covered, by bonds issued in Britain.

The CPR, by contrast, continued and improved upon its policy of attempting to avoid a fixed interest debt. From the time of its completion to the Pacific coast in 1885 until 1914, common stock issued rose four-fold, preference stock and debentures were issued to raise new money, and bonds outstanding were reduced to one-third their former level.

The decision to build two new transcontinental lines was an economic absurdity, but a political necessity following the failure of Laurier to effect a merger of the two new promotions in 1903 after a lot of strenuous effort. Pressure was mounted not only from Laurier and the government, but from Toronto financiers such as Edmund Walker, though without success.[90]

**TABLE VIII (1)**

**Canadian Pacific Railway Finance**

|                            | 1886          | 1914          |
| -------------------------- | ------------- | ------------- |
| Mileage                    | 4,651         | 13,280        |
| Capital                    |               |               |
| — common stock       | $65,000,000   | $260,000,000  |
| — bonds              | 47,785,019    | 16,492,642    |
| — 4% preference stock|               | 78,224,073    |
| — 4% debenture stock |               | 173,340,458   |
| Total cost of construction | $139,975,281  | $491,340,458  |

Source: U.K., Dominions Royal Commission, *Central Canada Evidence,* p. 403.

For the Grand Trunk Railway the year 1883 had marked the high-water-point of its prosperity; that year enough money was squeezed from the line to pay dividends on not only it guaranteed, but even all of its first, second, and third preference stock. It would never happen again. Not until 1900, apart from a fraction in 1887, was anything at all paid on its second preference; not until 1902 was even partial payment made on its third preference; the first preference share payments were irregular and seldom full; and even the guaranteed passed its dividend from time to time. In 1883, the par value of its securities was £16 million, while their market value was £12 million: by 1894, the market value stood at £3.5 million.[91] It was a ripe time for another shareholders' coup; Sir Henry Tyler was unseated, and Sir Charles Rivers Wilson, who had served under Lord Cromer in the reorganization of Egyptian finances and as a former Comptroller-General of the National Debt in England, was selected to replace him. A policy of renewed aggression against the CPR followed. And in 1902, a deal for a second transcontinental line was worked out with the Laurier government.

The Grand Trunk had been designed as a through line from Montreal to the American Midwest. Hence a total reorientation and the construction of a complete transcontinental system were necessary, the Grand Trunk Pacific in the West and the government-built National Transcontinental in the East. But first, of course, it was necessary to consult "the people."

It was like old times. The 1904 election pitted the Grand-Trunk-Liberal-Party nexus against the CPR-Tory machine. To build or not to build, that was the question: and all means fair, and more often foul, were employed in trying to answer it. Laurier tried to sell the arrangement to the electorate on the grounds that "Canada Cannot Wait." But one of his cabinet ministers resigned in protest, claiming it was Senator Cox, president of the Bank of Commerce, who could not wait; his bank was apparently so deeply involved in railway finance that only a flood of public money would save it from bankruptcy.[92] The CPR-Tory forces went to work purchasing newspapers and their editors, leading to a series of remarkable changes of editorial opinion. The former Liberal minister was eagerly cultivated by the Tory machine, and he co-operated to the extent of resigning from the chair of the Railway Commission.[93] CPR victory was expected to finally yield the elusive prize, the Intercolonial Railway. In the end, the will of the people was made known, and the GTR's transcontinental ambitions confirmed. A flood of British capital into Canada followed.

In addition to the bonds issued in London directly by the railway companies, large issues bore government of Canada guarantees, and not a few guarantees of the provincial government as well. For the Grand Trunk Pacific, the federal government guaranteed 50-year first mortgage bonds at three per cent for an amount up to $13,000 a mile on its prairie section and up to 75% of cost on the mountain section, while the remainder of the cost was to be met by the issue of four per cent first mortgage bonds of the GTP guaranteed by the GTR.[94]

The western construction led to a repetition of the national political battles in British Columbia, where the CPR put its new Premier, Richard McBride, to work against the project. The most effective technique was the banning of the import of oriental quasi-slave labour on top of whose broken limbs and bodies the GTR hoped to build its line at a minimum of cost. The federal government disallowed all the B.C. legislation; but nonetheless restrictions on Chinese labour escalated, and with them the labour costs of the line.

For the eastern division, the National Transcontinental, the government took direct responsibility for the line. A board of commissioners headed by a former Premier of Quebec, a close political ally of Laurier's, handed out contracts to the party faithful with an appalling lack of regard to the rank of the tenders.[95] A substantial amount of the contracting went to the Grand Trunk Railway itself. The GTR acted as middleman since it did not have a single piece of the equipment necessary for construction, and it sublet the contracts to a small group of favoured firms who in turn sublet to subcontractors. The sublet arrangements prevailed on the sections of the line let directly by the board as well. All of the layers demanded their share of the swag and construction costs soared. The contract awards bore no relationship to the amounts of the tenders,[96] and anomalies like

55,959 board feet of railway fence in the middle of a stretch of
primeval forest occurred with appalling regularity.[97] Numerous
frauds were pointed out by the chief engineer, but the Laurier
government's supposed investigation was such a farce that opposition members refused to take part in the hearings. All charges
of corruption were dismissed by the committee.[98] After the
change of government, a fresh investigation discovered the
scamping, doctored accounts, and irregularities in the tendering.
But by then the damage was done, for as early as 1910 the
Grand Trunk was publicly suggesting it might renege on its commitment to the National Transcontinental.[99]

# The New Railways: II

The story of the Canadian Northern Railway is astonishing even
by Canadian standards. It is essentially a story of how two men
created and realized upon political influence to build an enormous railway and transportation empire and a system of grain
mills, mines, and other enterprises without investing a penny of
their own money. It began in 1884 when two CPR contractors,
Donald Mann and William Mackenzie, met while working on
the Kicking Horse Pass contract under Herbert Holt, Chief Engineer. In 1886, one of the most powerful of the CPR contractors,
James Ross, brought Mackenzie, Mann, and Holt into a partnership with him. Among other monuments the united forces left
behind as testimony to their capacities could be numbered the
notoriously scamped and derelict Calgary and Edmonton line
and the fabulous promoters' profits of the Qu'Appelle, Long
Lake and Saskatchewan. The partnership dissolved in 1892 with
each member setting out for greener pastures, Holt to become
one of the dominant figures in Montreal's plutocracy, Ross into
a firm of consulting engineers, Mackenzie to dabble in farming
and politics, and Mann, after a short expedition in search of contracts abroad, staying in the West and running up a fair list of
slick promotions in B.C.[100] In some cases the new careers were
found wanting in charm and excitement. Mackenzie, for
example, joined up with Ross in a Toronto street railway swindle
before returning to the West and rejoining Mann in 1896.

That year they secured the charter granted by Manitoba to the
Lake Manitoba Railway and Canal Company in 1889, after the
CPR's monopoly clause had been cancelled. Their first three
short lines were bankrupt local railroads which they "purchased" at a very generous price from the Bank of Commerce,

which thereafter functioned as banker for the CNR in precisely the same way the Bank of Montreal functioned for the CPR. And the three short lines carried with them a land grant and a province of Manitoba guarantee.

In the new syndicate, Mackenzie and Mann held all the common stock, which corresponded to not a penny of actual investment, and financed all construction from bond issues backed by generous guarantees and huge cash subsidies.

The prairie provinces' railway guarantees began in 1885 with the Northern Pacific and Manitoba, followed by further Manitoba guarantees to the Hudson's Bay and Lake Manitoba lines in 1889 and 1892[101] in desperate attempts to introduce a modicum of competiton. The province, like Alberta and Saskatchewan after it, had no revenue from natural resources or land sales, since these remained the property of the federal government and therefore of the CPR, together with substantial residual holdings by the Hudson's Bay Company. This served to make them all the more excessive in their guarantees to competitive lines. And the land grants made from Manitoba lands were in fact often used by the railway companies to discharge their obligations to the province. Both the Lake Manitoba and the Manitoba and South Eastern, after their integration into the CNR network, "repaid" prior loans by "selling" Manitoba back some of its own lands.[102]

From Manitoba the promoters made their way into the chaos of B.C. politics around the turn of the century and reached deep into the muck to seize their share of the mineral booty. Under the terms of a deal worked out with the Laurier government in 1898, Mackenzie and Mann were to be contractors for a railway to the Klondike in return for 25,000 acres of mineral lands for every railway mile, a total of 37,500,000 acres in lands selected by them north of the 60th parallel. In addition, while miners working government lands paid a ten per cent royalty on minerals, those on the railroad land would pay the government only one per cent. The government further pledged that no Canadian railroad competitive with theirs would get any government aid for five years, and that for the next ten the syndicate would have first refusal in any line from Stickeen to a port in B.C.[103] Laurier had learned well from his years in opposition.

The Yukon miners immediately objected to the plan which would give Mackenzie and Mann the ability to cover all known gold lands with a blanket claim, and force all free miners in the area to deal with them.[104] But the arrangements proceeded. The next move was to secure a subsidy of $4,000 per mile from the Turner government in British Columbia for a line from a B.C.

port to Lake Teslin, supplemented by a Dominion subsidy of $6,000 per mile. For good measure B.C. added a monopoly guarantee. But the Tory Senate threw out the Klondike bill, the House refused to grant the $6,000 per mile, and B.C. withdrew its offer when the Turner government fell.[105]

Up to this point all of the Mackenzie and Mann projects had the backing of the CPR.[106] But once the B.C. deal failed, the scene switched back to Manitoba and relations with their mentor began to deteriorate shortly after. What Roblin meant by public ownership of railways now became clear. In 1898 the syndicate bought the Port Arthur, Duluth and Western Railway from the Toronto General Trust[107] and carried it into Manitoba, linking up with the Manitoba and South Eastern, one of the lines Manitoba had built in spite of Dominion disallowance. The new syndicate was now a direct threat to the CPR for with its Winnipeg-Port-Arthur connection it could now function as an independent wheat carrier.[108]

An interesting arrangement with the newly elected Roblin government followed in 1901. The government would secure from J. J. Hill's Northern Pacific 354 miles of its feeder line into Manitoba in a 999-year lease and then transfer the lease to Mackenzie and Mann, the government continuing however to assume all responsibility. In addition, it would guarantee 290 miles at $20,000 per mile. [109] Thomas Shaughnessy, then head of the CPR, was alarmed, and offered an immediate rate reduction to stop the deal. But it was off and running with Dominion sanction.[110] And a new transcontinental system was in the making.

Several key figures became associated with Mackenzie and Mann. In 1902, Edmund Walker of the Bank of Commerce was responsible for authorizing a three-million-dollar loan to aid them in the burst of feeder line construction they began that year. [111] The solicitor of the Canadian Bankers' Association, a leading corporate lawyer, Z. A. Lash, joined the team. And most important, R. M. Horne Payne was wooed from the CPR. A former member of a City of London stock brokerage house, Horne Payne, among other operations, founded the British Empire Trust Company to bring British funds to Canada, esepcially given the new trustee status for federal government debentures. It was claimed that Horne Payne alone was responsible for moving $500 million in British money to Canada, no small part of which flowed directly or indirectly into CNR financing.

The Roblin government's gifts to the CNR did not cease with the 1901 guarantee. More guarantees continued to flow, including one to build CNR feeder lines to some gravel pits of which Roblin was the owner.[112] And when the various pieces of the CNR system were integrated in 1905 in an enormous roll-over operation, the four per cent consolidated debenture issue that accompanied it bore a Manitoba guarantee.[113]

This by no means exhausted the potential for exacting guarantees, for in 1905 as well the CN's $30 million London issue carried a federal guarantee.[114] In 1906 came a thoroughly despicable public relations stunt when an attempt was made to get 90-year-old Henry Hind, the surveyor on many of the initial explorations of the West, and a man who had courageously exposed the corruption and fraud that surrounded the CPR and the Macdonald government, to ride on the CNR system to the Pacific.[115] Although Hind appeared to have refused to make the trip, it did not impede the onward march of the CNR. In 1908 Saskatchewan began to guarantee CNR bonds, followed by the other provinces.

Apart from Manitoba, it was in British Columbia that the CNR took the most active role in local politics. For some time it had been "business as usual" in the Pacific province. James Dunsmuir had left office under a cloud of railway scandal. His successor was dismissed unceremoniously by the Lieutenant Governor when it transpired that the honourable first minister had been busy opening tenders for work on a wagon road after they had been called for by his government, and then submitting his own tender at a lower figure than those he had found on the other tenders submitted. Former Finance Minister Richard McBride, who had broken with Dunsmuir, was now called to form a government, and quickly re-established good relations with Dunsmuir and the CPR, especially as the GTR construction proceeded. Then in 1907 McBride offered a railway charter to Mackenzie and Mann, a deal which led immediately to the resignation of two cabinet ministers. But McBride's victory in the 1909 provincial election led him to proceed with his arrangements with Mackenzie and Mann, which involved a guarantee of up to $35,000 per mile for 600 miles of line from the Rockies to the coast.[116] The only thing missing now was the money to cross the Rockies. At that point, relations with the Laurier government began to sour.

Up to 1911, the CNR had expanded at a truly phenomenal rate. From 1905 to 1911, the Laurier government alone had guaranteed $56 million in bonds for the line. But Laurier balked at the idea of the enormous expense of yet a third line piercing the Rockies, and refused to subsidize it.

Nor did his refusal to give them the Intercolonial Railway help relations. The 1911 election saw the CNR united with the CPR to defeat Laurier, and the Tory government that followed

**TABLE VIII (2)**

**Canadian Northern Expansion**

|               | 1897        | 1907          |
|---------------|-------------|---------------|
| trackage      | 124 miles   | 2,640 miles   |
| locomotives   | 3           | 190           |
| cars          | 87          | 7,279         |
| equity        | $200,000    | $37,750,000   |

Source: Stevens, *Canadian National Railways II,* p. 58.

was quick to show its appreciation to the CNR promoters. Bond guarantees and cash gifts from the federal government followed, concerning which the *Grain Growers' Guide* wryly commented, "The Government has called in the big bankers to ask their opinion on the matter, and has evidently received permission from the Kings of Finance to aid the knightly twins." However, London bankers began to advise some restraint, and the new federal gifts generally carried a greater government presence including holdings of voting stock.

Thomas Shaughnessy objected to the subsidies to the CPR's rival, but was successfully mollified and the arrangements proceeded with.[117] As for the use of the money, Mackenzie and Mann also functioned as contractors for the construction of the line, and it was charged at the time that they used the construction contracts to siphon the public money off into their own pockets. [118] In light of the size of their other business interests and the paucity of personal resources with which they commenced their careers, there was likely a substantial amount of truth to the allegation. By 1916 the line had amassed a total of nearly $212 million in guarantees over and above nearly $39 million in cash subsidies.[119] And of course the Grand Trunk was exacting its share of guarantees at the same time.

**TABLE VIII (3)**

**Canadian Northern Bond Guarantees**

| Granted By        | Par Value of Guaranteed Issue |
|-------------------|-------------------------------|
| Dominion          | $104,613,247                  |
| Alberta           | 18,950,361                    |
| Saskatchewan      | 14,762,546                    |
| Manitoba          | 25,501,865                    |
| Ontario           | 7,859,947                     |
| British Columbia  | 39,953,124                    |
|                   | $211,641,090                  |

Despite the guarantee by the federal government when the Grand Trunk tried to market its first issue in London, the bonds sold at a heavy discount, at 83, due to the fact that the CPR through Lord Strathcona had turned the tables on the GTR and discredited the issue among the leading private banks. This process was repeated when Sir William Mackenzie went to London to try to place the Canadian Northern's first issue.[120] Sir William apparently could not resist joining in the game, and began spreading disparaging rumors about the Grand Trunk among Scottish bankers.[121] However much fun this process might have been for the railway magnates, it was an expensive game for the Canadian taxpayers who ultimately bore the costs of the new lines. Later, R. M. Horne Payne of the CNR directorate domiciled himself in London to offset Strathcona's influence and spent his time urging British investors to place their funds in CNR bonds or those of related enterprises and avoid municipal and government issues.[122]

On top of all the other absurdities, the two new transcontinentals put the publicly guaranteed funds to work laying track over much the same areas, at the same time driving up construction costs, producing bottlenecks in the supply of labour and materials, and prolonging the period of construction, thus increasing their interest charges.[123] Moreover, the over-expansion of trunk lines did a great deal to increase the staple-extracting orientation of the economy, for the railroads were forced by the need to cover their fixed interest charges to abet the quick extraction of raw material for export.

# Notes to Chapter VIII

1.   *MT*, May 16, 1884, p. 1286.
2.   R. S. Longley, *Hincks*, p. 371.
3.   *Globe*, Oct. 3, 1873.
4.   Alexander Mackenzie *et al*, *Reform Government in the Dominion* (Toronto, 1878), pp. 103-113; 132;   *HCD*, March 8, 1878, p. 1004.
5.   D. Creighton, *John A. Macdonald*, II, pp. 8, 34, 38, 57.
6.   Pacific Railway Return: Charter, Correspondence, Etc., Canada, *Sessional Papers*,1873.
7.   *Ec*, May 4, 1872, p. 543; May 24, 1873, p. 622.
8.   *Ec*, June 7, 1873, p. 686.
9.   Sir Richard Cartwright, *Reminiscences*, p. 101.
10.  K. MacNaughton, *Lord Strathcona*, p. 79.
11.  U.K. House of Commons, Select Committee on the Hudson's Bay Company, *Report*, 1857, p. 3.
12.  B. Willson, *Lord Strathcona*, p. 99.
13.  W. Grenfell, *Labrador, The Country and the People*. p. 338.
14.  W. T. R. Preston, *Lord Strathcona*, p. 38.

15. M. Wilkins, *The Emergence of Multinational Enterprise*, p. 135.
16. House of Commons *Journals*, vol. V, 1872, p. 57, *Canada Gazette*, vol. V, Dec. 9, 1871.
17. *HCD*, May 14, 1872, p. 528.
18. *Ec*, Jan. 14, 1873, p. 714.
19. *Mail*, Oct. 22, 1873; *MT*, Oct. 17, 1873, p. 369.
20. London *Times*, Oct. 7, 1873; *Ec*, Nov. 1, 1873, p. 1327.
21. London *Times*, April 6, 1875.
22. G. R. Stevens, *Canadian National Railways*, I, p. 324.
23. M. Robin, *The Company Province*, p. 57.
24. See Richard Cartwright, *Reminiscences*, passim.
25. *HCD*, May 19, 1878, p. 1894.
26. W. T. Easterbrook and H. Aitken,  *Canadian Economic History*, p. 422.
27. Richard Cartwright, *Reminiscences*, p. 111.
28. Alexander Mackenzie *et al*, *Reform Government*, p. 171.
29. *CFC*, Oct. 14, 1876.
30. *MT*, Nov. 14, 1879, p. 576.
31. *Ec*, Jan. 15, 1881, p. 75.
32. *Ec*, March 27, 1880, p. 353.
33. *Ec*, Feb. 19, 1881, p. 227.
34. K. McNaughton, *Lord Strathcona*, p. 226.
35. Sir Charles Tupper, *Recollections*, p. 140.
36. W. T. R. Preston, *Lord Strathcona*, p. 316.
38. H. Gilbert, *Awakening Continent: The Story of Lord Mount-Stephen*, p. 94.
38. *MT*, Jan. 5, 1883, p. 739; Jan. 19, 1883, p. 795.
39. *MT*, Oct. 19, 1883, p. 431.
40. *MT*, Aug. 25, 1882, p. 205.
41. *MT*, April 20, 1883, p. 1177.
42. *MT*, Jan. 5, 1883, p. 739.
43. *MT*, Aug. 27, 1881, p. 1082; Sept. 3, 1881, p. 1110; Dec. 31, 1881, p. 1626.
44. W. Vaughan, *Sir William Van Horne*, p. 110.
45. *HCD*, Feb. 19, 1884, p. 380 *et passim*.
46. W. Vaughn, *Van Horne*, p. 77.
47. *HCD*, April 23, 1883, pp. 778-9.
48. *HCD*, Feb. 11, 1884, p. 222.
49. H. Y. Hind, "The Canadian Pacific Railway . . .," p.1.
50. *MT*, Feb. 8, 1885, p. 882.
51. *MT*, March 13, 1885, p. 1031.
52. *MT*, Aug. 26, 1887, P. 264; Sept. 23, 1887, p. 397.
53. G. R. Stevens, *Canadian National Railways*, II, p. 15.
54. *MT*, Oct. 14, 1887, p. 407; Dec. 30, 1887, p. 819.
55. H. Gilbert, *Awakening Continent* p. 216.
56. *HCD*, 1886, vol. II, p. 1000; See esp. G. Myers, *History of Canadian Wealth*, Chap. XV.
57. *MT*, Aug. 14, 1885, p. 177.
58. *MT*, Nov. 18, 1887, p. 639.
59. In fact James Beaty had a great deal of experience in these kinds of operations, dating at least as far back as a piece of highway robbery known as the "York Roads Job" of 1850. That year the Hincks administration put on the market in Upper Canada a lot of roads and other properties supposedly costing the government more money to maintain than they returned. Beaty on behalf of his York Roads Company bought up a number of roads into Toronto, the deal being consummated without parliamentary approval. He subsequently established a pro-Ministerial paper called the *Leader* an investment from which he reaped a major pecuniary advantage in the form

of government waiving of certain sums due as installments on the purchase price of the roads or interest thereupon. The initial purchase price was $300,400. By Beaty's own admission inside of a decade the returns had been well in excess of that amount. Earnings had been assured by his company running down the alternative roads until they were impassible, and thus diverting all traffic along the Dundas Street route to Toronto on which they could collect more tolls at less expense, at the same time jacking up the toll rate as their monopoly was consolidated. By 1860 Beaty was in arrears to the government some $149,508 on the purchase price, and still had another $180,240 in principal falling due in the future. The government then obligingly wrote off some $93,920 of the debt, and deferred until 1869 the date on which any of the purchase money would fall due. (See for example Canada, Seventh Report of the Public Accounts Committee; *Sessional Papers,* 1858.)

60.   J. S. Willison, *The Railway Question in Canada,* p. 52.
61.   Manitoba, Royal Commission on the Financial Affairs of the Province, *Report, Sessional Papers* 1900, p. 448.
62.   "Railway Statistics," *Sessional Papers,* Vol. 8, No. 13, 1888.
63.   *MT,* Aug. 28, 1896, p. 303.
64.   *HCD,* May 10, 1878, p. 2564.
65.   Cited in H. Gilbert, *Awakening Continent,* p. 98.
66.   *Globe,* Nov. 29, 1860.
67.   Macdonald to George Stephen, March 31, 1891, *Macdonald Papers.*
68.   M. Wade, *The French Canadians,* I, p. 468.
69.   W. T. R. Preston, *My Generation of Politics and Politicians,* p. 196; G. R. Stevens, *Canadian National Railways,* II, p. 270; W. Vaughn, *Van Horne, passim.*
70.   The best account of the chequered career of Chris N. Armstrong is in G. R. Stevens, *Canadian National Railways,* II, pp. 325 ff. See also G. Myers, *History of Canadian Wealth* and M. Wade, *The French Canadians,* I, on the Mercier administration and the Baie des Chaleurs affair. The reaction of the British financial press is reviewed in *MT,* Sept. 9, 1898, p. 344.
71.   See especially Martin Robin, *The Company Province.* This is a remarkably good piece of research.
72.   *MT,* Jan. 3, 1898, p. 1575.
73.   *MT,* July 8, 1898, p. 45.
74.   *MT,* July 22, 1898, p. 109; Aug. 12, 1898, p. 207; Aug. 19, 189g, p. 239; Aug. 26, 1898, p. 272; Sept. 2, 1898, p. 303.
75.   *MT,* March 2, 1900, p. 1145; July 13, 1900, p. 47.
76.   *MT,* Sept. 20, 1901, p. 367.
77.   *MT,* Dec. 15, 1899, p. 776; March 16, 1900, p. 1216.
78.   *MT,* April 6, 1900, p. 1318.
79.   Alberta Commission to Investigate the Organization of the Alberta and Great Waterways Railway Company, *Report* 1910.
80.   *Globe,* March 10, 1910; March 17, 1910; MT, Dec. 3, 1910, p. 233.
81.   W. Vaughn, *Van Horne,* p. 262.
82.   *MT,* Aug. 4, 1899, p. 141.
83.   Cited in E. B. Biggar, *The Canadian Railway Problem,* p. 109.
84.   *MT,* April 23, 1897, p. 1405; Sept. 9, 1898. p. 337.
85.   *Ec,* Oct. 26, 1901, p. 1572.
86.   *MT,* Feb. 25, 1898, p. 119.
87.   *CBC,* 1913, p. 578.
88.   *Ec,* Nov. 9, 1901, p. 1653.
89.   *MT,* Feb. 21, 1902, p. 1679.

90. Walker to George Cox, Sept. 23, 1902; Walker to R. Stuart, April 30, 1902, *Walker Papers.*

91. See especially O. D. Skelton, *The Railway Builders* on GTR finance and the second round of transcontinental railway building.

92. G. R. Stevens, *Canadian National Railways,* II, p. 144.

93. *Canadian Annual Review of 1904,* p. 221 ff.

94. *RCRTC,* p. XXIV.

95. G. R. Stevens, *Canadian National Railways,* II, p. 216.

96. Investigating Committee, National Transcontinental Railroad, *Report,* pp. 7, 21-24; *Globe,* April 14, 1906.

97. Investigating Committee, *Report,* p. 117.

98. *Globe,* Jan. 5, 1911.

99. *Ec,* May 21, 1910, p. 1132.

100. M. Robin, *The Company Province,* I, p. 111; G. R. Stevens, *Canadian National Railways,* II, pp. 24 ff.

101. S. Bates, *Financial History of Canadian Governments,* p. 208.

102. Manitoba, Royal Commission . . . Financial Affairs, *Report,* p. 448.

103. *MT,* Jan. 28, 1898, p. 986.

104. *MT,* March 25, 1898, p. 1257.

105. *MT,* April 29, 1898, p. 1417; May 20, 1898, p. 1813; June 3, 1898, p. 1577; May 16, 1898, p. 1449; June 17, 1898, p. 1645; March 3, 1899, p. 1156.

106. *MT,* Aug. 11, 1898, p. 206.

107. *MT,* Sept. 9, 1898, p. 329.

108. G. Roberts and D. Tunnell (eds.), *Standard Dictionary of Canadian Biography,* II, p. 267.

109. *MT,* Feb. 26, 1901, p. 1081.

110. *MT,* May 17, 1901, p. 1547.

111. Walker to J. H. Plummer, Sept. 15, 1902, *Walker Papers.*

112. *Globe,* March 10, 1910.

113. Canadian Northern Railway, *Annual Report,* 105, p. 4-5.

114. E. R. Wood, *Annual Review of the Bond Markets of Canada,* 1905, p. 6.

115. Walker to J. Hanna, Dec. 31, 1906. *Walker Papers.*

116. *Ec,* Nov. 13, 1909., p. 981.

117. *GGG,* April 2, 1913.

118. *GGG,* June 11, 1913.

119. *RCRTC,* p. XVI.

120. W. T. R. Preston, *Lord Strathcona,* p. 289.

121. G. R. Stevens, *Canadian National Railways,* II, p. 149.

122. *GGG,* June 23, 1913.

123. *RCRTC,* p. XXXI.

# Errata

p. 32, lines 17-21. E. H. King's letter did not "state" that Confederation was necessary for the restoration of the provincial credit; rather it implied it in terms intended to make the link clear to Galt. See also Canada, *Sessional Papers*, 1866, No. 35.

p. 36, line 38. "Tory whip" should be Tory Senate leader.

p. 44, line 11. Charles Tupper was "the leader" in the political arena, not the economic one. Tupper quite possibly had investments in coal, as he appears to have had in other fields of enterprise favoured by his own policies, but he was certainly not a dominant business figure in the coal industry.

p. 52, lines 21-38. A partial correction is necessary on the salt duty question. In 1879 the conflicting demands of the Ontario salt mine interests and the Maritime fishing industry produced a "compromise" whereby salt imported from the *British empire* in bulk for the fisheries was tariff exempt. However the exemption appears to have been quickly phased out.

p. 70, line 31. The question of who won and who lost in the struggle over the framing of the "first" Canadian Bank Act is confused by the fact that Bank Acts were passed in 1869 and 1870, yet the 1871 act is the one referred to as the "first" Bank Act in much of the literature. The 1871 act was not a victory for the Bank of Montreal except in a few elements, though earlier acts had been more powerfully influenced by that institution's views.

p. 71, line 34. The idea of a central redemption fund, which was indeed put into effect, came not from Foster, but from the bankers themselves, specifically from Edmund Walker. It was an attempt to circumvent the Foster-Bank of Montreal fixed reserve ratio proposal.

p. 72. An error with respect to the taxes on note circulation. The taxes on province of Canada banks existing at the time of Confederation were extended to the Maritime banks on Confederation. They were, however, abolished in 1871. In 1907 a new tax on the seasonal excess of circulation was imposed at the rate of four per cent. It was increases in the excess circulation tax rather than the long-defunct note circulation tax that the banks resisted.

p. 98, line 23. . . . Montreal *and Toronto*. line 29. *Toronto* not Montreal. In fact, the nominal headquarters remained in Halifax but the general manager's office shifted to Toronto.

p. 165, lines 19ff. In fact there were *two* Alphonse Desjardins in Quebec finance, and I have erroneously presented them as the same individual. One, the president of La Banque Jacques Cartier, was a well-known financial operator and a powerful ultramontane. The other, the true founder of the Caisse Populaire movement, was an obscure civil servant. I am indebted to Bob Sweeney of UQAM for pointing out this error.

p. 172, line 17. The report that Livingston retired to Hawaii may be false. Other reports have him remaining active in Canadian private banking.

p. 202, line 9-21. The Montreal Loan and Mortgage Company did suspend, but did not wind up. It limped along until the 1940's. However, its rapid growth phase did end during the 1884 suspension. Thanks again to Bob Sweeney.

p. 203, line 35. The size of the alleged pay-off was $28,000 not $30,000 as the *Monetary Times* claimed. (Indeed at one point the *Monetary Times* claimed it was $300,000!) Since the pay-off was reportedly to Chapleau and Würtele, I am inclined to doubt its existence, simply because there seemed no need to further ensure their cooperation in the operation.

p. 237, line 18. The statement was by Tupper, not Tilley.

p. 272, lines 27-28. Allan died the year before. The reference should have been to a 1876 bond issue.